AF244112

The Panthers Club

Four Original Stories

By
Alethea M. Pascascio
and
Lisa D. DeNeal

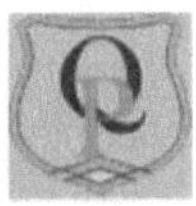

Queen Publications

THE PANTHERS CLUB

Copyright © Alethea Pascascio & Lisa DeNeal, 2011.

Queen Publications, P.O. Box 496 Antioch, IL 60002.
Website: www.queenpublications.com
ISBN: 978-0-9778377-9-3
First Printing December 2011
Library of Congress Control Number: 2011919758
Printed in the United States of America
Queen Publications' Paperbacks are published by
Queen Publications, P.O. Box 496, Antioch, IL 60002.
10 9 8 7 6 5 4 3 2 1

Acknowledgements

First and foremost, I am thankful and humbled to God for giving me life, love and the ability to be aware of the tools He's blessed me with so I can grow in His vision. I thank the DeNeal, Walton and Jacobs families for being loving and supportive over the years and for the support I know I will continue to receive. To my friends, especially Kimberly P., Dayon Burnett, Bridget J., Mark S., Toni C., Doris C. and Carolyn - the long talks whether on the phone or through e-mails and personal visits are appreciated above and beyond what you know. To the classmates and friends in Gary and beyond and the people of Gary – your support for me whether it's in the newspaper or during my debut as an author, you all show me love that's priceless…I hope you continue to do so with this novel!

Thanks to Karla aka "Pepper" for sharing a little bit on life as a flight attendant. And also thank you to Charles S. for sharing his life as being a younger man in the relationship. It help to shape the women and men behind "The Panthers' Club" easy!

Last and certainly not least Alethea S. Pascascio, the woman behind the idea for "The Panthers' Club." Although we did not become friends until long after receiving our high school diplomas, I cherish the connection we made while supporting mutual friend and author Sean D. Young. Thanks for the fun creating the women of The Panthers Club.

Acknowledgements

To my Lord and my Merciful Savior, Jesus Christ- Thank you for keeping me even when I don't deserve to be kept. Thank you for loving me unconditionally regardless of my imperfections. And thank you so much for your grace and mercy.

I am grateful for my parents, Ray and Margaret Sherls, who have supported me in all of my endeavors, and continue to challenge me to fulfill my purpose and use every gift God has given me.

I have been given the awesome responsibility of parenting two of the greatest, wisest, most beautiful children in the world- Alexis and Alaina. Thank you for keeping me focused and for your love.

Then there is the man who has helped me through one of the toughest transitions I've encountered to date. Shawn, what would I have done without you? I don't even want to know. I appreciate the 110% you give to me and the kids. You have no idea how much I love and adore you. Thank you for your unwavering love and support.

Sisters, Juanita Lafayette and Margaret Sherls..Nieces, Kennie Lafayette, Rinita Rankin, and Cherrita Rankin- I appreciate yall having my back and for coming from out of town to help me out, especially during my life's transition. That means more than I could ever express. For everything you've done to help my life run a little smoother…thank you.

This project took place during a difficult time in my life, but having a writing partner with the patience of Job made it a little easier. Ms. Lisa D. DeNeal, thank you so so very much for being understanding about me missing deadlines. You are an incredibly talented writer and I thank you also for editing the hell out of my work.

Contents

The Panthers Club

Prologue

"You owe me fifteen hundred dollars, Motherfucker!"

Ignoring the sudden rambling of disbelief on the other side of her cell, Chanale Arlington's red manicured fingernail tapped the silver Bluetooth attached to her right ear. She was not trying to hear another sorry ass excuse from the brother who canceled their date at the very last minute. No…No… canceled while she was sitting at one of the tables inside the art gallery's exhibit lounge waiting for him to arrive. Chanale immediately put her cell on vibrate before tossing it in her tiny purse not wanting to see the screen light up in case his name appears.

"I can't believe this shit," she mumbled while grabbing what would be her third apple martini for another sip. Her green eyes scoped the lounge through thick eyelashes and thicker wisps of long dark bangs. She put in a lot of maintenance the other day for tonight. New makeup to enhance smooth caramel skin, high cheekbones and lips that would make a certain award winning/man-stealing actress finally admit collagen enhancement. A facial, manicure and waxing of the eyebrows and her 'pleasure valley.' Three hours at the salon for the Rhianna inspired haircut with a light auburn rinse that hid some of the gray hairs popping up like loose strings. Calculate that with the barely knee length black, one shoulder dress and three-inch t-strapped stilettos with matching red toenails. You couldn't tell Chanale a damn thing. "Yeah…fifteen hundred sounds about right. I won't even show him the receipts. Just gonna mess with my money and time."

She finished her martini and gingerly picked up one of the fried chicken drummettes from her plate and dipped it in the spoonful of ranch dressing spread on the side. Leaning forward so not to waste any of the dip on her dress, Chanale took a bite.

The crowd inside the gallery was increasing as the voices got louder on various levels of engaging chat and excitement. It was her first time inside the art gallery and the impression of it was highly favored. Visonz was a wall to wall work of art, with floor to ceiling tinted windows and large steel doors that gave mystery and curiosity to those walking past the front of the building. Once inside, visitors were welcomed to calm earth tone backgrounds with a colorful explosion from elaborate displays of artwork from nationally and locally known African American, Latino and other minority artists. The first floor included the main gallery and the lounge area complete with a bar, buffet table, a small stage complete with lighting and sound systems. The seating areas leveled from plush, burgundy oversized sofas to black lacquered tables and chairs for two or more. Tea light candles and overhead light fixtures created a laid back intimacy.

Studios and classrooms were on the second floor as the owners gave back to the community with grants and scholarships that allowed young aspiring artists the opportunity to feed their muse. A café is also upstairs where juices, bottled water, fresh fruit, sandwiches and cookies are sold for a reasonable amount. Located in the heart of downtown Gary, IN, the two-story gallery was a department store in the 1970s and 80s. Once the ugly world of crack cocaine invaded the thriving Chocolate City, businesses and their owners packed up and hauled ass to greener pastures with whiter faces. Many of the buildings along the stretch of downtown Broadway became lifeless shelters to those who gave in to the crack pipe and its bitch.

The economy in Gary was already spiraling to hell and the Steel City was soon known as the Steal City and not just through break-ins, robberies and stick-ups. Many political figures over the decades stole from the poor and put it in their pockets. Grants from the government meant to help others were treated like loose change found on the street – picked up and never seen again. But in the first decade of the 21st century a change hit when long time citizens grew tired of the same old song and elected fresh, young politicians. Young adults who spent their childhood, teens and twenties witnessing the decay while struggling for an education decided it was time for a change. An African American man was the President of the United States who campaigned for new beginnings and the young politicians here felt that he should not be let down.

Chanale was happy to see the changes happening in her hometown. Hell, she was going through her own changes. She just turned 40! It was time for a different attitude; let go of the drama. Cut the bullshit and the bull-shitter. Turn over a new leaf…

"HUMMMMMM!" Chanale lowered her eyes to her purse as her cell went off and felt the twinge of her Bluetooth. "Turn over and land on a new man," she said while stabbing her fork into a Swedish meatball.

Chanale scanned the increasing crowd, which was mixed in race, age and possibly backgrounds. While race was easy to figure out as African Americans overwhelmed the gallery, age and professional backgrounds could be deceptive. Sloppiness was not allowed inside Visonz; depending on the events the dress codes was dressy casual to after five. Only when the children and their instructors were in session was the dress code slacked.

Chanale eyed two men having what seemed to be a deep conversation at the bar. The tall pecan tone brother with dreads wearing a crisp, white shirt and black pants was emphasizing with his hands. The object of his conversation, a bald, dark skin man with a goatee in a blazer, black t-shirt and jeans, nodded slowly every other second while nursing a drink. He looked at Chanale and delivered an uneasy smile her way. "Lovers' quarrel," she mumbled under her breath and diverted her eyes to another scene.

The Panthers Club

A group of women in too tight dresses switched their way towards Chanale's table, four pair of eyes zooming in on the remaining three empty chairs. Chanale immediately dropped the number to two after making sure her purse was seen in one of them. Smiling at the group, she mouthed "sorry, taken" and the women did a synchronized face scowl while walking past. She was just not feeling the need to share her table after having to dismiss another brother post-Desmond. And this guy seemed promising. Duke was 6"2 and 225 lbs of muscle, a former football player turned businessman living in Chicago. She met him when he stopped at an area drugstore and was in the aisle where condoms were locked in a case of all places. How do you promote safe sex and the condoms are locked up like a chastity belt on a virgin?

Duke was older than her by five years and just as she was much older than Desmond. After dealing with Desmond, Chanale thought it would be best to go back to someone closer to her age or older. And Duke seemed to fit the category. She thought they clicked right away, but now she knows it was a sexual click. And man was he making the right noises escape from her lips. Chanale thought she was on vacation every time she was with Duke; looking into those dark brown eyes and holding on tight from every thrust and pounding he gave her on his king size bed. He was her exodus and she escaped whenever she needed to.

But three weeks into their fling she heard less from Duke and he barely kept their dates. Two nights ago while lying in his bed he promised to meet her at the gallery since she had tickets. He would drive in instead of commuting on the South Shore and spend the night at her apartment. Chanale held on to that promise for no reason and was happy to spend money on herself for his approval.

"Can I get you another drink, Ma'am?" Chanale blinked out of her thoughts and snapped her head to the waitress standing in a uniform that was a black tie short-shorts combination with fishnet stockings and three inch heels. "Ma'am??! Baby, I am not a senior citizen, but yes, bring me another martini." The waitress smirked and walked back to the bar. Chanale watched the likely 20-something waitress walk away, passing a small cluster of men who shamelessly turned their heads in the girl's direction. Nearly all of them were old enough to be her daddy. "Little heifer," Chanale said. Blotting the grease from her mouth, Chanale contemplated leaving since she's already browsed through the exhibit. She considered purchasing a couple of prints as one of her ways to give back to the community. She had the means to do just that, along with volunteering for a couple of local organizations. The haters always try to find out how she is able to contribute financially, but always hit a brick wall. Chanale has never been one to brag about her background and it's nobody's damn business anyway. Can't a sister do some good in the community without getting the 'side-eye' inquiry?

The waitress returned with her fourth apple martini wearing the same smirk on her overly made up face. "That'll be $6.50."

Chanale grabbed her purse and pulled out a roll of cash that was visible enough for the now wide-eyed waitress to notice. Chanale smiled and paid the final $6.50 martini with a crisp $50 bill. The waitress gave her change and Chanale hit her with a $3 tip for being so smug. "Thank you, honey," Chanale said with a smirk and shoved the money back in her purse.

Nursing her drink Chanale noticed two women at the bar eyeing her table and quickly glanced around the lounge. Pretty much all of the seats and tables were filled, leaving her to look like one stingy bitch. "Damn it, do not come over here," she mumbled against the edge of her glass.

****

"**O**oh Denyce, it is so nice in here," Autumn said surveying the artistic expressions displayed throughout Visonz. "I am so glad you convinced me to come out instead of laying up under Denver tonight or should I say instead of him laying up on me," she giggled slightly hunching Denyce's arm.

Denyce stood up taller in her conservative black on black pants suite with matching patent-leather slingbacks and rolled her eyes toward the ceiling. "I'm not going to sit around tonight listening to you go on and on about you and your man's sex life. I came here to just relax and celebrate getting the marketing contract for the new Four Seasons hotel opening up downtown. The last thing I want to hear all night is about your wild sexcapades."

"Oh please, girl lighten up. Sometimes you are more serious than the swine flu," Autumn returned.

Denyce shifted her posture and tone again to sound and look more down to earth. She couldn't believe that as badly as she wanted to be free from the stiff shirts at work that she was actually turning into one herself. Not wanting to become anything like those she worked around, Denyce went for some levity. "No, I'm not being serious. It's just that your sex stories may start off different but they end up the same ole way… with your legs in the air. You need some new material."

Autumn laughed to herself knowing Denyce was nothing more than jealous of her uninhibited lifestyle and the *perks* that sometimes came with her being a flight attendant. Sure Denyce made more money being the VP of Marketing but to Autumn, even the title, *VP of Marketing,* reeked with boredom. It was no doubt that her friend was creative in the boardroom, but from their conversations, it was clear that her creativity didn't find its way to the bedroom.

Autumn, on the other hand, was a complete opposite from Denyce. Although she had finally settled down with one man, there was a time in Autumn's life when she nearly had a different man in each country. If she had not met and fallen in love with Denver, she might have become Gateway Airline's first card-carrying slut attendant who loved spending her layovers getting laid.

And Autumn enjoyed calling Denyce to give her all of the seedy details knowing when she described every thrust, every lick, every suck that Denyce was probably secretly imagining herself as the recipient of it all. Autumn always hoped that her wild stories would add some spunk to Denyce's boring stuck up life because she sat up in a high rise every day looking through her window down at people making far less money than her but were probably a hell-of-a lot happier. To Autumn, Denyce was definitely an example of a person having money but not being able to buy happiness or a man willing to get married... but that's another story.

A couple who looked to be in their 60s snatched Autumn's attention. She watched on with envy as they kissed and groped each other as if still teenagers.

"What's wrong with you," Denyce asked, glancing around to see what or who had captivated her friend's eyes.

"That couple over there," Autumn said, nodding her head in the lovers direction. "Do you see how he looks at her? Do you see how he touches her? Not one of her wrinkles or blemishes or gray hairs seems to faze him. It's like he can't see any of that. Their happiness seems to be pure...real. I want that kind of love when I'm that old."

"Well, you are only two or three years away, so you better hope Denver feels that way about you now," Denyce replied feigning serious before allowing a huge grin to cover her face.

Autumn glared at her friend. "O.K. bitch. So now you wanna be funny. Your ass is older than me. You better be making sure Brandon loves *you* for real. You are looking ok now but might be wrinkling soon. I can give you the number to my plastic surgeon, if you need some help."

For the first time since entering Visonz, Denyce felt the stress of the workplace drop from her like dead weight. Boisterous laughter burst from her mouth before she managed to stifle it with her hand. "You are always telling me to loosen up, now look who's being serious. Autumn, you are so vain that it's comical. Let's walk to the bar and get some drinks. I think we both could use one."

***

The ladies took a seat at the semi-circle shaped mahogany bar positioned across the room from the stage where the in-house band was setting up for a jazz performance. As if synchronized by an invisible force, the bartender immediately laid napkins on the bar top and asked for their orders.

"I'll have a Long Island Ice Tea," Autumn replied.

Denyce twisted her lips as if uncertain of what she wanted. "Give me uuuh. I want to try something different. Something risky that Brandon would drink, like a shot of Hennessy. No, a shot of Patrone."

The young bartender dressed like a penguin stood there awhile longer in case Denyce changed her mind again.

Autumn, in awe of her friend's sudden risqué decision, had to stop her mouth from flying open. She loved seeing signs of Denyce coming out of her shell and wanted the bartender to hurry up and pour that drink before the *other more conservative Denyce* took over. "Excuse me, Mr." Autumn leaned in closer and read the young man's name tag. "Mr. Elliot, you heard the lady. Bring her a shot of Patrone and bring the bill because we are going to find seats at a table."

Mr. Elliot scurried off like a mouse being set free from a trap and returned moments later with the drinks. He placed a glass of intoxicating liquid in front of each woman, and slid the check in the middle. "Enjoy," he muttered then made his way to the next customer.

Denyce snatched the bill before Autumn could even consider reaching for it. "You know tonight's on me." She slipped $30 from her jacket's pocket and fanned it in Mr. Elliot's direction. "Keep the change," she stammered before dropping the money down.

Autumn picked up her drink. "Let's make a toast."

Denyce took a whiff of her tequila and drew back from it in disgust. "I have no idea how Brandon drinks this stuff. Ok. What are we toasting to?"

They touched their glasses together as Autumn spoke, "We are toasting to your continued success, peace, love, and true happiness."

"Yes. True happiness," Denyce whispered before working up the courage to down her drink. The word *happiness* kept ringing in her head like an alarm clock in danger of being thrown across the room. But for some reason, maybe to portray the image of success to the people she imagined paying attention to her, she made herself believe she was happy. Well, at least happy about her professional life.

It had taken Denyce over 10 years to become the Vice President of Sherls & Hughes which was rated number one among all of the Marketing Firms in the U.S . She had worked tirelessly day and night developing strategies that would win over the top Executives and Board of Directors running the Four Seasons's empire. Putting her head together with a few outside connections who also worked in Marketing, she finally came up with a winning campaign. This landed Denyce a 6-figure bonus that almost surpassed her salary and tonight she wanted to spend some of her rare downtime with her best-friend, the one person she had neglected the most due to her extended work hours.

Of course, there was another person almost running neck and neck in the "who has been neglected the most by Denyce contest". Brandon, her long-term *boyfriend* … Denyce being an overgrown ass woman hated referring to him as her *boyfriend. That* term is for kids as far as she was concerned. She knew people whispered behind her back about him being over 10 years younger than her, but it didn't stop Denyce for wanting to marry him. The only problem is, he had not proposed to her. So until he graduated to *fiancé, boyfriend* was the only title for his position in her life.

Autumn took Denyce away from her thoughts. "O.K. I'm ready," she stammered after finishing off her brown-colored concoction. "Let's run to the restroom before we find a table."

Denyce spun around on her barstool a little too quickly and immediately began to regret stepping outside of her comfort zone. She held her head for a moment. "Autumn, what the hell was I thinking? I should have stuck with a simple glass of Moscato. That drink went straight to my head."

"You'll be ok, just drink water for the rest of the night," Autumn advised as if giving professional advice. Then she stood to test out her own level of sobriety. Feeling the strength of her legs up under her, she felt proud about being able to hold her liquor.

Autumn reached her hand out to Denyce. "Do you need some help?"

"No, sweetie. I'm alright. I really need to walk. Let's go find the bathroom."

***

Denyce stood in front of a porcelain sink in the bathroom. She glanced to her left at Autumn in the mirror putting more lip gloss on those collegan-filled lips. She wondered what it would be like to be like her for a day. Care free. Non-structured. Experimental in the bed. *Just plain nasty.*

A feminine voice with masculine undertones jumped right in the middle of Denyce's thoughts. "Excuse me, can I use the soap dispenser in front of you?"

Denyce stepped aside and gave the person invading her space a quick glance over from head to toe then did her signature eye-roll toward the ceiling before flashing her ebony eyes toward Autumn to see if she was paying attention. And not only was she paying attention, she had stopped reapplying her makeup to watch who she probably felt was her only competition in Visonz.

After washing and drying his hand's, the stranger shashayed out of the restroom but not before glancing over his should and saying in his best RuPaul voice, "Bitches!"

Denyce and Autumn fell into each other laughing harder than they ever had in years. Denyce composed herself as best she could before mocking the man's comment, "Bitches!" She snickered a little more then went on, "he has a lot of nerves coming in the women's restroom with hands and feet bigger than an NBA star's, and wearing that tight ass red dress. I tell you, it really does take all kind to make the world go round."

To Denyce's surprise, Autumn turned serious, "but did you see his legs? They were perfect. And his makeup? It was flawless. And those lashes made his eyes pop. They looked better than mine. And you know I would kill for a booty like that." Then suddenly, feeling a little more insecure about her own appearance, she began rambling around in her little Gucci clutch until found what she couldn't live without, Rimmel Volume Accelerator Mascara.   She meticulously applied it to her already lengthy lashes until reaching some level of temporary satisfaction.

Denyce looked on asking herself how could a woman who had paid top dollar for her plastic surgery still be so insecure. She could have saved that money and invested in something less temporal. Or even pay a psychiatrist to diagnose her and prescribe some unnecessary medicine. If she had done that then maybe, just maybe, she wouldn't be standing in those 4-inch heels looking like Janet Jackson wearing enough makeup for the entire Jackson family.

When Denyce saw Autumn reach back into her purse for even more lip gloss, she couldn't take it anymore. She had to pull her friend back to reality. "Uuuh, excuse me, Miss Thang," She said stepping close to see her own reflection in the mirror beside Autumn. Both of their eyes met in the mirror. "Autumn, I see I have to add one more thing to my list. I also didn't come out here to spend the entire night in the bathroom watching you bury yourself behind Mac and Maybelline. You paid good money for your face, now you want to hide it."

Autumn interrupted Denyce, almost sounding offended. "Excuse me? What are you trying to say?"

Not wanting to put a damper on the evening, Denyce released her words a little more carefully this time. "You are my girl and I love you. But sometimes it's hard for me to see you constantly trying to improve upon what's already perfect. You let a man in a dress walk in here and make you start second guessing your own beauty…and his legs were as hairy as my kitty kat. OK, I probably should have shaved and that's too much information, but you get my damn point."

Aututmn wanted to remain serious but couldn't hold the staunch look on her face any longer. The liquor wouldn't allow it. She dropped her head and smirked before turning to face Denyce. Composing herself a little she managed to say, "Hairy as your kitty kat? I see corporate America hasn't taken all of the ghetto out of you. So why don't you let Brandon shave you like Denver does me. I can't believe Ms.Corporate, Ms. Prim and Proper has an afro under that power suit."

"Well believe it", Denyce chuckled before leading the way out of the restroom.

***

Three clean-shaven male artists were dressed in all black. One sported a black Kangol. They all strategically positioned their art displays among the band's instruments. The tallest one with dreadlocks running from beneath his hat and down his back seemed to be in charge. He stood at the foot of the stage directing the others to move the arts piece to the left or to the right or having them switch one with the other. They swished about looking like designers on a home decorating show ensuring that view from the audience would tantalize the eyes as the music enticed the ears.

Finally satisfied with his design team's beautification of the stage, the leader extended his palms out in front of himself. "That's it. That's it. Perfect." He praised.

The artists left the stage and walked past Denyce and Autumn as they exited the bathroom. "Hello, ladies," they said in unison sounding like a male chorus.

"Hello," both women replied, a syllable off from each other.

Autumn continued to watch the men until they were no longer in sight. "That one with the dreads is too sexy. He reminds me of a man I met in Jamaica that made me have an orgasm by just whispering in my ear and caressing my back while we were slow grinding at a night club. Now that man had skills. Then we left and.."

"You don't even have to tell me," Denyce interrupted. "I told you that you need some new material. The stories end the same. You ended up with your legs in the air."

"Wrong! He ended up with his legs in the air. But you not ready for that story." Those words tickled Autumn on the inside and even more so after seeing the amazed stare on Denyce's face. She grabbed Denyce's arm. "Come on silly, let's find some seats."

Denyce stiffened up. "Wait. Were you serious? Why would the man have his legs in the air?" Not even giving Autumn time to answer she continued almost sounding defeated, "Why are you so damn nasty?"

"Please. Brandon might give you a ring if you take some lessons from me." She gave Denyce's arm a little tug. "Now, come on. Let's find some seats before the band starts."

Denyce finally gave in and let her freaky friend lead her through the maze of people and tables.

Autumn finally stopped and pointed across the room at a table with four chairs and only one was occupied by a woman who looked like she was ready to hurt somebody. "There's a table over there."

"Uuuh, Autumn. Does she look like someone willing to share her table with us? She even has her purse in one of the chairs."

"Maybe, she's mad that her purse is sitting in that seat instead of her man." Both women cracked up laughing. "I don't care what her problem is," Autumn interjected. "I need to sit down. My damn feet hurt."

"Well, come on. Let's go get our seats."

****

Camille Darwin blended with the crowd at the exhibit, introducing herself to the artists and collecting their media kits for further research and contact information. Keeping a pearly white smile on her face and a light, pleasant demeanor in her voice, mentally Camille was ready to go home. Any other time she would thoroughly enjoy the exhibit and mingle with the crowd, but tonight felt like a job. "I cannot believe I am doing this for him," she said to herself. But this is what you do for the one you…wait a minute. Shaking the last thought out of her head, Camille shifted her designer portfolio satchel filled with the media kits to her left shoulder and smoothed her outfit with her right hand.

Her red wrap-around blouse and black slacks complimented her figure perfectly. And it should…she worked out three times a week for two hours to keep a thick body tight without looking like a bodybuilder. Her dark shoulder length hair with touches of gray framed an oval shape face and brought out prominent cheekbones. A full, heart shape mouth painted with red lip gloss partnered with bright brown eyes defined glamour and maturity. Camille hardly looked 53 and approving glances from most of the men at the exhibit confirmed that notion.

Walking through the crowd like a runway model in three-inch sandals Camille came across a painting she felt would be perfect. Leaning towards the easel, Camille admired the theme of a pair of hands gracefully preparing a meal with a mirage of bright colors blending in. It was an abstract painting that stood out.

"Excuse me." Camille turned to the voice and smiled at a younger man who returned the gesture. "I'm the artist behind that piece. My name is Dayon."

Camille shook his hand and reached in her satchel for a business card and her platinum credit card. "It is very nice to meet you, Dayon. I would like to purchase this piece and have it delivered to the address listed on my business card."

Within ten minutes, Camille walked away from the overwhelmed artist and headed towards the bar. While waiting for her glass of champagne Camille scanned the lounge for a seat and noticed three women sitting at a table in the center of the action. She noticed how two of the ladies were enthralled in conversation while the third had a look of punching them in their throats. "Whatever the situation is, I am sure these young ladies would not mind if I join them for a minute," she said while grabbing her drink.

Camille

Chapter 1

The divorce papers arrived at Camille's house via certified mail at 1:15 p.m. By 1:17 p.m., she'd signed the tablet, thanked the mail carrier and locked her front doors. At 1:18 p.m. she ripped the large envelope open, yanked out the papers, skimmed over them and grabbed one of her fountain pens lying on the coffee table. "Free from your ass…free from your ass," she sang while signing the forms. She laughed aloud in her living room to keep from making a total mockery of the historical speech from the Civil Rights era. But she was indeed free.

However, for her now ex-husband, Elijah Xavier Darwin III there was no such thing as free. The divorce cost him a financial settlement of three million dollars, a couple shares in the stock market, a condo in downtown Chicago, the 2010 silver BMW(that was a present from her to him for his 60th birthday) and the beach house in Gary's Miller neighborhood. While the beach house was technically a summer home, Camille enjoyed the house almost year-round. Located on one of the meticulously cared for hills in the area, the two-story house was the last house on the street and seconds from a down-slope walk north to Marquette Beach where a personal gate allowed Camille and her neighbors to enter and take a stroll along Lake Michigan.

They purchased the house after the first year of their twenty years of marriage. "The first year anniversary is the paper anniversary," Elijah said while signing the lease inside the realtor's office. "This is the paper…the house is just a little something extra." Camille remembered that day, sitting next to her husband in that office, grinning herself to death about the dream house they would spend the rest of their lives in. May 1, 1990 was their wedding day after a whirlwind sex fling that lasted six months. He'd been married before and she never thought she would have a 5-carat wedding ring on her finger. It was a fairytale wedding per her request. He provided her with a church wedding that included a bridal party of ten, horse drawn carriage ride, a ridiculously expensive wedding gown, and a Grammy winning singer serenading her as she walked down the aisle. The outdoor reception was at the aquatorium by the beach with another Grammy winning singer and band, open bars, a five course meal and a towering champagne flavored wedding cake with butter crème frosting. The Jamaica honeymoon was 10 days long at a five star hotel. This was her reward for attending a mandatory party sponsored by the corporation where she worked at the time.

She was hired five years ago as a marketing consultant for the corporation which dealt with portfolios for their clientele. If the client wanted a major promotion package for his or her latest project Camille and her team were the chosen crew to hire. Her ability to charm clients into signing their names on contracts that ran up to six-figures with a fifty percent cut for the corporation made her a huge commodity to the administration.

It was mandatory for her to attend numerous social events and her bosses had no problem with her aggressiveness and sometimes intense sexuality when it came to the male clients. Camille knew the good old boys club all too well but she never slept with the clients; just delivered enough charm to make a man pull out his…pen to seal the deal. She gave sweetness without attachments and just enough spice to avoid getting burned. This changed however when she crossed paths with Elijah X. Darwin III.

Camille barely kept a moan from escaping her lips when she laid eyes on him. He had to be no more than 50 years old but you could not tell with his lean muscular physique. He looked as if he walked off the pages of an advertisement for whiskey where the handsome distinguished older man is standing by a fireplace with the glass in his hand. Elijah was at least six feet tall with broad facial features that included piercing dark brown eyes. His hair and beard were lightly gray and well kept.

Camille did not hesitate to introduce herself to him and would later catch Elijah sneaking glances at her hourglass figure that filled a long, spaghetti-strapped red dress perfectly. The long slit that revealed her curvy, left leg ended with her foot draped in silver sandals. It was a dress that one of her co-workers said was too daring for a corporate affair. "Honey, I am here to shake things up, not be a fucking wallflower," Camille said. With a tilt of her head and a smile on her lips, she charmed the man who would later be her husband. But right then she was going to make him her personal ATM.

"Shit! You sure do…know…how to …go…deep," Camille moaned as Elijah pushed further inside her as he held her tighter around her waist. They found a private restroom down the hallway from the party. Camille did not even bother to take off her dress when Elijah turned her around to face the marble sink counter, bend her over and lift the dress just over her round ass.

Camille steadied herself against the counter and stared at their reflection in the mirror above the sink. She smiled as she watched the many expressions develop on Elijah's face as he leaned over her, still wearing his white tuxedo shirt and black bow tie. His pants and briefs rested around his ankles. "Baby you feel so good," he managed to say between grunts. Elijah had the body of a man 15 years his junior and the libido of a 20 year old, minus the blue pills.

While working as an investor at a Fortune 500 company, Elijah was a rare sight in the world of millionaires; he was an African American male born into old money. His father was Elijah X. Darwin, Jr., a man who made his money off real estate that began when he went to Mississippi to claim acres of land inherited to him from his grandfather a former slave owner. The land, plus some private bonds under his grandfather's name had been held by an estate that was kept private for obvious reasons. The junior Darwin built on some of the land and sold the rest to a thriving casino owner years later. He passed it down to Elijah III, who kept the investments and business offers going under Darwin Development.

Within moments from eyeing each other Camille and Elijah were in the bathroom; dress up and pants down. Elijah was delivering heart stopping strokes in her slickness that turned into hard and rapid thrusts that damn near made her bang her head against the mirror. Camille bit her lip hard to keep from screaming until her vocal chords disintegrated. Blinded by locks of her hair matted to her sweaty face, she growled when Elijah found a tighter grip on her shoulders. "Am…am I…hurting…you?"

Camille let out a sigh. "I'll let you know when I am in pain…maybe," she said.

From that night on, Camille and Elijah were fuck buddies with no heartstrings attached. He would spend nights at her apartment in the Horace Mann neighborhood or she would be at his condo in downtown Chicago. He would take her on trips to New York, Las Vegas, Los Angeles and a couple of trips to London and Paris as time went by. When he first proposed to her, she refused because she did not want to settle down. Elijah convinced Camille that he would take care of her forever.

Forever ended August 5, 2010. "Hmph, I need to get my ten years back," she mumbled while shoving the signed divorce papers into a fresh manila envelope. Holding the envelope in her hand Camille sat on the cream toned sectional couch in front of the picture window.

The living room furniture and its fixtures added to the beach's gifts of comfort and relaxation. Set against almond painted walls, the coffee table was a combination of oak with a marble trim fitted perfectly in the space surrounded by the couch. Extra chairs of different structures spread out in the room and a fireplace was built inside the wall opposite the couch. A 42-inch flat screen hung above the mantel. The mantel had a few pictures of Camille over the years blending with antique candleholders. Pictures that included Elijah had been tossed in a cardboard box duct taped and tossed in the basement for now. The rest of the house included a dining room, a master bedroom and bath and two smaller bedrooms with 1 ½ baths, a fully equipped kitchen, walk-in closets, a den and a full basement with a bar and entertainment center. Camille already transformed one of the small bedrooms into a mini-gym, placing a stationary bike, weights, yoga mats and a television hooked up to Wi-Fi. The room was painted coral and the window supplied a view of the lake. The bathroom had a shower, a toilet and a full length mirror screwed to the back of the door. The den was now her office space where a desktop, printer and scanner rested on an executive desk complete with a hutch. The large but comfortable dark leather chair once Elijah's domain is now her throne. He picked up his belongings three months ago, allowing her to move her computers and office supplies from the corner office she created in the basement.

Camille rose from the couch, stretching her arms above her head with the envelope still in her right hand. She slipped into a pair of black flats, straightens her black cotton v-neck sweater over her jeans and snatches her purse, door and car keys off the coffee table. She unlocks the front, red door and its accompanying black security door and steps out into the cool afternoon breeze. Locking the doors and pushing the security alarm pad attached to her keychain Camille hears sounds of laughter coming from the children across the street. "Hi Mrs. Darwin!"

Camille turned to the direction of the voice and an eight-year-old boy with dreads shaping a dimpled face waved. "Hello Nathan," she responded and he gave her a smile and resumed playing with the other children. Neither Nathan nor the other children knew that as of that day she was no longer a 'Mrs.' She immediately became a 'Ms' once that ink marked the sheets of paper in the envelope she held as she unlocked the car door on the driver's side.

***

The drive to the main US Post Office was 15 minutes and a lot of flashbacks flowed in Camille's head as she hit Melton Road Westbound to her destination. With her left hand on the steering wheel, she dropped her right hand downward to the push button that brought satellite radio to life. The radio was already set on an R&B station that mixed old school jams with today's hits by singers whose record labels paid big bucks to sample some of that classic old school with their beats and make a 'hit' record. No sooner than she re-focused her mind to the drive, The Isley Brothers' "Living for the Love of You" flowed from her surround sound speakers. "Perfect…play our song while I close the chapter to this part of my life," she said aloud. She did not change the station, choosing to listen to the words as her destination was halfway there.

The beginning of their end evolved two years ago when Elijah was spending more time in Chicago, especially nights. He told her he was growing tired of living at the beach house and contemplated selling it. Camille immediately protested. "You can't sell it without my approval!"

Elijah was also working longer hours in the Chicago headquarters and had a partner supervise the Indiana office in downtown Gary. Camille offered to go to the Gary office from time to time to check on the 10 member staff and give him a report maybe even do some public relations work. "I told you, you did not have to work as long as we were married!" He treated her like the arm candy she was when they first met despite the fact that she had a bachelor's and Master's degree in business management. She was a consultant for the corporation that held that party. She still consulted businesses and organizations on the sly, keeping her files on coded flash drives. As time went by, he was barely at the beach house if only to stop through and prove his existence. He never packed a bag of extra clothes from the walk-in closet in their master bedroom, nor go through his underwear and sock drawers. Camille was becoming use to home cooked meals for one with leftovers dumped in the trash can and eventually frequented restaurants that lined both Lake and Grant Streets. She knew what was up and had suspected all along that Elijah is having an affair and was blunt in approaching him about it. "If you are fucking someone else, be a man and say it," she snapped at him as they stood around the kitchen island drinking coffee during one of the days he was visiting the beach house. "You're already a dick so just end the suspense!"

Elijah slammed his coffee mug on the marble top of the island and a chip of the ceramic mug bounced and slid away with the drizzle of dark liquid in pursuit. "Damn it, Camille, I am not fucking anybody! I have been working to keep your expensive tastes on point!" As soon as those words left his lips Elijah regretted it and frowned.

"Uhm… you pimped my ass," Camille said in a steady voice. "No one told you to stare me down, bend me over and toss money and jewels at me! I was making money long before you came into my life. You were the one showing out Big Daddy style." Elijah smirked.

"No one told you to wear that red piece of cloth with your titties fighting to get out and join your leg…"

"You must haved like it. Or maybe not since it was damn near over my head five minutes later," Camille said dripping with sarcasm and pride.

Elijah stormed out that day and never returned to the beach house. He continued to pay the utility bills, housecleaning and lawn care services so Camille never worried. When their 9th anniversary came and went without a phone call or a card, Camille decided to pay a surprise visit to their Chicago condo. She still had a few things there and still had a key card to get in. The doorman greeted her and held the door open as she walked in. She entered the elevator and pushed the button for the seventh floor. During the short and smooth ride she fiddled with the key card and wondered what would she say to him once she walked inside. The elevator stopped and opened its doors and Camille stepped into the hallway that would lead her to Unit 707.

Her two-toned brown pumps made eager steps on the carpeted hallway floor taking her closer to the door. Standing in front of the door wear a pair of tan pants with a cream colored button down shirt, Camille raised her right hand and inserted the key card into the lock and waited for the small button to turn green. As the green light flashed she twisted the knob and slowly pushed the door open. The scent of cologne and perfume invaded her nostrils immediately, causing her to fight a sneeze. Shutting the door behind her, Camille walked down the foyer where pieces of African art lined the walls. She tipped through the living room where his black leather furniture from his bachelor days remained. The bedroom where she once giggled, screamed and moaned against sound-proof walls was at the end of the hall past the spacious kitchen.

Camille paused at the kitchen and stared at an empty bottle of red wine and two empty glasses. She looked at the sink and noticed dishes piled up. She felt tears welling up and immediately wiped her eyes dry as she returned to the hall that ended with her life changing.

Knowing she could not be heard outside of the room, Camille's footsteps grew louder with every level of anger in her body. When she reached the bedroom door she took a breath and grabbed the knob, giving it a quick twist. "Oh yes, big daddy…Yessss!" The woman was on her back, dangling off the foot of the king-sized bed with her eyes squeezed shut and curls bouncing to Elijah's pumping. Sweat rolled off Elijah's face and on the woman's large breasts that jiggled absurdly.

Camille eyed the bottle of blue pills on the nightstand and then back to the scene taking place. And burst into laughter. "What the hell," Elijah said as he froze hovering over the woman; his eyes straining to be as big as her breasts. Camille laughed hysterically, wrapping her arms around her waist to keep from falling on the bed and on the stunned woman.

THUMP!

Within seconds, the woman brought her legs to her knees and used her feet to push Elijah off of her, causing him to lose him balance and hit the floor. "AAAAAAAAAAAAAAAAH!"

Camille looked down and noticed her husband landed on his stomach…and still erect penis. Camille stared in shock for a few seconds…and resumed laughing. The other woman snatched and wrapped the bed sheet around her, and running past Camille, snatched her clothes from the floor then darted into the bathroom. "Oh thank God this bedroom is soundproof," Camille said while pulling the desk chair close to her agonizing husband and sat while Elijah was now curled in a fetal position.

"You may need to take a trip to the emergency room," Camille said and waited for her husband to answer.

"Are you going to take me?"

Camille hopped up from the chair then walked out the bedroom to the bathroom door. "Hell no, I'm not taking you!" She banged on the bathroom door, then turned the knob and let it fly open.

The woman threw herself against the wall terrified. Camille smirked at the woman, savoring the look of terror similar to a stupid female meeting her fate in the hands of a serial killer. "Look, he needs medical attention and the only person who can fully describe what happened…is you," she said to the woman. "So get your shit together and go tend to 'big daddy.'"

Camille stepped backwards out of the bathroom and into the hallway as the woman rushed out and into the bedroom. Camille covered her mouth as she watched the woman try to help Elijah up and back on the bed before turning away and leaving the condo, tossing the key card on the floor of the foyer.

Camille pulled into the parking lot at the US Postal Service and killed the ignition. Unfastening her seatbelt and snatching the envelope and purse from the passenger seat, she climbed out and slammed the door. Walking through the post office automatic doors, she heads to the built in mail slots on the wall to avoid the long line at the counter to her right. She pulls the hatch open and drops the envelope without a second thought. Why should she give pause? Elijah made the decision to have an affair with a woman who turned out to be all of 17 years old. He also made the decision to withdraw some prime investments from his stock holders without alerting them. Both foolish decisions that would not have been revealed if Camille did not discover the disks he left in the desk drawer inside the den at the beach house. And he would have gotten away with keeping the woman-child a secret had Camille not recognized her as the daughter of one of Elijah's clients. She knew it all and let Elijah know it. Camille smiled as she spun around and exited the post office.

Chapter 2

It was not the first time Camille has been rewarded for keeping her mouth shut about her lovers. The settlement she received from Elijah was the icing on the cake. She learned from the best; well, her mother was one of the best business women in her eyes and a definition of one of those sixties soul sisters. Naomi Ross was one of those history makers thanks to diversity policies and worked as an administrative assistant for a major firm. She loved math and numbers and could type 75 words per minute. Everything she did she kept a proper file and her boss loved her for it. She was always professional about her work and dressed the part, shopping at the downtown stores that would allow black women to shop. Camille learned a lot of business operations from her mother. Naomi would save enough money from her job to create a wardrobe for business and for play. The latter resulted in Naomi being dressed to kill and the sixties and seventies fashions allowed her to show off her beauty.

Naomi was also the other half of various suitors so when she'd make a phone call to Camille's favorite babysitter or in later years give Camille some money to go to the show and spend the night with a girlfriend, Camille knew her mama was going for a night out on the town. And she deserved it after working hard all week. Camille loved watching her mother float around the house dressed to kill in short dresses that displayed long, shapely cinnamon legs. Her hair wrapped and pinned up with loose curls draping a face that was made like a supermodel preparing for a headshot. Whenever the doorbell rang at their modest, two -bedroom house at 1091 Harrison Street, Camille would watch her mother rush to the door. Camille would be excited too and stand in the hallway waiting for her mother to open that door. It was a guessing game to the young Camille as to who would be taking her mother out that night. She stuck around long enough to see the man step inside and then Naomi would give her the 'eye' to take her little butt back to the TV room with the babysitter. Naomi never let the men get close enough to her daughter and damn sure did not want Camille calling them 'Uncle' or 'Daddy.' Camille knew all about her daddy, Keith, who was killed in a car accident when she was six years old. Naomi also schooled her on how some men will use a woman and how women will only allow themselves to be used. "But not your mama, Camille, because just when they think they have you trapped…that is when you turn the tables on them!"

As Camille got older, her mother slowed her days of being the object of men's desires and instead focused on Camille. She became a more attentive mom- cooking, cleaning and making sure Camille did her homework. She had a decent savings and checking account but still held a part-time job as a clerk for one of the city administration buildings. When Camille graduated from Roosevelt High School in 1975 at 18 years old, her mother gave her an envelope that contained a card holding a $2,000 check and a set of car keys belonging to a used Chevy Corvette. Camille drove that packed Corvette to Bloomington and enrolled at a local university where she got a dorm room with no roommate. She went to a branch of the bank she had an account with at home and deposited most of her monetary gifts and spent the rest getting things she needed for her room. For the first year she concentrated on her studies, rarely went out and got a job in the cafeteria. By her second year Camille loosened up and went to more parties and concerts while keeping her grades up. And it was the year she started secretly dating one of her professors.

Allen Johnson was a sociology professor at the university and she took his introductory class the start of her second year. Forty-five years old and married with two kids, Johnson was a fairly good looking man with an average build that he kept in shape with weekend games of basketball and tennis. He was one of a rising number of black professors at the campus so a lot of the black student population signed up for his courses. Camille always sat in the front row of the large classroom, dressed in the latest short dresses or fitted t-shirts and designer jeans. She kept her long, black hair pressed and curled to frame her face which was always made up with cosmetics her money could afford.

Camille discovered that she caught professor Johnson's attention one fall day as she entered his classroom wearing a clinging cream toned turtleneck sweater that complemented her caramel brown suede skirt that stopped at her knees and tall, brown leather boots continued the journey below her knees. She smiled at him while taking her seat and resting her book bag and purse on the floor. She sneaked a peek at her professor while crossing her legs, revealing bare and full brown thighs spilling from the skirt's hem. Johnson's eyes damn near left their sockets as they strained to get a full view. Noticing Camille looking at him with a 'gotcha' smirk on her full lips, Johnson cleared his throat and directed his attention to the entire class and began his lecture.

Their secret fling began immediately after that fateful day; Johnson would meet Camille off campus at an apartment he once lived in as a bachelor working on his Masters years ago. He still had keys to the unit, having convinced the landlord to continue the lease so that he can have a place to be by himself...or with someone. The sex was OK, but Johnson also liked talking to Camille about his frustrations and daily attributes of being a professor. Camille grew tired of her professor by the end of the semester and stopped returning his phone calls and ignored looking at him when she'd exit his classroom.

Like a lovesick puppy Johnson showed up at her dorm room holding papers in his hand so to not get suspicious looks from the other female students in the building. He tapped on Camille's door and when she opened it and immediately tried to slam it shut, Johnson pushed himself inside. Wearing a pair of gray sweatpants and a t-shirt, Camille stared at her stubborn ex-lover in disbelief. "You really need to get the hell out of here, Allen!"

Johnson reached out to touch her but jerked his hands away when Camille folded her arms across her chest and stepped back. "I don't want you to end this Camille. I am crazy about you!"

Camille looked at the man and shook her head. "No…you need to go home to your wife and kids. I am tired of this," she waved her right hand around, "Plus, I am seeing someone else." She was not lying. She had moved up to seeing the assistant dean for one of the university's departments. He was an older gentleman with prestige…and more money.

Johnson's brown eyes darkened as he heard the last words. "I can flunk your ass!" Camille glared at him and smiled.

"You can…but you won't; I have everything I need to show your wife how big of a cheating motherfucker you are!" Johnson's eyes dropped to the floor and his shoulders slumped over.

"Besides, the university would not take kindly to hearing about one of the few black professors having a history of sniffing under some of the campus' female student population."

With that last remark Camille pushed past the defeated professor and opened her dorm room door. Taking him by the elbow, she firmly but easily moved him to the other side of the door and into the hallway. "Thank you professor Johnson for the last minute details of my final grade. I worked really hard for that 'A'!" Camille said loudly and smiled as Johnson's defeated look was joined with paranoia. Camille stepped back and closed the door. "It was a pleasure taking your class!"

Chapter 3

Camille slid back into the driver's seat of her BMW, closed the door and stuck the key into the ignition just as a car horn blasted to the left side of her. "What the hell?" Camille turned to the direction of the horn which belonged to a black Cadillac. She watched as the passenger window disappeared and jerked her head back to the even louder noise of gangster rap bellowing from the speakers.

Suddenly the upper half of a man close to her age leaned over the passenger seat from behind the steering wheel. "Hey pretty lady! Nice Beemer!"

Camille's face distorted in a look of disgust. "Is he fucking serious?!" she thought to herself. She turned her head away and started the car when the horn blasted again. Agitated, Camille hit the automatic button to lower her driver's side window. "You need to turn that mess down if you have something to say," Camille shouted while thinking, this Negro is trying to act young!

The driver was sporting a salt and pepper goatee, but his short haircut was the shade of Just for Brothers Black #2. His buttoned down black shirt that had three buttons opened revealed curls of chest hair he forgot to match with the hair on his head. He grinned like he was the only black bachelor available to appear on one of those reality relationship shows. "I'm just trying to holler at you, mama! Why don't you give me your address and number and you can take me for a ride in that BMW!"

Camille threw her left hand up where her former wedding ring turned designer diamond encrusted band sparkled on her ring finger. "Sorry, not interested!"

The wannabe youngster frowned at her rejection. "Oh, it's like that? You one of those gold-digging bitches!" Camille's eyes narrowed to slits as she stared back at the man. "Baby I did gold a long time ago and you can't afford platinum!"

As the man shouted obscenities, Camille rolled her window back up, put her car in reverse, straightened the wheels and screeched away from the Caddy and its vulgar soundtrack.

"The nerve of him, trying to hit on me," Camille mumbled as she continued to drive westbound deciding she needed to do some shopping downtown. As she got closer to her destination she laughed out loud, realizing that the fool thought she was younger than he was. "Naomi always said black don't crack in our family tree!"

Camille parked in front of the department store at 6th and Broadway instead of going to the parking garage behind the building. Closing the car door behind her and pushing the alarm button, she walked towards the parking meter and swiped a mandatory token card along a slot on the meter's right side. When the amount for her one hour parking digitally appeared on the small screen, she pressed the 'OK' button and a green light appeared.

Since there's been an increase in businesses returning to Gary, thus improving the economic development and all of its surroundings, the city has enhanced numerous things. The police and fire departments have improved over the years with renewed stations, squad cars, fire engines and more. The Internet and social networking sites are part of some of the operations throughout the city.

Camille put her card away and walked towards the department store's glass double doors. Stepping into the store, Camille was greeted with jazz music flowing through the sound system. Her body relaxed as she smiled and nodded at one of the salespeople saying hello. Camille walked past clothing racks of rich and colorful business suits, dress pants, blouses and dresses filled the "Professional Woman" section of the store's main floor.

Another area had discounts on casual wear in bright colors as fall was coming soon and summer inventory had to leave. Camille walked into that section and browsed through a rack of cotton Capri pants in neutral and pastels before picking out a pair in baby pink size 14. She glanced over to the wrap front blouses hanging on another rack and chose a printed blouse with pink splattered. "These will go great with my wedge sandals," she thought out loud.

Satisfied with her selection, Camille handed the saleslady her choices and instructed her to hold on to them until she finishes. Continuing her shopping spree with more casual pieces and a fitted after five dress in her favorite color…red, Camille headed to the escalators that will take her to the second floor for shoes, intimate apparel and more.

Stepping off the top of the escalator, the front of the second floor greeted Camille and other customers with displays and racks filled with bras, panties, slips and body shifting girdles in every color and style imaginable. Camille ran her fingers along the silk fabric of a black bra and started searching for her size when a voice from behind said, "Ma'am? Would you be interested in one of our premiere body shapers?"

Camille whipped her body to the direction of the voice. The voice belonged to a young, skinny as a rail sales clerk with a short blonde bob, wearing an all teeth and gums smile…until she saw Camille's facial expression. Camille then yanked her shirt up, revealing a bare, smooth, curvy and flat stomach. "Do I look like I need a body shaper?"

The girl turned beet red and began apologizing. "I am so…SO sorry, ma'am!" Camille pulled her shirt down, turned her back to the sales clerk and hung the black bra on the rack. "I don't think I want to purchase all of the items I have on hold downstairs because of the insulting attitude that belongs to YOU," Camille said as she walked past the girl and headed back to the escalators.

The skinny sales clerk rushed to block Camille with her hands raised nearly touching Camille's chest. "Please accept my apology and a 25 percent discount on your entire purchase," the girl nervously whispered.

Smiling, Camille accepted both offers and returned to the rack to get a couple of bra and panty sets from the designer label and with a printed coupon from the girl, goes back to the main floor and check out her entire supply.

Camille walked out of the department with shopping bags filled with discounted items thanks to an employee who will surely get reprimanded for her flippant tongue. "Some people still need training on working with the public," she said.

Within a few hours Camille went from celebrating her newfound freedom from matrimony to wanting to punch rude people in the throat all because of what they perceived her to be because of her age. She was proud of how she looked younger than her 53 years on Earth; she ate what she wanted, exercised and did not smoke. She believed in the media/medical and science research and statistics from whomever on drinking glasses of red wine in moderation…sometimes. And with the genes inherited from her parents, she had nothing to worry about in the beauty department. Cosmetic surgeons need not bother to send her pamphlets in the mail. One of her few vices, the hypnotic taste of caffeine. Camille could drink five cups of coffee a day without a second thought. While many coffee drinkers spend their days wired from the caffeine, Camille was totally relaxed from the elixir. Just thinking about coffee made her develop a taste for it and the coffee shop was next door. Not ready to head back home Camille adjusted her shopping bags while taking quick steps to the shop. The smell of fresh coffee grounds embraced her nostrils like an old friend and Camille inhaled and smiled. The sounds of casual conversations, newspaper pages rustling and laptop keyboards clicking joined in, making her feel at home.

Finding a corner table for two, Camille rested her bags in one chair and sat in the other chair just as a twenty-something female server appeared to take her order. Camille noticed the server was sporting a loose bun of micro braids, a pierced left eyebrow and a small heart tattoo on her neck wearing a burgundy and khaki uniform. Camille let out a sigh of disapproval upon the free spirited employee before smiling and placing her order. "I would like a medium hazelnut cappuccino, please."

The server smiled and scribbled the order and rushed off. Within two minutes the server brought Camille's order, steaming from a burgundy cup with makeshift coffee holder. Camille took a long sip, savoring the rich flavor before swallowing. She scanned the fellow caffeine drinkers taking a break from whatever madness they have in their lives or just getting some serenity. From the retired couple reading their novels of choice, the man wearing a suit and tie punching furiously on his laptop while giving his Bluetooth a workout to the a scattering of young people texting, tweeting and whatever other magic that can be done from their cell phones. Camille took another sip from her cup, sat back and looked at her shopping bags.

Thanks to the multi-million dollar divorce settlement and the other financial rewards granted to her by the divorce court judge, she could easily continue to live a carefree lifestyle. She could do some traveling and more expensive shopping sprees. But she knew better than that. What she was awarded accompanied the money and investments she saved up over the years from her under the radar consulting projects and her flings with men from her past. Camille watched her mother spend all the money her boyfriends gave up, even spending money on her for school clothes and so forth. But Camille made a promise to herself a long time ago that she would save some of those gifts for a rainy day, snow day, shit any day.

"I should broaden my freelance consulting work," Camille thought. She's not doing anything else at the moment.

The server returned asking if Camille wanted another cup.

"No thank you," Camille said and paid her bill before grabbing her bags to leave.

"Camille!" Hearing her name loudly in the coffee shop irritated Camille as she turned to the voice. A 45 year-old woman styling a reddish brown bob that complemented her pecan skin tone and wearing a tan blazer and pants set with a brown and cream print blouse and brown pumps rushed to Camille's direction.

"Sophia," Camille smiled and leaned in for an exchange of air kisses. Sophia Andrews was a friend in the level of business and social entertainment who entered Camille's life during the first five years of her marriage to Elijah. She knew of the divorce and knew money would be involved but never inquired on how much and how Camille got it. Camille could rely on Sophia to fill her in on upcoming social events in Gary, Northwest Indiana and Chicago. With the divorce finalized Sophia can get her further inside some great networks without clashing with Elijah.

Sophia's ability to connect with a diverse group of individuals, groups and agencies thanks to social network sites and old fashion communicating was more intriguing than Elijah always wanted to stick with the same old itinerary.

"Camille, I have a social calendar filled with events and fundraisers you may want to consider attending as the clientele can help you in many aspects," Sophia said while checking her cell phone. "You need to go ahead and open a page on that Interact website and create a networking wall for your consulting. I network with at least 2,000 friends on my page and have crossed paths with at least 500 of them. I can send you 'possibilities' links after you create a profile."

"Interact sounds like a singles website than social networking," Camille said with a laugh.

"I know you are not ready for another relationship, darling so I would not do that to you," Sophia responded. "However, things do happen, compared to what I see on some of my friends' profiles!"

"Yeah, well you are right about me not wanting to jump into another relationship," Camille said then leaned closer to Sophia. "I just mailed off the signed divorce papers to Elijah anyway."

Sophia's eyes widen. "Oh well you need a bottle of champagne, fuck the cappuccino!" Camille laughed and hugged her friend.

"I am heading home, sweetie. We will talk later." Sophia waved as Camille rushed out the door and to her car before the meter's time ran out.

Chapter 4

"I need some more fresh oregano and black pepper, please!"

The blur of professional chefs and young apprentices was dizzying as preparations for the lunch crowd was in full speed. The Menagerie, a hotel sitting smack in the middle of Grant Street's 35th Avenue, was one of the most talked about hotels in the Midwest. Ten floors with rooms that range from singles to executive suites with conference rooms and fully stocked bars according to the guests' desires, the design are modern comfort and elegance.

The Menagerie – with an exterior design of double side glass picture windows – is inspired by the classic novel and movie. The lobby and front desk are a mixture of mahogany and gold with a water fountain taking center stage. The Menagerie was Grant Street's crowning glory for a revised shopping district that included exclusive boutiques with an urban twist, hair salons, a convention center and a successful independent book store call Chocolate Pages that mainly showcased novels by local and nationally known African Americans and other minority groups. Another reason why the hotel receives amounts of publicity from travel, social and entertainment media is the five- star restaurant, "M" And its master chef, Roman Cane.

"Oregano and black pepper heading your way, Roman," yelled one of the cooks who walked over and placed both ingredients on the counter at Roman's right side. The tomato sauce simmered in the pot as Roman sprinkled a couple of shakes of each requested ingredient. He turned the flames off from under a skillet of perfectly seasoned ground lamb and sausage and rushed over to three plates of cooked spaghetti. In calculated timing, Roman brought the skillet of ground meat and spread spoonfuls of it over the spaghetti. Putting the plates on a wide serving tray he walked to the pot of tomato sauce and watched as another chef scoop and drizzle the sauce on top.

"Thank you," Roman said moving to another counter and placing basil on the side and a slice of homemade garlic/cheese bread on each plate. "Spaghetti and meat sauce, table 3 PICK UP!" Roman stood back as a server picked up the tray and rushed it to the table of three hungry clients. He watched as one twisted the fork into the spaghetti and indulged into a mouthful of the dish. Roman smiled when the client rolled his eyes in bliss and gave a thumb up to the server whom said he would tell Master Chef Roman of the compliment. In a scene of controlled mayhem Roman was a steady anchor for the restaurant and his crew of 10. He'd come a long way to realize that this was what he was meant to do.

At 40 years old, Roman became a rising star in the culinary arts after a childhood beginning of learning to cook by watching and helping his mother and two grandmothers. When he was eight years old he cooked his first Sunday dinner – under the watchful eyes of his grandmothers- fried chicken, candied yams, turnip and mustard greens and dinner rolls. The only physical contribution made by his grandmothers was a lemon meringue pie and 7-Up pound cake. In his teens Roman juggled playing with friends in the neighborhood, school work and getting dinner done three times a week before six p.m. From his sophomore to junior year, he worked weekends and summers as a busboy for a local restaurant and bugged the cooks on various recipes for meals. By senior year Roman wanted to take a break from working in restaurants for jobs other than a cook and found work elsewhere. He also found trouble hanging out with the wrong crowd and it showed in his grades slipping. His parents scolded him and told him the path he was taking was nothing but fire and brimstone but it fell on deaf ears. Then one day he was caught shoplifting a pair of jeans and some movie videotapes by a security guard at a department store in Merrillville. The sad look on Roman's mother's face when she picked him up and brought him home was nothing in comparison to the looks of sorrow on his grandmothers' faces. Roman decided right then that he was going to finish his senior year and graduate from Roosevelt High School. He went away to college deciding on a degree in communications concentrating on public relations. He worked in the campus kitchen as a short order cook and was so popular that many of the students made sure to be in the cafeteria during his shifts. Thick hamburgers stuffed with crushed peppers and cheese and breakfast eggs and sausage wraps were some of his specialties.

When he graduated from college Roman worked in the marketing and public relations departments for various companies. At one company the administration hosted an appreciation event for the employees and had the food catered. Roman could tell by the expressions on some of his colleagues' faces that the food was not all that. Tasting a forkful of a lobster salad resting in a bowl place at the center of the buffet spread, Roman frowned as a colleague watched. "Too much mayonnaise and you can hardly taste the lobster meat," he said. "I can do better than this crap!"

The colleague challenged Roman and a week later, he prepared a picnic lunch for the crew that included finger tuna sandwiches, crabmeat pinwheels, fresh lemonade, butter cookies and a lobster salad that was gone within the first 15 minutes. After being asked to do some more cooking jobs, Roman decided to apply for culinary schools in Chicago and ended up with a two year scholarship at a nearby college. Graduating at the top of his class, Roman was contacted for apprenticeship programs. He was accepted to and decided to attend a culinary academy in Tuscany, Italy, enrolling in hands on cooking classes on everything from pizza to various pastas and seafood dishes. While he was one of the few African American students at this academy, the reception was wonderful and he became a favorite with his teachers. When he returned to the United States he took a job at a Chicago restaurant preparing Italian and soul dishes. It was while there he heard about auditions for a culinary competition called "The Melting Pot."

The show called for contestants of various racial and social backgrounds to compete for the chance win a $50,000 prize and national recognition with references from the world's most notable chefs. Roman filled out the registration form and paid the $100 entry fee. After qualifying as a contestant, for the next seven weeks, Roman cooked and did presentations of every mandatory dish per category, from a garden salad to a four-course dinner. Roman placed second, winning $25,000 and decent mention in the Chicago area media. Roman was hurt and angry, until a few of the chefs attending the finale approached him and gave him references for any employment opportunities. When one of the chefs called him about the Menagerie needing a master chef, Roman jumped at the opportunity because it was in his hometown. That was five years ago with plenty of top reviews, magazine profiles and television appearances added.

Three hours later the lunch crowd had its fill and only people holding conversations at the bar remained. Roman plopped down in one of chairs belonging to a table in the back of the seated area and removed his chef's hat. Stretching his muscular arms to the back of his head, his fingers raked through his neat short dark twists. "Whew," he mumbled and did a full body stretch in the chair.

A server walked to the table with a wine glass and a bottle of red wine. Placing the glass in front of Roman, the male gingerly filled the glass near the rim. Roman grabbed the stem of the glass, did a mockery salute towards the server and took a long, thirsty sip. "I certainly hope you had some food first," a honey laced voice said in front of the table.

Roman smiled while putting the glass down, his hazel eyes capturing the beauty behind the voice. Evelyn was 30 years old, 5'5 in height with 36-28-39 in measurements. A caramel hued heart-shaped face with a shoulder length, layered bob of red highlights mixed with her natural dark brown. Wearing little make-up except for glossy, pouty lips, she was a natural beauty with no fuss. Roman drank in the curves that filled Evelyn's elbow-length sleeved t-shirt in a pair of boot-cut jeans that molded her ass, hips and thighs to perfection.

"Ahem! Mr. Cane, are you listening to me," Evelyn said while waving her hand in front of his face.

"What did you say, baby?" Evelyn pulled out the chair across from him.

"I said I would like for you to be with me tonight at this event..." Roman drew in his breath and picked up the glass.

"I told you, Wednesdays are one of the busiest nights here. Business dinners, post-Bible study meals, people trying to encourage Friday to hurry up and get here! I have to be here to cook and supervise the other chefs during the dinner crowd."

"But you can get one of your assistants to fill-in," Evelyn protested.

"No, I can't. I am the master chef and it is my responsibility to have things run smoothly here!"

Evelyn rolled her eyes and folded her arms against her chest. "Just once I would like for us to show up somewhere as a couple…"

The word 'couple' caused Roman to nearly choke on the last sip of wine. "Uhm, we've only seen each other for a couple of months. That does not make us a couple," Roman said, clearing his throat.

Evelyn glared at him in disbelief. "So all I am is a bed partner to you?"

Roman raked his fingers through his locks and shook his head. "I told you in the beginning we were just dating, no strings attached because I am too busy to deal with a relationship."

Evelyn jumped out of her chair and reached for the half-filled glass of red wine but Roman snatched it up and moved it away from her. "This wine is too expensive to throw away!"

Evelyn snatched her purse and turned from Roman stomping to the exit. "You arrogant old-ass motherfucker," she screamed.

Roman watched her storm out knowing he was not going to see that plump round ass naked again. "Good thing I took the bottle with me," the server yelled from a safe distance in the kitchen.

Roman drained the rest of the wine glass dry and placed it on the table. "Oh shut the fuck up!"

Chapter 5

Camille sat at her desk staring at the new Interact profile she created from her laptop. She chose a decent photo for her default and limited her information to wanting to clearly network and apply for consultant work. Within 30 minutes she had 50 requests from people she never met, some she had not seen in years and the usual spam. "Shit, some people really need to get a life," Camille said after deleting one person who wanted a partner for all of the junk games featured on the website. She dwindle her acceptances down to 10 people and focused on making the profile appealing to possible clients.

Within an hour, Camille's Custom Consulting was born on the profile with a direct e-mail address for more information. She already had a website – Camille's Corner – that she established years ago to handle private and secret clients that Elijah knew nothing about. Not that he gave a damn to wonder if she had a website, but she also wrote blogs and interacted with clients through the chat room. She decided to browse the profiles of the first ten friends on her list, see if they had any possibilities for clientele. While going through one profile she got a signal that another request was waiting for her approval.

Clicking the box, Camille chuckled as she recognized her offline friend Sophia wearing a big grin in her default picture. "Of course I will accept you!"

Seconds after her approval, Sophia sent an e-mail about lunch at M Friday. 'I told you I had some possible clients and I will forward some friend suggestions to you later tonight,' the message read.

Camille replied to a 1 p.m. lunch date at M, knowing that Sophia already made reservations. Turning off the profile, Camille went to her personal Mail Call account inbox to check new e-mails. She noticed one message from Elijah and opened it. 'Just checking on whether or not you got the divorce papers. Wanted to get them back right away and get things done and over with and I plan on going out of town for a couple of weeks.' Camille rolled her eyes and hit the 'Reply' box. "Signed, sealed and headed your way, as if I was going to let the envelope lie around for second thoughts. You should get in sometime in the morning." She hit 'Send' and shut the laptop off. "Hmph, I need to take off for a week or two myself," Camille said as she pushed back from her desk and stood up.

****

Turning the doorknob to his condo, Roman dragged himself into the living room and tossed his carry-on bag on his brown leather sofa and dropped his keys in the clay African design bowl on the glass end table. He did not even bother to change out of his uniform when he left M tonight rushing to get away from the madness that he loves so much. Roman grabbed a remote control; hit the button and the ivory vertical blinds opened on command to a scene of night blending with the lights coming from other buildings across the street. Twenty minutes from his career the matching condominiums with manicured lawns, 24-hour security and a small shopping district was perfect for him.

Residential homes complemented the neighborhoods and families gave a damn about how their exteriors looked. These were areas where abandoned and dilapidated homes and businesses once dwelled. Roman never thought he would return to his hometown, now at times he'd hardly recognized it. He did recall an elementary school was once part of the foundation where his home on the third floor now stands. There was also a park and playground area not used in years due to rust and tall weeds. All of the past was obsolete; young and successful blended with the middle class families and divorced individuals. There was still a ghetto on the far west side but even that seemed to be the wrong term to use as families worked hard to keep their homes tidy.

The sounds of John Coltrane softly waned from the speakers as Roman stepped out of his uniform and walked straight to the bathroom. The blue and brown tile floor was cold to his feet as he relieved himself of the bottle of wine he finished off after Evelyn stormed off. Flushing the toilet Roman stepped out of his briefs walked to the tub and snatched back the brown and blue abstract shower curtain.

Turning on the hot water he shut the curtain and let the steam build while standing over the navy blue sink. Roman starred at his reflection in the medicine cabinet mirror. Hazel eyes returned a stare as he gave himself an onceover; rubbing his face with his left hand. Some grey whiskers peeked from under his chin that will leave during his shower. A strong jaw line enhanced his profile with full lips and a narrow nose compliments of his Choctaw Indian/African American heritage. "I am not an old ass motherfucker…yet." The steam clouded his vision and Roman grabbed his soap and washcloth, pulled the shower curtain back again and stepped in the navy tub. The heat and steam from the water embraced him as he lathered his muscular build. His manhood thought of Evelyn and the few times it touched that round ass and inched up her back to show how happy it was to feel her.

Then again, it stood up for just about any damn naked ass chick. Roman stood under the shower head allowing the rush and sting of the hot water to pelt his body. After a quick shave, he turned the water off, grabbed a towel and stepped out to dry off. Wrapping the towel around his waist, he reached for the spray can of deodorant, but decided against it, since he was not having any company tonight. He grabbed a smaller towel to dry his twists while walking to the bedroom.

Flipping the switch, the lights exposed the extension of the brown and blue ensemble with a king size bed with a mirrored red oak headboard/hutch. The blue and brown comforter was folded back revealing navy sheets and brown and blue throw pillows. A red oak dresser and chest of drawers filled the room, as well as a book case adorned with crime novels, memoirs, sports, business and of course, cookbooks and books on entertaining. Framed pictures of his mother and family and a couple of framed certificates for his culinary accomplishments were strategically placed along the walls.

Roman sat at the chair by a small desk and greased his legs, feet and arms with Vaseline before he reached for a pair of drawstring pajama bottoms. Climbing on the bed he grabbed the TV remote and turn on the flat screen TV drilled to the wall facing his bed. It was on a sports network where he left it earlier that morning. With the volume turned low Roman slid further under the sheet and comforter, propping his head against two king size pillows. He hit another button on the remote and the bedroom light turned off leaving the glare of the television. Glancing to his left at the empty space in the bed Roman let out a sigh. The left side of his bed has embraced a number of young women in the last year. Evelyn was the latest to put a slight dent in the mattress. The ages ranged from early 20s to mid-thirties. Evelyn was not the only one who thought in due time, a relationship would develop. A couple of honeys turned bitter towards him when they saw nothing was happening beyond sex stunts. Others had an understanding and an invoice for their time. The ones in their twenties wanted their hair and nails done and some change for shopping, which Roman did not mind from time to time. What he did not have time for was someone bugging him all the time about things. His mother however, reminded him that he was getting too old for the games. "At point or another, you need to find you a woman and settle down," Shirley Cane-Marshall said during one phone call. "You know people get suspicious when a single, forty year old Black man with no kids and can cook, is still single!" "Mama! Now you know I am not on the down low or any type of feminine lifestyle," Roman said. "I am not ready for a relationship, let alone marriage! I am having my fun." The other line echoed a grunt of unsatisfactory with Roman's response. "I would love to have some grandbabies…the legal and right way! But I guess you are going to be my baby forever," she said. Roman laughed at his mother's attempt to make him feel guilty. "Mama you will always be my number one girl!" Roman smiled at the memory of that conversation and closed his eyes. "Nope, not ready for any type of commitment."

Chapter 6

Friday afternoon was the usual busy at M as out of town guests filled the tables after checking in for their weekend stays of business or pleasure. The sun reflected brilliantly against the wall to wall glass windows of the restaurant and made the tableware and flower vases sparkle. Ice cubes delicately splashed into tall glasses of tea or lemonade, eating utensils clinked in between the chatter from various tables ranging from whispers to bursts of laughter. Camille walked inside M wearing a lavender blouse and light grey pants with grey pumps. She walked to the front desk of the restaurant and waited for the hostess to greet her. "Good afternoon ma'am, table for one?"

Camille smiled at the hostess. "No I am here to meet someone. Her first name is Sophia, last name Andrews."

The hostess looked down into the reservations tablet. "Yes! Ms. Andrews," she said and stepped away from the desk.

Camille walked behind the hostess to a window table where Sophia was checking her cell phone for messages. Camille stepped ahead of the hostess and tipped to Sophia's blind side and pinched her upper shoulder. Sophia jerked her head around. "The fu...Camille! That hurts!"

Camille laughed and leaned in to kiss Sophia's cheek. "Had to snap you out of that cell zone, girl! Put it away for some live conversation!" Sophia snapped her cell shut as Camille sat across from her and placed her lavender leather purse at her feet.

A waiter walked over and immediately poured iced water in their glasses decorated with a slice of lemon and presented them with menus. "We want a few minutes, please," Sophia said with a smile big enough to be in a toothpaste commercial. The waiter smiled back and walked off.

"Uhm, Sophia," Camille leaned and waved her hand in front of her friend. "Huh? Oh girl how old you think he is?"

Camille glanced over her shoulder at their waiter who stood six feet tall, with a medium muscular build. "Sophia! He is a boy! He's probably not even 30!"

Sophia straightened up in her chair and grabbed her water glass for a sip. "I could teach him a few things," she said with a smirk.

Camille looked at her in shock. "You are old enough to be his mother! Since when have you been trying to rob the cradle?" Before Sophia could answer, the waiter returned and Camille got a better look at his face. He had light brown eyes and deep dimples appeared when he flashed a perfect set of teeth. Camille dropped her face into the menu but not before seeing Sophia pat her chest with a napkin.

"That's it, the bitch is in heat," Camille thought. She glanced over the menu looking at her friend's plunging scoop neckline blouse and rolled her eyes to keep from laughing.

"Excuse me? While my friend is having a private summer…"Camille said and bugged her eyes at Sophia whose facial expression alone could be the death of her. "I would like a fruit salad with raspberry dressing and a turkey club sandwich and an iced tea," Camille said while ignoring the glare.

"Ma'am? What would you like to order?"

Sophia regained her composure and ordered a chicken salad and lemonade. The waiter took their menus and walked away in time to Miss Sophia snapping her head in Camille's direction. "That was NOT fucking cute!"

Camille threw her hands up while laughing. "I could not stop myself! You were patting on your chest like you were Scarlett O'Hara! I'm the one who should be patting my chest like that; I'm older than you!"

Sophia touched her bob and rolled her eyes. "I could not help if I got a bit warm."

Now it was Camille's turn to roll her eyes. "Girl it is cool in this restaurant and cooler outside. Now," Camille lowered her voice. "You've been messing with some younger men?"

Sophia smirked and darted her eyes around as if anyone gave a damn about their conversation. "I've been with a couple," she said while toying with the water glass straw. "It is nothing serious; just a little fun."

Camille looked at her friend with a new pair of eyes. Sophia became a widow two years ago when Curtis, only 44, died of a heart attack. It was a shock because Curtis was physically fit as is Sophia. Camille was there for her friend and figured it would be awhile before she got back into the dating game. But she'd not expect Sophia to go for a younger partner. "Well…how old are these young men," Camille asked.

The waiter reappeared with their orders and smiled at Sophia before walking away.

Sophia grabbed Camille's hands. "Let's pray," she said and quickly bowed her head. Moments later Camille snatched her hands away and Sophia speared a fork into her chicken salad.

"SOPHIA!! Start talking!"

Sophia looked at her. "One guy was 40…and the last guy was," she put a forkful of salad in her mouth. "The last guy was…29."

Camille held one half of her sandwich in midair and suddenly looked over her shoulder at their cute waiter talking to a couple. "Oh no wonder you were staring at him! The waiter has to be younger than your last conquer," Camille laughed.

Sophia smacked her hand. "Shut up! Besides, I can't deal with the waiter anyway. I dine here too much," Sophia grabbed her lemonade. "And he is likely to stalk me later."

Camille threw her hand over her mouth and coughed...or laughed. "Oh, you're all that huh! Wow! I mean, I would never think you would go with a younger man."

Sophia looked at her. "While you will never find out, my goodies are priceless!" That drew laughter from both of them. Sophia then stirred the salad with her fork. "It has nothing to do with losing Curtis at his age. I mean forty-four is not old. Hell I am not old. But after a while I was noticing how some younger guys were checking me out more. And the 40 year old was at a mutual friend's birthday party and he asked for my number. I got his number instead and we went out for drinks a few times. The last time, which was a couple months ago, he came to my place and..."

Camille leaned over her plate, chewing rapidly on a bite of her sandwich. "And what!" She mumbled.

Sophia laughed. "And we had sex! He was very good and he was nice." Camille smiled and leaned back. "But he was not good enough." Sophia shook her head. "No, he wanted a relationship. I told him I was not ready and he said he understood. But I did not hear from him again."

Camille nodded, understanding. "Well, I know I am not trying to meet somebody right now because the ink just dried on my divorce papers. But I don't know if I would want a younger man when the time comes."

Sophia gave her friend a slight smile. "Well, I know you are not ready. But you never know when cupid or Mr. Right Now may show up."

Camille dropped her gaze from Sophia to her salad. "Let's move on to another subject," she said while shoving a forkful of strawberry and mango slices with pecans.

"Well, there are a couple of events happening within the next week, including a charity garden party Sunday."

Camille looked at her. "You mean this Sunday as in day after tomorrow?" "Yes! It's going to be a nice event, no need to panic. You can find something to wear. The crowd will be mixed in age and backgrounds and the pavilion in Miller is hosting it," Sophia said. "Proceeds will benefit a children's organization for upcoming summer camps that will be fun and educational. The consultation's already done but the guest list is promising with locals, Chicagoans and even some people from Michigan. I am sure you can get a good number of business cards exchanged and you can have some fun and good food." Camille went into deep thought while finishing her sandwich. "And you may run into a couple of Elijah's friends," Sophia whispered as Camille glared at her. "But Elijah and his slut...I mean...yeah, slut, won't be there."

Camille laughed. "Ok I will put it on my calendar. What else you have?"

They continued their conversation and when the waiter returned, both refused dessert and asked for the check. "I told you Camille, this is my treat," Sophia said while pulling out her credit card. After the waiter brought the receipt and card back, they grabbed their purses and headed to the exit.

"Sophia? You did not say anything about the 29 year-old you made love to," Camille said as she pushed the exit door open.

"Oh we did not make love," Sophia said while putting on her sunglasses and brushing past Camille. "We fucked."

Chapter 7

"Here comes Mr. Ladies' Man!"

The waiter rolled his eyes as he walked in the kitchen, trying to ignore the chants coming from his co-workers following Roman's lead. "What? I can't help if it the ladies love them some, Derek," he said.

Roman laughed while dicing a red pepper for fresh salsa. "Man I'm hearing from the other waiters on staff that you pick up a few numbers here. Better be careful with that shit. Mess with the wrong girl or woman staying here and your ass will be asking folks if they want that super sized!" Derek nodded.

"Well I heard your lady friend…" Roman stopped Derek mid-sentence with an icy glare that quieted the kitchen.

"That young lady was not a guest of the Menagerie. And you do not need to worry about my world," Roman said.

Derek raised his hands in defeat. "My bad, Roman, take it easy! I am not dealing with the hotel guests or the diners anyway. It is just harmless flirting. Part of the services we provide at the M."

Roman went back to chopping the peppers. "That does not include escort service…remember that," he said as the staff burst into laughter.

Roman checked his schedule from his cell phone for the next week and highlighted a few events. He was flying to New York Tuesday to tape a couple of guest judge appearances on two cooking shows and doing a newspaper interview about future goals in his career. He could have easily taken an offer a while back to host a reality TV cooking show like that vulgar talking British chef, but decided to return home. Besides, if he ever got the opportunity to host or create a show why not create it in Gary? He also highlighted his weekend schedule which included overseeing and preparing the menu for a garden party fundraiser in Miller. He made an extra note to contact the committee and go over the final approval for the menu. Just as he turned off the calendar the lyrics to "Bad Mama Jama" blasted from the phone. He cut the ringtone off and smiled because he already knew who that song was dedicated to. He let Evelyn's call go to voicemail, shoved the phone in his black pants pocket and went back to work.

****

Camille made a stop at the grocery store before heading home to stock up on fresh fruits, vegetables and poultry. She always limited her indulgence of sweets occasionally buying some glazed donut twists or a half gallon of mint chocolate chip ice cream. Since it was officially the weekend she decided to toss some ice cream and a small package of chocolate sandwich cookies in the cart. She grabbed a couple packages of frozen skinless chicken breasts and some wings along with a packaged bag of spinach and pre-washed turnip greens she will wash again before cooking. Camille pushed the shopping cart to the seafood counter and ordered a pound of perch fillets that she will bake later.

Moments later Camille packed everything into the BMW's trunk, walked to the driver's side climbed in and pulled off. Pulling into her driveway and turning off the engine, Camille popped the trunk and got out of the car in time to see one of the neighborhood kids grab a bag to carry. "Aw, thank you, baby," she said as she grabbed the other bag and led him to the door. "Your parents raised you right," she said as she unlocked the doors and they walked in. She pointed him to the kitchen and the boy hurried to the counter. He turned to walk out the door. "Hold on!"

The boy turned around and Camille handed him a five dollar bill. "Thanks Ms. Darwin!

"No, sweetie, thank you for helping me. You are a rarity in the world today," she said and walked him to the door. The boy shoved his reward in his pocket before running down the driveway, making Camille laugh at his secrecy.

Kicking off her shoes, Camille returned to the kitchen and began unloading the groceries. Opening the steel refrigerator she paused before placing the wrapped fish on a middle shelf. The refrigerator used to be stocked to the hilt with all kinds of leftover dishes, some of her favorite food items would join Elijah's choices. The door shelves would fill up with everything from a bottle or two of wine, condiments and other snacks for him. Elijah loved to cook on occasion, thinking he was a superior chef with his exaggerated presentations.

"Tonight we will have the best grilled steaks you've ever tasted," Elijah said one summer night last year. Wearing an apron with the words 'Too Hot to Handle" printed above an illustration of flames and cooking utensils, Elijah sang a Luther Vandross song while tenderly grilling their steaks on the pit in the balcony. Camille was sitting at the patio table holding a glass of red wine and watching Lake Michigan make waves at the shore. The white foam Mother Nature created as the waves rushed over under a star-lit sky was the perfect background that night. She watched as her husband rushed into the kitchen, listening to him opening and closing the refrigerator then return to the balcony with two bowls. "Here, let me help," Camille said placing her glass down. Elijah shook his head no and placed the bowls on a side table behind her. He then turned around and leaned over, placing soft kisses on the left side of her neck. "I got this baby." Camille turned to him and grabbed his face and gave him a full, deep kiss. Their tongues danced slowly then fast and she felt his hands brush across the fabric of her halter top. His left hand slipped into the cup of her right breast and squeezed her full flesh. She halfway rose from her chair for him to have better access when he stopped. "Can't let the steaks burn," he said in a ragged voice and stepped away from her.

Camille eased back into the chair and adjusted her halter, frustrated that he was focusing on grilled meat when she now hunger for a different kind of beef. He brought the steaks on a platter and fixed their plates with his homemade spaghetti and meat sauce and pasta salad. He removed the apron and sat at the table next to her and they ate in silence. Once finished he stood up and cleared the table and took the dirty dishes in the dishwasher. Camille walked past with the covered bowls and placed them in the refrigerator. Elijah went back outside and made sure the fire was gone from the barbecue grill and stepped back inside, locking the door and turning off the balcony lights. He walked past Camille, lightly patting her ass that filled the denim shorts before heading out of the kitchen. She took that as a signal to resume what went down on the balcony and smiled. Grabbing the remaining bottle of wine and their glasses, she rushed out of the kitchen and stopped. Elijah was sitting on the couch in the living room with his briefcase opened and business papers in his hands. His reading glasses were perched on the bridge of his nose and the television was on a news channel with the volume low.

Camille lowered her arms to her sides. "Baby." Elijah barely looked up. "Baby," Camille walked over to the couch and stood over him.

Elijah looked up. "What honey?"

Camille smiled seductively and leaned in enough for him to see her breasts spilling from the halter. "I want dessert."

Elijah looked at her for a second then lowered his eyes to the papers. "There's some strawberry cheesecake in the fridge," he said.

Camille straightened up and stared at him, the glasses clinking and threatening to break between her fingers. She held the wine bottle in her right hand which started slowly swaying and brushed against her thigh. "Elijah!" The only response he gave her was a grunt and rustling of the papers, ignoring her.

"CRASH!!"

Elijah jumped and turned to his right as a stain of red wine from one of the glasses splattered on the wall, the once full bodied glass now shattered on the floor. He looked at Camille who turned around and stormed off to their bedroom while filling the remaining glass to the rim.

Camille placed the wrapped fish and pre-packaged greens and spinach in the refrigerator and slammed the door. She pulled back the freezer compartment's door and placed the ice cream and poultry inside. Having that flashback was a hint that Elijah was cheating on her, but she was hoping against hope that he wasn't. When it came to a head, she was insulted and pissed off that he traded her for a younger woman. Not that she could not say anything, but when she learned of his infidelity it set her to reeling in anger. At least he could have picked someone who looked better than me, she thought while heading to her couch and plopping down. That fake, cheap, weave/color contact lens wearing, gap-toothed bitch!

The day Camille saw her in bed with Elijah she knew the girl was faking her passion. It was all about the money for her with her underage ass. Camille figured he wrote her a nice check to shut her up and she went partying with her friends and roughnecks. Camille shook her head to snap out of the funk and grabbed the remote control. Turning to a fashion network, she grabbed her phone on the side table and did a speed dial to her hair stylist, hoping for an emergency squeeze in appointment tomorrow. She had a full day to shop for an outfit for Sunday's garden party and wanted to look her very best.

Chapter 8

Roman smiled as his personal alarm clock got louder and louder. His eyes remained closed but his hands roamed Evelyn's familiar curves as she looked down at him with a glazed stare of intense pleasure. She was riding his manhood with moans matching each stroke. "Baby, you feel sooo...sooo good," Evelyn said as she picked up the rhythm.

Roman held her tightly and matched her with upward thrusts, sending her into delirium and then an orgasm. She lay on top of him fighting to catch her breath as sweat glisten her curves. Roman smacked her ass and moved her off of him. "Wha...wait! Where are you going," Evelyn shrieked as she ignored the sting from his hand and pushed her hair off her face.

Roman got out of the bed and his nakedness headed for the bathroom to remove the condom. After flushing the toilet, he closed the door and Evelyn heard the shower come on. "Oh no he didn't," Evelyn said loudly while jumping out of the bed not bothering to cover up. She banged on the bathroom door.

Roman frowned at the noise. "WHAT?"

"How are you just going to get out of bed and jump in the shower," Evelyn shouted.

"Evelyn....I have a busy day today! I have to get a menu ready for a party tomorrow," Roman yelled over the spraying of hot water.

"You could not even tell me that was great or shit, hello!"

Roman sighed under his breath while soaping up. "Girl we said hello last night! I told you when you came by that I had a busy weekend. Now you are going to have to get your clothes on and I will let you out in a minute."

Evelyn stood at the other side of the bathroom door, fuming. She turned around and snatched up her panties and bra from the floor and put them on. By the time Roman stepped out of the bathroom with a towel around his waist Evelyn was standing at the foot of his bed with her arms folded across her mid-riff top. Her left denim covered leg was jerking from the bouncing of her booted foot. "Not even breakfast?"

Roman looked at Evelyn and reached out to take her hand. She jerked away and walked out the bedroom. "Evelyn...you know what this is," Roman said while walking past her to unlock the door. "If you can't deal with it, then it may be best that we not see each other..."

SMACK!

Evelyn stormed out the unit as Roman placed his hand on the right side of his face. He closed the door and locked it, thankful he did not give her a key. He went back into the bedroom and stopped at the dresser mirror to check his face. "Good. She didn't leave a handprint," he said.

Chapter 9

Camille treated herself to a mini-spa day at Love Lee's, a quaint salon along the East Side of Gary that offered manicures, pedicures, massages and a team of hairstylists. The salon was designed to mimic a tropical getaway, with soothing tones of blues and greens being the chosen colors for the furniture and equipment, hanging waterfalls along the walls and a sound system flowing with soothing music. No televisions blaring the latest loud mouth ghetto dramas. A selection of books and magazines were made available if the clients chose to browse. She was accepted as a walk-in due to a cancellation and decided on a wash and curl and a mani-pedi.

Camille relaxed as soon as she sat in the chair attached to the shampoo bowl, feeling water run through her hair. As the shampoo girl worked magical fingers on her scalp, another employee began massaging her feet in preparation of the pedicure. Ninety minutes and $200 later, Camille walked out of the salon loving the lightness of her now shoulder length layered bob. The bob allowed her slightly graying hair to blend perfectly with her natural born black and the long bangs were a nice touch. She climbed into her BMW and placed French manicured tips on the steering wheel and the shift changer and pulled off, directing her car to the mall.

The department store of her choice had the biggest selection of dresses for a Sunday afternoon gathering that did not look matronly. Camille took relief that the selections were also on sale as fall and winter clothes filled the racks even though it was August. Going through the racks, she settled on medium tone green cotton shirtdress with elbow length sleeves and a wide, black belt with green prints around the buckle. The belt perfectly cinched her waist and the skirt area had just the right flow and length to show off her legs. She had a pair of black three inch open toe sandals at home that would be perfect with the dress. She also grabbed a bold necklace and earring set in polished black stones with reflective splashes of rainbow colors. Satisfied with her purchases Camille stopped at a deli on the mall's upper level, ordered a turkey Swiss on rye and headed home.

****

Roman rushed through M's double doors on a mission to make sure everything would be fine for the Sunday garden party. He OK'd the outdoor seating area at the right side of the hotel as it was closed off to diners so the staff can decorate the tables and background. He glanced and nodded at customers seated inside while making his way to a table in the back where

Sophia Andrews waited for him. They were discussing the finalizations of the food and drink menus for the party.

Roman brushed his hand on top of his locks neatly pulled and tied into a ponytail and brushed his other hand across the front of his long sleeved black t-shirt. He wore dark jeans as he wanted to be as comfortable as possible when he wore his chef jacket later.

Sophia looked up from the printed menu and smiled at the young man heading her way. She thought he was very handsome and well-built to be a chef. "He must taste his food then work it off…someway," she thought with a smirk.

Roman smiled at Miss Andrews and reached for her hand to shake before pulling out a chair next to her. "Roman, I am so glad you could meet with me one last time before you and your staff prepares the menu for my get together," Sophia said while scooting closer to Roman.

He kept his smile intact as Sophia's hand pats his right thigh. Is she trying to hit on me? She's old enough to be my mother! "No problem, Miss Andrews…"

"Sophia. Please call me Sophia," she interrupted his flow with a wink. She crossed her legs allowing the already short hem of her denim skirt rise a little higher.

Roman cleared his throat and focused on the menu. "So you want cucumber and chicken salad finger sandwiches, sweet and sour meatballs, ravioli stuffed with crab meat, fresh fruit and vegetable trays, a tower of small, red velvet cupcakes. And for drinks, you want pitchers of alcoholic and non-alcoholic mint juleps and fresh lemonade?"

Sophia leaned forward. "Yes, that is correct," she said.

Roman glanced at her and back to the menu. He knew good and hell well this woman was not flirting with him. It would not be the first time an older woman tried to get his attention, but he was not feeling that type of love. He was flattered of course with the little notes delivered to him by a smart aleck waiter. And more than once in his years as a chef he has been requested to visit the table of older women in plunging necklines, made up faces with the only fat on them was their credit cards. Many looked at him as if he was the main course offered exclusively away from the menu, but he would politely decline. And he would hear it from his colleagues or friends. "What! You would never consider hitting some older woman for sex? These are not old maids from a seniors cruise ship brother! These are women in their 40s or 50s who keep in shape and have money," he would hear some of his friends shout.

Roman focused back to the matter at hand and continued discussing the menus. Thirty minutes later Sophia was walking out the doors and Roman was wiping his brow and cutting his eyes towards the loud, smirking sounds coming from some of the waiters nearby. "You all enjoyed the show?" The waiters stopped and scattered to the dining area.

Roman got up and headed to the small office near the kitchen and grabbed his chef's jacket and a short white hat with his initials, RC, stitched in front. His assistant Cary looked up and smiled. "You may as well walk into the cougar's cage my friend," Cary said with a laugh.

Roman walked past him but not before slapping his shoulder. "Don't worry about who I dip," he said, returning the laugh.

Chapter 10

The outdoor party Sophia put together was underway and she could not have prayed for a more beautiful Sunday afternoon. A group of musicians from the local symphony played near the hotel's water fountain and the guests networked while nibbling on the delicacies and praised the refreshingly chilled glasses of mint julep, more so the alcoholic version.

Camille walked to a table served as the registry as two young women in floral sundresses and shawl sleeves smiled and offered her a pen and sign-in tablet. Once she signed her name and e-mail address, one of the women handed her a small gold trimmed white gift bag filled with floating vanilla scent candles, a business card holder, pens and a $25 gift card to use wherever Camille pleased. Sophia never disappoints, she thought to herself while taking the bag. "Thank you," Camille said as she walked away from the table and towards the party.

She eyed the tables draped with white tablecloths and table settings of gold and white. Fresh flowers filled glass centerpieces. The theme grasped at the last days of summer and the guests wore casual dress, enjoying the August sunrays. She spotted Sophia in a burnt orange off the shoulder blouse and light tan pants with orange and gold criss-cross sandals. Thin gold hoops swung gently from under her hair which looked to be clipped shorter than the last time they met. "Now had I known she was going to be Miss bohemian, I would have worn my pantsuit," Camille thought to herself. She shook it off and confidently sashayed towards her friend; nodding to some of the guests. A couple of them returned with a curt nod in Camille's direction, as they were friends of Elijah. Knowing they were watching her every move, she added an extra switch to her already sultry walk that not even the widest of skirts could hide.

Sophia turned away from one of the guests and smiled broadly as her friend made an entrance with her green dress and a fresh hairdo that complemented her chiseled face. "There's my girl," Sophia announced while rushing to embrace Camille. "Girl the couple on the left are practically glaring at you," Sophia said in Camille's ear while hugging her tight. Camille pulled back and glanced in the couple's direction. "Hmph they are a couple of Elijah's friends. I guess I am supposed to look 20 years older, slumped over and defeated," Camille continued.

She immediately faced them and threw a wide smile. "So nice to see you!" The couple, startled at Camille's cheerful greeting, turned away, awkwardly staring at a centerpiece on a nearby table. "That'll teach those petty motherfuckers," Camille said while still smiling as Sophia covered her mouth to stifle a laugh.

Sophia stood at Camille's left side and looped an arm through hers, leading her to a center table. "You have a seat and I will personally bring you a plate of goodies and a glass of strong mint julep," Sophia said as Camille sat down.

Camille watched Sophia dash off to the buffet table and sat against the wired frame of the chair taking in the scenario. She smiled when she noticed the hot, young waiter they talked about days ago as he checked the guests for refills. She also noticed there were more couples than singles at the event, but this was about business networking not getting a man. She reached inside her gift bag and pulled out the gold plated business card holder then reached inside her purse to grab some business cards from a side compartment. Her cards were red with gold lettering spelling out her name, consulting business, contact phone numbers and her e-mail address and website information. She placed 25 cards into the cardholder and shut it closed.

Sophia had returned with a plate, fork and napkins in her right hand and a tall glass of mint julep in her left. "Here you go, love." Camille took the items and placed them in front of her and glanced in the direction of the waiter. "You hired a couple of waiters to serve the guests. Were you afraid I would hit on young blood over there?"

Sophia plopped in a chair next to Camille and pinched her arm. "I was being a good friend, bitch," she snarled, then broke into laughter.

Camille raised a chicken salad finger sandwich to her lips. "Retract the claws sweetie, I don't want him," Camille said.

"Neither do I…I don't think," Sophia said.

Camille shook her head and took a bite from the sandwich and smiled from the richness of the chicken salad. "This is delicious! I've never had the chicken salad here," Camille said.

Sophia pointed in the direction where Roman stood near the buffet table. "The chef is right there with the locks in a ponytail. His name is Roman Cane."

Camille stopped mid-sip from her mint julep and glared at Sophia. "Roman Cane? It sounds like he made that up using the words Roman candle!"

Sophia pinched Camille's arm causing the glass to slip slightly and Camille to put a tighter grip. "Roman Cane is his real name! He was the young man with the story of coming from a family of women who taught him how to cook. This is a step towards bigger dreams he has," Sophia said.

Camille looked at Roman who was handing a waiter empty food platters from the table and replacing them with the help of another waiter. She had to admit this chef was kind of handsome…and young. She smiled while watching him charm a giggle from a young girl as he handed her a saucer balancing one of the towering red velvet cupcakes. The girl's parents smiled at the chef's gesture of personal attention. His eyes are definitely piercing shade of brown she thought to herself then snapped out of it. Sophia continued to gush about Roman. "He is truly a sweet, rugged young man…"

Camille looked at her friend. "You've fucked him already, haven't you?"

Sophia's eyes widened as big as the saucer the girl held in her hand. "I HAVE NOT!" Sophia looked around as people sitting at nearby tables stopped talking and eating to glance at her while Camille took a long sip of mint julep. She knew Sophia was going to cuss her out or cut her for being so blunt. Camille glanced at the table for any knives or sharp objects.

Sophia's skin reddened, making her pecan skin tone look warm but hardly toasty. "I am not a slut, Camille," she whispered in an angry tone.

Camille soon regretted asking the question, not wanting to hurt her friend's feelings. The last thing she needs to tease any woman about is the extent of her libido. She touched Sophia's hand. "I am so sorry. I did not mean any harm. Please forgive a new divorcee for being so cruel."

Sophia looked at Camille and offered a small smile. "All is forgiven and no, I have not fucked him, but I did flirt with him a bit. He seems to have no interest in older women because he totally ignored my ass," Sophia said with a laugh.

Camille laughed with her friend and took another sip of her drink. "Well, all jokes aside, Roman Cane does look like the type who has a long line of…what is the term, honeys at his command," she said.

Sophia stared at her friend and released a louder laugh and this time nearby table guests ignored them, assuming all was well between the two. "Actually, the term they use now is Dip. As in, he dips his, ahem, into plenty of holes," Sophia said.

Camille's eyes widened then tightly shut close as she shook her head. "Dips! Do women even bother to look into how men perceive them?"

Sophia kept quiet hoping her friend would not ask her to answer that question. She may not have known Camille all of her life but she knows the story of how Camille had her eyes set on Elijah from the moment she saw him. She dare not remind her because all Camille would say is all is fair in love and war. "I'm not saying Roman has a slew of women, but he probably keeps busy," Sophia said while grabbing a finger sandwich from her plate.

Camille shrugged her shoulders and pushed her chair back to stand up. "I'm going to walk around and pass out some of my cards, see if I can get a client or two. You behave while I'm gone," she said and walked away.

The musicians were taking a break eating and balancing their plates on their laps turn makeshift tables. Camille stopped at every filled table introducing and exchanging cards with a good number of people. A couple of the card takers bent her ear about what they needed and if she could offer the services. Roman was also walking through the crowd, stopping at tables shaking hands and handing out some of his cards. With Camille speaking to people at tables from the west end of the party and Roman moving his way from the east end, it looked like they were competing in giving out the most cards. Within 15 minutes both were chatting with people seated at tables side by side, dead center of the party. Another two minutes goes by and both were standing nearly back to back from each other, leaning in to talk or listen to their perspective clients. Three minutes later, Camille stepped sideways to her left, brushing her butt against his. Startled, Camille moved to turn and face the person she nearly knocked over. "Oh excuse me," she said while turning around.

Roman shifted his body to turn his head sideways in her direction. "Not a problem, ma'am," he said, returning his attention to the couple at the table.

Camille glared at the back of his head as if she could spark flames to strike his ponytailed locks. She knows he was being respectful and polite, but just hearing that word knowing it is for her burned her up. She rolled her eyes to his broad shoulders and allowed her eyes to continue rolling down his back in the fitted white chef's jacket. They then focused on the slightly narrow waist that would lead to his hips covered by a pair of pressed black slacks…

"Ma'am I said I was sorry for bumping into you."

Camille's eyes stared wide as she snapped her head to the voice in front of her. Roman had turned around after feeling like someone was burning a hole in his back. He looked at Camille with slight smile mixed with some frustration coming from believing this woman did not accept his apology.

Camille felt the heat rush her chest and scamper to her face. "Oh no, I am aware of your apology and I accept. I was just…thinking," she said while clearing her throat.

Roman dropped the frustration and offered a full blown grin. He gave her face a quick glance. She had a vibe of sophistication in her, he thought to himself. He stared into her dark brown eyes that returned a piercing gaze. He looked away, but not before noticing her full lips. Roman thought she could not be that much older than he was, because he did not see any smile lines etched from the corners of her mouth. She had cheekbones that rivaled notable black female superstar models. When she excused herself and walked to the next table of people, Roman found himself watching her switch off, her dress swaying at every step. "OK, what just happened," he thought to himself.

Chapter 11

Camille spent the next hour talking to other guests and occasionally walking past Sophia to give her a squeeze on her arm and a smile. It was a sign that she was getting some contact information from definite clients. Soon the musicians were packing away their instruments and the hotel's sound system was providing smooth jazz for lingering guests. The waiting staff was clearing the tables while some people chatted while draining the last of the lemonade and the two mint juleps. Sophia sat in another chair smiling at the success of her event while Camille sat across from her counting the money Sophia made from ticket sales. The young girls at the greeting table had counted the money earlier and turned over the cash in a metal cash box. But as soon as they left with smiles on their faces while stuffing their 'thank you' envelopes in their purses, Camille grabbed the box to do a double check. Sophia laughed at her friend but did not argue about her being presumptuous towards the ladies. "Four hundred and fifty dollars," Camille said as she slammed and locked the lid to the box, sliding it across the table to Sophia's right hand.

"Just like what it said on the sheet of paper," Sophia replied.

Camille winked. "You're welcome. So, I guess I will be going. You probably have a few more thank you envelopes to hand out to the chef and staff." Camille stood up and grabbed her purse.

"Hold up slick! What was all that staring between you and Chef Roman Cane earlier this afternoon?"

Camille gave Sophia a befuddled look. "There wasn't any staring! We bumped against each other in the narrow space between the tables and I said excuse me."

Sophia cocked her head up at Camille with an expression that read Bullshit. "You two looked at each other longer than 30 seconds!"

"Did you have a fucking timer in your hand, Sophie," Camille asked sarcastically. "It was nothing. Let it go." Camille walked around the table and leaned down to kiss Sophia on the cheek. "I will call you tomorrow…"

"WAIT!"

Sophia and Camille straighten and looked in the direction of the loud command. Roman was rushing towards them with two white paper bags neatly closed shut. He stopped in front of Camille and thrust his left hand in her direction waiting for her to take the bag. "I wanted to give you a take-home bag because I believe you did not have time to stop at a certain dessert table," he said flashing that grin.

Camille took the bag from him and opened it. Two red velvet cupcakes rested inside separate plastic containers. "Oh thank you so much! You are right I did not make it to the cupcake tower. Then again, I really don't need these."

Roman looked at her. "A little extra sweetness won't hurt your body." Camille looked away from the bag and right at his face which was now showing a little blush.

"Uhm, I did not mean it to come out like that! I was not saying you were mean," he stammered before shutting up. Camille smiled at him. He looked cute standing there embarrassed. Then she caught Sophia using her head like an observer at a tennis match, grinning from her chair.

"Thank you again Mr. Cane for the cupcakes. The rest of the food was also delicious and the mint julep was amazing," she said while closing the bag. "Have a good evening."

Camille turned to walk away, leaning sideways to pinch Sophia's arm hard before darting off causing her to yelp and rub the area. "Bye Sophia!"

Chapter 12

After saying goodbye to Miss Andrews and passing out the 'Thank you' envelopes his appointed staff that contained checks for their hard work, Roman walked in his office and shut the door. He placed his own thank you envelope in the side pocket of his jacket and walked around his desk to take a seat in the black leather chair. Bringing himself closer to the desk, he reached in his pants pocket and pulled out a handful of business cards from some of the guests. Sorting the cards one by one, he stopped at the red and gold card with 'Camille's Consultations' engraved. She had not handed him a card; he happened to spot one left on another table before she left and he snatched it up. Why he did that he had no clue. He flipped the card continuously between his left thumb and forefinger. And her image ran through his mind. And he smiled.

The silver BMW zipped eastbound towards home and Camille hardly focused on the possibility of getting pulled over by one of Gary's finest. With one hand resting on top of the steering wheel and the other on her right thigh Roman's face and smile flashed in her mind faster than the blur of other cars on the road. She could not help but notice how he was possibly built underneath the chef's jacket and black slacks today. And he had a slight pimp walk in his moves. Not too much, but enough to catch it. There was confidence in his stride and he looked like he worked out. That smile could charm the most evil bitch into a salivating, bosom heaving, panting…

"Ooh Shit!" Camille shouted and snapped out of it just in time to brake at a red light. The screaming front tires came from a red jeep that was crossing the intersection with the right of way on her side.

Camille cringed and mouthed 'Sorry' to the jeep's owner who glared at her and shouted 'Bitch!' before continuing on her way. Camille breathed a sigh of relief then cursed again for getting distracted by some young blood in a chef's uniform. "I don't need a damn puppy sniffing at my heels," she said aloud as if drivers in cars alongside of her could hear and nod in agreement. The light changed in her favor and she slowly pulled off this time and paced her way home.

Chapter 13

Camille drove into her driveway, put the car in park and turned off the ignition. She grabbed her keys; purse and cupcake bag and stepped out. She unlocked the doors and disengaged the house alarm then closed and locked the doors. While happy to be home, the feeling of not having someone to greet her with a pair of strong, loving arms ready to embracing got to Camille. She hated to think of her past as a Mrs. However, she was new to the divorce circuit and from talking to girlfriends who were veterans, they told her it would be a while before the ex leaves the mind. Especially the kind of flashbacks that involved naked bodies dancing with the glow from rows of candle lights. Camille had those thoughts every now and then when she and Elijah could not wait to tear each other's clothes off. At times they barely made it to the bedroom and a hardwood floor did not feel so cold when you're in heat. Camille felt herself having a flashback just from standing in the foyer holding a damn bag of cupcakes. "Shit," she said as she continued to walk towards the kitchen while an image of a man raced in her head. She expected to see Elijah's smiling face watching her as she performed one of her well known and loved strip teases. The image of the fine brother remained fuzzy but was just enough to make Camille think he was actually there.

Camille's walk became more confident with each click of her heels. She fingered the top button of her shirtdress and undid each button after while walking and switching to a bass line playing in her head. Each low hard beat captured the movement of her hips and Camille closed her eyes as her shirt dress draped open. An ivory lace plunging bra was exposed with matching boy shorts. Camille did not wear a slip because she hates them. She dropped her purse and keys onto a corner chair at the end of the foyer and shimmied the shirtdress off her body. The bass line pulsed deeper and louder to the point that they were in the room. Camille developed a grooving frown on her face as she rocked, dropped and swayed in her heels and underwear. When she opened her eyes the brother's image was clearer and the smile was miles wide. It was Roman.

Camille gasped, and then burst into laughter. She looked around the kitchen and at her near nakedness in front of the island. The fact that she thought about this young chef watching her do a strip tease amused her. "He does not want any of this. Not that I could not teach him some things," Camille said while placing the bag on the counter. She hopped onto one of the four chairs around the island and opened the bag, pulling one of the containers out with a trapped cupcake. Gingerly taking the cupcake out and raising it to her lips, she stuck out her tongue. Her tongue lashed out at the thick white frosting, removing a heaping amount from the deep red moist cake. Camille paused for a moment to allow her tongue to waver and lowered her eyes to look at the frosting. Then she rolled her tongue into her mouth and smiled as the frosting melted before she swallowed. And she laughed. "The boy would have an asthma attack if I did all of this and then some to him," she said and laughed again.

Chapter 14

"Ask him out."

Camille jerked her head back from the desktop screen as the words sat there waiting for additional words to join them. She forgot to hit the 'discreet' button on her Interact page that would hide her from friends who may want to talk to her. It was barely 8 a.m. Monday morning when Camille decided to turn on the computer after going to the bathroom. The three words came from Sophia who notice the 'online' button and opened the chat room. Camille cussed herself out for not going back to bed, but she was anxious to see if any of the people at the party yesterday sent her requests for interactions. Now Sophia was popping up in her imaginary business. "HELLO! I know you are still online," the next sentence appeared with a ;-) at the end.

Camille typed furiously on the keypad. "Ask who out?" and smiled, visualizing Sophia cursing her out. Sophia could have easily hit her with a message to appear on the webcam, but both were too vain to greet each other with stank breath face – that's when you look at a face and know that person did not brush and gargle yet - and do ragged hair.

Sophia's response blazed the chat wall. "DON'T PLAY WITH ME! You know who I am talking about!"

Camille burst into laughter and banged the keys. "LOL! I am not asking that boy out on a date! There was nothing going on…no sparks. No flirting."

"He gave you a cupcake to take home," Sophia typed.

"He gave me TWO cupcakes!"

"WHAT?!" That stingy mother… well, that proves he likes you!"

"It does not! He was being nice. Now go back to bed. I am!" Camille hit the logout button before another word from Sophia appeared and shut off the screen. She got up from the desk and rushed to the bed and climbed in for another hour or two of sleep. She thought about telling Sophia about the strip tease visualization and Roman 'watching' her, but changed her mind. There was no need in giving her friend more ammunition to push her into asking young blood out.

****

Roman and his staff were on Round Two of serving breakfast to the guests at The Menagerie. A line of guests surrounded the buffet spread of crisp pork and turkey sausages and bacon, scrambled eggs with or without cheese, slices of ham, pancakes and waffles, a variety of fresh fruit, pastries and pitchers of orange or apple juice. Those wanting their personal breakfast from the menu waited as he and his staff whipped up pecan pancakes, Spanish omelets, eggs Benedict, breakfast pork chops with applesauce. It was the type of hearty breakfast he would sometimes make after a night of fucking, a way to regain his strength. Usually he'd wait until his girl for the night left the premises before he'd head to his kitchen to prepare ham, steak or pork chops with eggs. Rarely did he make breakfast for an overnight guest because he would walk them to the door and get back in the bed. This morning as he mixed a bowl of pancake batter from scratch inside the hotel restaurant kitchen, Roman could not help but think about the older woman who brushed against him yesterday afternoon.

Even though she bumped against his hip, it may as well been his crotch. He was so glad he wore black pants to work because it hid his bulge well. And when he turned to face her, he meant to lean back against the chair to constrict his hard-on. He thought he was going to pass out when she walked away and the skirt of the dress swayed easily letting him know that she was not wearing a slip. Not even a half of a slip. Just the thought of the day before was giving him a rise. "Damn this woman is no one's granny!"

Her business card remained on his desk in his office and he contemplated calling her last night to ask if she liked the cupcakes but changed his mind. How stupid would he be to call about some cupcakes and not have anything else to say? Roman focused on the pancake batter, adding chopped glazed pecans and whipping the batter furiously. He walked to the large griddle, grabbed a ladle and poured perfect circles of the batter on the griddle.

Reading the card yesterday Roman knew she was a local person so there may be a chance of seeing her around. She was a friend of Miss Andrews who loved coming to The Menagerie for food and drinks. Roman shook his head back to the present and began flipping perfectly round pancakes. No more losing his train of thought on this Camille woman. "She's probably married anyway," he mumbled before another image of her walking off flashed in his brain. "That's one lucky motherfucker."

****

It was the crack of noon when Camille rose from her bed for the second time Monday. She stretched and walked into the bathroom and turned the faucets on her white claw foot tub. Another stretch and a brief look in the mirror, Camille handled her business while the tub filled. Disrobing and covering her hair with the shower cap, she carefully stepped in the tub, easing herself into the hot water. Camille willed her body to relax in the heat and grabbed a wash cloth and bar soap to work up a lather. In the midst of her routine, a ringtone of jazz filled the bathroom. Her cell phone lit up from the stand resting on the vanity table nearby and Camille squint to read the caller ID. "Unknown Caller" appeared on the screen and Camille resumed bathing. After four rings the cell went silent…until two minutes later when the jazz band started playing the same tune. 'Unknown Caller' appeared again and Camille again ignored it. By the time she rinsed off and was stepping out of the tub the 'Unknown Caller' was too familiar. "Who the hell is calling me?"

Wrapping a towel around her, the cell started singing again and Camille snatched it from the stand and hit the 'Talk' button. "Hello!"

"Oh! Uhm…hey. What's up?" Camille looked at her cell phone trying to figure out the deep male voice that greeted her like she was one of his willing to do anything for him hook-ups. Camille was not amused.

"Excuse you? You don't know how to properly greet someone you called? Are you the man calling my cell phone without leaving a voicemail?" There was silence from the other end for a few seconds, so Camille took a breath and began to hit the 'end' button.

"Wait! I apologize," the male voice said in a more respectful tone. "This is…Roman Cane, the chef at the M restaurant. Is this Mrs. Darwin?"

It was Camille's turn to give the silent treatment as she used her free hand to place a tighter grip on her towel. "Yes, yes this is Ms. Darwin. How can I help you?"

Roman fumbled for his next sentence while sitting in his desk chair. "Well…I wanted to say thank you for coming to the event yesterday…"

"It was my friend Sophia's event. There's no need for you to thank me."

"Right, I meant to say I hope you enjoyed everything we prepared for Miss Andrews' guests."

Camille lowered herself onto the vanity chair and snatched the shower cap off her head. She smiled while listening to this young man find words in a small telephone conversation. He sounded like a boy trying to talk to a possible crush for the first time.

"I enjoyed the menu very much, especially the red velvet cupcakes. Thanks for the extra cupcakes by the way," she said.

Roman smiled and straightened up in the chair. "Good, you're welcome."

Another moment of silence appeared and Camille began drying off while placing her cell on loudspeaker. "So, is there something else you wanted to say to me, Mr. Cane? You kind of caught me in the middle of drying off after a bath." Camille stopped moving the towel and stood up with a wide-eyed expression. "Why in the HELL would you say that?!" She froze to listen to the response from Roman and could only hear breathing and him clearing his throat.

"I'm sorry to interrupt you, Ms. Darwin. I was just doing a follow-up from yesterday. I'll hang up now. Good-bye."

Camille heard the click and a dial-tone and blew out a breath. "I can't believe I told him what I was doing!" Camille finished drying off and grabbed a bottle of cocoa butter lotion. Pouring a large dollop in her hand she began moisturizing her entire body.

Meanwhile Roman leaned back in his chair and a visual of Camille Darwin standing in a wrapped towel after a bath filled his head. Combining the memory of her brushing against his crotch at the party with imagining her letting the towel drop to the floor brought a smile to Roman's face. He had to admit Camille was one sexy woman, but also wonder how old she was. It was not like him to consider dating, let alone sleep with an older woman. And it was not like he hasn't been approached by older women.

In his time at The Menagerie Roman was often the subject of long, lustful stares from older women, some old enough to be his mother. And he has noticed more older women are dressing up and hitting the nightclubs and other events that lasted way past their bedtime. He normally smiled at the women and let them buy him a drink or two, but he almost always left the place with someone closer to his age or younger. One older woman who bought him several drinks a while back hunted him down to the restaurant and handed him a receipt with the number of drinks she bought him. She would not leave until he paid her back for, as she yelled, 'wasting her fucking time.'

But there was something about Camille Darwin that Roman could not shake. And he did not know whether he wanted to shake it off.

Chapter 15

Camille put on a pair of black straight leg jeans, a dark blue button down shirt with a wide black belt and a pair of black wedges. Combing her hair into a neat bob she put on a pair of small silver hoops and light application of makeup. She planned to do some errands before returning to spend time with the laptop. She hoped to have made a connection with some of the people from Sophia's party and get hired as a personal consultant. She was not hurting for money. She just needed something to fill her time.

Camille refused to be a divorcee doing nothing but spending her ex's settlement fund. She always made her own money even if some of it came from the hands and bank accounts of past lovers. Elijah always complimented on her ability to handle business and her workmanship with others. He knew she was not one to bow down and be quiet and that may have been part of his downfall. Camille had no plans on bilking her ex-husband out of more money. Keeping his underage sex secret under lock and safe deposit box key was insurance for her that she doubt will ever need. She opened the front door, stepped onto the porch and turned to her right where her mailbox was gaped open with mail and the daily newspaper.

Pulling the items out and shutting the mailbox Camille juggled the house keys in her other hand and turned to lock the doors. She walked to the car, got in and sat in the driveway thumbing through the envelopes for any piece of mail she needed to open right away. Bills, a couple of sales papers and one long, slim envelope with a return address from her attorney A. Adamson. Camille tossed the bills and sales on the passenger seat and leaned further to open the glove compartment. Grabbing a small, red handle pocketknife, she pushed the small silver button and a thumb size blade popped free. She placed the tip of the blade against the top left corner of the envelope and eased it into the tiny space. With one smooth glide the envelope opened as Camille pushed the button again to make the blade disappear. She dropped the pocketknife in her lap and widened the envelope's mouth and reached inside.

A smile hit Camille's face as the first check from the settlement rested between her fingers. She had insisted to her attorney and Elijah's attorney that the first check arrived at the house and the remaining payments would be directly deposited in her checking account. Apparently Elijah did not want to waste any time mailing the check. Surely he was not paranoid about her changing her mind and spilling all of his secrets like he spilled his semen into every condom he purchased? One hundred and twenty-five thousand dollars paid to Camille Elena Darwin. Camille stuffed the check back in the envelope, placed it in her purse, started and reversed the car out of the driveway. A new errand had to be handled, she thought as she directed her car to the bank.

Camille stayed on Roman's mind long after the impromptu phone call. He cursed himself for saying 'what's up' to a woman who was more mature than some of the women he's dated or hooked up with. He knew if he wanted to catch her attention he'd have to act like a grown ass man. Camille was a whole different ball game; sophisticated, elegant and confident. He knew she held her own. Roman left his office and walked to the kitchen pondering how to approach Camille Darwin again. Amidst the clattering of dishes and the aromas of meals being prepared for lunch, Roman decided he would probably not raise an ounce of interest from the woman. "She does not want to be bothered with my ass," he mumbled while tying on an apron.

***

After depositing her huge check, Camille made her errands to the post office, drug store and the mall. Before pulling out of the mall parking lot, she checked her e-mails through her cell and noticed the names of some of the guests from Sophia's party and additional messages from friends of those guests. Opening the unrecognizable e-mails the guests' friends said they were referred to her for possible projects. Camille smiled and closed her cell phone anxious to return home. On the way she made one last stop to pick up a carry-out dinner from an Italian restaurant because she had no interest in cooking later.

Arriving back home she rushed inside, place the carry-out bag in the refrigerator, tossed her keys and purse on the couch and walked inside her home office. Pushing a button on the stereo remote, old school R&B filled the room as she made herself comfortable in the oversized leather chair in front of her desk. The desk, a large mahogany with a hutch was the real deal and not something put together from a discounted department store. The desk was hers, passed down from her mother who spent many hours paying bills, reading the newspaper and writing or reading love letters from her suitors. A lot of those love letters ended up in the metal wastebasket that stood next to the desk. And that wastebasket had melted burn marks from the times her mother light a match to burn those letters and anything else that reminded her of a guy. Camille always wondered but never bothered to ask her mother if she'd burn any love letters from her daddy. And dared not to ask about any photos of him since all Naomi would do is clear her throat and start talking about something else. Camille knew who her daddy was but never bothered to look for him. As Motown tunes flowed from the speakers Camille's fingertips rapidly created the password to open the laptop and lead to her personal account. A total of 20 new e-mails waited to be revealed with what Camille hoped to be good news or opportunity knocking. Three e-mails were from the party guests who added their phone numbers and a request to call back immediately. Other e-mails were mixed; complimenting her website or letting her know they are considering contacting her. "Well, three call backs is a good start," Camille said while grabbing the telephone receiver.

Well into the evening Camille made appointments with two of the individuals and a callback promise with the third. Satisfied with her conquest she left the office and went to the kitchen to heat up her Italian carryout. Sipping from a glass of red wine as the microwave prepared her meal Camille returned to the office to log out from her account and check her Interact page. A new e-mail caught made her place her glass on the desk and plop into the chair. New message from Roman Cane. "Ok, he calls me earlier today and could barely talk, now I get a message," she thought. She moved the arrow to the link and opened the e-mail.

"Hi, Mrs. Darwin, this is Roman Cane from M. I apologize for my phone call today and interrupting you. I really wanted to know if you enjoyed the cupcakes. I also wanted to know if you would be interested in sampling some other dishes from our menu in the near future. I would personally prepare the dishes. If you are interested give me a call at 555-7942."

Camille could not help but laugh out loud at Roman's message. Taking another sip, she hit the reply button and began typing.

"Mr. Cane,

I did enjoy the red velvet cupcakes and I pretty much know most of the menu from M as my ex-husband and I frequented there many times. I am also sure that you are not trying to have me sample any dishes; if you wanted to ask me to dinner just say so. I am looking forward to your answer.

Camille."

Camille hit send and pushed her chair back just as the microwave announced her dinner was hot.

****

M was jumping during dinner as hotel guests and people enjoying an evening out filled the restaurant to capacity. Waiters rushed in and out of the kitchen balancing entrees, pushing dessert carts and carrying bottles of wine nonstop. Roman and his culinary staff barely looked at each other as their focus was to create visions of meals that would look beautiful until the slicing and dicing of silverware took them apart. It was this type of rush that motivated Roman to make every meal delectable for the consumers. Five hours later the pace slowed and the dining area was again dwindled to an intimate crowd of people chatting and sharing desserts.

The Panthers Club

Roman snatched the apron off and tossed it in the hamper in the hallway outside the kitchen and walked into the office. He collapsed into the chair, pulling the band that held his locks together and shook them loose. Cracking his knuckles he yawned and grabbed the car keys off his desk. This had been one of the busiest Mondays he and his staff ever worked. There must be a conference going on at The Menagerie along with the usual community clients and business people. Roman checked around the desk for anything else he needed and grabbed the mouse to shut down the computer when he noticed new messages on his account. One was from Camille and he dropped his keys to open the link. Reading the message put a smile on his face and he rapidly typed a reply and hit the send button. Roman shut off his computer, grabbed the keys again and left the restaurant whistling and throwing a peace sign goodbye to his staff.

****

Sophia's voice never hit the pause button and Camille felt the sweat grow on her left ear from the receiver of her cordless phone. She regretted not putting Sophia on the loudspeaker as she tried to thumb through the newspaper sprawled on her lap as she sat on her bed. The laptop sat on a bed tray positioned on what was once Elijah's side of the bed. Normally the laptop stayed in her office but Camille planned to research the backgrounds of the clients she communicated with earlier. Sophia's chatter delayed that plan. "Anyway, I am so glad they got in touch with you! They are very nice people and easy to work with, but you would not have a problem with that," Sophia rambled. "Plus, this will give you something to do and you won't be all pitiful and bored…"

Camille snapped her attention away from the newspaper. "Who the fuck said I was pitiful!"

Silence and regret hit the other line. "I am so sorry, Camille! You are not pitiful. I did not mean for it to come out like that. I meant you'd have something to do," Sophia whined.

"Uhm, Sophia, let it be known that I do not do pity parties. I have enough money to not do shit but travel and go shopping," Camille said.

"I know and I am sorry. I can tell when you don't like being bored is what I meant to say. Let's change the subject. Has Roman contacted you?" Camille stopped browsing through the newspaper all together at the mention of his name. She immediately wondered if Sophia had anything to do with Roman calling her earlier in the day. She wouldn't dare encourage him to call me! Camille decided right then not to tell Sophia about the phone call or the e-mail. It wasn't her business anyway whether or not she talked to the boy…man.

"No Mr. Cane has not contacted me nor I him," Camille said. She suddenly felt the need to disconnect the call. "Listen Sophie, I need to hang up now. I really want to start on my research on these people"

"Oh, OK honey! And again, I am sorry for ruffling your feathers tonight." Camille nodded and touched the pad on the laptop and noticed a new message on the screen from Roman. She leaned forward while still holding the phone to her ear as Sophia continued to say goodbye. Clicking the link Camille clamped her mouth shut.

"How does 9 p.m. Wednesday night sound?"

Camille put her focus back to the phone. "Sophia? I have another call coming in. Love you!" Camille hit the off button, threw the phone on the bed and typed her reply.

****

A familiar chime on Roman's cell sang from the right pocket of the pair of jeans he changed into when he got home. He was now standing a few feet away from the doors to a neighborhood bar when he heard the melody. He flipped the phone open and clicked the message link.

Wednesday night is fine. I will be at the bar waiting. Good Night.

Roman grinned, closed the phone and pulled the bar door open, walking in with a brand new wave of confidence. The cognac was going down good tonight.

No longer in the mood to do any research, Camille shut off and placed her laptop on her dresser, took the newspaper off the bed and hit the light switch. Pulling the covers back she paused at the realization that she agreed to have dinner with a younger man. He was not young enough to be her son…at least she did not think he was. What if he changes his mind when she arrived? What if this was some joke or bet between him and his adolescent staff? "If he makes a fool out of me," Camille thought while climbing in the bed.

"Girl snap out of it! He liked what he was seeing…and so did you," Camille said out loud in the darkness. She got comfortable and waited for sleep to take over as Roman's image flowed in her mind.

"What do you mean you can't see me this week?" Roman sighed and took a swig of cognac, trying to focus on the all sports channel blaring from a flat screen TV on a wall behind the bartender. He did not see Evelyn when he first walked in the bar. He was not looking for her, or anybody for that matter. He just felt like stepping out for a drink before turning in. Now Evelyn's right breast pressed against his left arm and whatever flavored martini breath was blowing in his ear. But she was not being flirty. "I can't follow you back to your place tonight, or I can't stop by period?"

"Look, Evelyn, you did not want anything else to do with me, remember? You slapped the shit out of me when I told you there's nothing serious going on. That has not changed. Now you're acting all needy and shit. And you know I can't stand neediness unless it is mutual," Roman said while keeping an eye on her to avoid another slap.

Evelyn reared back. "Mutual? Oh so you don't need me!"

Roman turned to face Evelyn. "Evelyn! Why are you talking like we have a monogamous relationship? I KNOW you are seeing other guys. We had our fun; we kicked it, the sex was good. You keep jumping back and forth and it gets tiring."

Evelyn glared at him and jumped from the bar stool. "You the one who is tired! I don't care if you are only 40 years old; you're still an old ass and too old for me!"

Roman shrugged and finished his cognac. "Maybe you are right. I need to stay away from the young girls. Or maybe you have not reached your potential of being a grown ass woman." After that last sentence the bartender gave Roman a look that said you know your back is facing this chick dumbass. Roman kept his eye on the TV and the reflection from the mirror lining the wall where the liquor was stocked. Evelyn frowned and stormed to the back of the bar where a table of young women looked anxious. Moments later, Evelyn's and her friends' voices grew louder as they talked about the lack of finding a good black man. Roman shook his head and ordered another cognac from the bar. He could still hear Evelyn's voice snapping furiously and emphasizing on how black men were dogs and older black men wanted to take advantage of younger girls. "I know her ass is not talking about me like I am some child molester," he thought. Evelyn was about to say another word when a few voices that were not her friends chimed in. "Maybe if some fast assed girls like you stop trying to find sugar daddies and act like you have some sense, a good man would talk to you!"

Roman smirked and watched the mirror as Evelyn and her friends stood up, grabbed their purses and jackets and walked quickly to the bar exit. Evelyn cut her eyes towards Roman who raised his glass to them.

Chapter 16

Wednesday could not get here fast enough for Camille. In the last 24 hours she sealed consulting deals with two of the people who attended Sophia's party and another from a referred individual. Each project would keep her busy for the next two months and she was inspired to get an early start on creating package offers for the holiday season. She rewarded herself with a shopping trip, purchasing a little black dress, sleeveless with a plunging v-neckline and a fuchsia shawl. She also found a pair of black pointy toed pumps with a three-inch heel and a pair of diamond teardrop earrings with a matching necklace. This would be the outfit for tonight's dinner with Roman. She'd texted him the other day on what should she wear on their date. She's frequented M on many occasions and was casual dressy, especially with Elijah. The few times they did dress up to go to M were during a benefit fundraiser or a formal in the upper level ballroom. She'd hope Roman would dress for their dinner and not still wear the chef's attire.

****

Camille returned home and drew a scented oil bath for her preparation. She also poured a glass of wine to calm her nerves. It had been years since she's been out with another man and she did not expect to get back into the game so soon. At the same time, Camille was not one to sit still for long when it came to the opposite sex. But this was a new game with younger interests involved. She took a sip and stepped in the steaming bathtub, placing the glass on a small table. She grabbed her washcloth and soap and gingerly lathered her body using circular motions to relax. Her nipples strained against the washcloth as she anticipated having dinner with Roman. By the time she was drying off and draining the glass of wine Camille was more than ready for the night. She covered her body with jasmine scented body lotion and generously sprayed the accompanying mist.

Walking to the dresser she pulled out one of the drawers where an array of bra and panty and bras and thongs were displayed. Camille decided against the usual black undergarments, instead choosing to match her shawl. She grabbed a set that included a fuchsia lace bra and thong. After putting them on she pulled another drawer open, grabbed a pair of black sheer thigh highs and sat at the foot of her bed. After carefully putting them on and sliding her feet into the pumps, Camille strutted to her full length mirror and struck a pose in her underwear ensemble. Smiling at her reflection Camille felt her former self on the prowl. "Nothing may happen tonight, Mr. Cane, but I hope a young blood like you can handle someone like me."

The Panthers Club

Camille arrived at M 15 minutes early, sitting at the bar watching a small crowd enjoying dessert or a late dinner like she will be shortly. Some of Roman's staff worked the dining area with a calm ease not anticipating another huge crowd before closing. Jazz flowed through the speakers and the conversations were barely audible. Camille scanned the restaurant for Roman but he was nowhere to be found. She glanced at her thin silver watch seeing that ten minutes passed.

"Excuse me, Miss?" Camille turned to the maitre d who smiled and offered his arm. "I am to escort you to your table." Camille smiled back and slipped her arm around the bend of his allowing him to lead the way. The maitre d walked her to the back of the restaurant and to a hallway she was unfamiliar with. Halfway, her escort stopped in front of a closed room. He turned the doorknob, pushed the door open and faced Camille. "This way Miss," he said and guided her by the hand into the room.

Camille smiled broader as she took in the view; a round dinner table clothed in white with a China plate setting and champagne flutes on top was centered in the room. A candlelight centerpiece glowed brightly. "Good evening Camille." Camille turned away from the maitre d and looked at Roman who wore a suit jacket and vest ensemble with a round collar button down shirt and slacks. His twists were neatly touched and his smile revealed dimples Camille had not noticed previously. His outfit framed his muscular build perfectly and when he walked towards her it was all she could do not to eye him up and down per step. The maitre d stepped away and disappeared into a side door and Roman reached out to her. "You look beautiful, Camille," Roman said as he paused and waited for her hand.

He stared at her, taking in her dress, long, shapely legs and the heels. He looked at her face and the bob that framed it. She looked far more seductive than any 20 or 30-something female he's seen or been with. She was not trying too hard and was comfortable with her sexuality. Camille placed her hand in his and he led her to a chair at the table. Holding the chair for her, she sat down and adjusted herself and he pushed her to the table. He leaned over her shoulder and Camille caught a whiff of cologne or aftershave that was not overpowering. Camille found herself whispering 'thank you' to Roman as he removed her shawl, brushing his fingers on her shoulders.

He sat across from her and the maitre d returned with a bottle of champagne. They took their flutes and toasted each other while a waiter came with an appetizer of lobster brusque soup. The rest of the menu included filet mignon, steamed vegetables, rolls and chocolate mousse with fresh whipped cream.

Throughout the meal they made small chat about each other. "So Roman, what made you want to ask me out," Camille said while taking a bite of filet mignon. "I am sure you have your share of young women to see. Exactly how old are you?"

Roman glanced at her. "I am 40 years old...I don't have a lot of women around me. I mean, I like to date and have fun. I am not tied down. If I was I would not have asked you out," he said.

Camille nodded and sipped champagne. "I think you are a beautiful woman and I was interested in getting to know you better. It does not matter how old you are...not that I would ask because it is not my business."

Camille smiled. "Well, I now know you are not old enough to be my son. Unless I had a child at 13 years old...which I don't," she said and soon regretted. This was not the time to talk about being a parent....I can't have children anyway," Camille thought as she briefly reflected on her menopausal years. Shut the fuck up, Camille! The remaining conversation stayed safe and by dessert they were working on a second bottle of champagne and laughing.

Roman had moved his chair closer to Camille so they were side by side and his arm draped the back of her chair. His suit jacket found a spot with her shawl in a chair away from the table. Camille relaxed her posture so to place her arm on the table and lean into him as they talked. The table was cleared and soft music played in the sound system. Camille found herself enthralled in Roman's story of growing up with women and learning how to cook. She was also enthralled with his full lips; wondering if they were soft. He looked well groomed; bright smile with straight teeth, deep dimples and piercing brown eyes. She watched him speak with a deep steady tone, his lips more inviting per word formed. "I wonder if he is a good kisser."

"Camille?"

"Uhmm...HUH," Camille snapped out of her fog and stared blankly at Roman. "I'm sorry, repeat what you said."

Roman smiled at her and she felt the heat in her cheeks. Then she felt his lips press against hers adding a little pressure. She returned the pressure and moments later he moved back. "I was asking if I could kiss you," he said. Damn was he telepathic or something?!

"Guess I said yes," Camille said with a laugh.

Roman leaned closer to her, cupping her face. "Nope, I just went for it," and he kissed her again with more pressure.

Camille placed her arms around him, her fingers massaging his neck and running through the twists above the nape of his neck. She felt her mouth coaxed open with the tip of his tongue and darted her tongue in return. Roman's free hand caressed the body of her dress while his other hand stroked her face and ran through her hair. As they pulled away from each other they caressed each other's arms and shared knowing stares. Camille dropped her eyes to her lap as Roman fingered the hem of her dress and brushed against the thigh high on her left leg. Just the feel of his fingers brushing her thigh had Camille's heart racing and she automatically crossed her legs. Roman's eyes scanned her body slowly and when she dared to look him in the eye he licked his lips. Any thoughts on the age difference shot straight to hell as Camille reached and brought his face close to hers and delivered an open mouth kiss that surprised him. She pushed herself from her chair sat sideways on his lap without breaking the kiss. All Roman could do was sit back and embrace her as she played with his tongue. A moan fought to escape from his throat as she shifted her hips in his lap and he found out she did not like slips. Camille broke away and placed quick light kisses on his lips while her right hand stroked his chest, fingering the buttons.

Roman's breathing grew heavy as he looked into Camille's eyes. "Uh, you want to get a room? We had a lot to drink and neither of us can drive," he said with a smile.

Camille sat on his lap and looked around. "We are in a room," she said with a smirk. Roman's eyes widened as Camille got off his lap and walked to the door where she and the maitre d entered earlier. She locked it and looked towards the ceiling, checking for camera monitors. "Just how private is this room?"

Roman smiled. "This and another room are private, usually for meetings and other things. This hotel has quite the history."

Camille nodded and turned to the side door. "Can this door be secured?"

Roman stared at her and jumped from the chair and went to the door. He opened the door and disappeared for a second. He returned and closed the door and revealed a key before locking it. He dropped the key in his jacket pocket and turned to face Camille who approached him with a gleam in her eye. Roman reached out and pulled her into his arms and kissed her, applying as much pressure as she had earlier. She matched him and pressed her body against him. Jerking away, she unbuttoned his vest and he let it drop while she unbuttoned his shirt. "Your clothes are in the way," she mumbled and then chuckled. She pulled his shirt out of his slacks and draped it open. She could see Roman was in the midst of having a six pack, but she was not complaining. She placed her hands on his chest, caressing his pectorals and then using her fingers to trail a path to his navel.

Roman smiled as his hands ran up and down her sides. "Your dress is in the way," he said. Bringing Camille closer to him, Roman reached around for the back zipper, kissing her as he pulled the zipper down to the end of her spine. His kiss went deeper as he cupped her round ass, giving it a squeeze. There was no sagging going on anywhere, he thought as he marveled at how firm Camille's body was. Camille unbuckled his belt and undid his slacks letting them hit the floor. He backed away and stepped out of them and Camille gasped at the physique standing before her in black cotton briefs. He was a single tone of chocolate with muscular thighs attached to slightly bowed legs. She thought he was beautiful before she'd get him out of those briefs, but the package aching to break free did not look disappointing. She looked at his face and he wore a raised eyebrow, a signal that it was her turn to step out of her dress.

Camille took off her earrings and necklace, placing them in her purse. She turned her back to Roman and reached up to pull the upper part of her dress from her shoulders. She pushed the dress to her waist, bent over and wiggled herself out of it. Straightening her body slowly she heard Roman mumbled 'Shit!" as she let the curves speak as a display of her lace thong not even covering her ass do the talking. She turned around so he could see the front side of the ensemble along with the thigh highs. Camille was proud of her 53-year-old physique and prouder that her body had Roman trying to catch his breath. She stared at him and like her daydream, began slowly moving to the beat of the jazz playing in the speakers.

Roman watched as she reached behind and unclasped her bra, yanking it off and tossed it in the chair. She slowly eased her thong over her thighs and legs and stepped out of them. Camille smiled at the expression on Roman's face; it was a combination of lust and a kid seeing presents lined around the Christmas tree. "I hope you have condoms," Camille said. Roman grabbed his pants, reached in his pocket and pulled out a handful of condoms. "Always prepared, huh," she said with a laugh.

Camille walked over to the table and sat on top. She went to start removing a thigh high when Roman walked over and stopped her. "Leave the thigh highs and the pumps on," he growled. Taking off his briefs and putting on a condom, Roman stepped between Camille's legs and gently leaned her back towards the table. Camille placed a firm grip to both sides as he rested her legs on his shoulders. She crossed her ankles behind his neck as he leaned to her and began kissing her. Pulling her hips further from the table Roman entered her slowly while kissing her harder. Camille did not know whether to hold on to him or risk breaking the table as she felt him push deeper inside her. He was reading her mind again as he shifted his weight so his arms could balance her and rest his hands on the table while she held onto him. If the table should give Roman could scoop her up without breaking rhythm. Camille held onto Roman for dear life as her body rocked and thrust upward to meet his pounding. "Damn, baby, damn," Roman grunted as he gyrated against her, his thrusts rotating from slow to fast. "Oh my...Oh my...,"was all Camille could muster from her throat between gasps and yelps. Both fought getting loud and overwhelming the music from the speakers.

The restaurant was long closed and the staff was cleaning up and following Roman's orders to not disturb him the rest of the evening. Little did he know the evening was going to include extra dessert that was not on the menu. The feast continued as Roman walked Camille to the sofa in the corner of the room as her legs were now wrapped around his waist. He laid her on her back and kissed her neck as she caught her breath. He put on another condom and flipped her on her stomach. "Get on your knees Camille," he said as he climbed the sofa. Doing as she was told, she bit her lip when Roman entered her. When it was over, the clock nearby read 1 a.m. and Camille sitting on the sofa wearing Roman's suit jacket and drinking a large bottled water. Her thigh highs were now holey from the tears during sex and her pumps laid by her feet. Roman returned to the room wearing his shirt and slacks and socks. He'd placed the tablecloth in a large plastic bag and in his car to wash later. The sofa he will place cleaning foam before they left. Roman sat down next to Camille and kissed her.

"Are you OK? You want a sandwich?" Camille laughed. "I thought it was usually the guy who demands the woman to make him a sandwich!" Roman took a swig of bottled water. "The way you put it down, I can open the kitchen and make you a buffet right now!!"

Chapter 17

Camille unlocked the front door and entered her house with an extra bounce in her step. Locking the door and flipping on the light switch she paused as an occasional flashback of what happened hours ago inside the restaurant. She appreciated the spontaneity in Roman who was a gentleman throughout the evening, including when he offered to get a room. The fact that he was not afraid to go with the moment thrilled her. She had to pat herself on the back, though. She still had it in her to go for what she wanted.

Rejection and humiliation glimpsed her mind for a second but when he returned the kisses and fondling all doubts died. Stepping out of her dress a second time in the night, Camille walked to her bedroom and entered the master bathroom and started the shower. Removing her undergarments and stepping out of her shoes, she put on her shower cap and stepped into the shower. Roman's touches and straight to it fucking replayed in her mind, causing her to spend a little more time under the water pressure. She finally left the shower and prepared to go to bed. Sleeping in without worrying about a 9 to 5 was a good thing. And she had no doubt Roman had plenty of energy left.

Roman made it back to his apartment an hour after walking Camille to her car. They shared another kiss before she drove off and he rushed back in the restaurant to do some quick cleaning in the private room. Cleaning the sofa, straightening the furniture while airing out the room and spraying air freshener, Roman had to dissolve all evidence of sex that happened. It would not be the first time the room was aired out and he knew he was not the only one to use the room. He was not expecting someone like Camille to thrown down like that! That's what he gets for making assumptions; Camille was the epitome of a lady in the streets but a freak in the sheets. The scenes between them ran in his mind as he got ready for bed, happy that he arranged to have the rest of the week off. He fell into a deep sleep from a workout that was worth the exhaustion.

"Where were you last night?"

Camille smiled and focused on making a late breakfast omelet, hash browns and turkey sausage while Sophia repeated the question through the earpiece. "All of my calls to you went to voicemail! I was wondering about your progress in the consulting packages and thought we would get a bite to eat."

Camille fixed her plate and grabbed a pitcher of orange juice out of the refrigerator and poured a glass. "I'm sorry I missed your calls sweetie but I was busy last night and did not get in until late," Camille said between bites.

"Busy? Where did you go," Sophia asked. Silence filled the air again until Sophia broke it with a demanding tone.

"WHERE DID YOU GO?!" Camille laughed at Sophia's frustration.

"I went out to dinner." Sophia sighed.

"Oh, you went to dinner with a friend! Well, I am glad you had a great time," she said. Satisfied with an answer, Sophia moved to another topic and chatted away while Camille ate.

Forty minutes into the conversation, Camille grabbed her cell and noticed five text messages. "Uhm, Sophia, I have to run, I will talk to you later. Yes let's have lunch tomorrow at one at Bistro on Lake Street. Bye." Camille opened the text messages, all from Roman, asking if she was OK and how much he enjoyed dinner and dessert. The last text asked if he could call her. Camille laughed at the last one and returned the texts. "Hi. I am doing well. I also enjoyed last night and of course you can call me."

Seconds later her phone rang and Roman's deep voice sent a chill down her spine. "Hey Camille, did I catch you at a bad time?"

Camille walked into her living room and sat on the couch. "No, I was talking to a friend and eating a late but hearty breakfast," she said with a laugh.

"Hearty breakfast, huh? I should be the one enjoying a big breakfast! I...I didn't hurt you, did I?"

Camille burst into laughter. "No you did not hurt me at all! I enjoyed every minute of last night, from the dinner to the extra desserts."

The last statement brought a smile to Roman's face as he relaxed in his recliner. "It's almost noon Roman; aren't you at work?"

"No, I am taking a four-day weekend. It's been a while since I've had a couple days off." Silence filled the air as neither one could not think of anything else to say. Roman wanted to ask her out again, but did not know if the status of their connection was just a one-night stand.

"Roman I am going to have to go. I need to get started on some projects." Roman stood up as if Camille was in his apartment.

"Oh, OK. I'll talk to you later...if that's OK with you," he said. "Yes, give me a ring before the weekend is out. In fact, maybe we can get together again," Camille said as she reflected on last night. "Take care, Camille," he said and hung up.

****

Bistro on Lake Street was full during lunch time on a sunny Friday afternoon, making Sophia glad she made reservations as soon as Camille said yes. She'd already ordered their lunches and sat at one of the corner tables by the picture window waiting for Camille to walk past before entering the restaurant. Lake Street was its usual busy scenario as people in business, arts and crafts, food and socialism blended like a world of their own. The outdoor tables were pulled inside for the season, leaving more room for window shoppers and people text walking their way into life.

Sophia was sipping a cup of coffee when she noticed a blur past the window and smiled as door chimes announced Camille's arrival. As Camille sat down the waiter arrived to set their meals on the table and take down her order for a hot apple cider. "So, how are the projects coming along," Sophia asked.

"They are coming along great! The Russell couple is throwing a huge charity event next month and the details are pretty cut to the chase," Camille said while plunging a fork into the grilled salmon. Sophia watched her friend, nodding to every word she said.

"Great, great. Who was your dinner date?"

Camille stopped and looked at Sophia who was barely eating her Caesar salad. "Why do you need to know about my dinner date? You're not old enough to be my mother. Sophia smirked.

"Your skin is glowing."

Camille took another bite of salmon and stabbed into her spinach salad. "It's a new exfoliating cream."

Sophia took a sip of coffee and laughed. "Exfoliate my ass! What's his name?"

Camille rolled her eyes at Sophia and put her fork down. "Ok, I'll tell you," she said while leaning forward. "But don't you dare scream in here!"

Sophia put the coffee cup down and leaned in. "I did go out to dinner…but not with a friend. I was with…Roman."

Sophia jerked back and did a fist pump. "I KNEW I saw a spark…"

Camille reached across the table and smacked Sophia's arm. "Shut-Up!"

Sophia covered her mouth but her eyes danced with joy at Camille's announcement. "Sorry, sorry! But you could not tell me I did not see something between you two during my party!"

Camille shook her head and laughed. "You are talking like we are a couple."

"Yeah a couple of horny asses," Sophia laughed. "I am not creating a future for you two; I just had a feeling that you and Roman were going to get together. It's not like you've never been with a younger guy, right?"

Camille paused and grabbed the iced tea, taking a long sip.

Sophia stopped chewing. "Oh hell, he is your first younger guy?!"

Camille glared at her. "Yes, he is. I've dated older men since my late teens. Guys my age never appealed to me and as I got older, the thought of going out with someone younger never crossed my mind. Older men meant power and maturity…well it did until I dealt with Elijah."

Sophia patted her friend's hand. "Now you did have some good times with Elijah but I guess he showed his true colors."

Camille sighed and took another bite of salmon. "Yeah, well he proved to be an arrogant ass. Why are we talking about him?"

Sophia smiled. "You're right! So are you going to see Roman again?"

"I don't know, maybe. This was nothing more than two people having a great time. There are no strings attached. For all I know he could be having sex with some young girl right now."

Sophia nodded. "That's true, or he could be wondering when he can get another serving of Camille! I know you put it on him, girl. You are not the vanilla type," she said with a laugh. Upon hearing that last sentence, it was Camille's turn to burst into loud laughter.

****

Roman stared as channels from his TV flipped rapidly from his thumb pressing down on the remote control button. He was stretched out on his bed in the middle of the day wearing drawstring sweatpants and a loose t-shirt with a graphic design. One of his favorite cooking shows just ended and he was searching for whatever else caught his eye. Camille's naked image danced in his head, well, both heads were affected. He fought not to place his right hand in his sweats but it was soon a losing battle and his hand and friend won out. The ringing of his landline broke his concentration and he dropped the remote to grab the cordless phone. He was about to push the Talk button when caller id placed Evelyn's name on the screen. Roman placed the phone back on the cradle and resumed concentration. He knew he was going to need to call Camille and see if they could meet. "What if this was a one night stand? What if she turns me down and not gets in touch with me again? Why am I panicking about this?!"

****

Camille was going through her e-mails when the phone rang. Checking the caller ID, she grabbed the phone. "Hey Camille, it's Roman. Did I catch you at a bad time?"

"No Roman you didn't. How are you?" Roman stretched across the bed.

"I am fine. Listen, what are you doing tonight?" Camille paused.

"I don't have any specific plans. Why'd you ask?" Roman took a breath. "I would like to see you again. Maybe we could go for a drive."

Camille smiled. "Or maybe I could just pay you a visit."

Roman sat up, the possibility of seeing Camille naked and in his bed had him standing at attention. "Yeah, yeah, you can come over if you want. I don't mind."

Roman recited his address and apartment number for her to buzz at the front door.

"I'll be there in an hour," Camille said.
"See you soon."

Roman hung up and nearly leaped off the bed and into the shower. In an hour he'd showered, put new bedding on, did a quick sweep around the apartment, tossed dirty dishes in the dishwasher and picked up every dirty piece of clothing lying around. The buzzer to his unit sang exactly one hour later. He hit the button that unlocked the front door of the building and watched Camille through a monitor as she entered the elevator.

When the elevator doors opened to the floor where his unit was, Camille smiled as Roman stood waiting to escort her to his apartment. "Hi," she said as she stepped out wearing a knee length coat belted at the waist and had a large, black satchel on her left shoulder.

Roman took her hand and looked at her, noticing she was wearing a pair of red stilettos without the thigh highs. "Hey," he said as they entered his apartment.

Camille walked away from him and admired the decorum of his apartment. "Very nice place, Roman," she said while standing in the middle of the living room. Roman walked into the kitchen and returned with a bottle of wine and two glasses. He poured her a glass and handed to her, then poured a glass for himself.

"Can I offer you a tour of the place," Roman said while taking a sip of wine. Camille glanced around, took a sip and smiled.

"You only need to show me," Camille then undid the trench coat and belt and let it gape open, "where is your bedroom Roman?"

Roman's eyes widened at the sight of Camille's nakedness underneath her coat. He could not believe the boldness that came from this older woman! Grabbing her hand and finishing the last two swallows of wine, Roman pulled her into his bedroom, taking off the t-shirt, jeans and briefs he wasted time putting on. Camille dropped the coat at her feet and slowly climbed on his bed, turning to prop her elbows beneath the pillows. She looked at him with anticipation and he climbed over her, reaching to pull the nightstand drawer open. Once he put on the condom, he laid on top of Camille, entering her at the same time. Her hands rested on his wide back and shoulders, holding on to him as he filled her up. Her wetness let him know that she had been thinking of him and he plunged deeper. "Ah yeah, baby…that's it," Camille moaned as Roman started a rhythm of slow, deep strokes. He lowered his face to her neck, planting kisses along the collarbone and the side of her neck. Low grunts left his lips as he alternated his thrusts from slow to fast and doing a circular grind in between. She wrapped her legs around him, closing them at the ankles where the stilettos bounced in the air. She raised her head and opened her mouth, flicking her tongue at his mouth. Roman flicked his tongue against hers, rolling his tongue until he pressed his mouth to hers. The pressure of their kiss ignited more force in their thrusts. She raised her hips to meet his moves, holding onto him tightly.

Caught up in the heated frenzy, Camille unlocked her legs and spread them as wide as she could, allowing Roman to go deeper. "Shit that's what I'm talking about, baby," Roman growled as he balanced himself on the bed. He lowered his body where he could take one of her breasts in his mouth. Camille arched her back as she felt Roman's teeth tug on her nipple then lick circles. He went to the other nipple and gave it the same treatment, driving Camille crazy with lust. Feeling Camille's fingernails rake the skin on his back encouraged Roman to thrust harder. Camille screamed with pleasure, panting and saying his name over and over. She came twice already and was not stopping for air. He turned her over and entered her from behind, pounding into her. "Am I hurting you," he asked. Sweat dripped from Camille's face as she shook her head. "NOOOOO! Baby I can take it!" She grabbed a pillow and held on as her body was pushed and rocked to depths she never experienced with Elijah. This was a new energy that rushed her body and she loved it. When he came, Roman eased out of her and went to the bathroom to dispose the condom. He returned with a glass of water for her. Camille gladly drank the water and looked at him. He was still erect so she grabbed another condom and signaled for him to come to the bed. He sat down and she rolled the condom on and climbed on his lap and proceeded to give Roman an unforgettable lap dance.

An hour later, Camille picked up her satchel and walked in the bathroom. Roman got up and stepped into the drawstring sweats and walked to the kitchen. Flipping on the light switch, he walked to the refrigerator and removed a carton of eggs and a package of bacon. Balancing them in one hand and pulled open the deli drawer to grab a small block of cheddar.

Pushing the door close he began whistling while placing the items on a counter near his stove and opened the cabinets above to pull out a bowl. He was smiling non-stop as he prepared to make a late night breakfast of scrambled cheese eggs and bacon. What he had was some of the best sex in a long time. If Evelyn had a twin sister and a freaky cousin join in, it would not have matched the sex marathon he and Camille had. He knew he wanted to get to know Camille better and hoped she felt the same way. Getting to know a woman was something he had not done in a long time; not since a relationship he had 10 years ago that went nowhere. Still, he had to be cautious because this was now just sex. Moments later, Camille walked into the kitchen wearing a pair of stretch pants and a short sleeved t-shirt with gym shoes. She was putting her stilettos in the satchel. "Well, I guess I will head home."

Roman stopped sliding the cheese eggs on a platter and looked at her. "You're going home?! It's almost 2 a.m. I can't let you drive home this late!"

Camille smiled and walked to the counter grabbing a strip of bacon. "I will be alright. I am not scared of the dark."

Roman put the skillet on the burner, shaking his head in disagreement. "I'm sorry I can't let you leave in the middle of the night. Please, spend the night. You can leave later this morning."

Camille looked at him. "So I guess this isn't a booty call?" "Look, we are two adults who had sex. But I am not going to be an ass and let you go home in the dark."

Camille nodded and sat down at the table reaching for the platter filled with eggs. "You win. Bring the bacon over here."

Roman grinned and walked over, placing the platter of bacon in front of her and pulled back the chair next to her. He filled his plate with a heaping of the late night/early morning breakfast then jumped up and headed to the refrigerator. "I have orange juice, grape juice, cola, milk and water," he said. "Grape juice, please," Camille said while breaking a strip of bacon with her teeth. Roman returned to the table with her glass and a glass of orange juice. They ate without speaking most of the time, Roman glancing at Camille every now and then. When she'd look back he focused on his plate.

Camille put her fork down. "What's wrong?"

Roman looked up and swallowed. "Nothing's wrong."

Camille looked at him and took a sip of grape juice. "What do you want to know about me Roman? You barely know a lot about me...unless you looked on one of those search engines on the Internet."

Roman smiled at her last remark, instantly giving away his secret. "I did look you up online. But I went to your website about your consulting business."

"I see. So now you know a little bit more about me," Camille said while grabbing another strip of bacon from the plate.

"You are divorced right? Your married name, Darwin...is this same Darwin who is the investor?"

Now it was Camille's turn to smile at him. "Yes, Elijah Darwin III is my ex-husband. The divorce happened this year, merely months ago."

Roman nodded and continued to eat. "So you were married to a rich man. That had to have been something," he said.

"Why? Because he has money? While he was rich when I met him, I am not a gold digger. I can hold my own," Camille said while shifting her weight in the chair. "And he is not a multimillionaire; but he held his own."

Roman nodded again and grabbed his glass of orange juice. Camille finished her plate and pushed it away, watching Roman and waiting for another question. "Why did you divorce him, if you don't mind me asking? It's not like they had your story all over the network news," he said.

"But there was a blurb about the divorce in the social pages of some publications here," Camille replied, making Roman stop eating.

"Yeah there was. But if you don't want to answer…"

"Elijah cheated on me with a younger woman. Some chick he met at a party," Camille said. Her mind wandered off to the scene of the extravagant corporate party where she and Elijah met and then got to know each other in the bathroom.

"Oh, sorry about that," Roman said and picked up their plates and walked to the sink to rinse them off before placing them in the dishwasher.

Camille waved off his apology. "It's fine. Either way things were handled with dignity before it got ugly enough to make the society pages' top story. It is what it is and a settlement was made."

Roman returned to clear the rest of the table. "And now you are starting over."

"No. I am having fun…with you," she said and stroked his arm. "Are you comfortable being with a divorced woman? A divorced woman who is 13 years older than you?"

"It does not bother me at all," Roman said, "I never would have guessed you were that much older than I am."

Camille laughed and stood up to stretch. "You are only as old as you act. And I've been known to not act my age!" Roman laughed, grabbed her hand and they walked out of the kitchen and back into the bedroom.

Chapter 18

The sun's rays peeped through the blinds in Roman's bedroom creating a silhouette of curves moving in a steady motion. He opened his eyes and watched Camille put on the clothes changed into hours earlier until he convinced her to stay the rest of the night. They did not repeat their heated sex romp before going to sleep instead they quietly climbed back in the bed like a familiar couple. "Morning," Camille said as she sat in the chair near the bed to put on her gym shoes.

Roman propped himself up and smiled. "Hey. Can I make you a second round of breakfast?"

"Nah, I will grab something on the way home. I remembered to leave the porch light on but now it is about…ten o'clock? I am sure a couple of well- meaning neighbors are wondering why I've not opened the door to grab my mail and newspaper." Roman watched her gather her things and got out of the bed stretching and walking to the chair.

Camille jumped up, standing face to face with him. "Last night…was great," she said.

Roman smiled and leaned to kiss her, then stopped and covered his mouth. "Hold on, I need to go to the bathroom," he said while jogging off.

Camille laughed at his realization that he had morning breath. They were not a couple so getting use to another person's dental and personal hygiene was another level. Roman returned after five minutes of brushing and gargling to see that Camille was already waiting at the door to make her exit.

"Wow," he said while walking towards her. "You are truly ready to get out of my place, huh?"

Camille shrugged. "It is what it is. And it's Saturday. I have things to do."

Roman nodded and grabbed the door keys, leaning in to unlock the door.

Camille placed her hand on his face. "I really did have a good time last night. You are a very good lover. You brought out the wildness in me and I did not have to resort to a lesson book for you," she said then cupped his face and kissed him.

He returned her kiss, wrapping his arms around her waist. With one move he had her back pressed against the door and began probing his tongue against hers. She ran her hands up and down his bare back and felt a growing erection fighting his pajama bottoms. He moved away and smiled.

Camille touched his face and turned around pulling the door open and both walked to the elevator. When the doors opened Camille stepped inside.

The Panthers Club

"You better get back to the apartment before a nosy neighbor decides to do a head to toe check on you," she said, winking at him.

****

Camille got home, grabbed the mail and the newspaper and walked inside to check for phone messages. Three messages were from Sophia, the last one saying she did not bother to call the cell phone because she figured she was too busy to answer. Camille walked into her bedroom, dropping the satchel on the floor by the bed and headed to the bathroom.

Stepping out of her gym shoes and peeling off her clothes she turned the shower on. After a quick shower she put on a pair of jeans, a cotton pullover and flats. Picking up her purse, laptop and grabbing a jacket, she stepped out of the house, jumped in the car and pulled off. She stopped at the downtown coffee shop, deciding this would be her out of office location for the day.

Camille secured a booth, placing everything she needed to work with on the table and left enough space for the barista to bring whatever she ordered. Fifteen minutes later the barista placed a ham and cheese on a croissant, chips and hot apple cider carefully in front of her.

****

Camille was already typing an agenda for the Russell couple's charity event. The entire package was nearly complete with everything they would accomplish in the evening. It was an event with an autumn theme so Camille focused on the metaphor of seasonal changes not only with Mother Nature but the attitudes of warmth and giving. This was the time of year when organizations and churches are asking for assistance from the community and the state, she suggested the Russell family choose one organization that could benefit from a shared interest.

The Russell family chose an area involving homelessness in the elderly. There was a center that catered to this type of problem and the family wanted to fund programs that would help relocate senior citizens in proper housing or certified nursing facilities. At the same time services would be assisted financially to keep the center operating. Camille called the promotional package "Transitional Leaves."

As time passed, the noise level in the coffee shop grew louder with parents coming inside with small children and teenagers pulling tables together to have live group chats. Camille put on a pair of headphones stashed in her purse, plugging it into the laptop to continue working.

"Earth to Camille."

Camille jerked her head in the direction of the person interrupting her. He stood over her, wearing a long sleeve button down shirt, dark slacks. His hair looked a little grayer on his head than what she was use to seeing and now sports a beard. He peered over his reading glasses and gave her a slight smile.

"Elijah." Moving the headphones so that they rested around her neck, Camille looked at her ex-husband and smirked.

"This is definitely a surprise seeing you around here. Are you looking for your latest young conquest?"

Elijah laughed and stepped aside to grab a chair. He moved the chair to her table and sat down. "No. I had a meeting today with some clients and figured I stop here to grab something to drink before I head back to Chicago. I noticed from the serious look on your face you still keep busy on a Saturday. But that was our routine anyway," he said.

"Yeah, well I am finding time to do things for me, at my own pace…not because you needed it done right away," Camille said.

"So how are you Camille? Or is it OK to ask?"

Camille looked at him. "I am fine Elijah, that's all you need to know. There is no need to ask me about my life because I am no longer in yours."

Elijah drew a breath. "Look Camille I know I made a mistake…"

Camille shot him a look. "A MISTAKE," she said loudly then leaned towards Elijah and brought her voice to a whisper. "You run around and fuck some younger chick who could not even match the looks, mannerism and professional attitude I have! Yeah you made a mistake alright. You lowered your standards. Are you still with Miss Thing or did she bother to hold your hand in the emergency room as you told the doctor how your dick got bent?"

Elijah jumped up and spun around and just missed crashing into the barista who was coming to Camille's table to hand him the coffee to go cup and a bag with two cheese pastries. Elijah faced Camille with a cloud of anger hovering above him. "You need to get off the bitch mode," he said. "Mmmm, I don't do women sweetie," Camille said then placed her headphones over her ears and stared at the laptop screen. "You just make sure those direct deposits show up on time."

****

Roman spent most of the day inside, taking time to clean up the place and catch up on laundry. Opening double doors to what could easily be mistaken for a closet he placed a basket of dirty jeans and darks on the dryer and opened the washer's door. Old school hip-hop filled the apartment as he shoved the basket of clothes in the washer, poured a cup of liquid detergent, shut the door and started the cycle. He walked into the bedroom to the sound of the TV broadcasting an action movie and began changing the bedding. The combination of exotic perfume and Camille's musk with his scent still lingered in the sheets. The more he worked on removing the bedding the stronger the scent became, but he was also reliving the other night which heightened his senses. He still could not believe this woman drove from her house to his place wearing a coat, heels and perfume! That's definitely confidence on her part. Roman's asked a couple of younger women to show up at his place naked under a coat and those girls looked at him like he was crazy. But at the same time those chicks are the first ones to try and twirl around a pole after a few drinks during amateur night at a club. Camille did not need alcohol to be bold.

Chapter 19

"You're fucking Roman?!!"

After deciding to tell Sophia why she has been extra busy for the last three weeks, Camille was glad she decided to invite her loudmouth friend to the house on a Wednesday night for homemade tacos and a blender's worth of strawberry margaritas. And she was just as thankful for thick walls, real brick exterior and a little distance between her and the neighbors. Not just to keep them from hearing Sophia screaming profanities at her for keeping this secret, but for the soundtracks from frequent day and night visits from Roman.

Two weeks ago she decided to allow Roman into her less than humble abode with the following rules: no leaving clothes in her closets or dresser drawers, no toothbrushes or shaving equipment in the bathroom. Come in with an overnight bag when necessary and take it with you when you head out in the morning – unless circumstances beyond their control had him hanging around until noon. While he never implied rules with her whenever she visited his apartment, Camille was not stupid and did not have time to play any games. They were not a couple, nor were they exclusive. She had a feeling Roman may still have a couple of side chicks despite his energy and agility between the sheets…on the floor…in the hallway.

"Use your indoor voice, Sophia," Camille said with a chuckle while checking the chopped pork and spices sizzling in the skillet. Sophia was already on her second strawberry margarita having lined her stomach with tortilla chips and salsa. She swung her legs back and forth while sitting on the chair by the kitchen island like an anxious child about to let out a flurry of questions. "When did this happen? Where were you and Roman when it happened? How come you are just deciding today to tell me? I thought you were my friend?!"

Her back to Sophia, Camille shook her head and laughed after each question. Turning off the burner under the skillet and stirring the pork with a wooden spoon, Camille ignored her friend for a few seconds, mocking serious concentration on the taco meat. "Four weeks ago. In one of the restaurant's private dining rooms after hours…"

"WHAT!!," Sophia sputtered as a sip of her margarita went down wrong causing her to tear up and cough and hack like a cat. Camille spun around, grabbed bottled water and handed it to her.

"Where did I leave off? Oh yeah, I was not sure if it was going to be a one-night stand or a continuation, so I wanted to be sure. And, of course I am your friend, which is why I saved the surprise until now," Camille said while bringing the skillet to the island and placing it on a cooling mat next to the hard taco shells. The rest of the island favored a buffet spread of sides to go with the tacos; bowls filled with salsa, sour cream, shredded lettuce, diced tomatoes and shredded cheese lined assembly style.

"El Tacos Camille!" Sophia glared at Camille and jumped off the chair to grab a plate. "Don't think I am finished with the questions because your damn tacos are ready. Even though they smell like I could eat this whole skillet."

Camille laughed again as they filled their plates and grabbed their margaritas. They went to the dining table, sat down and said a prayer before digging in.

"So, is this a relationship or is he a fuck buddy," Sophia said while chewing.

Camille cast a sideway glance at her. "Right now it is all about fun. We are enjoying each other's company with no strings attached," she said.

Sophia nodded and took a sip from her margarita. "And he is not catching any feelings? I mean, has he started calling you and trying to find out where you are and why he is not getting immediate callbacks?"

Camille shook her head while biting into her second taco. "As far as I can tell, he is not catching any feelings and he knows better than to call and play investigator. He calls and sees if I am doing anything and if I am free, he asks if he can stop by. If I feel like having him in the house I say OK. If not, that's the end of the conversation," Camille said. "Besides I have been focused on this autumn event for that couple and everything is falling into place. The event is this weekend."

Sophia laughed. "Yeah, yeah on the event, Miss trying to change the subject! So…how is Roman?"

Camille paused. "What do you mean?"

Sophia dropped her taco on her plate and pointed a finger in Camille's face, making Camille burst into laughter. "Heifer! You know exactly what I meant!"

Camille threw her hands up in defense. "OK, OK! He is very good in bed. I did not have to teach him anything. In fact, I think I surprised him! I have a feeling in the beginning he was not expecting me to be so aggressive and so full of energy."

Sophia laughed and poured another glass of margarita from the blender. "Ah, so he thought you needed a refresher course. Or maybe he figured the well was dry!"

Camille nodded while laughing out loud. "Yeah I think I kind of messed with his head. When I opened a drawer with condoms I believe he was trying to see if a tube of lubricant was in there. Not that there's anything wrong with some extra help. I wished I had a camera on me the night I showed up in my coat with nothing on but my stilettos."

Sophia screamed and leaned over to clink her glass against Camille's. "That's what I'm talking about! And speaking of cameras," Sophia said.

"Oh nooooo. No cameras. No recordings. I give him enough to keep everything a mental film he can play over and over in his head," Camille said. "Trust, I am not foolish like the ex. And no damn stripper poles either! I am willing to do some things to please him, but Roman is happy as hell that he is with an older, more experienced woman. We are each other's playground and I am swinging as high as I can go," Camille said with a laugh.

****

"So you are seeing someone," Evelyn said trying to sound sane long enough to rope me into confessing.

Roman drew a breath and made a mental note to knock one of his boys upside his head. He knew which one told on him; the brother who is dating Evelyn's best friend. The best friend who will sweet talk and fuck his friend into being a snitch about his personal business. Roman regretted the day he ran into old boy while having dinner with Camille two weeks ago. Already know how the conversation went back at his crib:

He: "Hey baby I ran into my boy Roman at this restaurant while I was having drinks with some co-workers.

She: "Oh yeah, baby? How are Roman and Evelyn? I'm going to have to give my girl a call!"

He: "Nah sweetie Roman was with some older woman. I thought maybe an aunt but they did not favor and I don't recall his mother having a sister."

She: "An older woman?! How much older? Maybe it was a business dinner. You know Roman trying to be like that foreign talking chef who makes the huge dinner party for the Academy Awards."

He: "No, they were dressed up but it looked romantic…shit…"

She: "ROMANTIC?! So Roman's stepping out on my girl!"

He: "Naw, baby! I mean, they are not going together. You know he and Evelyn are not an item…"

She: "Really! Well, we will see about that!"

Yeah, I'm gonna have to have a talk with that loudmouth real soon. Evelyn's deep frustrated breathing was getting louder in his Bluetooth.

"Evelyn, why are you acting like some crazy chick? We are not boyfriend and girlfriend. I have not seen you since you got all independent woman with your girls…including my boy's girlfriend…at the bar!"

"Well you could have called or e-mailed me to make it final," Evelyn whined. Roman paused in disbelief at what he just heard.

"Make what final? It was FINAL a long time ago!"

His last sentence created a screaming rant and Roman snatched the Bluetooth off his left ear and put his cell on loudspeaker.

"Evelyn! EVELYN! Stop being childish! You want closure? OK, it's over! It was nothing to begin with! We kicked it for a while but we both had other people! Don't worry about whether I was seeing her while with you! Isn't none of your business how much older she is (I am truly knocking him upside his head the little snitch bitch!)! "Click!"

Chapter 20

It was lunchtime at M and Roman and his staff have never seen the restaurant so full on a Thursday. There was no time for brief conversation as he and his chefs hurried to get order after order prepared and on the counter for pick up. The audio in the dining area was a loud overwhelming mixture of discussions, laughter and constant clinking of glasses and utensils against plates. The waiters were also overwhelmed but happy as the tips were generous. One waiter known to gossip rushed to the counter to pick up another tray of orders. "Hey," Roman whispered, "What's the crowd about?"

The waiter checked the orders. "A lot of businessmen, some corporate wigs and a couple of conference attendees. Something's going on this weekend at the center."

Roman nodded and let the waiter take off and returned to an island where he resumed dicing onions for a stew. Maybe some of the crowd had something to do with the weekend event Camille was talking about. He had not spoken to her this week, figuring she was just as busy trying to get everything ready. He is hoping to get with her later tonight or Friday but the way things are going it will be next week before he is back at her house or she swings by the apartment. Three hours later the madness calmed down and some of the staff went on a smoking break. Roman sat in his office going through messages on his cell phone. One text came from Camille asking him to stop by after the restaurant closes tonight. Roman grinned at the possibilities and returned her text with an OK ☺.

****

"Camille, I am not a catering service!"

Camille rolled her eyes as Roman plopped down on her sofa and opened his leather jacket. He shook his head while raking his fingers through his twists. He just knew it was going to be a night of sex that would relax his mind and stressed out body after a long and busy day. He was not expecting to be insulted.

"Baby, I really need your help! The chef who was suppose to prepare the main menu for the event was hit with the flu and her assistant is already hacking like a lung is about to leave her, Camille said. "I did not mean caterer, I want you to prepare the menu, hire a couple of your chefs and some of the waiters. I know they would not mind a little extra money on the side. I will take care of the bill, just please, do this for me!"

Roman stood up and faced her. "It's last minute Camille. I don't know if I can get some of the crew…"

"Bullshit! You just don't want to be considered below your means," Camille interrupted. "I mean, what the hell is the problem? You were catering when you did Sophia's party a couple months ago!"

Roman glared at her, shoving his hands in his jacket pockets. "That was not catering. Your friend had The Menagerie host and co-sponsor that party so the restaurant was part of the deal!"

Camille threw her hands up in the air. "So you can't do this for me! You are so fucking above being a caterer! You will not be doing this for free I said I will pay you!"

Roman stepped closer to Camille with a colder look. "Since you are all that, Miss Rich, go ahead and hire someone else to come in and save your event! I am not for sale!"

Camille returned the cold stare. "Yeah, you are right about that, sweetheart. I sure did not pay you for a piece of dick!"

A flicker of anger crossed Roman's expression, but it went away quickly as Camille did not flinch, another proof of the difference between her and younger women. She did not even raise her voice when she made that last remark. "You are right Roman, I cannot buy you into doing this one favor for me. You don't have to do it; I will find someone else. Being that this event will feature a lot of corporate people and it is a charity event you'd probably not have time to pass out business cards. The opportunities to expand your network and your net worth won't be there."

"You are not my boss or my mother, so don't talk to me like a stubborn child," Roman said.

Camille looked at him and laughed. "I am well aware that I am not your mother. Not trying to replace your mother. I respect what you went through over the years from what you've shared with me. I was throwing an opportunity your way while trying to save an event," Camille said then grabbed her cell phone. "I will call some other prospects and see what their schedules are and place my money elsewhere."

"So now it's your money…"

"Yeah Roman, it's my motherfucking money! Look, you need to leave. I am not trying to give you any ultimatum like if you don't do this, we can't fuck anymore. It is nothing like that. I am not trying to throw my money around because I have not done that to you. What we are doing is having sex. I am not trying to trap your ass!" And with that, Camille walked to the front door, opened it and stepped aside for Roman to make his exit. No fucking of any kind was going on that night because Roman knew he'd truly fucked up.

Chapter 21

Camille was up early Friday morning still hunting for a last minute replacement for the event's chef. While wearing a calm exterior, inside she was screaming like a madwoman as the hours were speeding against her will. She juggled her cell phone and the landline receiver while checking instant messages on her laptop. Why couldn't Roman just say yes to her offer? Why did the fucking male ego have to go berserk thinking she was hiring him as the help? Was he thinking about accompanying her to the event? Camille had to push those questions out of her head so she could find a last minute chef or else she was going to pull double duty as the consultant and cook. She put the receiver down and the phone rang immediately making her jump from her chair. "Shit! Hello?"

"Well, hello to you too, darling," Sophia's voice cooed on the other end. "What's wrong?"

Camille slumped in the chair and pushed her bangs from her forehead. "The chef and assistant had to bail because of the flu and I cannot find a replacement!"

Sophia paused. "Uh, sweetheart, Roman said he will prepare the menu."

Camille sat up straight and dropped her cell on the floor which she thanked the heavens that her opened purse was on the floor to cushion the landing. "Wait, what do you mean he's preparing the menu?"

"Roman called me and said he would be able to help out at no cost to us! He said consider the menu preparation and his assistants to be a donation to the event. Wasn't that sweet of him," Sophia said cheerfully.

"Yeah, that was really lovely of him," Camille said with sarcasm.

"Is there a problem Camille?" Camille stood up and shut the laptop close.

"No, no problem at all. The pressure is off my back. I will talk to Roman in a while. Got to go," Camille hung up barely hearing Sophia's confused good-bye.

"Son of a bitch," Camille said while walking down the hall to her bedroom to grab some clothes and take a quick shower.

****

An hour later, Camille was talking to the M's maitre d demanding to speak to Roman.

"Ma'am, he is in a meeting. I will inform him to call you when he is done."

Camille glared at the gentleman then reached to the side of the stand

and grabbed a menu. "I think I will have a salad or some brunch," she said in a calmer tone, "I would like a corner table please."

The maitre d drew a breath and led her to a corner table where she could see Roman leave whichever room he was having the meeting. She will catch his attention that way and when he sits across from her, she can calmly but firmly snap at him about the foolishness he displayed last night. Fifteen minutes after placing her order of a garden salad and grilled tuna, Camille kept watch on the door in the back near the kitchen while drinking a cup of herbal tea. The crowd was small as the lunch crowd was not yet here. Another five minutes and the door she kept an eye on finally opened and Camille prepared to stand up and wave for his attention. She was halfway out of the chair when she paused and watched a young woman with a shoulder's length worth of weave furiously walk out of the room. The angry young woman wore a short, tight denim dress with thigh high black suede boots. She had on enough makeup to do over three plain Janes and a pair of overly large hoop earrings. "Ma'am is everything all right? I have your order," the waiter stood at Camille's table with a concerned look on his face.

Camille blinked just in time to see Roman walk out of the room, raking his fingers through his twists. "Yes, everything is fine," Camille said and sat back down while smiling at the waiter.

The waiter placed her order on the table and walked off. At perfect timing Roman looked in the direction where Camille was seated and Evelyn was walking in that path. Camille placed her cloth napkin across her lap and keeping her head down rolled her eyes in the girl's direction. She then sneaked a peek past the girl and watched Roman, whose facial expression was beyond calm and more like fear. He never took another step and watch Evelyn storm past Camille's table. Camille caught a whiff of the floral perfume the girl was wearing and straighten up in her chair once she passed by. Camille stole another glance at Roman who looked like he has yet to take a breath. Only when Evelyn passed the maitre d and shoved the door open to leave did he close his eyes. No sooner than Evelyn stomped out of the restaurant, he saw Camille seated in a corner table, he felt as if the scene was happening in slow motion.

Camille took a bite of the grilled tuna and followed it with a forkful of the garden salad. She chewed and watched Roman who finally decided to take some footsteps in her path. He stopped and stood at the side of her table. "Hey Camille."

"Hello Roman, how are you? I was here to see you but you were in a meeting so I decided to grab a bite and wait," Camille said.

Roman nodded. "Oh. Sorry about that. The maitre d or the waiters did not come to the office to tell me you were here." Camille grabbed her napkin and dabbed the corners of her mouth.

"Well with the private meeting I would not expect them to interrupt you. But are you free now? Until a few hours ago I was frantically calling chefs in the area to still replace my sick chef for tomorrow night," she said in a calm voice as Roman pulled a chair to the table and sat down. "Then Sophia calls me saying you've offered to do the menu for free. You want to tell me why you did not offer this to me last night?"

Roman leaned in to Camille's direction and let out a sigh. "Look, Camille, when you texted me to come to the house after work I was not expecting you to throw a fit about what happened to your chef. You came at me frantic about 'I need a caterer! Can you cater my event?' It just hit me in the face."

Camille raised her cup of tea to her lips, stopped and smirked. "You did not race to my house to see what was wrong. You raced over there because you thought you were getting some," Camille said after taking a generous sip. "You were all ready for me to open my front door damn near naked so we could fuck all over the foyer, then the living room and to my bedroom. The last thing on your mind was to hear my emergency."

Roman opened his mouth to argue but thought best to keep his mouth shut.

Camille put the cup down and looked at him. "So when did you decide to contact Sophia? She barely knew what I was going through and I was trying to keep it quiet until it became desperate."

Roman looked at Camille and ran his right hand over his face. "I called Miss Andrews about an hour after leaving your house. I did not know she was fully unaware of your problem and I apologize for not offering my idea to you," he said.

Camille nodded and pushed aside her salad and plate with the half eaten tuna and dropped the napkin on the table. She waved for the waiter's attention.

"No Camille, don't worry about the bill for this," Roman said while motioning to the waiter to stop. "Look, about the girl you saw leaving my office. She is not…"

"What your meeting was about and with who is none of my business," Camille said as she stood up and grabbed her purse.

Roman jumped to his feet as Camille headed to the doors.

"Thanks for the free meal. I will see you tomorrow night."

****

Wearing a long, strapless bronze gown with sparkling gold trim along the bustier and a short gold shrug, Camille turned heads as she made her way through crowd inside the center's massive ballroom. Her hair was pinned up in an overflow of waves and curls and her makeup was flawless in light, fall colors of wines and gold. She wore a pair of teardrop diamond

The Panthers Club

earrings trimmed with her birthstone, ruby and a matching necklace. As ravishing as she looked, she was armed with a tablet and ink pen going over the operations of the night.   The theme of autumn colors – reds, yellows, tan and orange – blended in various shades with touches of gold for drama. The chairs were dressed with satin gold material kept together with bow ties of red, green or orange in the back. VIP tables for 5 that went for a $1,500 group fee, were draped with gold tablecloths and red and gold centerpieces, napkins and table settings. The remaining tables with ticket fees ranging from $150 to $25 each were draped with either velvet red, burnt orange or a forest green with gold accessories. Golden buckets of ice accommodated bottles of champagne, sparkling non-alcoholic grape juice or apple cider with cash bars in every corner for those wanting stronger spirits.

The host and hostess of the event held strong smiles as their guests talked about how everything looked amazing and they hardly recognized the center's ballroom. Camille enjoyed overhearing the couple mention her name and she discreetly placed Thank you notes inside the evening's program books that included her business card tucked in. Turning towards the buffet tables on opposite sides of the ballroom Camille did a quick glance for Roman. Not seeing him she figured he was in the kitchen with the staff. Roman brought a staff of five with him and the center's catering team had 15 servers available to help out during the night.

The tables were decorated to represent a harvest of delicacies including miniature spinach and ham quiches, turkey and cranberry kabobs, glazed orange chicken with chestnut stuffing, green beans, spicy vegetable soup and homemade bread with apple butter. The dessert tables included a tower of sweets like miniature sweet potato pies, apple crisps and fudge brownie cups. Martini glasses were filled with diced cinnamon apples with whipped cream topping.

Roman and his crew truly outdone themselves, Camille thought to herself. Before the evening's program began she made a quick dash into the kitchen to thank Roman. As soon as she pushed the swinging double doors, her sense of smell became intoxicated with the aromas of the buffet as fresh preparations were being made for tray refills. The sounds of cookware clattering and clinking blended with voices of the staff yelling orders in perfect rhythm. Roman was in the center of the melee, stirring the glaze for the next batch of chicken. The frown on his face was not of anger but concentration and he never bothered to glance up to see if someone was watching him. Camille decided not to walk to where he was and with the intense heat from the massive ovens did not want her hair to flop nor her face to melt. She eased out of the kitchen just in time to hear the hostess start the program and grabbed a handful of her long dress to take quick steps to the ballroom. Camille smiled as teenaged volunteers in short dresses and dark suits escorted the guests of honor to their tables. There wasn't a rush as many of the senior citizens benefitting from the event had canes, walkers and wheelchairs as part of their accessories. The crowds applauded wildly for the very important people as they took their seats and the hostess with her husband continued the program.

When the hosts' eight year old daughter announced at the podium from a footstool that dinner was served, the crowd waited as the volunteers and waiters brought dinner to the special guests. Soon afterwards the rest of the crowd was served by the waiters as the buffet layout was created to make it easier for the waiters to bring the dishes.

Camille continued to check with the hosts and various guests in the ballroom, only taking a moment to drink from her bottled water.

Sophia stepped away from her date for the evening to approach Camille. "Sweetie, you have done an excellent job with this program! Everything is gorgeous and you look amazing," Sophia said.

Camille hugged her friend who wore a red off the shoulder gown that showed off her curves. "You look ravishing yourself Sophia! And your date," Camille looked over her friend's shoulder and scoped the Hispanic male with an olive complexion and bodybuilder physique that made his tuxedo look painted on. He turned to Camille and gave her a flashing white teeth smile with deep dimples to match.

She fanned herself and winked at Sophia. "Whew! Where did you find him?" Sophia grinned at her friend's approving swoon.

"He was a guest at a corporate event earlier this week. We clicked right away," she said.

Camille glanced at her friend.

"No we have not slept together…yet. I am trying to take my time…oh, hello Julian," Sophia hurried and changed the subject as her date approached them. After a brief introduction, Sophia and Julian walked away from Camille, who guessed Julian to be no more than 30 years old. Camille resumed her duties of making sure everything went smoothly.

"Where is your table? You need to sit down and eat something."

Camille turned around and faced Roman who was standing behind her in a black chef uniform. She scanned him up and down and admired how a chef's uniform never looked so damn sexy until tonight.

When she looked at his face, Roman broke into a grin. "I was making the rounds with the buffet tables and seeing if the people were enjoying our food. I caught sight of you…" He leaned towards her with a smile. "…and you look like a deliciously rich, sculpted model of chocolate perfectly wrapped."

Camille was not wearing red until now when she felt her blood rush through her body and a flush overcame her cheeks. As cool as she has been towards Roman in the last 24 hours all of that disappeared with those words.

She kept her cool in the ballroom, however, with a sly smile on her wine colored lips. "I was in the kitchen earlier and I wanted to say thank you for helping out but you were busy," she said.

Roman's eyes scanned her body from the tips of her wine polished toes to the top curl on her head. "You can thank me later," he said in a husky, low tone before turning away.

He left Camille breathless without placing a finger on her. She watched him resume talking to the waiters and shaking hands with some guests marveling his cooking skills. Then Roman disappeared into the kitchen and she finally took a deep breath and signaled a waiter to bring a full plate to her table in the back.

The charity event was a success and the hosts presented Camille with an envelope and promises of using her consulting skills for future events. Camille thanked them and went to coat check and gathered her coat. Before shoving the envelope in her purse, she opened it and found a check with the remainder of her fee and another check with a $1,000 bonus. She decided that when she deposited her checks in the morning, she would write a personal check for $1,000 and send it to the charity organization. She rushed to the parking garage and jumped in her car and headed home. Camille thought about what Roman said about thanking him and she had no problem. But figured he was too tired to stop by her house tonight.

When she turned into her street however, she noticed a truck parked in front of her house. The closer she got, the broader her smile was as Roman was sitting in the driver's seat bobbing his head to whatever was blaring from the speakers. She drove past and into the driveway as Roman turned off the truck's engine and stepped out. By then Camille was out of her car and at the front door getting the keys out of her purse. She did not bother to turn around because she felt his presence behind her. She opened the door and they stepped inside. Camille pushed the 'Off' button on her alarm keypad and Roman closed the door and turned the locks. Words were useless as Camille took off her coat and draped it on the chair in the foyer and Roman closed the gap between them, jerked her forward and planted a hard kiss on her lips. Camille threw her arms around his neck and returned the kiss pushing her tongue into his mouth which made him grunt. Their tongues wrestled and occasionally she nibbled and pulled at his bottom lip. She jerked away from him and stared into his eyes. "We need to shower," she laughed. He grabbed Camille's hand and as he pulled her towards her bedroom both stepped out of their shoes and pieces of clothing and jewelry created a trail. By the time they were in her master bathroom they were completely naked. Roman pushed Camille against the cold bathroom wall and pressed against while devouring her mouth with another kiss. He reached into her hair and pulled out the two slim pins that held her curls and waves in place and then gather her hair in his hands. She felt his hardness press against the lower part of her belly and her vagina, making her grind against him. Camille pushed him away, giggling as she walked around him and yanked the shower curtain back and turned the water on. She straightened up and looked at the shower cap. When Roman followed her gaze and noticed the cap his eyes widen as if to say 'Hell No!"

"I'm joking, baby, joking," she laughed and stepped into the shower.

"Come here, sexy, let me clean you up." Roman stepped in and faced Camille who grabbed a gloved loofah and a bottle of lightly scented body wash. She put the glove on and with her bare hand poured the body wash on the glove as warm water sprayed on Roman's body. Camille began moving her hands along his shoulders and chest in a slow, circular motion and the combination of friction from Camille's gloved hand and bare hand created goose bumps on his skin. Roman's breath quickened as her hands moved further down his torso and on his abs. Camille suddenly moved her hands to his back, using the same circular motion on his butt and upward to his shoulder blades. Her body was pressed against his body and she kissed him. He grabbed her butt and caressed it while she continued to soap his back. They gingerly stepped under the showerhead and let the water spray over their bodies.

"Your turn," Roman said as he grabbed the body wash and poured some in his bare hands. He began massaging Camille's body with his hands, starting at her neck and working his way to her breasts. He gave each breast extra attention before moving to her belly and then her mound causing her to moan loudly. He rinsed her off and turned her around, bending her forward as she reached for the towel rack under the window. He grabbed a condom from the medicine cabinet and put it on. Placing a firm grip on her waist, Roman slowly entered Camille from behind. "Oh shit…oh shit!"

Camille drew a breath as Roman began delivering long, deep strokes inside her, first slow then fast. He leaned forward to get deeper inside and Camille cried out in pleasure. Roman held her tighter as he increased the rhythm of his strokes and they were more turned on at the sound of their flesh slapping against each other.

"Damn you feel so good," Roman growled as he pounded harder to Camille's delight. The water felt good against them for the next 20 minutes. Both stumbled out of the shower, grabbing the large towels on the rack by the door. They dried each other off and worked themselves up for another round. Rushing into the bedroom, Roman snatched the comforter back and pushed Camille onto her bed. He grabbed and put on another condom as Camille opened her arms…and legs to him. He obediently climbed on top and re-entered her as she wrapped her legs around his waist urging him to go deep. This went on into the early hours of Saturday until they fell asleep.

The Panthers Club

Later Camille turned her head and opened her right eye to glance at the alarm clock on her night stand. The clock read 11:15 a.m. In 45 minutes the bank with her accounts will close for the remainder of the weekend. Oh well, she thought. The deposits can wait until Monday. Camille turned over and moved closer to Roman's body. He moved slightly and dropped his arm across her body. "Thank you," she mumbled and fell back to sleep.

Chanale

Chapter 1

"Damn it, why am I so dry?!"

Behind the closed walnut brown bathroom door in her apartment, Chanale leaned towards the mirror and stared into her own irritating brown eyes after removing the green contact lenses. Every day she puts up with concealing what she always thought were boring, dark brown eyes that did not sparkle nor grab any man's attention. Her eyes were not the only things she concealed. "Ugh! C'mon now, shit," she mumbled while fighting her black spandex with lace trimmed Sister Hugs. This was the body shifter from hell she paid $125 for the one-piece body suit that pushed her breasts up and morphed her stomach into an hourglass shape for eight hours. It could do more hours than that but eight was all Chanale could stand without the fear of turning blue and keeling over. With the last clasp undone the upper part of Sister Hugs released its embrace and rolled down for her to push past her hips. Her once bound breasts and other pieces of flesh exhaled as if crying freedom. Chanale was not obese nor really plus-sized, just a little thick. Wearing these products – she has two dresser drawers filled with almost every item in the Sister Hugs label – allowed her to look smooth in her work, casual and going out wardrobe. And she's lost weight wearing the products under her clothes with all the contorting and sweating. If she just wore the panty/waist product Chanale followed a tip she heard on television from the lips of a singing superstar's mother. She'd take safety pins and pinned the waist part to four sides of her bra to keep the waistband from rolling under her belly. It had to work because that superstar daughter was definitely a thick sister.

She worked out, but not like an extreme fitness buff… it was more of an occasional routine and she needed to be in the mood or feel like she's gained an extra pound or two. Once an annual card holder of the area fitness club, Chanale began slacking on the visits and instead found comfort in her apartment with an entertainment system that included a stack of exercise DVDs, a yoga mat and a couple of hand weights. When the latest craze of line dancing and other routines that were packaged to not look like aerobics hit the fitness scene, Chanale jumped on it in the privacy of her home. She was not going to be trying to Zumba/rumba/cha-cha her way into shape with a group of women trying to evaluate her on the sly or blatantly in her face. She always got side eye glances and glares from women whenever shit entered a room. She knows they are trying to figure her out because she hardly enters with the same look. Her eyes are colors according to her mood for the day and her hair has grown in various lengths that she may as well been a replica of her Tiffany Taylor, her favorite childhood doll.

What she truly loved about that doll was with a twist and a pull, Miss Taylor went from blonde to brunette, sometimes with highlights. She kept the same color eyes of brown until Chanale took a blue marker and shaded over the brown pupils. She also styled the doll's hair until she decided to use a pair of scissors to do a blunt but uneven bob. That act got her ass whipped by her mother who eventually gave up on punishing Chanale for makeovers on the doll. What did her mother expect from her daughter, especially after naming her after a legendary socialite and fashion designer with her own perfume? And when her parents brought her home wrapped in a plush blanket and presenting their infant daughter on a satin and lace trimmed pillow, looks and presentation was injected in Chanale's plump cheeks. And she lived that name down, from wearing the latest in school fashion from elementary to high school. Spoiled? No, just dotted on from hardworking parents who had a budget but were not the type to let people see that dressed according to their earnings.

Daddy worked in the mill and Mama was a secretary for a corporate office. Mama worked part-time during most of Chanale's childhood so to be there for her. Whether she was going shopping, running errands or heading to work, Mrs. Arlington was kept together from her neatly pinned up hair to her makeup and blouses and narrow knee-length skirts that caught her curves. Mr. Arlington may have worked in the mill but you wouldn't know it from how he would enter the house wearing a clean shirt and slacks with a newsboy cap. He would shower and freshen up before he left the mill. And when they would go out for dinner or to a house party at a neighbor's house, they were in dressy casual outfits like they were going to a club. Daddy's closet was filled with enough clothes, shoes and accessories that you'd think he was a male model. If there was a way to look clean and sharp from casual to after five, Chanale's parents were a walking fashion show.

"Whew," she said while standing behind the bathroom sink massaging her flesh into normalcy. She turned her head to the right side of the bathroom where a full length mirror took over the door. Still in her heels Chanale slapped her own full, round ass, thankful she did not need any butt injections or fake booty cups. She also thanked the body angels for allowing her to inherit her mother's assets. "I swear if I did not have at least a decent piece of ass I'd become a hermit!" Turning her head to face the vanity mirror over the sink Chanale leaned forward and peeled away the fake lashes from her eyelids and tossed them in the wastebasket. Tying a scarf on her head she opened a jar of facial cream and dipped three fingers in to scoop out a small amount. This was her evening ritual when coming from work or from a night out. Taking off everything she could without bloodshed and washing the day away with crèmes and body washes. The evening ritual took all of 45 minutes, much less than her morning routine. Depending on which Sister Hug item and the outfit Chanale got up two hours early to stuff everything in and put everything on. Thank goodness her hair is short and done in an easy wrap or she'd have to put another hour in.

Chanale grabbed a shower cap and stepped in the tub for her shower using the massage showerhead to control the water pressure. She looked forward to the shower because the water pressure relaxed her flesh and muscles until the next time she needed it. For now it also took the place of massages from the opposite sex. She was taking a break from all of the dating. Just as she was picky about her wardrobe and looks, she was picky about the men in her life. They had to have money and a life of their own. Age wise, she preferred older men as some were not picky about how she looked. As long as she looked good enough to be seen with them, it was all gravy. And the money and gifts were nothing to complain about; if the guy wanted her to look good he had to pay the price.

This last guy, however, Duke, was a piece of work. Worth the time and money she spent on looking good for him, she felt it was time to take a break because he was getting a little bit too controlling. She knew this to be the case a while back but always seemed to find herself back to him. Now that she's not heard from him in a while Chanale hoped he found another young woman to follow and sniff behind. She could take some time out for herself or prepare herself for the next man to come into her life. Right now, it was all about her.

Stepping out of the shower and wrapping a towel around her, Chanale grabbed the bottle of body lotion and walked into her bedroom across the hall. She sat on the chair of her vanity table and rubbed the lotion into her skin. Dropping the towel to the floor, she stepped into a pair of yoga pants, pulled a t-shirt over her head and slipped her feet into her favorite flip flops and headed to the kitchen to warm up the small pan of her homemade deep dish lasagna. It was going to be a solo night and Chanale was not going to complain.

Chapter 2

Desmond Richards' lean, muscular six feet tall frame stepped out of the shower with only a white towel covering the lower half of his chestnut toned flesh. He was using another towel to roughly dry off his close to the scalp haircut as he walked to the locker area. Stopping in front of his locker, he whisked through tumbling the combination on the lock before giving it a sharp yank forward. His locker and those adjoining were a little taller than him and was like a mini apartment closet. He reached inside the top shelf for deodorant and aftershave. A quick glance to his right and his likeness appeared in a full length mirror glued into the locker door. He sprayed under his arms and slapped aftershave on his face and leaned closer to the mirror to check his head. Satisfied he returned his focus to the main locker space and took out a hanging button down black shirt and another hanger holding a pair of pressed black slacks.

Snatching the towel from his waist, Desmond grabbed a pair of silk black boxers and stepped into them. He sat down on the bench and grabbed a pair of black socks and pulled them on. He then stood up to put on the rest of his ensemble, concluding with a pair of black dress shoes, a watch and his hospital id in his shirt pocket. As a soundtrack of beeps, intercom announcements of visiting hours coming to an end, Desmond turned to the locker mirror again and after inspection grabbed his cell phone, pager, billfold and the charcoal gray blazer and slammed the locker shut.

Midwest Medical had Desmond's attention for the last 16 hours and he did not look nor feel like it. He loved his journey into the medical field, undergoing the residency after a sudden change in careers. He had considered a career in sales but the urge to work with people and helped make them healthy instead of trying to sell them something won him over.

At 35 years old he was a little late in the game but he did not care. This was his second year as a resident and Dr. Desmond Richards was the pride of his family. His mother was a retired nurse and dad was in office management. Different professions but his parents made it work, especially dad who said he found his Nightingale when she came and administered a shot in his ass nearly 50 years ago. Desmond worked hard and played hard, meaning the young women were always on the ready. He kept his dating private but staff at Midwest, particularly the female staff paid attention to him and few other handsome, eligible residents, doctors and surgeons who made rounds day and night.

Female nurses, doctors and a few supervisors could not wait for Desmond to enter the hospital doors, whether in a suit and tie, t-shirt, sweater and jeans, in scrubs or his white medical coat. As far as they were concerned Desmond was a photographer's dream stepping out of the pages of a magazine, sharp with a mega-watt smile to match warm, smiling dark eyes. He always greeted the staff and asked some about their wellbeing and that of their families. And if a couple of females caught his eye Desmond would discreetly wink or give a slight smirk while looking them in the eyes.

He tries not to be involved with women at the hospital but sometimes the urge wins over, like the certified nurse's assistant he was about to meet at a nearby restaurant. With a confident but quick stride, he waved and smiled his way out of the automatic double doors to jump into the black SUV parked in the side lot. The honey colored young lady was 28 years old, petite and curvy with shoulder-length hair and dimples that set off a plush, heart shaped mouth. He smiled at the thought of what the rest of the night could lead to while pulling off in the direction of the restaurant. If all went well and she was not too chatty about the wrong things (his or her exes, what he is looking for in a relationship, etc.)maybe they can have a nightcap at either her place or his. He smiled at the thought of what the remainder of the night could lead as he hit the highway to Merrillville. Within twenty minutes Desmond was parking in a space in front of the Italian restaurant. Walking inside the hostess led him to a table where the young lady was nervously waiting to see him approach the table. Desmond took in the red v-neck sweater dress that hugged her shape and the matching red stilettos that gave her an additional four inches when she stands up. She looks up and her dimples come out of hiding at the sight of him. Desmond smiles, thanks the hostess and walks confidently to the table.

Chapter 3

Desmond's head felt like half of a football team used it for practice. The dinner with the certified nurse assistant did not end well as she continued to ask every personal question she could imagine. He almost asked her if she was working for the CIA or FBI. She claimed she was nervous but damn! As she ordered an expensive dessert to conclude the meal she ordered, Desmond secretly dialed his pager from his cell under the table. Seconds later the pager went off and he dropped his head to check the message while placing a concerned frown on his face. As the waiter brought his date her dessert Desmond shook his head.

"What's wrong?"

"I got paged at Midwest to come in for an emergency meeting," he said, feigning a convincingly frustrated expression. "I have to cut our date short. I hope you don't mind," he said.

She looked at him and frowned, then remembered this is a doctor and if she wanted to hook up with a doctor she had to understand. They are in the same profession so she should understand. "No I don't mind," she said, putting her fork down from her dessert plate.

"No, finish your dessert! I will take care of everything," Desmond said while waving for their waiter's attention. The waiter brought the check and he placed a credit card on the tray. The waiter returned with the card, the receipts and an ink pen. "I am really, really sorry about this," he said while scribbling his name and snatching his card and copy from the tray and placing it in his wallet. "Text me when you get home so I'll know you are safe," he said and leaned down to kiss her cheek.

His date tried not to look disappointed as she smiled. "Maybe we can go out again, soon," she said.

He straightened his blazer and walked backwards smiling a fake promise. "Yeah, we'll talk."

Desmond rushed to his SUV and pulled out of the parking space. He took a deep breath and hit the gas away from the restaurant and directed his vehicle to Interstate 65 North towards home while his date sat eating an Italian dessert. He was thankful she worked for another hospital and met her at a health fair. He did not have to worry about running into her and after he received her safe at home text, he will block her access to his cell.

Twenty minutes later, Desmond pulled in front of the house he had a mortgage on in the West side of Gary. The brick house was thirty years older than he was and he and some friends renovated the interior within a two year period. A picture window in the front was one of many window replacements. The living and dining rooms had high ceilings and a fireplace. He knocked the wall between the two bedrooms and turned it into a master bedroom/home office suite. The kitchen was redone with imitation marble counters and lighter toned walls and cabinets to allow brightness. The bathroom included a standing shower with shelves and the necessary sink, toilet and medicine cabinet. The basement was renovated to favor a man cave with a 42 inch flat screen television with surround sound, large couch and recliners, a fully stocked bar and refrigerator A stereo system and pool table was also added. Desmond walked in his house and headed straight to his cave and the bar. He grabbed a bottle of cognac, a glass and plopped into the recliner grabbing the remote.

Chapter 4

The security guard looked up from the security monitors surrounding his station and smiled broadly at the sight of Chanale walking to the front door of the law office of Oscar Rollins & Associates. She kept her hair short and left her green contacts at home, allowing her natural brown eyes to shine…blended in with hazel contacts. She wore a medium blue scoop neck dress with a thin, black belt and three-quarter length sleeves under a waist length black blazer. She wore black open toe pumps with a three-inch heel and had an oversize designer bag hanging from her left shoulder. While she walked with a fast pace from the guard's vision and imagination, she was walking in slow motion, her round hips swaying to a sexy beat. Her shapely legs damn near gave his need to be retired behind a heart attack. He was at the door, holding it open just as Chanale reached for the handle. "Morning, Miss Arlington" the guard said as he stepped aside so Chanale could walk past.

"Morning Max and thank you so much," she said while giving him a smile that caused the man to take a breath. Chanale continued to the elevator doors knowing Max was watching and wishing he was twenty years younger. She walked in and turned around, waving at him as the elevator doors closed.

Chanale pushed the 5th floor button and hummed to the jazz music flowing from the sound system. She reached in her bag and grabbed her key card just as the doors opened. She stepped out to fellow paralegals and a couple of secretaries on their job. She smiled and kept walking, nodding hello to some and saying a few words to others. Oscar Rollins & Associates was one of the leading legal firms in Gary and Northwest Indiana, with a total of ten attorneys in criminal, corporate, bankruptcy and prosecution.

Chanale was a paralegal in Rollins' office and had been for ten years. She was one of the best paralegals Rollins had with her ability to perform accurate legal research for many of his cases. She interviewed witnesses with the level of an award winning investigative reporter, documenting every single thing they said.

She graduated at the top of her class in Paralegal School and had pondered going to law school to become an attorney. But she chose against the latter, finding herself pretty comfortable with the salary she earned, as well as the bonuses given in the middle of the summer and for Christmas. Rollins and his associates collected enough from winning cases that bonuses ran from an extra paycheck to weekend getaways to ski or tropical resorts. The holiday parties were the talk of Gary with flowing champagne and extravagant buffet prepared by a top chef with live entertainment flown in.

The fact that this was a law firm owned by an African American with a multicultural roster gave their recognition within the legal system.

Rollins owned the seven story building and ran the firm on two floors while the rest of the building leased out space to small business owners. Rollins made sure the businesses were sound and staying afloat; he refused to have someone lease space only to shut down a month later, leaving the space abandoned. Over the last ten years only one small business shut down, but another business opened immediately and remains flourishing to this day. A café, independent bookstore, art shop and other businesses owned by young, Internet savvy individuals were vital in the building. And the building security was top notch thanks to some of those digitally trained professionals and a group of security officers who were retired from the military.

Max Walters was a family friend of Rollins and a former Gary police officer who was devoted to Rollins when given the job. Chanale swiped her key card to enter Rollins' office, walked in and placed her bag on her desk. The blinds were already open and the coffee machine was brewing, meaning the secretary was early or Rollins started the machine. She looked at her desk frowning at the portfolios in the center. Work was already waiting for her before she could get her first cup of coffee. "Shit! I hope Oscar is already in court," Chanale said while walking to the sink to rinse out her coffee mug. She was pouring the coffee when she heard the door open and a man whistling.

Oscar walked in whistling a Stevie Wonder song. "Chanale," he paused to greet her and resumed to whistling. Chanale turned around and looked at her boss. He was five feet, nine inches in height but walked like he was ten feet tall. Forty-eight years old but looked 10 years younger with a shaved head that complemented a strong jaw line. He worked out but was not obsessed with it and wore tailored made suits.

Oscar came from a family of lawyers, mill workers, nurses and teachers. He was likeable and respectable. And a couple years ago, a great lover. Seven years into the job, in an environment that was professional and family friendly with the employees thanks to a great benefit package, some flirting developed between Oscar and Chanale. No one raised an eyebrow because it was discreet. And anyone who figured something was going on knew better than to enter Oscar's office and question him.

One evening after hours of research and documenting a major case, Oscar and Chanale ordered Chinese food and he opened a bottle of red wine for them to consume. After two hours of drinking, eating and non-legal conversation, Chanale was spread eagle on his mahogany desk, blouse opened, bra unclasped from the front, skirt pushed up, panties on the floor and Oscar holding her ankles. The fling lasted six months and was hardly scandalous since he was divorced. But the fact that he slept with one of his paralegals was enough to set him up for a trap. Chanale, however, would not consider blackmail because she knew he would not fire her. She was without question, one of the best paralegals working for him. She told him not to worry about having to show extra attention to her; their fling was all it was, a fling. Besides, she gained plenty of frequent flier miles from flights to wherever she pleased. And she did not bug him for a lot of things except for the occasional spa weekend and some extra money for clothes and hair salon appointments.

Oscar did not give her extra treatment, obvious by the pile of portfolios on her desk this morning. "Oscar," she said while taking a sip from her mug and gesturing if he wanted a cup.

Oscar shook his head and waved some folders in his hand while heading to his private office. "Before you get started on those portfolios I need you to come inside for an update on another case." Chanale took a gulp of her coffee and followed Oscar into his office, waiting for another lengthy update.

****

"You need to leave those disposable contact lenses alone."

Hours after a more than usually long meeting with Oscar, the last thing she wanted to hear was criticism from another paralegal. And this had nothing to do with research on a case or office gossip. Nope, this was about Chanale caught blinking her eyes too many times in the visibility of a coworker. Chanale closed her eyes, praying tears would not form from the pressure and not prove to be another reason for one of the other paralegals to open her damn mouth.

"I like variety in eye color."

"No, you don't like your brown eyes. And those lenses are probably irritating the hell out of your pupils." Gabrielle, a petite, green-eyed, chocolate sister said while going through some files. Gabrielle's green eyes were God-given and Chanale wanted to know what deal did her and her parents make with the angels in charge of hookups in order to give a dark-skinned girl almost emerald green eyes. The scientific ability to order the makeup of your kids before the doctor slapped their asses just hit the medical journals a couple years ago, so that wasn't it.

Gabrielle caught the attention of plenty male lawyers stopping through Oscar Rollins & Associates with those smiling green eyes, perfect white teeth and hourglass shape. Chanale did side glances at Gabrielle who wore suits that were reasonably trendy and priced in comparison to the designer labels she wore. Gabrielle also exuded confidence when she entered a room; her personality was on point with her attitude. It was that type of combination Chanale would mock. But for now, Gabrielle needed to shut the hell up.

"You have beautiful brown eyes, Chanale. Remember, I caught you sans contact lenses that day in the restroom," Gabrielle said while continuing to go through a file. "Why you would hide your natural eye color is a mystery to me. It's like you are trying to be someone you're not."

Chanale glared at her. "Well, at least I am not wearing blue contact lenses (at least not during the daytime)!"

"Oh then you would look like a fucking idiot." The last sentence had Chanale ready to walk over to Gabrielle and slap all of her pearly white teeth out of her mouth, but she took a breath and walked to the conference room door. Gabrielle did not even raise her head to apologize for what Chanale considered an insult. Then again she was the type to say what was on her mind no matter whose feathers she ruffled. Gabrielle would be a great lawyer, if she wasn't so damn honest.

Chapter 5

Desmond strolled through the automatic doors of Midwest Medical in black slacks, a white fitted t-shirt and denim jacket, looking nothing like the hung over damn near oversleeping bachelor he was earlier in the day. The day nurses at the first station he walked past gave him their biggest smiles and highest pitch voices. "Afternoon, Dr. Richards!" Sounding like a choir of prepubescent teenage girls…some of the nurses were old enough to be his grandmother.

He returned their greetings and added a wink but did not slow down for small talk. The nurses inhaled the scent of his cologne blended with an earthy soap he used in his bathroom shower. Desmond walked into the men's locker room shaking out of his jacket and stopping in front of his locker.

"So, how'd it go?"

Desmond spun around to the direction of the questionable voice. Another medical resident stood at the end of the lockers smiling. The guy and Desmond were about the same height and began their medical residency at the same time but similarities ended there. This guy was married with one kid walking and another baking in his wife's oven. He seemed to get a kick out of hearing Desmond's tales of one honey then another, so he was looking for a story today.

"How did what go, man?" The guy scoffed at Desmond's attempt to be oblivious to his query.

"You know what I'm talking about, Richards! How did it go with that young nurse's aide last night?"

"She's a certified nursing assistant and I ended up home alone with another curvy object…a bottle of liquor," Desmond said with a laugh.

"Oh," the guy said and shoved his hands in his white coat pockets. "Well that's a downer," he said.

Desmond slipped into his own white coat and clipped his id to the lapel. "Aww, I'm sorry, man. I did not know you were looking for another one of my illicit stories of how sexy a chick was. How big her breasts were and how she was in the kitchen making me breakfast after screaming all night," Desmond said and laughed even harder. He did not share all of his personal business but this guy acted as if getting married and having kids was a death contract he did not sign. Desmond walked past and slapped his fellow resident on the back.

"Richards! You ever think about settling down? Seems like you are slowing down on the one night stands or short flings," the guy said.

Desmond paused at the locker room exit door before answering. He was not ready for marriage but maybe he was slacking off when it came to dating and flings. The certified nursing assistant was not a bad woman; she just seemed to push the wrong buttons last night. Going home to continue drinking was not a way to brush it off but he needed the edge taken off. "Marriage will hit me at the right time," he said and pushed his way out of the locker room.

Midwest Medical was in the heart of Gary, Indiana. In fact, it was the only hospital in the city period. Additional medical buildings were nearby clinics and rehabilitation centers. Regardless of its spotlight, the hospital was one of the strongest in the state and trained some of the best doctors in the United States. Only a few of these successful doctors remained at Midwest Medical while others took residency in other parts of Indiana or transfer to another state. Desmond wanted to stay in his hometown and be there for the citizens, many who were like family and even family members.

When he told his parents he was changing careers from management to medical, they were ecstatic. His mother never pressured him to be a doctor; she just wanted him to be happy. His dad was proud…but told him there were pressures in going into the medical field and a good reputation is part of that pressure. Desmond knew his dad was hinting at the constant partying and dating he was involved in. But he made some changes to prove he was serious in becoming a doctor. The long, studying hours in medical school knocked the partying nights out, but his dating spree was still thriving. That is, it was thriving.

****

Chanale decided to leave early so to get ready for her date with a corporate vice-president who came for a free consultation a week ago. The man had to have been in his mid-50s and average build, but he had a confidence about him. And he could not take his eyes off her when she interrupted the consulting meeting to grab some full binders. Mr. Williams had salt and pepper hair in a neat cut with a full beard to match. She did some research on him and discovered he was a widower with two adult children who could be her younger siblings. He was vice-president of an engineering corporation and was featured in numerous business and marketing magazines.

One prestigious magazine that highlighted successful African American entrepreneurs and moguls named him one of the Top Ten financially successful businessmen. After playing dumb to his advances she finally accepted a dinner invitation. "I just could not stop looking at those hazel eyes," he said during a telephone conversation sealing the date. In her mind, she'd already picked the short, black strapless dress and silver, three inch heels she would pair with a silver purse, the diamond tennis bracelet that was a gift from a couple guys ago and a diamond and silver choker. She highlighted her hair earlier that week so all she needed was a quick self-styling. Chanale jumped in her car and raced home, trying to remember if she has a set of hazel contacts in her kit.

****

Desmond finished his rounds, visiting patients and having conversations with some of their immediate family members on the conditions. He made a stop in the Emergency Room to see if some of triage staff needed assistance. The afternoon was slow as far as emergencies and ambulances rushing to the area of the parking lot leading to the ER. It was one of those rare afternoons that few people were waiting in the lounge area waiting for an examining room. Other than the occasional stomach pains and complaints thought to be major, there wasn't any action going on. Desmond grabbed a chair in the ER's nurses' station and began going through charts, occasionally throwing a smile at one of the nurses who stopped in between examining rooms.

Another physician 'hottie' entered the double doors in a dramatic fashion as if a film crew was a few feet away capturing every second before the director yells, "Cut!" Dr. Monroe was 5 feet, seven inches in height, but you could not tell him that. He walked like he was taller than Desmond and any member of a professional basketball team. He wore designer eyeglass that suited his strong square jaw line and had wavy hair with touches of gray along the edges. His physique was proof of a strict health regimen that included boxing, tennis and jogging. He was 42 years old and considered one of the best physicians in Northwest Indiana. He was also one of the most eligible.

Desmond sat up and tossed a patient's tablet on the counter. "Afternoon, Dr. Monroe," he said. The physician stopped at the station, inches from where Desmond was seated and grabbed a couple of charts, opening one of them and began reading. Desmond stood up and walked to the counter, facing Monroe who had yet to look up.

"Ahem. Dr. Monroe, will you need any help?"

"I am going to always need help…"

Monroe stopped and glanced at Desmond's id tag. "Dr. Richards. The question is, are you ready to be of assistance when I need you to be?"

Desmond looked at him. "Well I usually make the rounds on the other floors. I was just here because it is kind of…" he stopped when he noticed Monroe was giving him a glare that was cold as steel. "Yes sir, I will be ready!" Monroe shook his head and walked off with the tablets in his hand.

In the midst of being cool and collected nearly all of the time, Desmond was now looking like a punk who tried to stand up to the neighborhood bully. He felt the eyes of the female…and a couple of male…nurses bore into his back. His charming young looks were bashed by a doctor who was only seven years older, but had more maturity in him that he could be mistaken for a 52-year old man.

Desmond hung around the emergency room for another hour, hoping Monroe would bark his last name in the midst of the examining rooms. He decided to head to an upper floor when he noticed another resident on the heels of the mature doctor writing notes and handing Monroe extra anything from his pockets. While waiting for the elevator doors to open, Desmond felt someone slap his shoulder. He spun around in time to see Monroe's back walk past him towards the ER's entrance. "Richards we have a single car accident arriving!"

The ambulance eased backwards to get as close to the emergency doors as possible before coming to a complete stop. Monroe and Richards rushed to the red and white vehicle as the passenger medic and driver jumped out and rushed to the back to open the doors. "I told you, I can walk out of this damn ambulance if you take me off the stretcher!" The medics stepped in to grab the foot end of the stretcher and eased it out of the ambulance. "I am fine! I do not need to be here! I bumped my head but I am not dying! Shit, give me some pain killers and let me go. I have an appointment!"

Desmond grabbed the side of the stretcher while they rushed through the emergency room doors and Monroe listened to the medic spit out vitals in rapid speed. Desmond looked at the patient who seemed to be wearing a dress but was covered to the neck with sheets. The heels of her shoes poked out from the end of the stretcher and her face was made up like a model prepping for a fashion shoot…with the exception of the big, rising bump on her forehead. Desmond smiled down at her. "Well it looks like you will be missing that appointment, Miss," he grabbed the driver's license from the medic's hand. "Miss Arlington."

Chapter 6

"I need my cell phone!" Chanale shouted while the medics lifted and laid her on a bed in one of the triages. They made a quick exit after handing Desmond plastic bags with her belongings. Chanale noticed her cell phone in one of the bags. "Give me that bag! I need to make an important…shit," she stopped trying to sit up when she felt light headed.

Monroe grabbed her and eased her back on the bed, resting her head on the thin pillow. He then snatched the guardrails up and locked them. "Miss Arlington, I'm Dr. Monroe and you may have a concussion. We are setting you for an X-ray and other tests if needed. You will have to calm down. That bump is pretty big and your appointment is now canceled," he said.

Chanale looked at the handsome doctor but was in no mood to flirt. "Can I at least make the phone call?"

"No ma'am," Desmond chimed in. "You can't use the cell phone in this area. But I will place your belongings on this table near you. Do you have anyone to call in your immediate family? I can go out and call him or her for you." Chanale looked at the young doctor and gave up.

"You can call Oscar Rollins. He is my boss. My parents are deceased," she said. Desmond nodded and waited for her to recite the number and left out of the room. Monroe began examining her.

"So, you are late for an appointment? From the looks of this dress, you look like you were going on a date," he said. Chanale glared at the older doctor for getting in her business.

"I happened to be driving to a business social, asshole!" Monroe cleared his throat."

"My apologies, Miss Arlington. It was not my intention to insult you," he said. Chanale continued to glare at this arrogant doctor, whether he was fine or not, he was smelling himself. The triage curtain pushed back and Desmond entered with a smile that calmed Chanale.

"Miss Arlington, Mr. Rollins is on his way." She looked at Desmond and smiled until she felt the coldness of the stethoscope touch her chest. "Sorry, Miss Arlington," Monroe quickly said.

A nurse walked in to inform them an X-ray machine was ready for Chanale and they prepped the bed to roll to the room. Desmond stayed behind to watch the bags.

Within 15 minutes, Oscar was speed walking into ER, peeping into each examining room. He peeped into the last room and rested his eyes on Desmond. "Excuse me, young man I am looking for Chanale Arlington?"

Desmond smiled. "She's in X-ray right now. Are you Oscar Rollins?"

"Yes I am," Oscar said with a concerned look on his face. Is she going to be alright?" Desmond walked over and placed his hand on Oscar's left shoulder, leading him to the nurse's station.

"I believe she is going to be fine. Looks like a minor concussion and a nasty bump on her forehead, but she is alert…and bossy," Desmond said.

Oscar smiled, relieved. "Yeah, she will be fine if she was bossing people around!"

Desmond continued to fill Oscar in on the accident and her condition. "She said she was going to an appointment? Sounds like a date to me," Oscar said.

Desmond chuckled and handed Oscar Chanale's things. "Yeah, she was definitely dressed up!"

Five minutes later, the orderly and nurse brought Chanale back to the examining room. Monroe strolled in soon after, stopping when he noticed Oscar and Desmond at the station. "Oscar Rollins?"

"Yes sir," Oscar said while straightening up his posture.

"I'm Dr. Monroe and Miss Arlington will be fine. She is staying overnight for observation. That bump is going to be around for a few days and she is sore from the impact but no broken bones."

Oscar sighed in relief. "Good. Thank you doctor," he said.

Oscar walked in the examining as Chanale filled out papers and answered the nurse's questions. After the nurse walked out Chanale looked at Oscar. "Don't even start," she said.

Oscar raised his hands in defense. "I'm not saying anything except I am glad you are OK."

Chanale looked at him again, then grabbed her purse from the table and opened it. "Can you do me a favor and call this number on this business card?"

Oscar took the card, looked at it and glared at her. "You were going on a date with a possible client?"

Chanale glared back. "He was not going to be your client. That's why he called and asked me out. He wasn't stupid!"

Oscar shook his head and walked out of the examining room with the card in his hand.

"And find out if my car is worth driving," Chanale shouted in the air.

Desmond took his visual from the frowning gentleman in the expensive suit and refocused on the curtain that hid the interesting female patient. He leaned against the counter of the nurses' station and chuckled at the thought of the exchange between her and this attorney, her boss. He was relieved the man was not her pimp, but still, she is bold enough to go on a date with a possible client?

One bold chick. Desmond pushed off from the counter and approached the curtain from the side of the room. "Excuse me, are you decent?"

Chanale looked up and adjusted the thin white blanket and waved Desmond in. "I'm as decent as I'm going to be," she said.

Desmond walked to the bed with a smile, which became wider when he noticed she'd combed her bangs forward to cover the bump. "I hardly notice the bump," he said with a laugh.

Chanale glared at him until he cleared his throat and stopped laughing. Got a lot of nerve to be laughing at me, she thought.

"I'm sorry Miss Arlington," Desmond said as his voice tone turned serious. "Exactly how did the accident happen?"

Chanale carefully adjusted herself into a sitting position and let out a sigh. "I made it to my apartment just fine so I could get ready for my...appointment. After two hours of preparation I noticed I was running late to meet the gentleman so I jumped in my car and took off. I am not a bad driver and I normally don't speed, but I really needed to get to the restaurant and it was 30 minutes away. Since there was too much traffic on the main streets, I decided to take a shortcut. When I made the turn on 21st and Grant Street, some fool on a bicycle was zigzagging..."

"The white guy with the stringy hair and crazy looking hat," Desmond interrupted.

Chanale's eyes widen and she pointed at Desmond. "Yeah, him! Anyway, I call myself watching him and that bastard swooped by my driver's side and moved his bike like he was going to cut in front of the car! I did a sharp turn to the right and before I could straighten the wheel, jumped the curb and hit a part of a metal fence. I was able to completely brake before I went through the fence, thank God. I guess when I slammed the brakes I bounced my head off the steering wheel," she said.

"Your car doesn't have airbags," Desmond asked.

"Yeah but the steering wheel airbag did not jump out," she said, "I guess the impact wasn't hard enough."

"Well, I am sure the car is good enough to drive. Did someone call towing?"

"The police called the towing service that works for them," Chanale replied. Chanale gave Desmond the onceover as he flipped through her chart. Damn, he's kind of cute! Pretty brown skin tone, medium build, nice voice...and younger than I am, she thought. He has to be in his late twenties; that's usually the age pof these residents after spending a lot of years in medical school. Probably a chocolate version of George Clooney with plenty of women...or that brother who was in the other medical show created by the sister and got his ass bounced from the cast. Hmmm, if I was 10 years younger...WAIT! Why am I thinking like I'm somebody's damn grandmother! I'm 40 years old not 80! But he probably doesn't dig that older woman, younger man scene anyway...

"Miss Arlington did you hear what I said?"

Chanale blinked and realized the doctor was leaning forward and staring into her eyes with a concerned look on his face. His brown eyes sure are deep! And those lashes need to be on a woman! "Huh? Uhm, no, what did you say?"

"I said the nurse's aide is here to roll you to your room," Desmond said with a smile. He picked up the plastic bags with her belongings and eased them on her lap and bent over to release the wheel locks on the bed. "There, you are all set Miss Arlington. You take it easy, get some rest and Dr. Monroe will check on you tomorrow," Desmond finished while pushing the curtain back so the aide could push the bed.

"Thank you," Chanale said as she waved at him. He threw his hand up and turned towards the station. Damn he ain't cute...he's Fine! She thought.

Chapter 7

As soon as the nurse's aide and the nurse for the night shift got Chanale comfortable, checked her vitals and left out of the room, she grabbed her cell phone from the bag. The tips of her French manicured nails hit the pad to dial Oscar's cell number. "Are they keeping you?"

Chanale hit the loudspeaker button while frowning at the attitude coming from Oscar. He has a lot of fucking nerve acting like her husband or a pissed off boyfriend who uncovered a secret. "Cut the tone, Oscar! Yes I am staying overnight for observation," Chanale said then stopped and leaned forward to see if her door was closed. The last thing she needed to be was the subject of overnight gossip from the night shift. Seeing it was closed she moved the phone closer to her face. "Did you check my car?"

"Yes and I will pick up my assistant and come back to the tow yard and she can drive it back to your apartment," Oscar said. "It's a minor dent, no major damage."

Chanale breathed a sigh of relief. "Good! I really don't need to invest in a new car anytime soon!" She heard Oscar clear his throat. "What?"

"Aren't you going to ask me about your...date?"

Chanale was about to roll her eyes towards the ceiling but thought better of it. "Did you call him?" Oscar huffed.

"Yes I called him and told him you were in an accident but you will be fine. I also told him there was no need for him to visit you...you need your rest," he said.

Chanale jerked up from her bed and just as quickly laid back down when her head began throbbing. "Motherfucker no you did NOT tell him what to do, she shrieked.

Her outburst caused the door to fly open with the nurse and another doctor rushing in thinking something was wrong. "Miss Arlington is everything all right," said the doctor who stopped at the side of the bed. He and the nurse suddenly changed their concerned facial expressions into one of irritation as they noticed the cell phone.

Chanale felt the blood rush in her cheeks and her head was pounding. "I am so sorry," she said as she pushed the End button disconnecting Oscar shouting her name.

The doctor stared at her and shook his head. "Miss Arlington being that you are under observation for a possible concussion...and I am sure that bump has given you a headache, you need to be calm," the doctor said as Chanale rested her phone on the night stand. "And you need to be quiet," he continued. He then told the nurse to bring Chanale some pain relief medicine. "If possible, I will need for you to not be on your cell phone Miss

Arlington. You definitely need to rest," the doctor said as he thumbed through her chart and walked out as the nurse returned with a pill in a cup and a cup of water.

Chanale sheepishly took the pill and water, shooting both down her throat. "Thank you," she quietly said to the nurse who smirked and walked out, closing the door behind her.

"Bitch," Chanale mumbled before hitting the button to turn off the overhead light.

****

"Well, that dressed up patient was definitely paying attention to you."

Desmond looked up at the supervising nurse seated in the ER station. The older woman grinned as he shook his head. "She was something else! But she looked nice." The nurse laughed.

"Oh you could tell from the blanket draped on her?" Desmond laughed back.

"Well from the high heel shoes she finally let them take off her feet and place in one of the bags, she was looking nice for a night out on the town!" "Honey, we almost threatened to cut her out of her strapless dress…and the Sister Hug body shaper," the nurse chuckled.

Desmond twisted his face in confusion. "The Sister huh? What?"

"The Sister Hugs," the nurse continued, "it's like a smoother version of a girdle and supposedly better and more comfortable. They cost a mint though. Personally I rather pay for a health club membership."

Desmond shook his head. "The torture you women go through for us men!"

"Only because you men holler about Beyonce or those stick skinny models all the time," the nurse shot back.

"Humph, glad I'm married to a man who appreciates meat on the bones!"

Desmond laughed again. "I don't have a problem at all with curvy women! And honestly from what I could see without peeping under the blanket and getting my teeth knocked out, Miss Arlington did not need that hug or whatever you call it. If she is trying to look skinny she needs to quit and accept her body!"

The nurse smiled at Desmond. "So she's your type? Or do you have a certain type because I know you have these girls tripping over each other to get your attention!"

Desmond backed away from the station and stared at his watch. "Oh look at the time! I have a few more things to do and patients to check before my shift ends!"

"Uh-huh. See you later," the nurse said as Desmond jogged off to catch the elevator.

Chapter 8

Desmond smirked as the elevator doors closed to take him to his destination. Despite the nurse teasing him about the 'dressed up patient,' he did find the car accident patient a bit humorous and intriguing. He got a chance to glimpse at the strapless dress she was wearing before he was put out of the examining room so that the nurses could help her out of that body shaper. A garment she did not need to be wearing as far as he was concerned. She was dressed to kill but thankfully she did not do it in a literal sense, nor was she a fatality. A very attractive woman with beautiful brown…no, maybe they were hazel? Whatever color they were, they were beautiful. The loud 'Bing' of the elevator doors let Desmond know he made his stop, the fourth floor.

After greeting a couple of visitors who were stepping in, Desmond walked out and strolled down the hallway leading to the nurses' station in the middle of the floor. He smiled as a couple of nurses looked up to see who was standing at the counter.

"Dr. Richards," one nurse said and returned a smile. The other nurse looked at him and refocused her eyes to the monitors just underneath the counter. Desmond took notice to the light brown skin beauty wearing a ponytail with a pink and green band holding mid-length hair in medium brown with blonde highlights. Her heart-shaped face with round cheeks complemented a small, full mouth covered with medium rose lip gloss. Desmond focused on her ID trying to read her first name. "Evening…Melanie," he finally said.

Melanie looked up, revealing almond shaped brown eyes with long, thick lashes. "Evening, sir," she replied dryly before pushing her chair back and rising up to walk away. Desmond watched her circle the counter with folders in her hands and emerged to the hallway without saying another word. He shrugged it off and walked to the back of the station to check the logs.

While checking the logs, Desmond looked to his right and scanned the large washable bulletin board with the list of patients, their room numbers, assigned nurses and doctors' names. He noticed a patient's name, Chanale Arlington on the fourth row of the board. He walked over to get a look at the room number and the nurse assigned to her. It was not Melanie, but Drs. Monroe and Jackson were playing tag team with this floor's lineup and Miss Arlington was one of the subjects.

He memorized Room 410 and placed the medical logs on the table. As he walked past the counter where the pleasant nurse greeted him earlier he nodded a goodbye. "Oh Richards," the nurse called out just as he made the turn in the hallway leading to 410. Desmond took four steps backwards and stopped at the station counter.

"Yes nurse?"

"You are not going to try to catch up with Nurse Melanie are you," she asked.

Desmond looked at her with confusion. "No."

"Oh, good," the nurse said and lowered her voice, "because she's kind of ticked that you blew off her cousin the other night."

Desmond jerked his head back. "Her cousin?"

"Yep. The certified nurse assistant you have yet to call back," the nurse said before returning to her workload.

Desmond sheepishly walked away from the counter to return to his destination…peeping in on Midwest Medical patient Chanale Arlington. He stopped in front of the hospital room door and knocked lightly. When he did not get an answer he slowly opened the door and stepped in to the sound of slightly loud snoring.

The room's lights were on but Chanale was fast asleep with her right hand resting on her cell phone which was on the moveable tray. He tipped further into the room and stopped at the foot of the bed. He eased her chart from the folder at the end and thumbed through it before easing it back into the slot. Desmond walked to the left side of the bed and reached to hit the button on the wall above the nightstand to turn off the bright overhead light. "What? Who's in here," Chanale blurted while blinking her eyes as soon as the overhead light went out. She turned her head and was startled to see the medical resident who was asking her questions in the emergency room. The FINE medical resident who was too damn young for her taste.

I am so sorry," Desmond said as he turned the overhead light back on. "I was trying my best not to wake you up. I was just checking to see how you were doing."

Chanale pushed herself in a sit-up position and pushed the 'up' button on the guardrail to raise the upper part of the bed to support her. She automatically checked her hair only to stop when she realized she was wearing a thin and ugly hospital gown. She was not even going to imagine what her face looked like since the makeup is a few hours old and half gone from the nurses and doctors checking on her. "Well, I am doing fine. I can't complain because it could have been a lot worse," Chanale said, realizing that her mouth was dry. Great…just great.

Desmond reached for the Styrofoam cups and yanked one from the stacked pile on the nightstand. He turned around and grabbed the pitcher of ice water and poured water into the cup then handed it to her. "Thanks," she said and took big gulps from the cup before handing it back to him.

Desmond nodded towards Chanale's cell phone. "Did your boss call you back about your car?"

Chanale frowned and shook her head. "No and he did not text me either. I would call him but I don't want to end up yelling and cussing again and the nursing staff come rushing in here like they did earlier," Chanale said.

Desmond chuckled at the discovery that she was the one the nurses were mumbling about earlier. News had traveled quickly. Desmond checked his watch. "Well, it looks like you are doing fine. Sorry I disturbed your sleep pattern," Desmond said, walking away from the bed.

"No problem doctor," Chanale said as she lowered the bed a little to get readjusted. "Please turn off the main light."

Desmond obliged and hit the switch with one hand while grabbing the door handle with the other. He pulled the door open…and nearly collided with Nurse Melanie who greeted him with a cold glare that would match the coldness of the pitcher of water on Chanale's table.

"Excuse me," Desmond said and swiftly walked around the nurse as her head damn near did a full circle revolve in watching him. And he was not going to look back to see if she'd succeeded.

Chapter 9

The next morning Chanale woke up sore and stiff with a slight headache. A couple of blinks and she noticed the day nurse pouring a cup of water. The nurse put the pitcher down and handed her that cup and a small child dosage cup with a pill in it. "Pain killer," the nurse said as Chanale happily grabbed both. She tilted her head back slowly to take the pill and followed with sips of water while watching the nurse's aide draw the window curtains back. The sun shined brightly in her room and was a beautiful sight above the scenery of red brick structures that were part of the hospital.

Chanale shifted her body and the rhythmic sounds of age responded in bone cracking and popping beats. "Shit, I'm forty, not one hundred and 40," she mumbled.

The nurse smiled while checking Chanale's blood pressure. "Other than the need for a pill and your bones talking, how are you feeling, Miss Arlington?"

"I'm alive and grateful to be walking on top of the Earth," Chanale said, "I guess this soreness and stiffness will be with me for a minute."

The nurse finished checking Chanale's vital statistics and recorded them on the wall board. "Yes, you will be sore for a few days. The aide will bring you some adhesive heating pads for your body and I will bring you a muscle relaxer after breakfast," the nurse said before leaving.

The aide walked over to the bed. "I will bring the pads in a minute, Miss Arlington," she said.

Chanale nodded and noticed her cell phone screen was blinking bright fuchsia, alerting her of missed calls. She opened the phone as the aide left the room and began checking messages. A couple of messages were from Gabrielle and another message from another paralegal offering word of concern and quick healing. Another message came from the landlord who heard about the 'awful accident' then reminded her that rent was due in a few days. Hmph, she must think I'm about to die without giving her that $850 check, Chanale thought. The next message was from Oscar telling her the car was taken out of the towing lot and is being looked at by a mechanic. Don't worry about the repair cost. "How sweet of him," Chanale mumbled, knowing he will eventually take it out of her paycheck or ask her about a payback later. Another call came from the non-client she was rushing to meet last night. No voicemail, but a text wishing her a speedy recovery. That's it? No question asking for a rain check on dinner? Chanale hit the 'End' button and placed her cell phone on the nightstand just as a cafeteria employee walked in with her breakfast tray.

"Morning," the young lady said while placing the tray on the table and lifting the lid. She walked away from Chanale like a runway model making the best out of that ugly, dull burgundy uniform with the hairnet for accessory.

Chanale stared at the powdered scrambled eggs, dried white toast, crispy bacon and fruit cup before grabbing the utensil kit to begin dining. "I have to go home today," she said.

****

Desmond was up and fixing a Spanish omelet complete with red and green peppers, goat cheese and a mixture of spices. A plate of turkey bacon rested on the counter next to the stove as he carefully folded the omelet over in the nonstick skillet. The small flat-screen TV was attached to the upper right corner of the wall at an angle where he could watch from the medium length marble top galley. Placing the omelet on his plate Desmond grabbed it and the plate of bacon and walked to the galley where he put them down. The TV was turned to "Good Morning America" with one of his favorite black newswomen, Robin Roberts talking about the latest in current events. He went to the refrigerator and grabbed a half gallon of orange juice and closed the door.

Returning to the galley, he poured a tall glass and placed the carton on the counter and bowed his head in a quick prayer. He leaned against the galley, grabbed a fork and began eating while standing up. Even though the galley came with a set of metal back chairs covered in soft leather, it was a habit of Desmond's for years to eat standing up. Due to always being in a hurry, especially as a child, rushing to eat breakfast before the school bus showed up at the corner. As soon as he noticed a piece of yellow Desmond would drop his empty plastic cereal bowl and spoon in the sink, grab two strips of bacon and run out the front door while snatching his book bag. His mother, Missy Richards would be yelling for him not to miss that bus or it was going to be a long walk. Those words would float in the wind as he ran knee to chin to the corner before the bus doors could get a chance to open.

He rarely missed the bus and when he did, he would curse under his breath, throw the book bag on his shoulder and start speed walking four blocks to the elementary school. As he got older the four blocks grew to eight for the middle school and 10 blocks to the high school unless a parent of one of his friends would pity him and give him a ride the rest of the way. When he got his driver's permit then his driver's license, his Dad, Daniel Richards provided him with half the money to purchase a used car while Desmond had to save money to cover the rest of the cost. He worked a lot of part-time jobs and saved enough to match his dad's amount, plus the money for registration and plates.

College and working in retail stores pushed him into sales and marketing but as the years went by, he felt a calling to go into the medical field. His mother thought he was crazy to go to medical school at a late age but supported him nonetheless. His father was happy Desmond was alive, healthy and doing anything positive instead of being a newspaper's statistic of violence, drugs and gang-banging. Mama made her transition after Desmond completed his first semester in medical school. But Dad was still around, living in one of the nicest senior complexes his pension and Social Security checks could afford.

Silver Linings were about 45 minutes west from the family home and convenient for Mr. Richards or Danny as he was always addressed by friends and family. Desmond visited him at least three times a week and called him just as much. He gave his father a cell phone that was easy enough for the elder Richards to operate and he loved it.

Glancing at the clock on the corner of the TV, he finished the rest of his breakfast and washed the plate, empty glass and utensils in the sink. He stretched and grabbed the remote to shut off the TV and walked out of the kitchen and to the bathroom for a shower and shave. He did not have to go to Midwest until that afternoon and wondered if Chanale Arlington would be released to go home by the time he showed up for work.

Why was he thinking about this woman was beyond him. From studying her chart he saw she was five years older. That wasn't too old but older than women he usually dated…wait. Why is he even thinking about this patient and dating? Desmond shook his head under the water pressure coming from the showerhead and continued to soap up his lean and muscular body. The thought of adding her or any older woman to his list of flings was far from reality…or was it? "She's got a nice, thick body, bruh," his conscience said loud enough to make you think that another person could be in the bathroom with him. "What's a few drinks and dinner? It will make up for her missing out on her that with that dude." Desmond shook his head again to clear it.

Finishing his shower, he snatched the towel from the rack and began drying off before wrapping the towel around his waist and stepping out. He opened a jar of petroleum jelly from the sink counter and start moisturizing his arms and legs. After spraying deodorant, Desmond opened the medicine cabinet and grabbed a razor and a can of shaving cream and began removing the quickly growing shadow on his face. Ten minutes later he walked out the bathroom and down the hall to his bedroom of mahogany wood with black, blue and silver decorum. He turned on the TV centered on his entertainment system and finished dressing. Grabbing his laptop and other belongings to place in his backpack, Desmond put on his coat, strapped on the backpack and left the bedroom. Grabbing his car and house keys he unlocked the front security doors, stepped out on the porch, locked the doors and hit the alarm keypad button and jogged down the steps to his SUV. He jumped in, started the engine and pulled off to do some errands before heading to Midwest.

And Chanale Arlington was still flirting with his conscience.

Chapter 10

Chanale fought to stay awake despite the effects from the muscle relaxer. She was not in the mood to go back to sleep only to have the nurse or doctor wake her up and piss her off. She was ready to go home. She glanced at the TV in the upper corner and the female motor mouths were arguing over some stupid shit that will be on a tabloid show later in the day. Chanale pushed the TV button on the right guardrail of the hospital bed, changing to a channel that aired game shows 24 hours a day. "Knock-knock," a voice near the door said. Chanale turned to the direction of the voice and smiled as Gabrielle walked in with a single yellow tulip in a slim, plastic vase in her left hand. She was dressed in a cream toned shawl collared blouse and chocolate brown draped skirt that hugged her curves with brown sling back pumps under a swing coat that matched the skirt.

"Hey G," Chanale said with a laugh as Gabrielle placed the vase on the table and leaned over to hug her.

"Hey speed demon! Shit, I know your date was not worth you jumping a curb and damn near missing a house," Gabrielle said while looking at the bump on Chanale's head.

"You got that right! The man did not even call to ask if I was alright or in the morgue! He left a text for a speedy recovery," Chanale said.

Gabrielle burst into laughter and pulled up a chair closer to the bed and sat down. "Oscar told me he called the guy for you and canceled the date," Gabrielle continued.

"Canceled? Hell Oscar pretty much ran the man off," Chanale frowned. "Oscar's acting like that TV character the children love. And acting like we are still dating."

Gabrielle was the only one who figured out Oscar and Chanale were seeing each other a while back and kept it to herself even when other colleagues were trying to snoop around. "So when are you getting out of here?"

"Hopefully sometime today," Chanale said, "I do not like hospitals! I have a feeling I might still be here for lunch, let alone dinner."

Gabrielle visited for thirty minutes and got ready to leave in time for her lunch break. "Well, I am going to get some real food, sweetie," Gabrielle said with a laugh.

Kissing Chanale's cheek she grabbed her purse when both heard the door open. Dr. Monroe walked in and smiled at them. "Afternoon, ladies," he said.

Gabrielle returned the greeting and stepped aside to head out the door. "I'll check on you later Cha…" Chanale noticed that Gabrielle did not finish her sentence and looked past the doctor to see why.

Gabrielle froze in front of Desmond who strolled in a few steps behind Monroe, with a light scent of cologne replacing the smell of disinfectant and alcohol. He stopped in front of Gabrielle who stared at him like he was a personal meal delivered to her. "Hello," he said to Gabrielle who had yet to take a breath.

Desmond smiled and walked around her and stopped again at the foot of Chanale's hospital bed. Chanale dropped her head to avoid Desmond looking at her with a smirk trying to hold a laugh in. "Goodbye, Gabrielle," Chanale said loud enough for her to snap out of her trance.

"Huh? Oh, yeah, bye," she said while carefully walking backwards out of the room watching Desmond.

Desmond smiled until he felt Monroe's stare and quickly changed to a serious expression. "Now then, Miss Arlington I see through X-rays and tests that you are not in any health danger. We see no need to keep you here another day and night," Monroe said, making Chanale smile.

"Just take a couple days off and rest. I will prescribe you a muscle relaxer and pain pill that you can take only when necessary and you can do a follow-up with your physician or healthcare provider next week."

Chanale listened and nodded as Monroe added information and told her she should be out of there before dinner. She also sneaked glances at Desmond who remained quiet and serious during the checkup. Monroe excused himself and walked out of the room with Monroe following him, making Chanale frown at a missed opportunity to talk to him. She sat back against the pillow and started to change the TV channel.

"Ahem," a voice came from the front of the room. Chanale turned her head and the fine medical resident stood there smiling the cutest smile she's ever seen. "He's a boy," she thought to herself. "Not a little boy but a boy just the same!"

"Miss Arlington," Desmond said as he walked back to the bed.

Chanale took in the resident doctor's handsome and freshly shaved face which made him younger than what she guessed. His tall and lean build was just right as far as she was concerned. While there is nothing wrong with a beefed up muscleman, sometimes a medium slim build in a tall glass did just the trick…what the hell is wrong with me? "Hello…Dr. Richards," she finally managed to say. A long silence filled the room and Chanale suddenly felt her eardrums throbbing, or pounding. Was she nervous around this boy, uh, man?

"Well I know you will be glad to go home later today," Desmond said while glancing at her.

"Yeah, I can't wait to get out of here," she said faster than she wanted to. Another moment of silence filled the air until a buzz from Desmond's coat pocket disrupted the uneasiness.

"That's my work cell phone," he said while reaching in his pocket and pulling the phone out to read the message. He turned away from the bed and quickly walked out, tossing a 'goodbye and be well' over his shoulder as he yanked the door open.

As soon as he disappeared the pounding in Chanale's ears disappeared and her body calmed down. She lay back on the bed, hoping the day nurse would not walk in to do her last blood pressure reading. She was not going to stay another night in Midwest because of Dr. Desmond Richards.

Chapter 11

"Who was that fine ass brother," Gabrielle repeated over the phone hours after Chanale was released from Midwest Medical and back in her apartment. Chanale was barely situated when her cell phone was jumping from Gabrielle constant calls and texts. She turned off her cell when Oscar returned to the hospital driving her car to take her to the drug store for her prescriptions and then home. He walked her to her unit and after she settled in, Oscar took an envelope from her with the rent check and dropped it off at the landlord's office before leaving in a cab he called for.

Chanale was glad Oscar did not stick around for fear he would bug her about the non-client now non date. He knew he overstepped his boundaries ordering her around and fussing, so he also knew to leave her the hell alone. But she appreciated his friendship and concern. When she did not turn her cell back on, Chanale's landline went to singing.

"That fine ass brother is a doctor. Right now he is in his residency," Chanale said while sitting on her couch. She was ready to pop a muscle relaxer in her mouth to ease the muscle tension from the accident, and Gabrielle playing nosy reporter. "That is all I know about him, G! I am not trying to find out about him so let it go. You act as if you've never seen a good looking man before," Chanale said.

"Oh I know how to act around a fine man..." Chanale interrupted Gabrielle with a loud laugh. "Yeah, OK! You were calm as hell when you blocked him from walking to my hospital bed!"

Gabrielle laughed in agreement. "OK, you got me! But, Mr. Soon to Be Doctor was not paying any attention to me," Gabrielle continued. "He was eye balling you!"

Chanale rolled her eyes, thankful she was not wearing a pair of disposable color lenses. "That man doing no such thing! Besides, he looks kind of young. I'm old enough to be his big sister!"

Gabrielle chuckled. "Maybe a few years difference, but who the hell cares? You know that old cliché, 'age ain't nothing but a number.' You better go catch that young blood!"

Chanale stared at her phone receiver in disbelief. "Girl, younger men are not my thing! I like older and experienced...and money!"

"Not a damn thing wrong with a younger man Chanale! What does it matter to you, anyway? You trying to be younger than you are with the fake color eyes and wearing oxygen cut off spandex to fit into younger looking clothes!" That last sentence stung Chanale. Again, Gabrielle was being true to her outspoken nature.

"Look, G, you don't need to insult my ass! There is nothing wrong with my having some variety and flare in my looks! Besides, you dress to impress and get attention too!"

"I'm younger than you," Gabrielle deadpanned.

Chanale jumped to her feet and stomped to her dinette set where her purse sat open and the prescription bags stuck out. Grabbing the bottle of muscle relaxers she stretched the phone cord on her walk to the kitchen without saying a word.

"Hello? Chanale," Gabrielle said from the other end. "Chanale, I was wrong to say it like that, but you need to just be yourself! You are a beautiful black woman and you are only forty years old…but you are acting like you're 15 years older trying to fool people!"

Gabrielle could hear Chanale snatch a cabinet door open and the slam of a cup hitting a counter or table. "C'mon, Chanale say something," Gabrielle pleaded.

"I need to take a pill. Bye," Chanale said and hit the 'End' button on the receiver. She took the muscle relaxer and gulped down the cup of water then walked back to the landline and slammed the receiver on the cradle. The fucking nerve Gabrielle has to talk about her style and looks. She is just mad that medical resident did not give her the eye, Chanale thought as she stepped out of the gym shoes Oscar brought to the hospital for her along with the jeans and light sweater. She guessed she would have looked ridiculous getting wheeled out of the hospital in her strapless dress and high heels. And no way was she going to try to squeeze herself into that Sister Hug getup again.

Padding the hallway in her socks, Chanale peeled off her sweater and reached back to unhook her bra. She placed both items in her hands and unbuttoned and unzipped her jeans. By the time she walked into her bedroom she was only wearing her socks and flung the clothes into the closet hamper. She walked to the bed to grab a pair of pajama bottoms and a t-shirt from the foot, but not before stopping in front of her stand-alone mirror. Staring at her naked reflection Chanale placed her hands on her hips and turned side to side, posing in between. Her full breasts were still perky and she had a firm but soft belly. Her arms were fuller as well which meant more exercise routines. She ran her fingers through her medium length bob, glancing at the flash of color and let out a sigh.

Chapter 12

Desmond finished an eight hour shift and wasted no time leaving Midwest. He exchanged a double with a colleague because he wanted to visit his father and maybe take him out for a coffee and dessert. It was after seven o'clock so he knew Dad ate dinner two hours ago like clockwork. Desmond loved the small restaurants in the Silver Linings community that gave Dad a choice in healthy dining. He also knew Dad loved the kitchen in his unit because he loved cooking his own meals. But tonight he convinced Dad to let him take him out and away from the 'community' to a nice little spot.

Desmond drove his SUV to the guard house in front of the black iron gates with "SL" engraved in silver. He gave the guard his name and the guard checked the monitor to see if Daniel Richards sent a notice of Desmond's arrival. Seconds later the notice appeared next to Mr. Richards' unit number. The guard hit the 'approved' button and then pushed another button that opened the iron gates. "Go right on in, sir," the guard said with a smile and Desmond waved and drove forward.

He drove along the smoothly paved road until he met a 4-way stop sign and turned on the right signal light. He made the right turn and continued into a circular path that led him to the second brick unit on the left side of the road. He turned on the left signal light and moved the SUV to the driveway of the unit. His father no longer drove a car so it was convenient for Desmond or some of his father's friends to park. Danny relied on the free transportation from Silver Linings when he was not walking to his destination. He cut off the engine and jumped out of the SUV, locked it and walked to the front door. Before he could push the buzzer, his father pulled the door open and greeted him with a broad smile. "Hey son, come on in," Danny said while pulling Desmond towards him for a handshake and a hug.

"Hey dad, how are you?" Desmond asked while hugging his father tight. Desmond stepped back and looked at his father who stood at the same height and build as he. He sported the bald look and had a slim mustache and goatee of salt and pepper. His eyes were a piercing brown and he had a dimple in his left cheek. He was 62 years old and retired four years prior thanks to a great plan put together by the corporation where he worked in senior management. He stopped driving when he had a mild stroke around the time of his retirement and his left leg still bothered him. But to look at him – plus the months of strenuous physical therapy – no one could tell he was sick once.

"I am doing just fine Desmond. Blessed, truly blessed," Danny said while patting his son's shoulder.

They walked down the foyer and past a wall of framed family pictures. An 8x10 gold framed photo of Desmond's parents served as a centerpiece for the smaller pictures of them and Desmond through the years. They entered the living room that was a simple decorum of a large wine color sectional couch with a recliner at the end. Patterned throw pillows enhanced the couch and a large wood and glass coffee table was the centerpiece. There was an entertainment center complete with a hidden flat screen and surround sound stereo system was against the wall facing the couch.

A picture window was on the left side of the room. Books, CDs and DVDs were neatly stacked on the center and surrounding bookcases. Desmond helped his dad pick out the furnishings for the unit and was allowed to purchase some of the stuff. He was glad his father had comfortable living quarters, even though he could have stayed with him. "Grown men need their own space," his father said a few years ago when he gave Desmond the deed to the family home. "If you were not able to take care of yourself, you'd have not received the deed."

"Well are you ready to go out for coffee and dessert?"

His father waved the suggestion off and sat down on the couch. "I have some pound cake in the cake holder on the kitchen counter and coffee's already done. And a bottle of scotch if you want something stronger," he said with a laugh.

Desmond laughed and took off his coat and walked to the hall closet. After hanging up his coat he went to the kitchen and grabbed a bottle of soap dispenser and proceeded to wash his hands over the sink. He opened a cabinet and took out two saucers and two coffee mugs. He went to the cake holder and lifted the cover from the pound cake.

Five minutes later Desmond entered the living room holding a tray with two slices of pound cake, coffee and cream and sugar packets. He placed the tray on the coffee table and handed his father a slice of cake and a coffee mug. "Careful Dad it's hot," Desmond said as his father took a sip and winked at him.

Desmond sat next to his father and immediately picked up his fork and separated a piece of the sliced pound cake. "Man, this is good! When did you make it?" His father smiled and sat his mug down.

"I didn't cook this one. A friend made it and dropped it off the other day." Desmond cut his eyes towards his father, who did the smirk Desmond inherited.

"A friend made the cake huh? What's her name," he said. His father laughed and picked up his saucer and fork, digging into the slice.

"Don't you worry about what her name is! She lives in another unit and she is a nice woman," he said while taking a forkful of cake into his mouth.

Desmond sat back into the couch and smiled at his father. "Dang, dad I don't get a hint?"

His father waved him off. "Just a nice woman is all you need to know," he said and reached over to grab the TV remote. He searched until he stopped on the jazz channel where vintage footage of Miles Davis playing filled the screen. He returned to eating the cake while Desmond took a sip of coffee. "Besides son, you don't necessarily indulge the names of the women you take out," Danny said while turning to face his son. "If you take them out at all."

Desmond coughed to keep from choking and placed his mug on the table.

His father patted him on the back. "I know you are a player son and you may be having fun. But just as you decided to change careers, you may want to consider how you are with women."

Desmond straightened up and looked at his father. His father respected and loved his mother to the highest of highs and through the lowest of times. But he also knew Danny was a charmer pre- Missy Richards from the stories he told when he engaged him with "that chat" as a pre-teen. The fruit had not fallen far from the tree. "I just hope you will start thinking about some strong minded and well-meaning decisions…if you decide to become a one-woman man in the future," Danny Richards continued while lifting his mug for another sip.

Desmond sat quietly while listening to the sounds of Miles Davis who was probably a major player back in his heyday. But he was a changed man when he met and married Cicely Tyson, staying with her until his death. He also thought of his parents and wished Missy Diane Richards had not left this Earth, dad and him. He had a lot of inspiration when it came to relationships. But could he be inspired?

Chapter 13

Two hours later Desmond left Silver Linings and directed the SUV back home. While talking to his father, Chanale Arlington crossed his mind. He thought better not to mention this woman to dad; besides, she was a patient from a single vehicle accident, not someone he'd taken out! He reflected on the certified nurse assistant he bailed out on during a date because she was too jumpy in conversation topics. At least, that's what he thought. She probably was nervous around him and he should have made an effort to relax her instead of lying and getting his drinks at a nearby bar.

When he cornered Nurse Melanie about her cousin, Melanie snapped that she seen him at that bar slinging back drinks. And that her cousin, Terri, was texting her in between a couple of trips to the restroom about being excited to be with him. So when Melanie noticed him at the bar she texted her cousin to see if the date was over with and that was when she got the text about Midwest Medical 'paging' him and he had to leave.

While he did not feel bad that night at the bar, Melanie's revelation made him feel worse than shit. It would serve him right if he did not get the chance to cross paths with Chanale Arlington again. Desmond pulled up in front of his home and cut off the engine. While unlocking the front door his work cell phone chimed. He went inside, reached in his coat pocket and looked at a message requesting he come to the hospital during the 8 a.m. shift. He sighed and punched his reply and walked into his bedroom. He was done for the night.

Chapter 14

"Hey G, I just want to apologize for my shitty attitude on the phone last night. I had no right snapping on you like I did. I know you meant well. Call me when you get the chance," Chanale said to Gabrielle's cell phone voicemail and hung up. It was after 9 a.m. which meant Gabrielle was either parking in Oscar Rollins and Associates' lot to begin her workday or she was on a frantic, last minute pace in her house getting ready to leave. Either way she was probably not answering her cell phone right now. Chanale hoped Gabrielle will check her messages once she was settled in the office.

Chanale did not sleep well during the night and figured it was because of her attitude and not the lack of the muscle relaxer's effect on her body. She knew there was nothing wrong with her body, let alone being 40 years old. But she had been playing the got to look younger game for a couple of years. The older men who chased her were not as frequent as in the past; while she still got some looks and conversation, it was the younger paralegals gaining the full package. And they did not even have to try. Oscar Rollins and Associates was starting to look like new cast of characters who were younger, firmer and dressed more than the part of someone starting in the legal system.

All of them were worked harder and adding social media to the law firms to further promote their employers' expertise with elaborate websites. Oscar scoffed at the changes but soon gave in to the suggestions from some of the younger paralegals – including Gabrielle – who said if he wanted to keep up this was the way. He compromised with them, keeping the standby of walk-ins while hiring an online content assistant to prepare conference calls via Skype and establish a website that informs the public about them.

Consultations were still handled in person by appointment only. This pleased Oscar who also added health packages to bonuses, including a one year membership to a health club within Northwest Indiana. Chanale noticed how many of the attorneys, secretaries and paralegals were taking advantage of the club packages, even Oscar's lost some weight and was looking better in his suits. Chanale chose to exercise in the privacy of her apartment, at her own pace, which was pretty slow.

She got out of bed and stretched, allowing bones to pop and her muscles to loosen. She was feeling better than a few days ago and figured she can return to work in another day. She scratched and walked into the bathroom and turned on the sink faucet to allow the water to get warm while she sat on the toilet. Moments later, she leaned over the sink washing her hands and then grabbed a bottle of facial cleansing cream, pouring a generous amount in her hand. She washed her face, checked the now small bump on her forehead and then brushed her teeth. She left the bathroom and walked to the kitchen and opened the refrigerator, grabbing the jug of milk, two eggs and a loaf of bread. Leaving the door open, Chanal placed the items on the counter near the stove and returned to the refrigerator to grab a package of bacon and a stick of butter. Placing a skillet on the stove and turning the fire on underneath, she walked to the living room and grabbed the remote, turning on the TV.

The talk show queen was busy giving away something that gave her audience coronaries while Chanale fixed a breakfast of French toast and bacon with a side of mixed berries and a tall glass of milk. As she sat at the dining table where she could see the TV, Chanale reached for the stick of butter and sliced four squares to crown the French toast and followed with the bottle of warm syrup. Chanale watched the syrup collide with the pats of butter already melting in the toast and stopped half pour. "This is too much," she said out loud as if Miss Talk Show heard her. She stared at her plate, then sat back and looked at her stomach. The round bulge rested and waited to feel the contents of her breakfast to arrive. Chanale sighed and grabbed her knife and fork and began satisfying her stomach's desires while feeling empty everywhere else.

I got your message," Gabrielle said, "I accept your apology. We're cool."

Chanale had answered the phone five minutes after placing her dirty dishes in the sink and lowering the talk show sound. She sat on the couch cradling the phone receiver. "Thanks, G. I will make it up to you with lunch on me when I return to work."

"Don't worry about it, Chanale. Anyway, how are you doing?"

"I am feeling better, thanks," Chanale said, "I am going to make an appointment for a follow-up, but I plan on finishing the work week when I return Thursday." They talked for ten more minutes and hung up. Chanale grabbed the remote and began flipping channels eventually turning to the AUX channel and switching to the DVD player.

She walked over to the DVD tower, skimming for a movie she's yet to watch. She decided on an action thriller that's been in the tower for a month and inserted the disc into the DVD player.

Chanale sat back on the couch, grabbing the throw blanket from the corner and sprawled it across her lap. As she watched the movie, one of the black male lead actors emerged in a chase scene and the camera did a close-up. Damn if he did not favor that Richards brother! The actor was a little shorter but still the resemblance was striking. Chanale continued to watch the movie but her mind wandered off into a steady mental image of Desmond Richards. She found herself wondering how he would please her sexually; his strong but gentle hands caressing her body and unzipping her dress. She could almost feel his full lips pressing against her neck and occasionally nibbling her skin.

Chanale smiled as he stood in front of her, unbuttoning his shirt to reveal a broad chest with a six pack for a stomach. Desmond wore a tight pair of dark denim that she could not wait to undo the button, pull the zipper down and slip her hand inside to grab his hard and eager member. She stepped closer to him while her hand moved up and down, squeezing and releasing. Desmond's breath shortened in gasps as she leaned forward to slip her tongue in his mouth. They kissed with such passion as she removed her hand from his crotch and he lifted her up and wrapped her legs around his hips. Desmond walked her to her bedroom without breaking that passionate kiss. He gently placed Chanale on her back on her bed and leaned over her, kissing her neck then her breasts. He placed gentle kisses on her full stomach and looked up and smiled before lowering his head. Suddenly all she could see was the top of his head; and all she could feel was heat rising…

"CHANALE !!"

Chanale nearly fell off the couch and onto the floor when she heard her name. She looked around frantically before realizing it was the sound of her cell phone. She recorded her own voice yelling for her to answer her cell as a ringtone. She must have chosen that ringtone by mistake as she only uses that ringtone for an alarm clock. She snatched the cell phone from the coffee table and checked the screen. She cursed when the screen read, 'unknown caller' and deleted the call without listening to the voicemail.

The TV had a black screen with instructions to replay, pause or go to extra scenes blazing across, so Chanale grabbed the remote and ejected the disc from the DVD player. She walked over and removed the DVD and placed it back into the jacket and into the tower. She tossed the remote on the couch and walked to her bedroom to grab some clean underwear and headed for the bathroom for a shower. She needed to get some air.

****

Dressed in jeans, black Henley t-shirt and denim jacket with a pair of short heel boots, Chanale drove downtown to the shopping district. It was late morning which meant people were finishing early morning rituals and wondering if they would hang around for lunch at the café or the area diner. She found a no-fee parking space near Wake-Up Call, a café-bookstore squeezed between a furniture store and a department store. She climbed out of her car and hit the alarm deciding to do some browsing in the department store. Chanale walked in the store which had the winter apparel up front and center on numerous clothes racks and tables. She walked over to a display table loaded with cashmere blended turtlenecks in rich and various tones of brown, red, blue and pumpkin.

Happy to see sizes going beyond 12 in the sweaters, Chanale picked up a turtleneck in every color. She wanted to get ready for the true change of fall since Mother Nature was playing a trick on everybody with global warming. Using the crook of her left arm, she cradled the folded sweaters and continued to browse through various racks. "May I help you?"

Chanale turned to the voice and faced an older female with a forced friendly look on her face. Chanale gave her a truthful smile and handed her the turtlenecks. "Yes, you can hold on to those and follow me around the store while I pick out more clothes."

The saleslady looked at her and tightened her smile. "Miss, I am not a personal shopper," she said. Chanale looked at the woman.

"Why else would you be following me? I assume you get a commission per sale and you look like you may need that extra money. Besides, it would look much better than me telling the owner of the store that you followed me because you thought I was going to shoplift."

The woman's expression turned horrific and confused. "I, I was not assuming…"

Chanale flipped through a rack of expensive corduroy jeans, picked up a tan pair then checked the size. "I am going to need this, and three more pairs in black, dark brown and grey," Chanale told the woman about the corduroy jeans that cost $45 each. The turtlenecks carried a tag of $90 each.

Chanale looked at the woman who suddenly turned around and searched for extra pairs of the jeans. Within 45 minutes, the saleslady rested on the cashier counter turtlenecks, jeans, a black wool pea coat, two pairs of boots, three suede blend hoodies and draw string pants, three dresses and two designer purses.

A phone rang and the saleslady excused herself to answer it. A younger saleslady approached the counter. "Are you ready ma'am?"

Chanale opened her mouth to say the older woman would ring her up. Then she smiled at the young lady. "Yes, please!"

Five minutes later, the once timid saleslady rushed over in time to see the young lady hand Chanale her bags. "I was returning," she said, knowing she still got the commission.

Chanale grabbed her bags and thanked the young lady. Turning to the older saleslady, she gave her a 'fuck you' grin. "I am in a hurry," Chanale said and left the store. Shee stuffed the bags in the trunk, locked it and re-set the alarm. She then turned around and walked inside Wake-Up Call.

The Panthers Club

Chanale loved the atmosphere of Wake-Up Call, an independent café/bookstore with current and used books lined wall to wall. The place was designed with Earth tones and various colors splashed throughout. One standout was the availability of current and classic novels and nonfiction pieces written by African American, Native American and other authors of various nationalities. There was also a magazine and newspaper stand filled with papers and publications local and across the U.S. And smack in the middle of it all was a café section with tables and chairs of all sizes and a menu listing sandwiches, coffee, teas and fruit smoothies.

The owner of Wake-Up Call was a relative of the owner behind the other independent café/bookstore, Chocolate Pages inside the Grant Street shopping district. Each table had a bowl of fresh fruit available to customers for free. Chanale sat at a side table and picked up an orange and instantly started peeling the skin. A waitress placed a saucer on the table and Chanale put the skin on top, looked up and placed her order. The waitress nodded and walked away as Chanale pulled a slice and bit into it, relishing in the sweetness.

"Feeling better?"

Chanale stopped mid-chew and tilted her head, looking right at Desmond who was in scrubs and a denim jacket. And Chanale tried her best not to choke on the slice of orange now sticking out of her mouth. Mortified, she dropped her head, bit off the slice and placed the remaining piece on the saucer. "Uhm, yes, yes, I am doing better," she said as she tried to chew the orange slice without grossing him out…or choking.

"I'm sorry Miss Arlington, I did not mean to scare you," he said with a laugh. Chanale shook her head no. "It's fine! I was not expecting you here at this time of the day. I guess you are on your way to Midwest Medical?"

"Actually, I started an 8 a.m. shift and slipped out to pick up something for lunch before they find out I am gone," he said. He excused himself to go to the counter to pick up and pay for his call-in.

Chanale could not believe she would run into him and found herself wondering if looked decent. Who am I kidding? The man's seen me in a hospital gown sleep with drool running down my chin!

Desmond came back to her table and smiled. "It was good seeing you out and about," he said.

The waitress arrived with Chanale's order, placing it on the table and walked away.

"It was nice seeing you, too."

Desmond walked out and Chanale prepared to take a bite out of her turkey sandwich.

"Miss Arlington?" Chanale looked up and he returned to her table. "Before I catch you with your mouth full, again…are you doing anything

Friday night?" Chanale's eyes widened and she suddenly forgot how to talk. Desmond took her reaction for shock. "I'm sorry, never mind," he said and turned away.

"Wait," Chanale said a little too loud. Desmond looked over his shoulder. "I'm free Friday night."

He came back to the table, smiling. "Would you like to go out to dinner? I don't always ask a hospital patient out, but, I would really like to take you out," he said.

Chanale smiled back and put her sandwich down and grabbed her purse. She pulled out a pen and notepad and scribbled her address and apartment number and home phone number. She tore off the sheet and handed it to him.

"OK," he said, folding the paper. "I will pick you up at seven."

Chanale nodded. "And you can call me Chanale." Desmond took a couple steps backwards and smiled at her before turning to exit the café.

It was all Chanale could do not to draw attention to herself with a scream. She took a long sip of the hot apple spice cider to try and calm her nerves. Taking a deep breath after swallowing Chanale managed to finish her turkey sandwich without choking on reflections of what happened moments ago.

In a couple of days she was going to dinner with this guy who is five years younger. Damn the fact that he will become a doctor; this was the first time she would go out on a date with a younger man. Ever since she was 17 she was all about older men and what they could do for her. She held her own with working but she wanted to be treated like someone special. And if that meant money and gifts along the way, who was she to say no? Now she was going to test the waters with a young blood. Chanale finished her drink and passed on dessert when the waitress returned and paid her bill. This date changed her plans on returning to work tomorrow to finish the week. She left Wake Up Call and jumped in her car to head home.

****

Desmond headed back to Midwest Medical blasting 90s hip-hop from the sound system of his SUV, nodding his head to the rhythm. Every now and then a smile hit his face at the thought of the former hospital patient saying yes to his date offer. The supervising nurse in the emergency room was right back then when she said Miss Arling…Chanale was checking him out from the examining cart. Now in a couple of days he will pick her up at her apartment and take her to a nice dinner. He could tell by the look on her face that she'd never dated a younger guy. It would be an experiment for her. Besides, it's not like she's ten years older.

He pulled into the employees' parking lot in time to have 15 minutes left for lunch so he decided to eat in the car. The music blaring from the speakers was sounding too good to shut off and the windows were up so to keep security from walking over and tapping his window. He watched the scenery surrounding the hospital; honked at passing vehicles with co-workers behind the wheel. And young nurses and too young candy stripers waved flirtatiously as they walked across the lot. He waved back or winked on occasion, but his mind was fixated on the possibilities of this Friday night date.

****

Chanale made it home and grabbed the cordless to call the law firm. She purposely called Gabrielle's line to give her the news of not returning to work until Monday.

"Good afternoon, Oscar Rollins and Associates, how may I help you?" Gabrielle's professional tone was a mixture of serious with a hint of subtle sensuality, a combination sure to get a male client's attention.

"Hey sexy," Chanale said in a deep voice and then bursts into laughter.

"Chanale you are not right chick!"

Chanale calmed down while Gabrielle talked about her. "OK, OK! Anyway I was calling to tell you to let Oscar know I will not return to work until Monday," Chanale said.

"Are you all right," Gabrielle asked.

"Oh yeah, I'm getting better, but I am going to rest up a few more days."

Gabrielle paused then chuckled. "Ok, because usually when you call off before the weekend, it means you have a hot date!"

Chanale was slow to respond and when she did, she coughed first.

Gabrielle laughed. "Oh, OK! So it is a hot date! When is the date and who is the guy?"

Chanale paused a few more seconds. "Friday night and Desmond Richards," she said.

"Who?" Gabrielle said with a high pitch in her voice.

"Dr. Desmond Richards! He is the medical resident you blocked when you were leaving my room at Midwest Medical."

"GIRL SHUT UP," Gabrielle shouted then slapped her hand over her mouth and glanced around Oscar's office. Remembering that Oscar was in a meeting out of the building Gabrielle jumped from her chair and rushed to close the door. She rushed back to her chair and readjusted her head set. "I'm sorry Chanale, I thought I was at home for a second," Gabrielle said as Chanale blew out a breath from the opposite phone line.

"You are going to make me choke you yet," Chanale said then went on to tell Gabrielle about running into Desmond at the Wake Up Call.

"Girl he looks young," Gabrielle said while logging on to the Internet from the office laptop.

"Yeah well I don't know how much younger he is…"

"He's 35 years old and originally from Gary," Gabrielle interrupted.

Chanale paused. "You typed his name into the search engine?! Nosy heifer!"

Gabrielle laughed at Chanale's so called insult knowing her friend would do the same thing for her. "Don't worry, there's not a lot of information on this engine. He probably disabled a lot of stuff for privacy reasons. He's no one's baby daddy, that much I can tell you," Gabrielle said with a laugh.

Chanale shook her head. "Well at least I get to go by his mystique until Friday night, Miss Scoop!"

Gabrielle laughed out loud and typed an e-mail to send to Oscar about Chanale returning to work Monday instead of tomorrow. "So any idea where this young blood is going to take you for dinner?"

"He said he will call me later tonight and give me the information, but do dressy casual," Chanale said.

"Well I just shot Oscar the email of you resting the remainder of the week so you are all good," Gabrielle said. "I hope you let him see your natural dark brown eyes," Gabrielle chimed in before Chanale could hang up.

"I have hazel eyes…today. So that is pretty close," Chanale said while ignoring Gabrielle's loud sigh.

"Girl you need to listen to that Mint Condition song and let your true self show! And don't wear any of those damn Sister Hug getups. Show off your natural curves!"

Chanale rolled her eyes while holding the phone receiver. "I have not even decided on what to wear and here you go already tripping!"

Gabrielle decided not to say another word about her friend's preparation session when it comes to going out.

They said their goodbyes and hung up and Chanale immediately called her hair stylist for an emergency hair appointment Friday morning.

Chapter 15

Thursday became Spa Day and Chanale was glad she was able to benefit from a cancellation at Intensity Free, one of the best spas in Northwest Indiana. The exterior of the spa building was a modern brick with plain double doors, but beyond the doors was a lobby and waiting area complete with an indoor waterfall and surrounding rock garden. Wind chimes announced her entrance and soft music flowed from hidden speakers. The lobby was painted a pale yellow to blend with the earthly presence of the spa. The front desk registry was a half circle glass and sand wood counter with two employees dressed in a uniform of pastel colors.

Chanale wore one of the hoodie and drawstring pants sets she purchased the other day, gym shoes and a baseball cap controlling the short hair. She was greeted warmly by the front desk registry and approved all of the treatments she called in for. She was allowed by the doctor to get a soft tissue massage and a facial. She also registered for a manicure and pedicure and eyebrow wax. The treatments would also take away some of the nerves of excitement she had about the date. Why is she being nervous about this date was beyond her understanding. He's a man; a fine, sexy, young, man. Whew!

As soon as she was handed a robe and a pair of spa sandals Chanale walked to the dressing room to her personal locker with the combination in her hand. When she found her locker, she opened it and removed her baseball cap and began removing her ensemble and gym shoes. She folded her pants and placed them on the top locker shelf and hung her hoodie and camisole together. The jacket she carried over her left arm was also hung with care. She stuffed her black satchel inside the locker but not before taking a slim identification carrier out. It contained her license, insurance card and folded bills and a credit card. She slipped the fold into her bra, paying no attention to the stereotype of Big Mamas stuffing items in their bosom. She slipped on her robe and stepped into the sandals and closed the locker door. She left out of the dressing room where the masseuse waited for her at the door of the private room.

Chanale removed her robe and bra and climbed on the massage table. Placing her forearms and card holder under chin, she let the male masseuse work his magic on her upper back with scented coconut oil for the extra pleasure. She closed her eyes and it did not take long for her to imagine the massage was being delivered by Desmond. She smiled as she thought about his hands gently but firmly rubbing her muscles from top to bottom, appreciating her full, curvaceous naked body. It would not be long before he would tell her to turn over and she'd feel his fingers delicately massage her breasts. "Mmmmm, that feels so good, Desmond…"

"Excuse me, ma'am?"

Chanale opened her eyes and looked at the face of the male masseuse who looked puzzled. His name tag had Ivan neatly printed. "Uh, nothing, never mind," Chanale said as she felt the heat of embarrassment build in her neck and face.

Chanale was quiet the rest of the massage and hurried up and exited the room for her next treatment without looking at the employee. Her day lasted a good three hours and she went back to the dressing room, jumped into her clothes, grabbed her things and went to the registry to hand over her credit card. She made sure to include the tips for each employee who worked on her, with an extra tip for the masseuse. Chanale jumped in her car and headed to the café to pick up a carry out lunch and head back home to eat and catch a nap from being so relaxed. As soon as she walked into her apartment, the phone started ringing. She checked the caller ID and Oscar's cell phone number appeared on the screen.

"I've been trying to reach you at home and on your cell phone all morning," Oscar said, his voice filled with concern and nosiness. "Are you OK? I was checking on you."

Chanale dropped her satchel and jacket on the couch and sat down beside them. "I am fine. I had to do some errands this morning but I am home. I picked up something to eat and then I am going to take a nap."

"Oh," Oscar said.

Why was he suddenly so involved in what I was doing on my time off, Chanale thought to herself.

"Well, I was just checking on you," Oscar continued, "You go ahead and eat your lunch. I will see you Monday."

He hung up and Chanale stared at the phone. She knew good and damn well Oscar was not trying to play keeper of her personal business. Just because she almost went out with a guy who almost but did not become one of the firm's clients. Oscar needed to let that shit go. They were not an item anymore and he needed to respect that. "He keeps this up I'll leave and work for his competition," she said out loud as she walked into the kitchen with her carryout bag.

****

Desmond breathed a sigh of relief that he was able to switch schedules at Midwest with another resident. The other person was thankful to get extra hours on Friday and Saturday and Desmond would take two of the colleague's midnight shifts next week. He wanted to make sure nothing would stand in the way of his date with Chanale tomorrow night. He'd already made reservations at a steakhouse near Lake Michigan and ordered the selected red wine to go with their meals. He figured they would not go too far from the area and maybe, if she felt like it, they could go to a late movie or a nearby jazz club. Meanwhile half of his day shift was over and the hospital had calmed down for the moment as far as ambulances racing into the designated drop off area.

"So what are you doing this weekend that made the other resident happy to take your place?" Desmond looked up from the chart he was holding and Dr. Monroe looked at him. He knew Monroe did not have a problem with his taking time off. But he also knew of his reputation of dating in the workplace.

"Nothing spectacular, sir, I just have some things planned," Desmond said.

Dr. Monroe nodded and remained standing near Desmond. "Is there something wrong?"

Monroe looked at him. "No, no…I just hope you cool your heels here at Midwest…"

"Not meaning to disrespect you, Dr. Monroe but, didn't you meet your wife here about 20 years ago? If I remember what was told to me by your supervisor, it was pretty much a big conversation here," Desmond said.

Other nurses and doctors walking in the hallway where Desmond and one of his bosses stood suddenly slowed their walking paces to try and hear the answer from Monroe.

Taken aback, but not stupid enough to lash out, Monroe cleared his throat. "My apologies if I seemed too personal, Richards," Monroe said and walked off. Desmond watched him walk away and then refocused on the chart. But not without taking a breath and praying Monroe does not change his weekend schedule before his shift ended today.

Chapter 16

Friday night could not arrive soon enough for Chanale. Her hair was freshly cut and styled into a bob with the sides shaved close and full wisps of bangs. She opted to go without color or a temporary rinse since what little strands of gray was not visible to the naked eye. Her makeup was flawless and the red wrap dress with plunging neckline and elbow length sleeves was the perfect dinner outfit. She chose a pair of black pumps with the red soles that she found online for a steal.

She rested her black lined trench coat on the back of her living room chair with her purse in the seat of it. She wanted easy access when he pressed the buzzer. She'd already decided that she would take the elevator to the lobby instead of letting Desmond come to her apartment. She took one more look in the full length mirror to make sure everything was in place including the Sister Hugs one piece made like a sleeveless leotard. At seven o'clock the buzzer sounded off.

"He is on time," Chanale said as she grabbed her coat and purse. "I'll be right down," she said into the intercom.

Chanale rushed out, locked the door and did a quick step to the elevator. Her heart pounded during the ride to the lobby and she felt as if she was meeting Desmond for the first time. Of course this was different than the actual first time; she was disheveled in a strapless black dress that night bugging the hell out of the paramedics trying to help her. The elevator doors opened and she walked out and headed down the hallway to the building's front doors. The doors were half glass but it was tinted, one side glass so people standing there could not see the tenants but the tenants could identify you.

As Chanale got closer to the doors she caught her breath at the glimpse of Dr. Richards. He was wearing black pants and blazer with white shirt opened at the collar. His hands were shoved in his pants pockets and he had a boyish look on him; younger than he truly is. But he also looked sexy as he raised his head and looked straight ahead at the door. For a moment Chanale thought he had X-ray vision and could see her taking him all in. His dark eyes were piercing the glass as if he was willing it to let him see her.

"Wow," Desmond said when Chanale pulled the apartment building door open and he caught a head to toe view of her. "You look amazing, Chanale."

Chanale smiled and felt blushed as he unapologetically scanned her from the flyaway strand of a curl on top of her head to the square toe of her pumps. He rested his eyes back to hers and flashed a smile while offering his hand. She placed her hand in his and he led her to his SUV and opened the passenger door, helping her step inside. He closed the door and jogged around to the driver's side when he noticed Chanale leaned to the side and unlocked the door.

When he stepped in, she straightened up and put on her seatbelt. He turned the ignition and pulled off. The ride was quiet except for the radio station playing R&B slow jams. The fall night air was crisp but not cold. Chanale enjoyed the calm but her brain was mentally scrambling to start some small talk. "Are you feeling better since the accident?"

Chanale turned to Desmond and caught him sneaking a quick glance at her before resuming to keeping his eyes on the road. "Yes, I am feeling much better. The bump on my head is gone and I am not as sore," she said.

They went quiet again and stayed that way until they pulled into the parking lot of the restaurant. Desmond drove up to the valet who immediately ran to the passenger's side and held the door open for Chanale. Before she could turn to step out she heard the driver's door open and close and saw him step in front of the valet and take her hand. She held onto Desmond's hand and stepped out of the SUV and onto the sidewalk. Desmond gave the keys to the valet and they walked inside the restaurant.

The hostess walked them to their table towards the back and near the night scenery of Lake Michigan. The waiter arrived with a pitcher of water and filled their glasses. Another waiter appeared with the first bottle of red wine, pouring it into the wine glasses. Desmond told the waiter to return in ten minutes to take their orders as they picked up the menus already resting on the table.

"This is a very nice restaurant," Chanale said as she looked at the decorum that included cherry oak and neutral tones.

The lighting was dim for evening to create a romantic atmosphere. She wondered if this was a frequent dating spot for Desmond and the younger women he probably dated. After browsing the menu when the waiter returned both ordered filet mignon with cream of lobster soup and baked potato with fresh sour cream and chives. The waiter took their menus and walked away.

Desmond raised his wine glass to Chanale. "You really look beautiful tonight," he said.

Chanale raised her glass and nodded in appreciation. "Thank you and you are handsome."

He smiled.

Awkward quietness hit them again until the waiter returned with their food. Once they settled and said a short prayer, they dug in. "Tell me,"

Chanale said after swallowing the first bite of filet mignon," what made you decide to become a doctor?"

"Well, I was in sales management for a while and one day I felt I could do something better for people than get them to buy something. I want to make people better health wise instead of them letting go of their money for something with a temporary warranty," he said.

"OK," Chanale said, "but health care is expensive so are you going to be one of those doctors who will help people no matter their financial status?"

Desmond took a sip of wine and nodded. "I am pretty much doing that now at Midwest Medical being that a lot of the patients are not fully insured. My focus is to be able to get them as healthy as possible and educate them on things they can do to prevent from having to see me or my colleagues every single time."

Chanale nodded as Desmond continued talking. She was impressed with his mission, but even more impressed with his deep voice and full lips that were inviting per every word pronounced; every syllable broken down.

She feasted on the filet mignon and visibly feasted on his young muscular body filling that outfit...

"Chanale," Desmond said, leaning forward to get her attention. She blinked and noticed that he was holding the half bottle of red wine at an angle to pour more into her glass.

"Oh I am so sorry," she said and quickly held her glass for him to pour. "I don't know if you heard me ask, but do you plan on being a lawyer or is paralegal pretty much it?"

Chanale smirked as she clearly did not hear a damn thing he said to her because she was too busy eyeing him for an extra meal. She had to admit that she's never felt this way about previous dates with other men; much older men. With them she feigned interest and if it led to sex that was usually the most enjoyable part of the date. Desmond, however, was sexy and inviting without putting a lot of effort into it. "I enjoy being a paralegal although I also hold a degree in communications concentrating in mass media. I do some freelance work with editing and writing about legal issues for the firm's website and a few articles on law for some business publications," she said.

Soon they finished their meals and another waiter arrived with a dessert cart. Chanale hoped her Sister Hug would not go against her when she selected a strawberry torte while Desmond chose a slice of devil's food cake. They also ordered coffee and Desmond told the waiter that he would be taking the other bottle of wine with them.

He watched Chanale off and on as they ate dessert and sipped coffee and was definitely enjoying the view across from him. When they walked into the restaurant earlier he purposely walked behind her as they followed the hostess. He smiled appreciatively as she walked with a switching motion and her shape filled the dress in all the right places. He particularly watched her full hips sway per step and the four-inch heels made the vision more enjoyable.

Throughout dinner Desmond had to shift in his chair as his manhood also took notice to Chanale's figure and fought to leave his briefs and pants. He has been with a few older women, purposely ignoring the older female employees at the hospital. The few he did take out he met while hanging out at the area nightclubs and bars. Many times Desmond reconsidered the advances and compliments he would receive and instead chose not to take them seriously. But Chanale was different. In fact she always looked different.

"Chanale? Excuse me for asking, but, aren't your eyes dark brown?"

Chanale was about to consume the last bite of strawberry torte when Desmond asked about her eyes and the fork stopped halfway towards her mouth. "Uhm, yeah, they are dark brown," she said and lowered her eyes to focus on the saucer that once held her dessert. "I wear color contacts on occasion for variety."

Desmond smiled, "I did not mean to embarrass you, but I knew they were not hazel because I looked directly into your eyes in the emergency room," he said. "You don't need the color contacts in my opinion. You have beautiful brown eyes."

Chanale looked at Desmond and the subtle attraction spoke volumes at that moment. Maybe it was the wine but she was ready to consume him, damn waiting for another two or three dates.

The waiter arrived with the check and Desmond handed him a credit card. Upon return with the card and receipt, Desmond stared at Chanale with such intensity that she was afraid she would explode in heat. At the same time, she was full from the meal and the heavenly dessert and the Sister Hug was getting just a little too tight for her comfort. She smiled to hide the uneasiness she felt.

Desmond smiled back, deciding it was time to leave for the next part of their date. "I thought maybe we could listen to some live jazz at this nearby club. They probably just started right now so we won't miss much," he said.

"Ok, let's go! But first I need to go to the ladies room." She rose from her chair and he stood up- such a gentleman! – and watched her head to the restroom. Once inside, she adjusted the dress and the shaper to get comfortable again. She looked at her reflection and checked her hair then patted her belly.

While Chanale wanted to get with Desmond, looking at her shape made her think otherwise. *What if he does not really like women to be this thick? What if I undo the dress and the shaper and he suddenly has to get home because of an early schedule or some bullshit excuse?* Chanale snatched a paper towel and pat her face as she felt anxiety rise. She took one more look in the mirror, washed her hands and returned to their table.

When Desmond saw her coming back he stood up again and went around and grabbed her coat. "Are you ready to go?"

Chanale noticed a drop in his voice tone; it was dripping with rugged sexuality...or maybe it was the wine. Either way he was sounding really good and as if he did not want to go to the jazz event. Truth is she was not trying to go either. Chanale looked at him as he helped her with her coat and took the opportunity to invite Desmond back to her apartment. "Desmond, I hope you don't get upset but, I don't feel like hearing any jazz music tonight," she said.

Desmond brushed his hand lightly on her shoulder. His fingers tickled the nape of Chanale's neck as he fixed her collar and afterwards his hands brushed downward on her sides before grabbing the belt and moving it to the front for her to grab and tie. A chill ran down Chanale's spine from every single touch and heat engulfed her hands when she touched his hands while grabbing the coat belt. She grabbed her purse and Desmond grabbed the drawstring pouch that concealed the wine bottle and they walked out of the restaurant arm in arm.

They got in the SUV and pulled out of the lot. Chanale sat back and watched the lake's waves crashed against the shore as they drove by. She loosened the front of her coat and relaxed as slow jams flowed from the speakers. A Marvin Gaye hit, "Sexual Healing" began playing and she chuckled at the irony of being in a doctor's ride on a date. Desmond glanced over and laughed with her. He also freed his right hand from the steering wheel and placed it on top of her left hand resting on the hump separating them.

Chanale looked at his hand which completely covered hers and raised her eyes to look at him. She was already burning with desire so when he placed his hand on top of hers and caressed it she felt as if he struck a match. She definitely wanted his ass now! And she found herself not wanting to wait until they arrived at her place. She did not know what she was waiting for; she's been spontaneous many times with some of the men she's date and was attracted to. *Why should this younger man be any different? And she could tell he wanted her...or at least she hoped.* They were still along the shore away from the restaurant, heading towards the wooded area of their route back to her apartment. *No time like the present, girl.* "Can you pull over?"

Desmond glanced at her and started steering the vehicle off the road in a dimly lit area. "Are you OK," he asked, ready to aide her if she was about to be sick from the wine.

Chanale smiled…and undid her seatbelt. She leaned forward and with her right hand reached behind his neck and moved his face closer to hers. "I am just fine," she said and pressed her full soft lips against his.

Desmond was startled but that did not last long as he returned her kiss. He reached down and un-clicked his seatbelt and wrapped his arms around her, adding pressure to the kiss. Within seconds Desmond slipped his tongue into her mouth, tasting the wine and strawberry mixture. He moaned as their tongues fought with each other resulting in passion rising between them. His left hand reached down to the front of her trench coat and he pushed it further open and slipped his hand between the front sections of the wrap.

Chanale broke the kiss with a gasp and he stopped, fearing he'd gone too far. Instead, Chanale wiggled out of the coat and slipped her hand to the tie that held the dress together and loosened it, causing the area that covered her breasts to gape open. She leaned forward, encouraging Desmond to grope and feel on her full breasts.

Feeling as if they were being watched Desmond suddenly glanced around for passersby and flowing traffic, especially a squad car. Seeing that the area was practically deserted, he pushed the front of the dress open and saw the body suit. "Don't worry baby it's easy access," Chanale said and undid the front clasp of the bra section.

Desmond licked his lips and cupped her breasts. He dropped his head and circled his tongue around one nipple before clasping his mouth on it, gently tugging and pulling the nipple. He treated the nipple with equal intensity as Chanale moaned and stroked the top of his head. His caresses and tongue drove her crazy and she was getting wetter by each touch.

She felt his hand slip under her dress and between her legs and thought she was going to bang her head through the passenger window when his fingers stroked against the fabric of the body suit. He found the clasp to open the crotch panel and slid two fingers inside. He moaned again when he felt her wetness cover his fingers and looked into her eyes. Chanale was hypnotized by Desmond's lust filled stare and found her hips struggling to move against his hand. Desmond reluctantly moved away and reached over her. "I'm going to recline your seat," he barely got out of his mouth.

Chanale nodded and set herself to fall back with the front seat. She also pushed pack so the seat could move further from the dashboard.

Now that she was laid back, Desmond eased across the hump and positioned his body to take off his blazer and undo his pants. He pushed down his pants and briefs. Chanale opened the dress completely and slipped out of it. She suddenly pushed her body further back to where she was off the recliner part of the front seat and in the back of the SUV. She parted her legs and propped her upper body against the interior.

Desmond smiled and reached in the glove compartment and pulled out a wrapped condom. He tore the wrapper with his teeth and placed the condom on his long, erect penis and climbed towards and over Chanale. He entered her slowly, cupping her ass and lowering his body closer to hers. She wrapped her arms around him, her hands planted on his broad back. She took a deep breath and let out a loud moan when he plunged inside her and began to slowly pump in and out. "Damn, you feel so good," Desmond grunted and he continued a slow, rhythmic pace. He picked up a little speed when Chanale wrapped her legs above his hips. He leaned forward and pumped deeper, rocking her body each time.

"Oh. My....My...Oh yes, baby, yes," she moaned as her body surged with heat. Desmond responded with fast and slow pumps, gentle then hard, continuing when Chanale raised her hips to meet his rhythm.

He kissed her deeply as the friction between them got rougher. Chanale felt herself building towards an explosion and her body bucked underneath him. Within moments she cried out, holding on to his shoulders as her body released her pleasure. Desmond pumped harder as his own passion was igniting for released. "Aaah Chanale...Chanale," he shouted before filling the condom. He pulled out and rolled onto the back seat.

Chanale breathed heavy and held onto her chest. She'd never felt such intensity in her life! The full moon beamed into the back window and she looked at him sitting up and carefully removing the condom to dispose it. Chanale got back into her dress as he yanked up his pants and put on his shirt. She stayed in the back seat as he climbed over the front seat and got out to place the used condom in a nearby city trash can.

Rushing back into the SUV he noticed she was not in front and looked over his shoulder. "Are you OK?"

Chanale nodded and sat up to put on the back seatbelt. "I did not feel like re-adjusting the front seat. Let's go back to my apartment," she said.

He faced forward and started the SUV and pulled off. Desmond glanced at Chanale in the rearview mirror and nearly drove off the road as he could see Chanale hike the dress up and play with herself. She had positioned herself so he could see her reflection and even better, what she was doing. Chanale smiled as Desmond forced himself to keep his eyes on the road...but the SUV picked up speed.

They made it back to her apartment in one piece and eagerly got inside the building and in the elevator where Chanale pulled Desmond to her and kissed him. When the elevator opened they stumbled to her apartment door and she grabbed the keys out of her purse and unlocked the door. Rushing inside, Chanale was stepping out of her dress and the bodysuit.

The Panthers Club

Wearing only her pumps, she walked the hallway to her bedroom as a completely naked Desmond was at her heels. She laughed as he pushed her forward onto her bed and he hovered over her and entered her from behind. Her laughter turned into gasps and then loud moans as he pumped in and out of her again. He grabbed the edge of the bed and she held on to the bedspread moaning as he did pushups on her. Their sexual exercises lasted another hour before they climbed under the bedspread and sheets to fall asleep.

Chapter 17

Chanale's left eye opened and darted left and right above the bed sheet. That was when she felt it. "Shit," she mumbled and sat up pushing the covers back. She stopped when she remembered Desmond was also in her bed. His back was to her slowly moving to the rhythm of his breathing pattern. She carefully got out of the bed and smoothed the covers forward. She snatched her robe and tipped out of the bedroom straight to the bathroom. Turning on the light, she slowly walked to the mirror over the sink and opened both eyes. Both disposable contacts were still in. She forgot all about them when she and Desmond stumbled into her apartment.

No doubt there is a trail of clothes and shoes from the living room to her bed. She washed her hands and carefully removed the contacts and tossed them in the wastebasket. She opened the medicine cabinet and grabbed the bottle of eye drops. After blinking and washing her hands again, she used the bathroom and decided to take a shower.

Feeling the hot water hit her body, she smiled at the memory of what happened last night. "I was really bold," she said to herself while lathering up with a lavender body wash. She continued to think about how they ravished each other as she rinsed off. Stepping out of the shower Chanale grabbed a towel and started to dry off when she heard a knock on the bathroom door.

Wrapping the towel around her Chanale opened the door to a naked Desmond standing in the hall rubbing his eyes. His long, lean and muscular body was beautiful; he almost had a six-pack but what he was working with was fine with her. He was not even covered with a tattoo or a piercing, just a beautiful sculpted piece of living art. He opened one eye and smiled at Chanale. "I need to use the restroom."

Chanale held on to her towel and walked out as he began walking in. She peeped at Desmond's small but firm ass and muscular legs before he closed the door.

Chanale sat on her bed and grabbed a jar of cocoa butter to moisturize her arms, stomach and legs. Opening the towel, she began rubbing cocoa butter on her breasts and massaging it in her skin. She heard the shower come on and figured he opened the linen closet where the towels and wash clothes were stacked on the middle shelf. Bars of soap rested on the rack hanging on the door. She finished moisturizing and grabbed a bra and panty set from the drawer. By the time she was in her closet searching for a pair of jeans, Desmond re-entered her bedroom wearing the towel around his waist. Chanale felt his eyes on her because she was still in just the bra and panties and became self- conscious because of the little roll of fat just underneath the back of the bra. She even hated he was seeing the curve that led to the shape of her round ass. She wished she had the body suit on…and the robe.

"Morning", Chanale said over her shoulder. She grabbed a pair of stretch jeans and a long buttoned down shirt and turned to face him. She also blocked the front of her body with the articles of clothing as she headed back to the bed.

Desmond watched her attempt to cover up. Why was she acting shy? Hell, he's seen everything…and loved every inch…now she's hiding? He walked over to where Chanale stood and grabbed the articles of clothing and tossed them on the bed. Pulling her to his body, Desmond wrapped his arms around her waist and kissed her deeply. Chanale relaxed and put her arms around his neck and returned the kiss. Desmond held her tighter and she could feel his erection against the towel. She slowly grinded against him and he lowered his hands to her ass, caressing. They broke for air and he nuzzled her neck. "Morning," he mumbled against her skin.

Chanale laughed and rubbed his shoulders. "Morning to you again. Are you hungry? I can fix us some breakfast."

Desmond moved his head away from her neck and squeezed her. "How about you be my first course," he said with a smile and moved her closer to the bed.

Chanale lightly slapped his shoulder and broke away from his grip. She grabbed her jeans and bent over slightly to step in them. She could feel his eyes scanning her body and with her side vision caught him licking his lips. She straightened up and zipped and buttoned the jeans. "I'm kind of starving for actual food Desmond," Chanale said, "I mean, the dinner and the wine was, ahem, burned off and my belly is empty!"

Desmond playfully pouted and looked to put on his clothes. "Damn I can't wear my briefs from yesterday and my carryon bag is in the jeep!"

Chanale looked at him wondering why he'd have a carryon bag filled with fresh underwear and other clothing. She shook the thought out of her head figuring as a doctor he probably has extra items in case he does extra shifts. Then again it's probably his booty call bag too. Stop it!

"I will put on my gym shoes and jacket and get the bag for you." Desmond went in the living room and found his keys and handed them to her and she put on her jacket. "Be right back," she said and unlocked the apartment door. Five minutes later Chanale returned and handed Desmond the bag and he went back to her bedroom.

Chanale walked into her kitchen and opened the refrigerator door, grabbed the carton of eggs, milk, package of turkey sausage patties, a cup of diced green peppers and slices of cheese. She placed everything on the counter next to the stove, opened an overhead cabinet door and took out a box of pancake mix. She figured Desmond had to be just as hungry as she was so she decided on pancakes, scrambled cheese eggs with peppers and turkey sausage. She grabbed a large bowl and measuring cup from another cup and snatched a couple of large spoons from a nearby drawer. She turned the burner on underneath the medium nonstick skillet and poured a dab of vegetable oil into the skillet to heat for the sausage patties. She blended the eggs, milk and pancake batter in the large bowl.

Desmond entered the kitchen and immediately grabbed the package of sausage patties, taking them out and carefully placed them in the skillet. "Desmond I got this," Chanale said while smiling and pouring the batter on the hot griddle on the other side of the stove.

Desmond was dressed in a long sleeve grey t-shirt and jeans. The aroma of the turkey sausage blended with the scent of the aftershave he had in a grooming pouch inside the carryon bag. It was so intoxicating to Chanale who did not say another word about his helping cook.

Desmond removed the cooked patties and drained the skillet, cleaned it off and added oil for the eggs. He reached into the cabinet for a small bowl and pulled a drawer open to see if she had a whisk. Finding one he took the eggs out of the carton and broke two at a time into the bowl. "Oh so I am dealing with a chef, huh," Chanale said while flipping the pancakes.

"I can do a little something," Desmond said with a laugh. "My daddy pushed me in the kitchen one day while mama was cooking dinner and said it was time for me to learn how to cook for myself. I was nine years old! I thought he was telling me mama was not going to cook for me ever again!"

Chanale burst out laughing while placing the pancakes on a platter and taking it to the dining table. She grabbed a couple of plates and utensils to set the table.

Turning to head to the refrigerator Desmond walked by Chanale balancing the plates of sausage and scrambled cheese eggs and peppers. He'd also had a bottle of syrup in the bend of his right arm. "I don't have any coffee but I have orange juice, apple juice…ginger ale, she said.

"I'll take the orange juice please," he said. Chanale brought two glasses and a half gallon of orange juice to the table and sat down. As soon as she placed them on the table, Desmond grabbed her hand and bowed his head in prayer. She bowed her head and listened as he said a short blessing for the food. It kind of surprised her to see him pray. Not that it was weird, but sometimes younger people would just dive right into the food. Why am I thinking of this man like he is an underage boy?!

They ate silently and damn near cleaned all of the plates. Chanale at first was afraid to grab three big and fluffy pancakes to go with the heaping spoonful of eggs and two sausage patties. But seeing Desmond get into every single thing she no longer felt shy. Hell he's seen her naked! And made love to her naked body in his SUV and in her bed! She watched Desmond take a final swig of orange juice and push back from the table. "Whew! That was a great breakfast," he said while patting his barely bulging stomach and grinning at her.

"Yes it was delicious," Chanale agreed and placed her fork on her empty plate. They looked at each for a moment.

Desmond reached over taking her hand. "I really, really enjoyed our date Chanale; every last minute of our date."

Chanale smiled at Desmond and squeezed his hand. "I had a great time, too; from dinner to right now."

They cleared the table and Chanale put the dirty dishes in the sink and turned the faucets on. Desmond grabbed the dish cloth before she could. "I'll take care of this, you sit down."

Chanale looked at him in disbelief; a guy on a date who turns into a one night stand, is washing my damn dishes? I have to be dreaming, she thought to herself. She went back to the kitchen table and sat in one of the chairs."Desmond…do you normally do minor chores for the women you date?"

Desmond chuckled while pouring the dishwashing liquid in the sink of water. "No I don't. But I don't want you to think I am some messy jerk. I mean I was not expecting us to go this far, but we did."

Chanale nodded. She too, was not expecting Desmond to be an overnight guest, let alone washing dishes before he got ready to leave. Overnight guests in the past would jump in the shower, kiss her on the cheek – maybe – and haul ass out of her apartment. Sometimes they would just put their clothes on in the middle of the night and wake her up to unlock the door. Those times she had no problem getting up, unlocking the door and slamming it shut without mumbling "bye" or "see ya!"

Desmond's parents would be proud of him…aw hell wait! The last thing she would want his parents to know is he slept with an older woman!

"What are you thinking about," Desmond said while placing the wet dishcloth on top of the faucet. The dishes were drying out in the drain rack sitting in the next sink.

"Nothing," Chanale said and glanced at the clock on the wall of the stove. It was already 10 a.m. Saturday morning.

Desmond walked over and looked down at her. "I think I will leave now. I have some things to do," he said while rubbing her shoulder.

"OK," Chanale said while getting up.

Desmond went in the living room and picked up his slacks, socks and dress shoes. He walked into the hallway and picked up his dress shirt from the floor and laughed when he noticed his blazer draped on the bedroom doorknob. He went to the bed and stuffed everything in the carryon and zipped it closed.

She walked him to the door and unlocked it.

Desmond opened the door and stepped forward; then turned around and kissed Chanale. "I hope to call you before the weekend is over," he said.

"You most certainly can," Chanale said with a smile. She watched Desmond walk to the elevator where he smiled at her again before stepping in. Chanale closed her door after hearing the 'bing' of the elevator doors closing. She did not walk to the living room window because that side faced away from the parking lot. Chanale was glad she could not watch him pull off. It would only make her look more like an unlikely high school girl losing her mind after sleeping with the captain of the football team.

Chapter 18

Desmond stopped at his house before taking off again to do some errands since he had some time off. He jogged up the steps and bent over to snatch up the newspaper and check the mailbox before unlocking the door. He stepped in and turned off the alarm which beeped loudly as soon as the door swung open. He walked down the foyer and dropped the carryon bag on his bed. He sat down at the foot of the bed and browsed the newspaper when he heard the ringtone of his cell phone. He reached in his bag and noticed five different messages and texts blazing on his screen. He checked all of them including three from a couple of younger women trying to see what he was doing for the weekend. One woman in particular was an exotic looking woman who worked for one of the pharmaceutical companies in partnership with the hospital. He remembered seeing her eating a salad in the hospital cafeteria a few weeks ago.

Within ten minutes of conversation he knew her name was Arianna, she was 27 years old and a consultant working on a degree in pharmaceutical medicine. And she was 5'10 and all legs. Legs with beautiful, small ankles he held onto while hitting her spot on his bed. She left his house at 3 a.m., tipping out like the neighbors were going to catch her and call her parents. He read her text. She wanted to meet for lunch and maybe head back here.

He sent a return text saying he was busy, maybe a rain check and stood up. He walked to the closet and pulled out a leather jacket, shoving the phone in one of the pockets. He grabbed his keys and left out of the house to do his errands. His stomach was still full from that large breakfast. And his mind and body was still full from Chanale.

****

So how was the date?"

Chanale had just changed the bedding, smiling as a mixture of Desmond's natural scent and hers remained on the sheets and pillow cases and used bath and wash towels that she tossed in the washing machine before pouring the detergent. She lit a scented candle on the dresser and cracked the window open. She was cleaning the bathroom while talking to Gabrielle through her Bluetooth.

"The date was alright. We had dinner at the steakhouse near Lake Michigan, ate filet mignon, baked potato and everything. Then I had strawberry torte and he had devil's food cake and we drank a bottle of red wine. And we were going to listen to some live jazz but pulled over and had really hot sex."

Gabrielle chuckled. "Yeah right, quit playing!"

There was a long pause and Chanale could hear the beginning of a scream…

"BITCH YOU ARE LYING!!"

Chanale had to grab the side of the tub to keep from falling in as she was on her knees scrubbing it out. She laughed as Gabrielle was still shouting and demanding details. "Giiiiirrrrl, we were looking at each other during dinner and that wine was kicking in," Chanale said as she got up and sat on the vanity chair. "We got to his SUV and were heading back to my place and he touched my hand and I told him to pull over!"

Gabrielle could barely breathe as Chanale gave her the rest of the story.

By the time Chanale was finished Gabrielle was screaming at every complete sentence Chanale delivered. "And we cooked breakfast together!"

"Shut the hell up," Gabrielle shrieked as Chanale went to the living room and flopped on the couch.

"He was so good in bed and we just went at it! And he was just sweet!"

Gabrielle paused and Chanale knew what that meant. "No I am not telling you how big he is!"

"Dang Chanale! OK, so are you going to see him again," Gabrielle asked.

"If he asks me out again…maybe," Chanale said.

"And if he just wants to come by and hit it…are you going to let him?"

Chanale got quiet and thought about it. "I don't know where it is going after this date. I mean the sex was good but it's not like we are going together. We just felt the attraction and let it played out," she said.

"OK I understand, no pressure for either of you," Gabrielle replied. "Damn I need to start visiting the hospital and seeing if anymore young doctors or soon to be doctors are roaming around!"

Chanale laughed at her friend. "Girl, that's another reason why I am not sweating on the outcome on Desmond. I know he has a lot of those young nurses and probably older nurses' noses wide open. He's young, fine and knows what he is doing. He is considered a catch and he is probably tossing those chicks left and right," she said.

"I know that's right! Well I still say I need to join in on the hunt for a doctor," Gabrielle said, "maybe I just need to rent one of those short, costume nurse's uniforms with the thigh highs, garter belts and white stiletto heels and march right into the emergency room!"

Chanale screamed with laughter. "G they would have to rescue your ass from the lunatics and dirty old men in the waiting room if you show up in that!"

They said their goodbyes and Chanale went back to cleaning around the apartment.

Chapter 19

It was late afternoon when Desmond returned home from running errands. He unlocked the front door and walked in balancing grocery bags and other items. Placing everything on the dining room table, he went back to the front door, opened it and reached in the mailbox for the handful of mail. He tossed the mail on the table, slipped out of his leather jacket and carried the bags into the kitchen to load up the refrigerator and cabinets.

Desmond walked back to the dining room, grabbed the phone and checked the voicemail. Two calls were from Dad checking on him, along with messages from some friends. The last call gave him news from the hospital that he did not have to show up for work until Tuesday morning, meaning an extra 'weekend' day. He decided while on the phone that he would schedule the extra hours that will fill in the trade he made with the colleague.

As soon as he hung up from the hospital the phone rang. "Hello? Oh, hey, Arianna," Desmond said and listened to the pharmaceutical consultant's attempt to invite her to the house. He pondered the idea of letting her come over but Chanale's image played in his mind. The more insistent Arianna was getting, the more he thought about Chanale.

"I'm sorry, Arianna, I am just not in the mood for company right now. No, it's not you. I just have a lot on my mind," he said and listened to the dial tone that came without a goodbye first. Desmond just could not brush off the passion he and Chanale shared the other night, which was totally different from what he is used to doing. His one night stands were just that, one night stands…booty calls. But Chanale put it on him last night; enough to make him hang around her apartment help cook breakfast AND wash her dishes!

It was only a five year gap but she was as freaky as a woman in her twenties along with women in her age group or older. Desmond just did not feel right having another woman with him after Chanale. Staring at the phone, he picked it up and dialed Chanale's number. The line rang three times and he was about to hang up. "Hello, Desmond," she said.

He laughed figuring she would check the caller ID box. "Hey Chanale, how are you? Did I interrupt something?"

Chanale was watching television and grabbed the remote to lower the volume. "No, I am just relaxing. What are you doing?"

"Nothing really. I've been out running errands, taking advantage of the long weekend. I have Monday off too," he said.

An awkward pause that had no business showing up did just that.

Desmond did not want to ask if he could come back to the apartment, although he really felt like he could.

"Was there something you wanted…Desmond," Chanale asked.

"Uhm, no. I just felt the need to call you. I'll let you get back to watching television. I think I am going to visit my dad before it gets too late." Desmond said his goodbyes and hung up, then turned to hit his head on the wall. He had to shake Chanale out of his mind for now. There weren't enough cold showers to calm his horny ass down.

****

Chanale held her laughter in until she heard the dial tone from Desmond's phone line. Hanging up, she could not believe how tongue tied this young doctor was in regards to her. I wonder if he was trying to see if he could have another date or maybe trying to have a booty call before returning to work, Chanale thought. She resumed to watching television but found that she too was unable to shake Desmond out of her mind since the phone conversation. Her body definitely reacted to his voice…hell her goodies betrayed her from the moment he said 'hey.' She found herself shifting her body on the couch as Desmond talked. He definitely proved that he was no beginner in the bedroom.

At the same time she was proud and shocked at how she was able to keep up and then some with his energy. Chanale continued to mentally analyze the overnight romp as she rubbed her stomach and occasionally pinched at her waist. He did not seem to have a problem with her extra pounds. And he did not shy away when she was naked or in her regular underwear this morning. Girl, he was not giving a damn about the pounds! He was all over you like an extra chocolate dessert personally ordered!

Chapter 20

The weekend went too fast for Chanale but at the same time she could not wait to get back to work. She walked past the security desk where Max Walters grinned as he looked away from a copy of the newspaper. Chanale was wearing a burnt orange sweater dress fitted with a wide imitation brown crocodile belt and knee-high brown leather boots with patchwork designs of tan, caramel brown and burnt orange. A chocolate brown trench coat, an oversized burnt orange purse and a pair of small gold hoop earrings completed the ensemble.

In Walters' eyes she was never in a car accident and the pep in her step proved it. "Morning Miss Arlington," he said while standing up out of respect and to get a full view of Chanale's outfit. "You sure look beautiful today! But that is every day. We miss you! Are you doing better?"

Chanale flashed a big smile just for Walters. "Thank you so much, Max! I am glad to be back; it gets kind of boring at home," she continued with a poker face.

She took the elevator to the fourth floor and stepped out to the usual Monday morning madness of paralegals rushing to get fresh coffee, files and flash drives filled with client information. She took out her key card to let herself into Oscar's office but the door was slightly ajar. Chanale tapped on the door. "Knock, knock," and pushed the door back and stepped in.

Oscar was focused on the computer desk monitor and talking through his headset. Without looking up he waved Chanale inside. She walked in and removed her coat and grabbed a hanger from the closet. After placing her purse on her desk, she grabbed her mug and went to the coffee machine.

By the time she was stirring her two sugars and one cream in the full mug Oscar had removed his headphones. "Welcome back! Are you doing better?"

Chanale raised her coffee mug to him in a mock salute. "I am doing much better, thanks. And thanks for taking care of business for me with the car and my potential date. Even though you were acting like papa bear on the prowl."

Oscar sat back in his oversize leather chair and laughed. "Yeah, sorry about that. But you made up for the date later, right?"

Chanale took a long slurp from her mug and raised an eyebrow in confusion. "What do you mean?"

"Well I am assuming you took a rain check and called ol' boy apologizing for my rudeness and went out anyway over the weekend."

Chanale's mind raced as she wondered why in the hell would Oscar be inquiring her about a weekend date...

"Earlier this morning, I kind of overheard Gabrielle talking to someone about you had a hot date..." The rest of Oscar's words warbled in the air like the anonymous grownups you hear in the Charlie Brown cartoons as Chanale kept her composure. But she was plotting to leave out of the office, go down the hall, walk in Gabrielle's office....and punch that big mouth heifer in the throat! "...I did not stick around to hear the rest of the conversation because I to do a conference call – when you walked in I was finishing it – but I guess you made up for it," Oscar continued.

Chanale placed her mug on her desk and cleared her throat. "No, I did not go out with him. In fact I did try to contact him to apologize and he would not return my calls," Chanale said, lying through her teeth. "I did go out. I went out to run errands and get some fresh air and eventually relax."

Oscar straightened up in his chair and shrugged his shoulders. "It's not my business to know what you are doing in your spare time. I did not pry even when we," he stopped himself as that too, was a private matter.

"Anyway, Gabrielle was yapping and you have to be careful around her." Chanale nodded while keeping a calm face. She could not wait to see Gabrielle and take her aside.

****

"Let's have lunch."

Gabrielle jumped, slammed the office refrigerator door shut and spun around so fast she almost fell against Chanale's body. Gabrielle straightened up and looked up at Chanale, who was staring her down like a killer would moments before the machete slashed or a gun magazine emptied. "Girl you scared me! I brought my lunch today..."

Chanale leaned in on Gabrielle and clenched her teeth. "We are going out to lunch...your treat...I'm driving."

Gabrielle forgot all about her insulated lunch bag and went back in her office and grabbed her coat and purse. She walked out of the office and noticed Chanale standing by the elevator, looking calm and smiling at passersby. They got on the elevator and quietly rode to the main floor, walked past and waved at Walters then headed to the parking lot.

"I CANNOT BELIEVE YOU TOLD MY BUSINESS!" Chanale's mouth was going a mile a minute, escalating into profanity then slowing down just enough before charging up. She was driving in the same manner which scared Gabrielle into making sure her seatbelt was on extra tight.

"I am so sorry, Chanale! I did not know Oscar was near my office; I had no idea he would have heard..."

"Why in the HELL are you talking about my business Gabrielle? What your weekend was so fucking boring that you just had to tell my stuff? Or what, it's a shock that Dr. Young, Fine and Sexy looked past you and focused on me? I...was...a...patient," Chanale said while hitting the steering wheel with the right palm of her hand for emphasis.

Gabrielle clamped shut as Chanale continued to drive and shake her head. They headed to Broadway's shopping district and got caught by a train. Chanale put the car on brake and shifted her body against the seat belt to look at Gabrielle. "I am so waiting for your answer!"

Gabrielle looked at her. "I am sorry Chanale. I...I was so outdone by the fact that you went out with the brother! I mean, from what you've said in the past, you only dated older men. And then you go out with a guy who damn near saw you naked in the emergency room."

Chanale threw her hands up. "So, I suddenly can't have a change of pace? I suddenly can't say, why not go out with him? You know Gabrielle I am not even worried about that. What I want to know is, who were you telling my business too?"

Gabrielle dropped her head. "I was talking to another paralegal on the phone. When Oscar walked by my office he apparently did not look inside. I was on the phone."

The train finally passed and the gates rose as Chanale put her foot on the brake and moved the steering to drive. She shook her head in silence and drove the next couple blocks to Wake Up Call and parked in front of the café. The café's name and seeing what Gabrielle did made for a perfect reality check.

"The paralegal does not work in Gary so you don't have to worry about running into her," Gabrielle said, trying to soften the blow.

Chanale unbuckled her seat belt and faced Gabrielle. "Do you not get what I am saying? I don't give a damn where the paralegal was working or who she is. You had no business telling MY business! Hell, we work for attorneys; do you not know about confidentiality? I mean, what's the explanation...are you jealous?"

Gabrielle glared at Chanale. "I am definitely not jealous of you! I'm not the one wearing false eye colors and changing my hair and wearing girdles trying to look younger than I am," Gabrielle said with attitude.

Chanale was ready to push back into her seat, lift her leg and kick Melanie out of her car...closed door and all. "You are sitting here right now with those fake ass green eyes and extra hair for bangs! Can you breathe with that Sister Hug or whatever spandex and Lycra get up you squeezed into? You are the one with the issues!"

Chanale hit the 'unlock' button for the passenger side. "Get the fuck out of my car...NOW!"

Chapter 21

Chanale reversed her car, yanked the steering to forward and whipped out of the parking space making Gabrielle jumped further away from the curb. Gabrielle stood on the sidewalk with her purse in her hand, gawking as Chanale did a U-turn in the middle of downtown Broadway and gunned the car back to the office. "Your ass can catch a bus or hoe yourself a ride back to work," Chanale mumbled as she took one last glimpse at Gabrielle in her rearview mirror. She knew confiding in her was no longer an option and made a mental list of what she needed to do when she got back to the office. She was going to leave the online accounts that pertained to the law firm open, but block Gabrielle from her personal social networking sites.

Not that she put her business on the walls, but Gabrielle was going to get the 'dismissed' alert from myace.com and will eventually be removed from her cell phone contact registry. It was only one date and Gabrielle put it out there like she was going to get a big ass check for gossiping! Chanale stopped at a fast food joint and ordered a cheeseburger with everything, fries and a strawberry milkshake, not giving a damn if her girdle ripped at the seams. She left the drive-thru and headed back to the office.

By the time she rushed past Walters and two more security officers rode the elevator and marched down the hallway sipping from the thick shake, Oscar was in his office doorway. Chanale stopped in front of him and glared. "So you left Gabrielle in front of the café'," he said and scrunched his nose at the smell of onions. "Uh-uh, you are not eating that loud cheeseburger in here…" Chanale stormed off and went into the lunchroom and dropped her sack on one of the tables. She held on to the shake while coming out of her trench coat. "Gabrielle called me shouting all kinds of craziness and I told her to hail a cab," Oscar said as he walked into the lunchroom. "Had I known you two were going to act crazy I would have kept my mouth shut!"

Chanale cut her eyes in Oscar's direction while snatching the sack open and pulling out the huge piece of foil that covered the cheeseburger. She popped a fry in her mouth and opened the foil. She wondered if during the shouting in Oscar's ear if Gabrielle mentioned Desmond?

"Look," Oscar said as he pulled back a chair and sat down, "is this going to be a problem? I mean you two aren't dating the same brother?"

Chanale took a bite of the cheeseburger and shook her head. "No! And I am not going to have a problem with Gabrielle. It's business from now on," she continued.

Oscar sighed and got up from the chair. "Well like I said before, you really should not let Gabrielle in on all of your business. I mean, you pretty much keep to yourself with the other colleagues and hardly doing any water cooler talks."

Chanale looked up at Oscar and rolled her eyes. "She does not know anything about us Oscar," Chanale whispered. Oscar cleared his throat and walked out of the lunchroom. She looked at her cheeseburger and re-wrapped it and tossed it in the garbage can. She finished her fries and took two more sips of the shake and tossed the rest of the stuff in the garbage. Chanale washed her hands in the sink and brushed the crumbs off her dress.

Turning around to leave, she was face to face with Gabrielle. They looked at each other and Gabrielle walked by and opened the refrigerator and grabbed her insulated lunch bag from the shelf. Chanale walked out of the lunchroom knowing that it will be a long minute before they do any friendly chatting.

****

Desmond spent his extra day off being lazy. He slept until 10 a.m. and stayed in the bed watching game shows until noon. Throwing the covers back he grabbed the remote and turned to a sports network and enhanced the volume for background sound. He pulled a t-shirt over his head and with drawstring pajama bottoms walked to the front door and turned off the alarm so to grab the newspaper on the porch. He headed to the kitchen and dropped the paper on the table and went to the sink to wash his hands with the antibacterial soap. Heading to the refrigerator Desmond opened the door and grabbed a loaf of bread, a package of salami and Swiss cheese, a jar of mayonnaise and a jar of pickles. He placed all on the table and made a sandwich and added a small bag of salt and sour potato chips. He went back into the refrigerator and grabbed a bottle of beer.

It was a little early for a beer but he felt deserving of it since it helped relax him. He walked back into his bedroom with the plate and the bottle and placed them on the nightstand to grab TV bed tray from the closet. He climbed in the bed, adjusted the tray and placed his sandwich and beer on top and propped the pillows behind him. Halfway into eating the sandwich the doorbell rang. Desmond cursed under his breath for the interruption. By the time he was in the hallway, the doorbell was being leaned on, which annoyed the hell out of him.

"I'M COMING!" Desmond looked into the peephole and unlocked the door.

"Hey baby," Arianna said with a big grin. She was wearing a leather blazer over a fitting lavender turtleneck sweater with a tight pair of jeans and black suede boots. Her hair was styled in a long bob with bangs done in a blunt cut.

Desmond's eyes roamed Arianna's body from head to boot and his other brain was reacting behind the pajama bottoms. "Hey. What are you doing here," Desmond said as he wiped his hand over his face and discovered he has yet to shave.

Arianna placed her hand on her hip. "So are we going to have this conversation through the glass door?"

He blinked and noticed he had not unlocked the security door and paused on whether or not he should. Damn if she did not look good enough to eat. He decided to unlock the door to let her in. "Be forewarned…I am funky," Desmond said as he stepped aside to avoid Arianna brushing against his body and better yet, his hard on.

"And we have been funky and sweaty together once upon a time," Arianna threw back over her shoulder and followed the sound the TV. She walked into his bedroom and sat on the bed as Desmond walked behind and watched her take a swig of his beer.

"I was driving through and noticed your SUV in the driveway," Arianna said while removing her blazer, "I figured you would be home and thought you were sick or something."

Desmond looked at her and walked to the bed and sat on the other side of the tray. "I have today off. Go back in for an extended shift tomorrow," he said. "Well, I was in the middle of running errands, but…" Desmond watched with glazed eyes as Arianna stood up and walked over to him.

Standing in front of him she yanked her turtleneck out of her jeans and over her head. She stepped closer to him and unbuttoned and unzipped her jeans. Desmond threw his hands up. "Whoah hold up, Arianna! I told you I am funky and what makes you think I want to have sex?"

Arianna answered his question by reaching down and placing her right hand into the waistband of his pajamas and dropping her hand lower until she wrapped it around his hard on. She looked him in the eyes as he drew a deep breath. "I believe you are outnumbered on the decision," she said as she moved her hand up and down.

Desmond moaned when she gave it a quick but sharp tug which also made him stand to his feet. He reached down and removed her hand from his pajama bottoms and then in one swoop, picked her up and walked into the bathroom. "I will pay for your next hair appointment," Desmond said and kicked the door closed.

An hour later, Desmond was stepping into a pair of jeans while Arianna was still wrapped in his bed sheet watching him. "Are you OK? Seems like you were focusing on something else," she said to his back as he pulled a black v-neck sweater over his head.

Desmond said nothing at first; he frowned as he adjusted his sweater. He was focused on something, or rather, someone else. Having sex with Arianna felt different and hearing her voice felt…annoying. "Are you going to get dressed?"

Arianna sat up straighter and her own frown developed. "Well I guess I better get dressed being that you are fully clothed."

Desmond turned around. "You invited yourself here," he said.

Arianna unwrapped herself out of the sheet, her naked body angrily jumping out of the bed to head for her clothes. "You could have easily slammed the door in my face! If you did not want to fuck…"

"I told you I was funky and you should have taken the hint that I did not feel like doing anything!"

"Well your other brain did not seem to mind," Arianna snapped while yanking her turtleneck over her head and over her jeans.

"It is what it is," Desmond said, "you opened the door and I walked right in."

Arianna paused and glared at him. "Well I don't need to be treated that way!" She stomped past Desmond and walked the hall to the front door. He was on her heels and reached around her to unlock the door. She glared at him one last time and walked out. This time Desmond slammed the door hard enough to shake the room.

****

Chanale was so happy to walk inside her apartment later that evening she did not even bother to hang up her coat instead she tossed it and her purse on the couch. She removed her boots and reached for the buckle to her wide belt, allowing the sweater dress and her stomach breathing room.

Padding into the kitchen Chanale opened the cabinet stocked with glasses and grabbed a wineglass by the stem. She went to the refrigerator and yanked a bottle of red wine from the side door, slamming it shut. Within seconds she filled the glass damn near to the rim with the dark red elixir and wasted no time bringing the glass to her lips. That bullshit she dealt with at work was not how she wanted to start her first week back.

She walked into her bedroom with the bottle in one hand and the glass in the other and sat on the foot of her bed. Placing the bottle on the dresser Chanale paused as she realized there was still a faint scent of the cologne Desmond wore when he spent the night. She inhaled the aroma as she took another sip of wine, closed her eyes and reflected on last weekend.

Damn that Gabrielle for running her mouth in the workplace with Oscar overhearing a little bit. Thankfully he did not hear Gabrielle say Desmond's name or he would have put two and two together and ride her about sleeping with a doctor. As far as Oscar was concerned when it comes to doctors they get in the way of lawyers like him winning cases and getting nice percentages. Which is a stupid ass theory but Chanale just let Oscar run his own theoretic on the situation. She put the glass down and went to the bathroom to draw a bath. After making sure the water temperature was just right and pouring a little bit of lavender bath salts in, Chanale walked back to her bedroom and began removing her dress. She undid the Sister Hug body slimmer and stepped out of it. She retrieved her wine glass and poured a little more wine into it and grabbed her cell phone heading back to the bathroom.

She placed the phone in the charger resting on the vanity table and turned on the small portable radio/CD player that rested on the shelf above the table. She still had one of her Mint Condition CDs inside and immediately hit 'Play.' The tub was full and the lavender filled the entire bathroom. Chanale stepped in and sat down ignoring the reaction her skin was having to the water's heat. She sat back and rested her head against the satin pillow and let the water relax her. "This feels so damn good," she murmured while grabbing the wine glass from the edge of the tub.

Chanale was in her own world for two minutes before her cell phone's ringtone interrupted her CD's flow. "Shit, who could that be," she said as she turned to look at the id from the charger. Seeing Desmond's name on the screen surprised Chanale who put the glass down. She could not grab the phone from the tub so she let the call go to voicemail.

Twenty minutes later Chanale stepped out of the tub and wrapped a towel around her body. She placed the glass on the vanity table and grabbed her cell phone, hitting the password and loudspeaker buttons to play Desmond's message."Hey Chanale, it's Desmond. I hope you are doing well and your first day back at work was OK," he said. "Call me back today if you can."

Chanale disconnected the message and wondered what did he want? She dried off and moisturized her body and headed to her bedroom to put on a pair of sweatpants and a t-shirt. Picking up the landline phone she dialed his number. "Hello," he said.

"Hey Desmond its Chanale," she said and sat on the bed.

"Oh hey! I'm glad you called back."

"I was taking a hot bath when you called my cell. How are you doing? Aren't you getting ready to get back to work yourself?"

"Yeah, I head to Midwest in the morning. What are you doing right now?"

Chanale paused at his question wondering if she should make something up or tell the truth; that she really did not want company. "Well...I am not doing anything. I am in for the evening."

"Can I stop by?"

"I really don't feel like having company," Chanale said.

"Have you eaten dinner? Desmond asked, oblivious to her reply. "I can bring some Chinese takeout."

Chanale sighed, but at the same time she was hungry and any more wine on an empty stomach will be disastrous and a fun way to enter the job in the morning. "OK Desmond you can stop by and bring some Chinese food. I like sweet and sour shrimp, rice, vegetable egg rolls…"

"I'll bring that and more so we can have choices. See you in thirty," Desmond said before hanging up.

Chapter 22

Chanale stepped aside as Desmond walked inside her apartment with two bags of Chinese food and a six pack of beer. He smelled freshly showered with cologne as an accessory. "I take it the beer is for you because I refuse to touch the stuff," she said closing the door and walking to the kitchen where he placed the bags and beer on her table.

"Yeah the beer is for me and I will take the remaining cans home when I leave," he said as he slipped out of his leather jacket.

Chanale grabbed his jacket and walked to the closet, wondering why Desmond wanted to pay her a visit. He was not actually looking at her in a lusting manner; he was acting more like a friend ready to hang out. She headed back to the kitchen as he was grabbing plates from one of the cabinets. She went to the utensil drawer and grabbed two forks but when she turned around Desmond was removing two pairs of chopsticks from one of the bags. "Guess you won't need these," she said while waving the forks in the air.

He smiled and opened a can of beer while she returned the forks in the drawer and went to the refrigerator to grab a can of pop. She joined him at the table as he passed her the containers of sweet and sour shrimp, rice and vegetable egg rolls. He opened a container with orange chicken, stir fry vegetables and pork egg rolls. They piled their plates and grabbed the chopsticks and began eating in silence.

"So what brings you here on the evening before you return to work? Chanale asked while using the chopsticks to gather some of the shrimp fried rice.

"I just felt like stopping by for a little while. I wasn't interrupting anything, was I? I mean if you were not in the mood for company I would have understood," Desmond said while taking a swig of beer.

"I don't mind you visiting. I just had a bit of a rough day," she said. "What happened?"

"It's nothing. Just had it out with a coworker," she continued. Silence grew between them for another five minutes. Desmond watched Chanale from the corner of his eye as she put a lot of focus on her plate and seemed to over concentrate on the chopsticks.

"What happened if you don't mind me asking you? This was your first day back at the firm right?"

Chanale pushed her food around with her chopsticks and took a breath. "I had an argument with Gabrielle."

"The one you call G," Desmond said thinking that's what he heard Chanale refer to the woman he encountered in Chanale's hospital room.

She nodded. "Yes, we had it out over her talking too much, particularly about my business."

Desmond paused before putting a heaping of orange chicken and rice in his mouth. "What was she blabbing about?"

Chanale began focusing on her plate with more intensity, making Desmond look at her again. "Oh she was talking about me! How was she talking about me Chanale," he said.

When Chanale cut her eyes in his direction Desmond had a devilish smirk on his face. She shook her head and then laughed. "Last weekend I mentioned I was going on a date and she keep nudging until she figured it out," Chanale said. She chose not to admit to going into detail about their date. "Anyway when I entered Oscar's office he mentioned overhearing Gabrielle talk about me and a date but he assumed it was the guy I was supposed to meet for dinner the night of the accident."

"So Oscar has no idea that it was me Gabrielle was talking about?" Chanale shook her head no while finishing off her plate.

Desmond took another swig of beer. He was flattered that Chanale even talked about them to someone else, even if it was a first date. He watched her take her empty plate to the sink. She turned on the faucet and started adding dish washing liquid, making him jump up and empty the rest of his plate. He stood next to Chanale as she took his plate to wash. He sensed that there was more to the story than she was letting on. "Are you having second thoughts about what happened last weekend, Chanale?"

Chanale looked at him and shook her head. "No I don't regret what happened between us. I guess I should not have told Gabrielle about the date and with whom I was going out. It's not like she and I are best friends."

Chanale scalded the dishes, dried her hands with a cloth and went back to the table to close the containers.

Desmond joined and continued watching her. She looked at him and smiled. "Am I the first younger man you've been with?"

Chanale paused and then grabbed the closed containers and walked to the refrigerator. "Yeah you are the first younger man I've been with," she said stacking the containers on a shelf and closing the door.

"Are you taking the other containers home with you?" Desmond nodded and placed them in the bag with the beer. "Are you putting me out already," he said and faked a pout until Chanale laughed.

"No you can stay as long as you like!" She grabbed her pop and walked into the living room and sat down on the couch. He joined her with a second can of beer. Chanale picked up the remote and turned on the TV, flipping channels until she rested on a network showing a horror movie.

"Aw now c'mon! I know you want to watch one of those all chick networks with the tissue box theatre or some type of male bashing talk show," Desmond said while laughing.

Chanale shoved him and he playfully keeled over in mock pain.

"I happen to like horror and suspense and action flicks and shows," she said.

They remained quiet for ten minutes and Desmond sat closer to Chanale. He placed his can of beer on a coaster on the coffee table and rested his arm on the back of the couch behind her. Chanale felt her heart flutter at the touch of his body leaning into her and when his fingers ran through her hair her nerves jumped.

"Am I the first older woman you've been with?"

"No," he said, which made Chanale lean away from him to look him in the face.

"Really? You have a history with older women?"

"Yeah, I mean age does not matter to me, but I have dated or gone out with a couple of older women in the last ten years," he said. "I just like to have a good time and if the chemistry is right then we can have some fun."

Chanale flashed back to the chemistry they had last weekend. There was enough chemistry to summon a bomb squad! She could understand the fun in dating someone older; she's been doing that for at least 20 years and rarely did she date a man who was the same age or close to it. But this was not dating going on between her and Desmond. It started as a date but in the end it was passionate sex.

She turned her head to Desmond to say something and he leaned in and kissed her. His lips pressed hard against hers and she let a moan escape as he pulled her into an embrace. When she felt his tongue lick across her lips, Chanale parted them and flicked her tongue against his. She shifted her weight and moved so that she was on Desmond's lap. They necked for nearly thirty minutes and she soon wiggled out of her pants. Desmond shifted his hips and reached in his pocket for a condom while she opened his fly. He took off his V-neck sweater and then tore the wrapper with his teeth and rolled the condom on his erection.

Chanal turned her back to him, grabbed his thighs and slowly sat on Desmond's lap, relaxing against his chest as he leaned into the back couch cushion. He wrapped his arms around her and placed his hands on her breasts as she rode him up and down. She moved her head so that she was cheek to cheek against Desmond whose quick breaths and moans filled her ear. Getting a stronger grip on his thighs Chanale balanced her lower body so to go up and down and grind on him, giving him one hell of a lap dance. If he'd ever been in the 'champagne room' he did not experience anything like what Chanale was doing to him. "Damn Chanale...Damn," he kept repeating while squeezing and rubbing her swollen breasts. He kissed the nape of her neck while grunting every time she bounced on his lap. Chanale continued her pace of fast then slow, her body temperature rising with each stroke. She got hotter when she felt Desmond's right hand move over her stomach and to her heat and jerked forward when his fingers rubbed her clit. Electric waves of shock surged from her hips to her breasts as she cried out and rode him harder until she climaxed.

Chanale stood up and reached down to grab her pants and panties before disappearing into the bathroom. Desmond was left on the couch trying to catch his breath from what just went down. He sat still with his jeans and briefs scrunched around his ankles and his erection slowly fading. He removed the condom and tied it so he could get up and yank his jeans and briefs up.

Figuring she was in her master bathroom, he walked into the hallway bathroom and properly disposed the condom. Desmond looked into the mirror and washed his face. When he looked into the mirror again, a broad smile hit his face as Chanale was standing behind him. "Are you OK," she said smiling at his reflection.

Desmond's reflection returned a smile as he grabbed a towel to dry his face. He turned around as she stood wearing her pants and the pink lace bra he barely got to see in the living room. "I think you almost gave me an out of body experience, sexy!"

Chanale laughed and exited the bathroom to give him more privacy. Hell she had to walk away from him when they were finished or else she'd have to go to the emergency room from hyperventilating. She'd never been that hungry towards a man like that in a minute, know if she'd acted like that with an older man he would probably go into cardiac arrest.

Desmond was like an elixir that was twice as powerful as the fountain of youth. She enjoyed every inch of him earlier and was willing to go at him again. She threw on her t-shirt and walked back into the living room where she noticed the carry out bag on the coffee table. She turned and caught Desmond removing his jacket from the hanger to throw on. "As much as I would like to stay, I have an early schedule on my first day back at Midwest and I would not want to wake you up at 4:30 a.m. trying to slip out of bed to get ready," Desmond said as he walked past and grabbed the bag.

They walked to the door and Chanale unlocked and opened it. "Later," he said and kissed her lips.

"Thanks for dinner…and dessert," Chanale replied and closed the door.

****

Desmond stepped inside the Medical Staff entrance at Midwest at 6 a.m. with his bag filled with his doctor's uniform. The smell of disinfectant filled his nostrils as he walked the hallway recently clean by the maintenance staff. The lights in the ceiling appeared to be brighter than usual, then again the mid fall season made for darker mornings. Early staff nurses and lab technicians were getting adjusted to a new day with coffee cups in their hands and gossip being the first topic of choice before the doctors appear and start ordering them around.

Some of them looked up and quieted down as Desmond walked by and nodded an acknowledgement to him. Desmond smiled and nodded back and picked up his pace towards the locker room as the group resumed blabbing. He made it to the locker room and spun the combination on the lock and with a yank noticed a folded sheet of paper land at his feet. He looked around to see if any colleagues were nearby so to ask who slipped a note through his locker door vent. No one else was there so he kneeled and picked up the note and unfolded it.

You need to slow your roll, Doc, the note read. Desmond jerked his head up then glanced left and right along the row of lockers. He looked back at the note and flipped it over to see if someone left a name on the other side. The handwriting was in print so he could not tell who the author was and that pissed Desmond off to no end. He shoved the note in his jean pocket and proceeded to change into his scrubs and lab coat. Desmond exited the locker room with a stone expression. His mood had changed within the first 45 minutes of being in the hospital because someone wanted to play childish games.

Nurses who were set to greet him with a friendly hello squashed the gesture as Desmond grabbed patients' charts without even looking at the nurse's station. He only calmed his expression when he visited the patients. Finishing those rounds, attending two meetings and doing another set of rounds in the ER had Desmond focused on his work instead of flirting. When the clock struck 1 p.m. Desmond was sitting in the hospital cafeteria with a plate of chicken tacos and fries in front of him. He had yet to take a bite of any of the food as his mind drifted on the mysterious note.

"What's wrong with you?"

Desmond looked up as Dr. Monroe stood at the other side of the table. Desmond did not answer right away; instead he drew a long look at the older physician and wondered if his hating ass was the author of the note. "Nothing's wrong. I guess I don't really have an appetite," Desmond said.

Dr. Monroe shrugged his shoulders and walked over to one of the counters to order his lunch from one of the cafeteria workers. Desmond looked at his plate and picked up a taco, forcing himself to start eating since breakfast was long gone from his stomach.

****

Chanale spent all day assisting in legal briefs with Oscar and some of the other attorneys from the firm. Gabrielle sat in on a couple of the sessionsbut stayed on the other end of the conference table. Those sitting between the two women were aware of the fallout and Chanale leaving Gabrielle downtown at the curb yesterday but deemed themselves too professional to chime in. Instead it was business as usual.

When lunch rolled through, Chanale stayed at her desk with the leftover egg rolls and sweet and sour shrimp from home. She warmed a plate in the office microwave and grabbed a bottled water from Oscar's refrigerator. Taking a plastic utensil set from her drawer she stabbed her fork into the shrimp. "I guess you and Gabrielle are not speaking," Oscar said while passing Chanale's desk with a carryout bag in his hand.

Chanale silently ate while he unwrap the foil from a cheeseburger removed from his bag. He pulled out the large order of fries and placed them on top of the bag and opened the can of pop already on his desk. "Look I am going to need some form of communication between you and Gabrielle..."

"I will communicate with her, in a professional setting and matter," Chanale interrupted. "I represent the firm and will always honor that. Beyond that no one should give a damn whether I speak to Gabrielle or not –including you."

Oscar shook his head and took a bite from his cheeseburger. "I just wanted to make sure you and Gabrielle understood what is more important. I remember when you lashed out at me after what transpired between us," he said, then regretted when he heard Chanale's fork hit the desk. He felt her stare without looking up. "I should not have said that..."

"You're fucking right you should not have," Chanale shot back. "I realized how we were acting unprofessional back then; that's why I let go of your ass! And I turned in my resignation letter in case you've forgot. Oh and who was the one to try to get back together," she continued.

With the cheeseburger in his left hand Oscar threw both hands up in surrender. "I'm sorry I brought this up. It's just that Gabrielle was all down about this issue between you two," he said.

"That's her problem, not mine," Chanale replied while taking a bite from an egg roll. They ate their lunches in silence as Chanale thought maybe it was time to consider working for another law firm. She'd actually thought about it a while back...after her liaison with Oscar but when she received a raise and extra vacation time she pushed the thought to the back burner.

Now the thought re-emerged and this time nothing she believed would push it back. Chanale suddenly heard a ringtone acknowledging a text message was sent to her and she grabbed her cell phone off her desk.

"Thinking about U" appeared on her screen. It was from Desmond. Chanale stared at the text, surprised he would send something like that to her.

"Is there something wrong," Oscar said as he watched her focus on her cell phone.

"No, there's no emergency," she said while deleting the text and placing her phone back on her desk.

****

"I got your text today," Chanale said to Desmond later that night.

"I did not send you any texts," he said, cradling the cordless phone between his head and shoulders while fixing something to eat.

"You didn't? Well, someone sent me a text during lunch and your name popped up."

Desmond stopped slicing the onions he was going to caramelize for the steak. "That's real strange unless you know another Desmond…do you?"

Chanale laughed, "No I don't! But it is kind of odd that you did not send a text and yet you name appeared on the screen."

Desmond finished slicing the onions and quickly went to the stove turned the fire to medium under the frying pan. While waiting for the pan to heat Desmond thought about the note he shoved into his jean pocket at work and reached into his right pocket. He pulled out the note, unfolded it and re-read the message. "You know Chanale it's funny you mention a text message. I got a folded handwritten note slipped into my locker at Midwest today," he said. He tossed the note on the counter and grabbed a bottle of vegetable oil and a large spoon, adding three spoonfuls to the hot pan. "I don't know who wrote the note because they did not leave a name and the message is written in print…hold on," Desmond said. He threw the sliced onions into the pan and began stirring them. "OK I'm back. Like I said I don't know who could have written the note and that is crazy about the supposed text from me."

He turned down the flame and continued stirring the onions until they were a perfect brown. Turning off the fire Desmond added a heaping of the caramelized onions on top of a well done tenderloin steak that rested on his plate. He added a couple of spoonfuls of mixed vegetables and a small baked potato stuffed with sour cream and chives.

"You sound busy," Chanale said.

"Well I was fixing my dinner. I did not eat all of my lunch because I was a bit frustrated about this note along with a crazy shift so I am kind of starving."

"Oh well don't let me keep you," Chanale said, "I will talk to you later."

"OK, later it is." Desmond pushed the end button and placed the cordless phone into the cradle and picked up his plate and a can of beer. He walked downstairs to the basement entertainment area and placed everything on a TV tray and grabbed the remote. Finding the channel he wanted, he sat down and pulled tab from the can and began eating.

Thirty minutes later Desmond pushed the tray to the side and finished off the beer before smashing the can and tossing it into the tall wastebasket on the right side of the bar. His mind was still on the note and now the phantom text message with his name. He sat back into the couch and closed his eyes as the TV volume spoke of a car chase scene in a movie. "I'll be damn," he said in a jolted thought five minutes later.

****

Chanale picked up the phone and almost dialed Gabrielle's number. "Shit," she mumbled while putting the receiver onto the cradle. Getting a mysterious text message and thinking it was from a guy you're seeing is a topic that called for a girlfriend conversation. But Gabrielle's blabbing was what pissed Chanale off. Not that she did not have additional friends. But she did not know if she could count on them to keep their mouths shut either.

One thing Chanale did know, she was not going to be a part of some foolish drama on Dr. Richards' part. Maybe it was one of those outside texts that got into her phone from someone else. Or maybe Desmond's phone account was hacked. But now there is the mysterious note he got today at the hospital. Chanale then realized Desmond did not tell her what the note said. She did not ask and he did not offer to read it, instead he was focused on fixing his dinner. What did that note say?

****

The doorbell rang and Desmond ran up the stairs two at a time and jogged through the kitchen and hallway. When he made it to the door and looked into the peephole he smiled and opened the door. "Hey girl, come on in!"

Adrianna walked in and looked at Desmond who put on a sincere smile while closing the door. "Have a seat," he said while he plopped on the living room couch.

Adrianna walked over to the couch and sat in the corner, turning her body to face him. "What's up Desmond? A couple days ago you were distant and let me walk out of here talking that 'it is what it is' crap," Adrianna said.

"Oh it still is sweetheart, nothing's changed," he said while reaching in his pocket.

Adrianna watched his hand and shifted her weight, making Desmond stop. "What's wrong with you? You act as if I am about to pull a piece out of this narrow jean pocket!"

"I don't know what you are about to pull out," Adrianna said with a smirk. "Your hand is not close enough to pull out your dick. So the only other things I can think of are a condom, some money or a credit card."

Desmond laughed and removed his hand from his pocket and placed his hand face down on the empty section of the couch that separated them. When he moved his hand Adrianna's eyes widen then narrowed within seconds. Having caught her expression changing Desmond stared at her, a frown developing on his face. "You wrote this note," he said.

"I don't know what you are talking about," Adrianna said as she began to stand.

"Sit your ass down," Desmond commanded. His tone startled Adrianna who sat back down and looked away. "You wrote this note telling me to slow my roll and slipped it in my locker! How in the hell did you get into the male staff locker room without getting caught?"

"I did not go inside the locker room," Adrianna shouted. "I gave the note to someone to slip it in."

"WHO," Desmond shouted, his face showing more frustration.

"I gave the note to one of the nurses and I guess she gave it to one of the doctors and lied about it being an important note. So the guy slipped it through the vent," she said.

Desmond was fuming and could not wait to kick this nut job out of his house. "Wait, a female friend of mine got a text message earlier today and thought it was from me. Did you do the text?"

Adrianna got quiet.

Desmond stood up and looked down at her. "Get up and get out," he said while unlocking the door.

"Desmond I did not mean to get access to your account! Remember you gave me a phone as part of your package plan when we were tight!" Desmond remembered and at the same time decided it was time to get out of that contract and buy a new cell phone, no package deals for other folks either. "I would not have done all of this if you weren't running around with another chick," she continued and further admitted to doing what she did after one of the nurses told her.

"I don't recall us or whoever I am with being a relationship Adrianna! We had a past in the past and were supposed to be friends but you kept bringing yourself to me. And I am not one to turn down something offered."

Adrianna blinked after that remark and walked to the door. "It was Melanie," she said, "It was Melanie who happened to see you at the Wake Up Call talking to a former patient! Melanie was coming out of the restroom in the back and saw you smiling and talking to the woman. And she figured something was up when you left and walked back to that woman's table."

Desmond shook his head and pushed his security door open. "Bye Adrianna. This friendship…is done."

Chapter 23

Desmond was working the overnight shift so he did not show up at Midwest until 8 p.m. for the 9 p.m. sign-in. Just as he was walking the hallway towards the locker he noticed Nurse Melanie leaving one of the surgery waiting rooms. Her eyes were going over an open folder. "I can easily report you and that male colleague of yours for harassment."

The nurse froze in her tracks and looked in the direction of the voice. Seeing Desmond standing inches from her with a stone expression shook her off kilter. It was obvious that Adrianna called or text her to warn that Desmond knew about the game. "I should write out a report and keep it on file for leverage if your nosy ass pisses me off again," Desmond said as he stepped into her space and lowered his voice. "I am a grown ass man and you need to grow up instead of playing the helpful sidekick to Adrianna and your cousin. Find something else to occupy your time. Go get you a man and open your legs once in a while to relax because your fingers or that vibrator is not working. But stay out of my business!"

Nurse Melanie's face was so red it looked burgundy, but she did not open her mouth to argue or give a smart remark. Instead she nodded and stepped away from Desmond and quickly walked away.

Chapter 24

"I solved the mystery behind the text message you received and the note that was in my locker."

It was Friday evening and Desmond got the weekend free after working extra shifts to compensate for last week. He called Chanale who was about to put some coated catfish nuggets into a deep skillet popping with hot vegetable oil. A medium size pot of spaghetti with meat sauce was already cooked and waiting to be served with the nuggets.

"What was the solution detective," Chanale asked while laughing.

"The note and the text were from the same person. A girl I once had a relationship with a while back," he said.

Chanale listened while carefully placing the nuggets into the hot oil. She grabbed a strainer spoon and turned the nuggets over as they browned before stepping away from the stove to let them cook. As he talked Chanale wondered if she should even bother keeping contact with Desmond. She already figured he was a player because of his looks and the fact that he was in the beginnings of being a doctor.

Doctors meant money and prestige and women, mostly those in the medical field who are single, divorced or looking for some side action, are always eyeing the good looking doctors. She knew this for a fact; one time when her mother was in the hospital there were nurses and nurse aides always hanging around the floor where her mother was. It was more than the appointed staff at times and the reason was this male specialist who was really good looking. And he happened to have her mother for a patient. The doctor looked to be in his late forties and had wavy hair, a beard and dimples. She noticed whenever she visited her mother how the nurses made sure they were on call during his shift. They would act like they were so extra attentive to her mother.

Even her mother noticed how good looking the doctor was and she was not fooled by the nurses who drooled when he was on the floor. So it did not surprise her that Desmond would have his share of fans and this Adrianna chick was just bold and stupid. "Chanale are you still there," Desmond said.

"Yes, I was listening while frying these catfish nuggets," she said.

"Oh this time I am the one interrupting your cooking," he said with a laugh. "I'll let you go but...can I stop by so we can finish the conversation?"

Chanale paused while taking the nuggets out of the pan and placing them in a bowl lined with a paper towel. "I really don't feel like company tonight Desmond. I just want to eat my dinner and relax because it's been a crazy and busy week."

Desmond tapped his fingers on the coffee table thinking he should have gone to Chanale's first before telling her about Adrianna. "OK well you have a good night and maybe I can call you tomorrow."

Chanale said her goodbye and hung up. She went to the cabinet and grabbed the hot sauce and went to her plate where she put a large spoonful of spaghetti and meat sauce covered with melted American cheese slices on top. She scooped some of the catfish nuggets and grabbed a fork from the drawer and went to the table. She went back to the refrigerator for a pop.

Grabbing the remote Chanale pointed towards the flat screen and clicked on a channel with nothing but old school cartoons and plopped in the kitchen chair. Cartoons, fish and spaghetti was her escape tonight and the fuel for what she needed to do about Desmond.

****

Desmond woke up just before noon Saturday, jumping out of bed and walking to the bathroom. An hour after his daily routine he walked back into his bedroom and dried off as the television gave him a weather report on a midseason fall day. While finding something to wear and then making up his bed Desmond thought about Chanale and last night's phone conversation. Just from the tone in her voice he knew she was having second thoughts about him. At the moment he could not blame her but he also wanted to prove that he did not have a bunch of crazy women chasing him. He thought about stopping by her apartment unannounced with a bottle of wine and some flowers. Just as he was about to call a florist to create a bouquet the phone rings. "Hello? Oh hey dad," he said.

"Hey son I was just checking on you. I had heard from you in a few days but I knew you were working so I did not disturb you," the elder Richards said.

"It's not a problem dad. If you ever need me you have all of my numbers on speed dial," Desmond said with a laugh.

His father laughed harder. "Listen son what are you doing today? Are you working later or is this a free weekend? I figured we spend some time together; see one of those matinees and get a bite to eat." Desmond paused before answering. "Or do you have an afternoon date?"

"No dad I'm free. Can we get something to eat first? I woke up about an hour ago and I am really hungry."

"Fine by me but hurry up; you know my stomach has an eating schedule!"

Desmond arrived at Silver Linings twenty minutes later noticing his father waiting in the security building. Danny Richards was standing at the picture window and spotted his son pulling up at the gate and signaled the guard that he was leaving. The guard nodded and watched him walk to the car and waved at Desmond. Desmond jumped out of the driver's side of the SUV and walked around to the driver's side to open the door for his father. "Thank you Desmond."

Desmond got back to the driver's side, climbed in and fastened his seatbelt. "I figured we stop at that restaurant that serves the liver and onions you enjoy so much," Desmond said while backing out of the gate entrance, shifted gears and pulling off.

Danny nodded while patting his knee to the jazz station his son found on the satellite radio. They arrived at the restaurant twenty minutes later and settled into a booth.

A waitress stopped at their booth pouring water in their glasses and handing them menus before walking away. "Well you already know what you are ordering," Desmond said while smiling at his father. The waitress returned five minutes later and Desmond ordered the liver and onions special for his father and chicken and waffles for himself and iced tea for both. The waitress took their menus and walked away.

"So…are you dating," Danny asked.

Desmond looked at his father and chuckled. "Not really. I mean I would not call it dating…"

His father raised an eyebrow and then nodded. "Getting free milk I see."

Desmond's eyes widened at his father's bluntness.

"I'm old son not ignorant. I had my fair share of free milk before I met your mother. But your mother was not passing any free milk my way. She had to be courted and chased so I put on my running shoes," he said while laughing loudly.

Desmond tilted his head back and joined his father's laughter on that remark. "Missy Lewis was not trying to give up anything without a reason so I worked hard to keep her attention on me. She was seeing a couple of guys every now and then but I stepped in and proved to her that she could tell those other brothers to go somewhere. And within a year that's just what she did."

Desmond nodded at the knowledge his father shared. He did not know his mother had it like that. Then again she was a gorgeous woman and men always did a double take, even when his father was with her. His father did not mind the looks because she was focused one hundred percent on him and he never had to worry.

"I guess I take a little bit after her huh? Maybe I have not found the one to grab and keep my attention," Desmond said.

The waitress returned with a tray and placed their orders and glasses of iced tea in front of them before leaving. Father and son said a brief prayer before digging in.

"Well you are a mixed combination of both of us," Danny said while cutting into a piece of liver. "You favor your mother, especially with the smile and the cheekbones and those dark eyes. I am in there somewhere. You have a lot of energy and when you make up your mind on something you usually go after it. I think that's a little bit of me in you," his father said with a wink.

Desmond laughed and raised a forkful of chicken and waffle to his mouth. "Well there is a woman I've taken out and spend a little time with," Desmond continued between bites. "She works at a law firm here as a paralegal. In fact we met at the hospital."

His father looked up. "Was she at the hospital helping her boss chase ambulances?"

Desmond had to fight choking from a mouthful of food. "No dad," he said while laughing. "She was in a car accident and I was assisting Dr. Monroe! She wasn't seriously hurt but they kept her a couple of days just in case. And during her stay I was always assisting her well- being."

"Mmmhmmm," his father said as he continued to eat his liver and onions with garlic mashed potatoes and broccoli on the side.

"So you just happen to hang around and help with the monitoring of this female patient."

"Well I am a medical resident," Desmond said ignoring the slight sarcasm from his father.

"Well it sounds to me that she may be a nice young lady."

"Well, she is five years older than I am dad."

"She's still a young lady as far as I am concerned," his father said with a wink. "Another older woman huh? Sounds like you are bouncing between age groups. What happened to that Adrianna girl?"

Desmond rolled his eyes at the mention of her name. "She's out of the picture for good."

His father looked at him and shrugged his shoulders. "OK so are you just seeing this paralegal for fun?"

"Yeah, there are no strings attached." Danny Richards took a sip of iced tea while watching his son's face.

Desmond was pausing more than usual, especially since the conversation subject was the opposite sex. "Looks like she is on your mind, Desmond."

Desmond looked at his dad and grabbed the small hot pitcher of syrup for the waffles. "She is; but it's no big deal. We are just kicking it," he said.

His father nodded officially ending that conversation. He knew when Desmond was ready to have a complete talk about a female it will happen. "So I was thinking about seeing one of those action movies playing right now. I feel like seeing some explosions and car chases," Danny said.

Chapter 25

Chanale spent Saturday cleaning her apartment and doing laundry. She thought about calling Desmond and telling him to stop by but changed her mind. He was probably busy or hanging out with friends; maybe even on a daytime date. Why was she even thinking of him! Well for one, she was having flashbacks of all of the times they had sex. The sex was great but what did she expect from a younger man even if only by five years? She had lucked out in getting with a younger man who knew what he was doing with what he had. And undoubtedly other women benefitted from that carnal knowledge. "What'd you expect? He had to learn how to have sex from a girl or a woman! Can't expect him to just know all of the moves naturally," she thought to herself.

While folding another load of laundry the phone rang. Chanale checked the monitor screen which read unidentified caller and decided to let it go to voicemail. Two minutes later the phone rang again and again no identification appeared on the screen. Five minutes later…

"Hello! Who is this?"

No one responded from the other end. Chanale repeated the greeting and eventually hung up. She checked to see if any voicemail messages were recorded and none appeared on the screen. She resumed folding her laundry when the phone ranged again. This time Chanale snatched the receiver off the cradle and hit the loudspeaker button. "Who the hell is this messing with my phone?" She looked at the monitor and it still read unidentified caller. "Whoever this is you need to stop fucking with me! I am not the bitch to mess with," Chanale shouted and hit the button to disconnect the call.

Another 15 minutes went and the phone was jumping again. Chanale picked up the receiver and held it while silence filled the phone line. "Adrianna!"

Within seconds the other line disconnected and Chanale slammed the receiver down. She picked up the receiver and dialed Desmond's cell phone. Desmond had dropped his father off an hour ago and was home checking e-mails on his laptop when his ringtone blasted. He knew it wasn't Adrianna because he blocked her numbers and ability to access his cell and land phone lines. He smiled when he read Chanale's name on his screen.

"Hey Chanale! How are you…?"

"When Adrianna hacked your cell phone the bitch must have pulled my number from your directory," Chanale said angrily.

"Wait, what happened?"

"She's been calling my phone in the apartment Desmond. Someone was calling here and they blocked their number. There were four calls and by the fifth call something told me to yell Adrianna. When I did, a dial tone hit real quick!"

Desmond ran his hand over his face. "I am sorry about that Chanale."

"See sorry is not going to cut it Desmond! You need to call and tell her real quick that I am too old to play high school bullshit! I am not blocking or changing my numbers. If that childish bitch is so bad she needs to come and see me. Then she will end up being one of your patients," Chanale shouted in Desmond's ear.

Desmond tried to calm Chanale down, promising her that he will talk to Adrianna. "I will call her tonight Chanale right after I hang up from you. Then maybe I can come over and we can talk…"

"NOPE," Chanale interrupted. "You are not coming over here Desmond! I don't feel like talking or doing anything else. In fact, we need to just keep it moving. I've thought about this situation since last night and I am not trying to be in a triangle, square, circle, nothing."

Desmond tried to interject but he could tell Chanale was not in a negotiating mood. "What we had was fun but I am not trying to get caught up in some shit or shall I say, some more shit! It was nice getting together with you but no, I am staying drama free. You just talk to that little girl!"

Desmond held the cell phone as he heard Chanale hang up. He immediately called Adrianna who blocked his access. Desmond flung the phone on the couch and suddenly remembered he could use the work cell phone since she did not have that number. He walked in his bedroom and grabbed that phone off the nightstand.

Adrianna picked up on the second ring. "Hello?"

"I told Chanale to file a police report against you," Desmond lied. "She will file in the morning unless you tell me you will stop with the damn prank calls. Not only will she file a report, I will visit your job and talk to your boss about your childish behavior."

A slew of cuss words assaulted his ear but she said she would stop calling.

"I mean it Adrianna. I will have a talk with your boss if you continue to trip out!" Desmond hung up and made a mental note to turn in his cell phone an end the package contract Monday before going in to work.

He called Chanale back.

"Yes Desmond," she said still angry.

"I talked to her and she is not going to harass you anymore," he said.

"Thank you, goodbye," Chanale said.

"Wait Chanale; I really don't want us to stop talking to each other."

"Desmond I've been on this planet five years longer than you and I have been through the game playing and messing around. While you are the first younger man I have dealt with, right now I am ready to just count this as an experiment."

Desmond looked at his phone. "Damn…an experiment? You sound like you were some chemist and I was a lab mouse in a cage."

"Look," Chanale sighed, "it is what it is."

Desmond recognized that saying in an instant. "Well, all younger men aren't like what you think Chanale."

"Yeah but Desmond…are you the type of younger man I think you are?" Desmond got quiet and hung up. He stood in the living room in deep thought and came to the conclusion that it was what it was. And she was not the first older woman…and will unlikely be his last.

Denyce

Chapter 1

Denyce slowly opened her eyes. Rays from the sun trickled through delicately thin lace curtains and onto her tawny-brown skin. This was the first morning she had allowed herself to forget her alarm clock in God knows how long and it felt so good. Entangled in crème color satin sheets she glanced at the time: 7:00 am. God, she thought, only I would think of waking up at 7 am as sleeping in. She closed her eyes again and embellished in the sweetness of lingering sleep.

Seconds later a hand touched her and began tracing a line from her hip to her ribs and back around her waist. Denyce let out a contented sigh. *Brandon Gordon.*

Their clothing lay strewn across the floor, evidence of last night's passionate romp. Their first official 'date' was a success. They went out to eat at *Mon Ami Gabi*, a French Bistro that Brandon's boss recommended and talked about life, love and about dreams. They even went as far as talk about their exes. She had put him off for quite some time, worrying over their age differences.

Denyce reminisced about the 48 hours before her hot session with Brandon when she hosted a 'girls' night in' with friends, Charlize and Natasha.

"Oh, get over yourself, woman!" Charlize said. The drinks flowed as Denyce endured her friends' drilling her to let that young, fine piece of chocolate work her body. "Have you seen the ass on that man? Damn! Women would literally kill to catch his eye!"

"I just don't know!" Denyce replied. "He's just so…"

"Young?" Natasha said. "Girl, listen: nowadays, there isn't 10% of the population out there that would be offended by a woman of your maturity," she winked for emphasis, "to seek out a sexy younger man like Brandon. A woman has needs!"

They had all laughed then. "I guess," was all Denyce could reply. And wasn't Natasha right anyways? A woman does have needs, and who are those 10% to tell her how to live her life and who to love? Yet she was still torn: she had spent her life working her ass off for her position at the company, setting aside all that lovey-dovey crap for independence, power, and wealth. And at $150K a year she couldn't complain.

"Woman, I know you have got to be lonely," Charlize added. "I don't know the last time you actually had a companion in your life. And you know how you chew men up and spit them out once they've seen your bed and tasted a bit of that cocoa."

Natasha choked on her drink and playfully slapped Charlize's arm. "Girl you're gonna kill me with this drink!

Denyce has every right to take a man into her bed, and I personally think she has been smart about every decision she's made. She's forty-five …"

"Forty-three!" Denyce interrupted. "At least let me stay 43 until my next birthday, please!"

"Forty-three," Natasha emphasized, "look at what she has made for herself. This beautiful townhouse didn't just remodel itself, that Porsche Cayenne she has in that garage didn't drive itself off the lot, and those men that find their way into her bed aren't holding this woman back from being or having anything she wants in life. Far as I can tell, she's got it made."

"Thank you, Natasha," Denyce said while tapping her wine glass to Natasha's. "And you're damn right!

No one tells this woman what to do, and you can bet your life I ain't washing no man's dirty underwear!"

Laughter filled the room, but Charlize's comments drummed Denyce's ears like a bad hangover. Loneliness and companionship are two words that are complete opposites and yet she knew one of those words too well.

A full week didn't go by before she'd finally decided to call him. "Hello, Brandon?"

"Denyce?" *How did he know it was me? Did he seriously know the sound of my voice already?*

Her pause must have given her surprise away. "Sorry," he exclaimed, "Caller ID."

"Right," she faltered. "I was just calling… "

"To tell me that you are turning me down yet again for another date," Brandon said and sighed heavily through the phone and in her ear.

"No. Actually I wanted to know if you are still interested in taking me out."

Brandon paused as if waiting to hear Denyce yell, "Psych!" and hang up laughing at his ignorance. "OK…you're serious? Me and you going on a date?"

"Well, maybe not a date. More like a casual get-together," she said.

"So it would not be a date?" Clearly he was confused. *What is this woman getting at? Does she like me or not? It's not that complicated.*

"Sorry," she finally blurted out. "Yes, a date, I guess. Are you still interested?"

"Absolutely, I am. Let's meet at the French Bistro on the lake. See you there for dinner at 7 o'clock," he had answered.

Her hands shook as she hung up the phone, and she fell back onto her bed in convulsive giggles. *I'm so glad this man can't see me right now*, she thought, *I am such a fool*!

On the other end, Brandon let out a roaring "HELL! YEAH!" and leapt into the air, his yellow hard hat nearly falling off his head. His foreman Nick glanced up from his tablet, looked at Brandon and smiled, assuming exactly what had transpired.

Despite their nerves, the date had run smoothly. They chatted awkwardly at first, but as the night went on and the wine calmed their nerves and made them more confident, the conversation was easier and much bolder.

"So how old are you exactly?" Brandon asked.

"How young are you, exactly?" Denyce asked.

"Does it matter?"

"It might. Do you really want to be with a woman who is almost fifteen years older than you?"

"You're only twelve years older than me," he said. He looked at her, his dark eyes piercing her soul. "Someone once said 'love knows no boundaries.' If you're really asking me, I'd say age is just another boundary created by society, by culture, to make us afraid. I'm not allowing so-called boundaries to keep me from doing those things. I do what I want, and I do it with all my heart. Then again, it could be the wine talking," he winked.

"But doesn't that leave the door open for you to get hurt?" Denyce asked. "I know I haven't been living like that, not in that way." She paused when Brandon gave her a quizzical look. "Don't get me wrong; I am a strong woman. I know – or at least I knew – what I wanted, but when you open yourself to that kind of vulnerability, that level of trust –" she glanced away, looking out towards the darkness of the lake, "It's so daring, yes, but it's also dangerous."

"So you're saying you've never let anyone in before, in here…" Denyce watched as Brandon placed his right hand on his heart. She inhaled sharply when he reached over with his right hand and grabbed her hand and gently placed it on his chest. "I'll let you in here Denyce…but this time, I'm not going to be the only one trusting. You got to let me in, girl. Let me in."

Her hand was cold against his chest, but as he held her hand to his heart he felt it warming. She felt it too, the coldness leaving, the resistance falling away. His heartbeat beneath her fingertips was melting her own heart. She was letting him in.

Her bed was a little over six blocks away, and she could feel it calling. He had no idea where she lived, and he didn't care; it was enough to finally be close to her, this woman who had stirred up his mind like fall leaves on a windy day. He couldn't get enough of her. There was something about her. She was frigid in a sexy way, strong, and fierce. Guarded in a way that he wished he learned to be. He had watched her walk the first time they met, that cat-like saunter hidden beneath all the professionalism. *Mmm-mmm-mmmm!* he thought. *What I wouldn't do to get beneath that suit and figure this woman out.* She was like nothing he'd ever had before, that was for sure. She's beautiful, older, mature, powerful – and not to mention financially set. And she obviously had class that went beyond her corporate position as well. She was a woman who took care of herself, which also meant she was high maintenance. *A woman like that would probably eat up every penny I have for her hair alone*, he laughed to himself, *but damn, she can sure put on a performance in those heels*. A woman like that would toss him out on his ass like a misbehaving schoolboy. But all he could think was, *Yes, Teacher. I'll obey every word that drips out of your honey lips.*

He was hired for a six-month stint at Walsh Construction as a temp worker, they called it. Most jobs Brandon previously held teetered between six months to yearlong contracts. It wasn't that he was a bad worker; on the contrary, he was always highly recommended. Unfortunately, with the economy struggling, so were many hard-working men. Foreign laborers were often willing to work for far less than he could settle for, and so the majority of permanent positions often went to lower paid workers. But this job at Walsh would have a higher payday than he'd ever anticipate, and it came the day Denyce Wright stepped on site.

Nick had approached him only two weeks into the job. "Brandon! Get your ass over here!"

Brandon set down the nail gun and walked over to the foreman's table. "What can I do you for Nick?" He asked.

Nick had his hands on his hips. A smaller man by nature, Nick was a nearly a foot shorter than Brandon's 6'1" frame, but Nick was also a second generation Russian with plenty of competence and power to make up for what he lacked in stature. "I got the Vice President of Sherls & Hughes popping over here in about ten minutes, and she's bringing the board with her. They want to size up the progress we're making and see whether or not we're on track as far as construction and scheduling is concerned."

Brandon threw Nick a puzzled look. "So…"

"So I want you to manage the crew while I'm leading the suits around. Keep it clean and the work movin', alright?"

"Sounds good, Boss."

"Get at it, then."

The Panthers Club

Brandon was on his way to supervise the construction crew when Denyce showed up. Nick handed her a hard hat and walked her to the window front. Eighteen floors up gave them a mind-boggling view of the city. Before Brandon could get his hands too dirty, Nick called him over again. "Brandon Gordon, this is Denyce Wright, Vice President of Sherls & Hughes and the person we answer to."

Brandon extended a rough, weathered hand and felt the cool, slender fingers slide into his palm. With a firm shake Denyce greeted him, "Pleasure to meet you, Mr. Gordon."

Five foot five, slender build, gorgeous shoulder-length, chestnut brown hair, with piercing green eyes and dressed in a dark navy blazer and knee length pencil skirt that fit her curves perfectly, Denyce left him nearly speechless. Yet he had managed to say hello. "Pleasure's all mine," he replied with a glimmer in his eye.

"Brandon," Nick interrupted, "what Ms. Wright here needs is a capable and strapping young man such as yourself to put on a good show for the board members when they get here."

"I see," Brandon replied.

"Basically, Mr. Gordon," Denyce started, "I'm going to need you to work in an area within eyeshot and earshot of our meeting, so that the board members can see that we've hired an efficient and competent contractor to handle the furbishing of our new offices."

"Furbishing," Brandon repeated while gazing a bit too long at the beautiful VP.

Sensing Brandon's inability to communicate properly, Nick cut in. "Ahem, Brandon just haul some of those two-by-sixes over here and build a partition during their talk. Nothing too fancy, but don't look stupid, either. We're trying to impress these guys."

"Got it, Boss," Brandon said with a wink at Nick. I'll get on it."

Several minutes later the board was on-site meticulously surveying various areas of the project until finally making their way to Brandon. Denyce let her eyes shamelessly follow his movements while the board members also watched him, albeit for business purposes. Denyce thought of earlier, how was courteous during their brief conversation and at the same time, letting a lingering moment occur. *Was he flirting when he said 'pleasure's all mine'? He couldn't have been; I'm old enough to be his mother for sure.* But the more she looked, the more she liked. And his brawny frame was certainly making its mark on her mind: muscles rippling with every movement, sweat glistening on his reddish-brown skin, and a face to go with it – he looked like he stepped out of a magazine. He was younger than her, yes, but he was far from a boy. His hands deftly handled the wood and by the way he handled the perfect lines in an efficient manner, it was obvious that his skills and mannerisms stood head and shoulders above the rest of the crew. If anyone was going to impress the board members, it would be Mr. Gordon.

After an hour the board members seemed pleased and found their way to the elevators. However, Denyce lingered, opting to catch up with them later. She wanted to thank Nick for his cooperation and let him know that the board members were pleased with what they saw. But mostly, she wanted another moment with Brandon, no matter how brief.

She walked over to the foreman and stretched out her hand. "I wanted to let you know how much we appreciated the last minute tour," she said as Nick shook her hand. "Be sure to thank Mr. Gordon for his participation. He seems to be a great employee.

Nick let go of her hand and waved towards Brandon. "Just head over there and tell him yourself, Ms. Wright. I'm sure he won't mind the break."

Denyce turned in the direction of Nick's hand and glimpsed at Brandon. She cleared her throat as if in need of a glass of water. "Yes, Nick, you are right," she smiled, "it's only fair that I personally thank him."

Denyce then drew a breath and began walking towards Brandon with what felt like mock confidence. The closer she got to him, her stomach began to flutter and she felt a touch of perspiration on her forehead. Each step she made felt like lead yet her knees were ready to give. I know my ass is not about to fall out! She shook her head to snap out of it. Thankfully the man was too focused on the power drill to hear her coming, let alone see she was falling apart. "Mr. Gordon!"

Startled, Brandon set down his drill and stood up to meet her. Denyce glanced quickly at his muscular arms as the veins in his biceps worked to calm down. "Ms. Wright. I thought you and your colleagues were already gone." He tried to hide his surprise that she would be singling him out yet again.

Denyce gave him a warm smile and hoped he would not notice her bottom lip was quivering, just a little bit. "I wanted to thank you personally for your efforts here. I know it's a bit unorthodox, but you've made quite the impression on the board today," she said. Denyce noticed that her palms were now sweating and fought the urge to wipe her hands on her skirt.

"Did I make a good impression on the board…or just, you?" Brandon said. He knew it was a bit cocky of him to be this bold with the CEO and he usually wasn't that bold with women. Denyce made him want to risk getting fired.

Denyce stifled a smile. "I was also very impressed with the work you did today, and again, I think about you."

Brandon laughed. "You do, do you?"

"I mean," she stammered, "I meant I thank you." *Damn it! What am I doing!*

"Ahhh," he smiled, "I see. Well, it really was my pleasure."

Wow! So he did mean it in a flirting way! Denyce tried to keep her composure, but she could feel her cheeks burning. "Have a good day, Mr. Gordon."

Denyce coolly and quickly turned away to hide her embarrassment and nerves. She rushed away from the construction worker, no longer caring that her four inch navy pumps were giving her feet hell with pain. She had to get away before she made a bigger fool of herself.

As she reached the elevators she pushed the down button with a growing intensity. *God, please send this elevator up here right this minute!* But before the elevator arrived, Brandon jogged up beside her again.

"Ms. Wright," he asked, his own voice feeling shaky.

"Yes, Mr. Gordon." She felt weak in the knees again. What had gotten into her? A strong, assertive woman like herself shouldn't be this shaky with men. What was it about this man?

"Can I have your number?" *Bold move, playa. This could literally cost me my job; what the hell am I thinking?*

The elevator doors dinged open and without hesitation Denyce nearly leaped forward onto the marble flooring before her. Before the doors could close, she held her breath and passed him her business card, their eyes meeting one final time before the doors shut.

****

After dinner at *Mon Ami Gabi*, they walked to Denyce's house, taking the scenic route along the lake. A light breeze suddenly picked up and Denyce pulled her coat a little tighter. As warm as she felt inside, her skin was covered in goose bumps, half from excitement and the other from the night's chill. They talked for a while, but soon a peaceful silence overtook them. Brandon's heart raced as he thought of taking her hand, but she folded her arms across her chest to block the cold. His chance had passed.

"Listen," he cautiously started, "I know what you meant about getting hurt."

Denyce looked up at him in the darkness and bits of streetlights and the light of the moon reflected in his eyes. She struggled to decipher if it was sincerity or naivety in his words. Either way Brandon moved her in ways she couldn't imagine with any other man.

Brandon continued, "I have been hurt – many times - because I put myself out there, because I trusted too many, too much. I wish I could say that it was worth it every time." He peered out at the blackness of the lake, a thousand stars reflecting off the waves. "I don't know what it is that makes me that way, but I don't think it's a bad thing, to love like that, regardless of the hurt. I think every woman deserves that kind of love." He looked at her then, willing her to understand that he was already loving her as much after such a short time. As a matter of fact, Brandon had started loving her from the first moment he'd laid eyes on her. He wanted her to know that she was worth it and that she didn't have to be afraid. He gently grabbed her arms, unfolding them and placed her hand in his.

Despite his gentleness Denyce was still afraid of him and his intense nature. It was one thing to let someone in for the first time; it was another to have someone so full of love look at you that way while walking beneath a moonlight sky and on a first date nonetheless. For God's sake, she felt like a teenager with the way he made her feel. It was all encompassing, and wonderful, and terrifying all in the same moment.

When they reached her townhouse and stopped at the door, it was a good five minutes before Brandon finally said something. "I better be sending you off to bed, Ms. Wright; you've got a long day ahead of you no doubt. Miss Big Time VP of Sherls & Hughes can't take a day off, can she?" he smiled. "God knows it was hard enough just getting you away from work to take you to dinner."

Denyce flinched at his attempt to be lighthearted. She had been extremely busy lately; managing the building project for the expansion along with her usual business dealings had literally overtaken her life. "You're more right than you know, Brandon," she conceded, "I can't remember the last time I slept in. I'm up every morning at five, and its go-go-go until eleven at night. This is honestly the first breath of peace I've had in a very long time."

"Peace is good, Denyce. Sleeping in would be good for you. You got to let your hair down once in a while." With that he ran his hand through her shoulder-length, chestnut hair. She looked up at him, her hazel eyes meeting his as his hand gently rested on the back of her neck. "You're an incredibly beautiful woman. You deserve more than this in life; you deserve to have peace... and love, happiness."

Denyce felt her body gravitate towards him and needed to wrap her arms around his firm body. She wanted to feel his lips pressed gently yet firmly against hers. Men prior to Brandon were nothing but one night stands...a thing she tossed away with the slam of a door behind them. But with Brandon she understood that he loved without restraint and by going forward from this point on meant commitment. It meant companionship. She wouldn't be able to toss him out in the morning, and she might not want to.

She handed him the door keys and as the last lock was undone, Denyce used her body to push the door open while pulling him inside.

Sunlight peeked in through Denyce's bedroom blinds. Brandon head nuzzled into her neck. "See, I told you," his smooth voice whispered in her ear, "Sleeping in is a good thing, Love."

"Mmm-hmmm," Denyce mumbled in happiness. "But you know what's better than sleeping in?" She bantered as she turned her body to his, "Waking up next to you."

"That's my woman," Brandon smiled as he pulled her closer, burying his face in her neck. "You smell good in the morning," Brandon panted as his mouth moved to her breast. He grabbed her leg and brought it up over his waist. "I could just eat you up. Mmmmm-mmmm." He returned to her neck and released a low growl against her skin.

Denyce smiled as the heat from his words and mouth traveled throughout her body.

"Having you off work for just one day is enough to make me the happiest man in the world."

Denyce felt her lower body pulsate against his thigh as his hands clutched at her body. She nudged her mouth close to his face, letting her lips brush his, the anticipation building. Suddenly, his hand reached around the back of her neck as he pulled her mouth onto his. Her tongue explored his mouth as his tongued teased hers in return. She indulged in the eagerness and passion not felt with a man her age or older. She gripped Brandon's muscular back, pulling him closer until he was on top of her. She tenderly wrapped her legs around his waist, her ankles locked just under his firm buttocks. At that moment their eyes locked on each other, listening as they inhaled each other's air. His hand moved down her waist, slowly inching lower until he felt her heat on his fingertips. Denyce's body moved into his hand, desperately begging him for more. He answered her body's pleas, and together they moved, her body writhing beneath him, his masculine frame rocking with her and bringing each other to another world.

Brandon shifted his body so that his mouth would hover to her breasts and immediately took one in while his tongue caressed her nipple.

Denyce tensed up as Brandon continued to take turns giving her breasts his utmost attention while his fingers moved rhythmically further below. She moaned loudly, a signal that he was hitting the right spots. He suddenly pulled his hand away, letting his body meet hers. Feeling him enter her, Denyce arched her back in pleasure encouraging Brandon to push her threshold further than she's ever been. Wanting her to truly feel every inch of him, Brandon sat up and pulled her on top of him and eased her into a straddling position. They embraced as she moved up and down, pulsing rhythmically. Feeling him throb inside of her, Denyce cupped Brandon's face, her expression contorting in satisfaction as she gazed into his eyes, her pleasure feeding his. Slowly their panting began to harmonize and they moved faster, harder. Brandon guided her while gripping her bottom as she rode him; reaching, grasping, until together they cried out, their bodies achieving orgasm together, pulsing, letting each entry flood over them like a wave of euphoria.

Chapter 2

Brandon walked into the house nervous as hell. He could hear Denyce in the shower and his heart beat faster. *Damn, she's home early*, he thought, *what the hell is she doing here?* He considered leaving before she'd hear him and call his name but that would be a waste of time, so he stayed. The guys would be here any moment and he prayed she'd keep the water running until he could get everything hidden. Denyce might work an unbelievable amount of hours each week, but it was nearly impossible to sneak anything by her.

As Brandon was about to lose his cool, two figures appeared at the door. Before they could ring the bell he threw the door open with his VISA card in plain sight. The delivery guys were about to strike a conversation with him but caught a look on his face clearly reading 'Don't say shit!' They rushed inside with the boxes and within seconds of Brandon swiping the card and signing the tablet they watched the door shut in their faces. As Brandon locked the door he heard the shower shut off and pondered rushing the stairs to block Denyce from coming down when her cell phone signaled for attention. He soon heard her muffled but angry voice as she blessed out who he could only assume was her Chief Operating Officer Trevor Langfield. Brandon mentally thanked the asshole for giving him at least 15 minutes to complete his surprise mission.

Denyce stood in the middle of the bedroom with a towel tightly wrapped around her body. Her hair was dripping wet but she was oblivious to the dampness as she lit a stream of profanity in Trevor's ear. Trevor dropped the ball on a major contract – one of the largest ever – from Powell and Sons and before one drop of ink could land on the signature line, the company was about to go with another marketing firm.

She had to jump in on the eleventh hour and take the client on a very expensive lunch meeting to get a second chance. And with that second chance came longer hours attached to an additional two-week deadline to smooth things over. This and trying to adjust to Brandon moving into her house was too much to bear. Or so she thought until she realized Brandon forgot their six-month anniversary.

Just the thought of him letting this important day slip from his mind made her hot enough to dry off from head to feet. She remembered Brandon talk about plans to be with the work crew and celebrating the halfway mark of the building project for Sherls and Hughes. She frowned as she recalled him saying in a nonchalant tone to work late since he would not be home until well after midnight. So Trevor had to feel her wrath against Brandon.

"Janice was responsible for contacting Greg Powell about the details, including the negotiated price," Denyce said as her voice pitched higher. "Trevor, I don't care about whether or not Greg contacted Ravenhouse while we were negotiating! I don't care whether it was before we met with him, whether it was after or whether it was during…"

Brandon flinched from some of the heated conversation his girlfriend was having with a colleague and decided he need to move quickly on this surprise.

"Yes, of course this is very important…I am saying that Powell & Sons' negotiations with Ravenhouse are not our concern. It was our responsibility to make the client happy, to meet their needs and Janice failed to make sure that happened." Denyce rolled her eyes, snatched the towel off and paced back and forth in the bedroom as drops of water from her hair were airborne. "And you can bet your ass there will be repercussions for this complete fuck up come Monday morning! I don't have the time or the energy to discuss this with you right now, Trevor. I'll see you tomorrow, and we'll sort it out then!"

She slammed the cell phone shut and nearly threw it across the room before regaining some composure. She resisted the urge to throw herself onto the bed in a screaming fit. Everything seemed to be falling on her shoulders, and for the first time she felt she might not be willing to carry it. She wanted something, anything, to make her disappear, to make her forget the stress of her career. She smoothed her face with her hands and let them slide over the upper half of her nakedness then she stopped. She wanted Brandon.

Denyce sat up, grabbed her towel and used it to dry her hair while eyeing her phone on the bed. Should she interrupt his guys' night out with her drama or should she just wait until tomorrow. Working late hours always makes for awkward scheduling to get together. If she waited until tomorrow, he'd still be in bed by the time she was out the door heading to the office and their talk would have to wait until tomorrow evening. She could wait up tonight until he got home, but then he'd probably be drunk and incoherent, and fall asleep before she'd be able to get out what's going on. It also didn't help that he'd forgotten their anniversary. Should she bring that up as well or just keep him in the 'dog house' until he figures it out for himself? Six months in and basic relationship tactics still eluded her.

"THUD!" Denyce jerked her head up towards the ceiling just in time to hear a low scraping sound. She jumped from the bed and rushed to pick up a large African sculpture of a female that was long enough to make a weapon. Wielding it like a sword before her, she slowly made her way to the rooftop stairs, pausing at every step, eyes wide with terror. She threw open the roof door and screamed out, "Whoever's up here, I'm warning you! I'm armed, and I've called the police! So you better get the hell off my roof before I take your ass out!"

She had barely placed her front foot on the snow laden top step when suddenly a dark figure came around the corner. Denyce immediately closed her eyes and swung blindly with all her might.

"DENYCE!" Brandon's hands gripped her arms as he shouted for her to stop swinging. "WOMAN! It's me!"

Denyce opened her eyes and looked with shock at Brandon who stood half smiling, half terrified before her. "Mutha… Damn it, Brandon, what the hell are you doing home? And what are you doing on the roof?!"

"What the hell are you doing coming after a potentially dangerous robber in your bath robe and a $1,500 sculpture?"

Instantly they were overcome with relief, and Denyce threw herself into Brandon's arms.

"I thought you were out with Nick and the boys," she said.

He took her by the hand. "Come here," was all he replied.

Around the corner a pathway of white rose petals on a red carpet led to their rooftop greenhouse, where a candle-lit dining table with two chairs draped in fine linens awaited them. Bouquets of white and pink roses, mixed with fresh tulips and hyacinths, ferns and green hydrangeas surrounded the table creating a lush summer arrangement, the icy world outside looking in with envy. Tiny lights glimmered in thin netting covering the setting like a million stars lighting their meal. Candles were strategically placed throughout the greenhouse and added a warmth and glow that softened the mood. Music played quietly in the background and the table was perfectly set with gold-rimmed porcelain, gold place settings, and crystal wine glasses. On one of the plates lay a narrow, black velvet box.

Denyce felt her mouth fall open in surprise. "I … I don't know what to say," she stammered, half frozen in her bath robe, half at a loss for words.

"Don't say anything, baby," Brandon cooed in her ear. "I know you thought I was out with the boys tonight; I'm sorry I lied. I only wanted to make you happy."

Denyce felt her eyes get hot with tears. Brandon pulled her close and gently kissed her. "Baby what's wrong? Why are you crying?" He asked as he held Denyce tighter while kissing her tears away.

"I just had the most horrible day!" She began to sob. "Oh, God, I know I sound like such a drama queen right now, but Honey, I thought I was going to lose it. First work, and then you forgetting – "She let herself melt into his chest, the tears coming hot and fast.

"Oh, Baby, I am so sorry," he scooped her up in his arms. Denyce buried her face in his neck. "All this can wait," he stated, and carried her down the stairs to their bedroom. He gently laid her on the bed and gently untied her bathrobe. "Let me pamper you, woman." He raised her body and removed the bathrobe and eased her back on the bed. He stood by the bed and took off his shirt before climbing on the bed and lying down beside her. "Turn over, sweetie," he said and she did what she was told. He sat up and leaned down to place his hands on her smooth and curved back.

Denyce felt her body relax as Brandon's hands began to firmly massage her back. He then placed his hands firmly on her shoulders and used his weight to straddle above her hips. He resumed massaging her back and then moved to her neck. Unable to resist he lowered his head and placed his lips on her neck, lighting her skin with kisses. Without missing a beat, Brandon kissed her neck, shoulders and the delicate spots between her shoulder blades while kneading the tension away. He smiled as he heard her release a sigh from her lips. "That's it, baby, let me take care of you," he said. "You just relax in my arms, sweetie." His lips lightly kissed her spine and his hands moved steadily over her tired back. He could feel himself wanting more, but he refrained himself from giving in to his urges. This time it was all about Denyce and what she needed. His kisses and caresses continued down her back and he moved further down and leaned sideways to turn her on her back. He then began to massage her feet. Denyce felt the weight of work fall off her body and leave her mind. She opened her eyes and watched her man give her all the passion any woman could ever imagine. *How could this man possibly care so much for me?* She thought. *That sexy body, that face: my man is beyond good-looking. And he has an incredible heart, too. He's intelligent, thoughtful and insightful. He could have any woman he wants. Why me?*

Brandon continued to rub her feet, running his fingers between her delicate toes. "What's my girl thinking about?" he asked as she gazed at him so intently.

"I was just thinking: how the hell did I get such a good man?"

He released a low laugh. "How did I get such an amazing woman?" He placed her feet on the bed and crawled up to lay beside her. He adjusted his body to face her and rest a hand on her firm but smooth stomach.

Denyce moved closer to Brandon and reached to caress his chest before resting her hand against his now rapidly beating heart. "Mr. Brandon Gordon, I think I love you," she whispered while looking into his dark eyes.

"I think I love you, too," he replied, a smile playing at the corners of his mouth. He leaned forward and wrapped his arm around her until their bodies were pressed against each other. Without hesitation he let his mouth find hers and they explored each others' mouths…then bodies, as if it were the first time.

The next morning Brandon woke up and briefly watched Denyce sleep without disturbing her. After their time in bed last night, they had gone back up to the roof to enjoy the private dinner he had ordered for her. The five course meal was followed by a private dance, just the two of them under his makeshift blanket of stars. When Brandon thought about how far he and Denyce had both come since first starting out, he could only smile. *She was so uptight*, he remembered, *Woman walked and talked like she was some kind of futuristic robot.* In time his free-spirited nature rubbed off on her and she relaxed more. Mornings like this, when she allowed herself to sleep in, was becoming consistent in her life. Weekends, holidays, even the possibility of a vacation, was replacing her workaholic schedule. He knew that prior to coming into her life, Denyce would not think of being spontaneous. Now, only six months in and both of their lives were changing right in front of them for the better.

Brandon gently slipped out of bed and grabbed his running shoes nearby. He tipped to a chair across the room and grabbed a pair of sweats, stepping into them and the shoes. After throwing on a long-sleeved thermal shirt and hoodie, he eased out the room and walked to the back door. The November air hit him as soon as he opened the door but he rushed out and quietly closed the door behind him and took off towards Lincoln Park. Unlike Denyce, who felt when Old Man Winter shows up it was time to jog on a treadmill in a warm, toasty setting, Brandon preferred the sharpness of harsh winter air hitting his face, challenging him to either run harder or give up like a bitch. Brandon loved a challenge and the winds felt like a close friend pushing him, even when it was minus 10 degrees.

Brandon kept a steady pace as the sounds of his feet on the snow covered sidewalk were muffled with a slight crunch. The sky was still dark and despite the occasional sight of lit rooms in a few houses he passed, the silence was loud…and welcoming. He treasured running time like this as it was the calm before the storm of commuters, workers and vehicular noises. Even on a weekend morning the city would be bustling but at a slower pace. Brandon jogged until he reached South Pond and stopped to stretch his loosening muscles. His mind was clear, nearly blank as he focused on stretching his muscles, the tendons releasing their stiffness, the blood pulsing through his ears.

He took the path that would lead him to the lakefront trail because he wanted to run on the beach today. He could already feel his body temperature rising. If he were inside he'd be sweating with nothing on, begging the fan to turn its pitiful breeze into a frozen gale. He'd have to sit his head in the freezer for a good ten minutes afterwards, just to keep from getting brain fever if he had stayed home. But here, in the freshness of the chilly out of doors, he had automatic air conditioning. He pulled off his hood and let the steam escape, feeling the wind licking at his ears.

The lake was beautiful in the morning; its dark and mesmerizing countenance changed now into a frozen, parched, desert-like landscape with ice chunks forming at the shoreline. On the horizon the sun was fast approaching: hues of orange and red spilling out from what seemed like the other side of the Earth. Gordon continued to catch his breath, waiting for the white of the sun to peak over the edge and illuminate the darkness once more. As the sun light began to creep closer above the horizon, Brandon took off in a sprint, running as if he was challenging the sun to keep up. The faster he ran the higher the sun descended until its warm rays touched his face and his body. The winter sun's glare did not bother him as he picked up speed. The feeling was intense and comforting; it also opened Brandon's train of thought. Denyce…what was once frozen is now warm. Her icy demeanor is melting away and changing into something better, comforting. It was the perfect metaphor! He would have to share this with her when he returned. He resumed spending time with his other woman, Mother Nature.

Brandon entered the house an hour later and heard the shower running. He removed his running clothes while walking through the kitchen and to the laundry room where he tossed them into a hamper. Returning to the kitchen he opened the fridge and looked until he found the protein shake in the middle of the top shelf. He grabbed the carton and was about to drink from it when he remembered that Denyce hated when he did that. So he stepped over to the dishwasher, opened it and took out a clean glass. "Two brownie points for me," he said to himself before guzzling the glass down with a slice of whole grain bread.

"Brandon, is that you?" Denyce shouted down from the bedroom.

"Who else would it be, woman? You're expecting someone this early?" Brandon laughed.

"Actually, I am," she replied with sass. "Can you please let Trevor Langfield in when he gets here? He's dropping off some things, and I don't want to come down in my towel."

"Got it," Brandon said while trying to hide the disdain in his voice. *Trevor*, he thought with a sneer, *I can't stand that slime bag always trying to get his grubby little fingers all over my woman.* "Can you please let Trevor in?" He mocked. "You bet your pretty little ass I'll let him in. And if he so much as looks towards the stairs I'll…"

DING-DING-DONG-DING! The doorbell stopped him before he could finish his sentence. He strode over to the front door and swung it wide open, standing in front of the unwelcome guest with nothing but his Calvin Klein briefs. The expression on Trevor's face was between shocked and disappointment. He'd obviously hoped to see Denyce at the door…even went so far as dreaming to see her in a towel coming out of the shower. Brandon appearing in front of him in a pair of briefs and a scowl on his face slapped his wishful thinking on its ass. Trevor wore a pair of dark denim jeans and a grey cable knit sweater under a black wool coat. His closely cut hair was covered with a charcoal grey newsboy cap. He was a chestnut brown in skin tone with a strong jaw line and dark features. He kept his eyes on Brandon while removing his black leather gloves.

"Good morning, Brandon," Trevor managed to say through gritted teeth. "Is Denyce home?"

"She's busy," Brandon responded curtly.

Trevor shifted his weight. "Well, I'm supposed to drop off some work material. She said I could swing by."

Brandon didn't move. Beads of sweat glistened off his well defined body, his muscles still tense and pulsating from his run.

Trevor swallowed uncomfortably in the silence.

"Brandon" Denyce suddenly called down from the balcony. "Let the poor man in already! It's freezing out! I'll be down in a second."

Brandon stepped to the side, allowing just enough space for Trevor to awkwardly squeeze by. He didn't let his eyes drop from Trevor's gaze, but he struggled to remain steady and tried to be just as intimidating.

Brandon did a quick roam over Trevor's body and did not see a briefcase as the man entered their home. "So where's all this important work stuff. I don't see anything," Brandon huffed.

"It's in the car, Brandon. I wasn't about to haul it up to the house without first making sure I could leave it inside."

"Right," Brandon sneered, "and you just HAD to bring it over at seven in the morning on a Saturday."

"I'm assuming that's a rhetorical question," Trevor responded coolly, "but maybe that's too complicated a term for someone like you to understand."

"What's that supposed to mean?" Brandon barked, stepping closer to Trevor.

"Good morning, Trevor!" Denyce said as she wedged her body between them. She ignored the fact that Brandon was standing in his underwear as if they were a pair of heavyweight boxing shorts. She turned and faced Brandon with a fixed smile and glaring stare. "Brandon, baby, why don't you go hop in the shower. I'll take it from here."

Brandon was oblivious to Denyce's mock innocence and was still staring Trevor down. However, Trevor was unabashedly gazing at Denyce as her back was still facing him, his smile spreading as his eyes roamed to the curve of her hips. Denyce could feel the leech's eyes but needed to keep her man from being on the Saturday night news broadcast.

"Baby? Shower?" Denyce prodded, and Brandon reluctantly turned away and headed to the staircase. He slowed his pace while trying to catch what words was spoken before he closed the bathroom door.

"Sheesh!" Trevor exhaled. "You got to keep a leash on that one, Denyce!"

Denyce gave him a look of amusement. "Brandon? Oh he is just a bit protective. Plus, your timing is bad as he likes to relax on the weekends," Denyce chuckled. "And he likes to relax with me…his woman. He has nothing to worry about; we're good…real good." Trevor nervously cleared his throat after her last emphasis on being good.

"Yes, yes you two seem to be…real good. The lucky happy couple; a beautiful, intelligent woman and clearly a well built muscle of a young man living in their own beautiful world. Like that popular children's fairytale involving an over protective monster?"

A wave of discomfort washed over Denyce following Trevor's words and the arrogant smile he ended with. It was unlike him to be so petty. She masked her uneasiness with a smile. "So Trevor," she said, "the items?" Trevor walked backwards to the front door. "They're in my car. I'll run out and get them."

"Yeah you do that. That would be great."

Denyce hugged her body as she watched Trevor from the living room window. He pilfered around in the back seat for a minute or two before returning to the house empty-handed.

"So?" Denyce asked when he came back inside.

"So, it looks like I somehow grabbed the wrong box from my office yesterday. I'll have to just get you the files on Monday."

Denyce dropped her arms at her sides in frustration. "Seriously, Trevor?" Denyce asked. "You drove out all this way and brought the wrong box? That's quite an oversight."

"I'd say so," Trevor replied. "Sorry to bother you, Denyce. I'll see you Monday then." He turned for the door, and then paused. "Unless you want to just pop over to the office for a minute with me and grab the file so you can get started this weekend?"

Denyce looked at the clock. If she went with Trevor she couldn't possibly be back before Gordon was out of the shower, especially with the streets still needing to be plowed. He wouldn't be very happy about the arrangement.

"I tell you what, Trevor, it can wait." Denyce replied. "I'll see you Monday morning."

"Will do," he answered, and with that, he was out the door.

Denyce immediately headed upstairs to the master bathroom. "What the hell was that?" She shouted at Brandon while throwing the shower door open.

Brandon finished washing the soap off his face and turned to look at Denyce. "What do you mean, 'what was that'?" he played, a smirk creeping over his lips.

Denyce wasn't smiling. "You know what."

"I don't like that way that asshole looks at you," Brandon said.

Denyce put her hands on her hips and began tapping the tile floor with her foot. "What are you talking about?"

"Oh, come on, Denyce. You are the most intelligent woman I know and you're trying to play dumb at a game you already mastered." Denyce looked away.

Brandon turned off the shower and stepped out. "That asshole is just waiting for you to spread your legs so he can crawl in between them." Denyce shot a horrified look at him. "And in the meantime, he's undressing you with his eyes every chance he gets."

Denyce stormed into the bedroom with Brandon following close behind. He grabbed a towel and wrapped it around his waist.

"So you think I'm some kind of whore?" She suddenly exclaimed. "You're saying I can't keep my legs crossed tight enough to keep out someone you are only *assuming* is interested in me."

"No!" he replied instantly.

"Then what are you saying?" she shouted.

"This has nothing to do with you, Denyce," Brandon replied, "It's about that jerk of a co-worker of yours, and about all the crass things he's probably doing to you in his mind."

"Probably?" Denyce let out a sneer. "See, your problem is that you're just *assuming*. You just picking on someone who happens to work closely with me and you are letting jealousy get the better of you. You are a jealous child and you are trying control me. To top it off, you have no idea if he's interested in me or not, and you certainly have no clue as to what's really going on in his head."

Brandon threw his hands up in disbelief that Denyce was oblivious to Trevor's intentions. "Woman, you are blind. You are so blind! He is going to pounce on you the first chance he gets; wait and see, wait and see!"

Denyce felt her ears ringing and blood rushing in her face. Now she was the one in disbelief. After a night like last night, how could he be so ignorant just a few hours later? "How dare you!" she screamed at Brandon. "How dare you insult me in my home about a man with whom I am not interested! That man is my co-worker, my employee, and my friend. He has never done anything questionable to jeopardize our work relationship, and you honestly have no right to treat him the way you did this morning."

Brandon threw his hands up again. "Fine."

"Fine? That's your response?" Denyce gawked. "I want you to apologize."

"Apologize? Apologize for what?" Brandon laughed. "The day hell freezes over is the day I'll apologize to that creep."With that he walked into the closet and threw on a quick pair of jeans and another hoodie.

"What do you think you're doing?" Denyce blared.

"I'm getting dressed and I'm getting out of here." Brandon exited the bedroom and headed downstairs to the front door.

"Where are you going?" Denyce chased after him.

"Anywhere but here with you screaming in my ears!"

Brandon slammed the door, leaving Denyce standing there and fuming. The blood pounding in her ears along with the throbbing headache now developing was louder in the silence of her home. "SHIT!" she screamed and grabbed a crystal vase off a table by the door and hurled it at the wall in the foyer. Thousands of tiny shards of glass showered across the floor upon impact. Denyce's heart felt as if it were going to leap right out of her chest. *OH, that man pisses me off sometimes!* She thought. *I could just strangle him; wrap my little hands around his neck or slap the fire out of him! She roughly ran her hands through her hair and tried to take a deep breath. The effects from that massage the other night was long gone.* She stormed back upstairs to the master bedroom and threw herself on the bed.

By the time Brandon came home Denyce was sitting in the dining room at the table staring blankly out the window. She was wearing her silk robe, and she had her legs tucked up underneath her. In her hands she was lightly fondling the emerald and diamond necklace he had given her the night before. Brandon took off his shoes and walked quietly to the table. He knelt down besides her and rested his head on her lap. Denyce let her hand come down on his head, stroking the close cut of hair, feeling his cold ear against her thigh.

"I love you," he said.

"I love you too, baby," she replied.

He raised his head and looked at her. "I just get so angry when I think of another man having a part of you," he explained, "I get all crazy and I just can't control it. I'm not trying to control you baby…I'm trying to stop him from taking you away from me."

Denyce cupped his head in her hands. "Honey, no man is going to take me away from you. I am all yours. You don't have to be angry when you think other men are looking at me, just be proud I'm your woman."

Brandon nodded. "I know you think it's that easy, Denyce, but it's not. I feel like I barely have you in my life. Sometimes I feel like you're just going to slip away soon as some good-looking, intelligent, successful man comes along. I know I'm not good enough for you."

"Baby, you are more than enough man for me, trust me!" Denyce replied, running her hand over his head and down to his neck. "Look at me," she demanded, pulling his face up at her. "Never… never again do I want you to think that you are not good enough for me, or that I'm going to just up and leave you, alright? Don't you ever think that way again!"

Brandon looked into her bright hazel eyes, searching for her honesty and devotion. Gordon smiled when he found it in her eyes and body language. At that moment he knew she belonged to him. Denyce lowered her head and slowly kissed his eyelids, cheeks, his forehead and then the corners of his mouth. Brandon stood up and pulled her up to him. He wrapped his muscular arms around her waist, not wanting to let her go.

Suddenly he lowered his head and pressed his mouth hard against hers, engulfing the breath she tried to release from surprise. His tongue forced her lips to part and they soon exchanged their anger for passion as their tongues lashed against each other. She broke away from the kiss, panting as she yanked Gordon's shirt over his head and kissed his neck then licked his earlobes. She reached down, unbuttoned his jeans and pulled down the zipper. Brandon moaned when her hand slipped inside his jeans and wrapped around his erection which became harder to her touch. He stepped out of his jeans and bent his knees, signaling Denyce to jump in his arms. She wrapped her legs around him and he cradled his arms under her butt. He entered her, rocking her against his body as she tightened the grip in her arms and legs. He took a couple steps forward and lowered her on the dining room table. She relaxed her body enough to lie on her back but her legs were still wrapped around him. He was going to miss this weekend's Sunday morning jog.

That Monday morning Denyce was at work but her mind stayed on the weekend, particularly Saturday. Orgasmic bliss took over them and they were pleasantly exhausted when it was all over. She smiled while reflecting on how Brandon always managed to loosen her up, take her away from the controlling apprehensive woman she's been for years. As many lovers she's had, Denyce was always routine…the bedroom was the place to have intercourse. Brandon introduced her to other rooms in the house like she'd never lived there. The dining room table, the floor…while holding on to the kitchen sink and her looking out the window above the faucet! She wondered why it had taken her forty-three years to finally become uninhibited. Hell, she became a straight up freak!

Trevor's knock at the door interrupted her pleasurable trip down memory lane. "Ms. Wright may I come in?"

"Trevor? Yes come right in." She swept the lingering feeling of Brandon's hands on her body from her mind.

Trevor carried in a box of files and placed them neatly on Denyce's desk. "Here are the files I forgot when I came over on Saturday."

Denyce looked past Trevor and noticed her assistant Cheri standing in the doorway. "Yes, Cheri?"

"Joan Ridlock is on line 3 for you, Ms. Wright."

"Please take a message for me, Cheri. I'll be busy for the next half hour with Mr. Langfield."

Cheri nodded and closed the door. How long had Cheri been standing there? Denyce shuddered to think what Cheri might have heard before announcing a phone call. That chick could have alerted her on the intercom! Denyce hoped Cheri did not hear him mention stopping by her house over the weekend. And if Cheri did hear it, have sense enough not to run her mouth to her peers. Although she worked hard to keep Trevor at a 'friends only' distance, she could not help noticing they've grown closer. And as much of an ass he was acting towards Brandon – who was going along and adding his share – Trevor was noticeably awkward after Brandon stormed off.

"Trevor," she began, "there's something I would like to speak to you about, and it might be a bit uncomfortable for the both of us."

Trevor stopped rifling through the box of files and tucked his hands into his pant pockets. He slowly looked at Denyce and instantly knew where this was going.

"Trevor, we've always had to work closely together. Most VPSs and their COOs do…you know that."

Trevor nodded, still watching her closely.

"And lately," she paused, wringing her hands, "Well, lately we've just had to work a bit closer under the present circumstances, and I just want you to know that…"

"That this is, and always has been, strictly business." His eyes were still locked on her face.

"Yes," she responded quietly.

"I know," Trevor said. "Look, about Saturday. I'll admit there were some feelings unfolding that I didn't realize were there." Denyce's cheeks was suddenly feeling flushed and she shifted in her executive chair. "But I want you to know that I completely agree. Our relationship is about business…this business, and I want to apologize for my behavior. And for letting my feelings get the best of me. I promise you, it won't happen again," he said.

Denyce sighed lightly, a bit of relief escaping her lips. She felt suddenly grateful for such an understanding partner. "Thank you, Trevor," she smiled, "I knew I could count on you to always act professionally."

He smiled, turned and walked to the door. He grabbed the doorknob then looked over his shoulder. "So, we're good here?" he asked. "You have your much-needed files and we're still the best team this company has ever seen."

"Absolutely!" Denyce said with a smile.

"Great. Then I'll see you at the meeting this afternoon." With that he walked out of the office and gave Cheri a flirtatious grin as he headed down the hall.

Denyce let out a breath she felt was held the entire time Trevor was in her office. She spun her chair to face the wall to floor windows and looked at the city's landscape. She wouldn't tell Brandon about this discussion. If Brandon knew Trevor had let his feelings towards Denyce evolved into something more it would send Brandon over the edge.

Yet if Trevor's behavior resurfaced in an argument again, she would know beyond the shadow of a doubt that his actions were unquestionable. It wasn't that she felt the need to hide Trevor's feelings from Brandon but revealing them would only cause more complications. Plus, Trevor was her partner in business and her friend. For twelve years now they worked side by side, and she wasn't about to let go of the relationship they've built just because of Brandon's insecurities. She leaned back in her chair. Yes, it was good to know that Trevor would remain professional from now on. She couldn't afford to lose him...or Brandon.

Chapter 3

Denyce scurried through her walk-in closet. She was running late for work again and the culprit still dozing peacefully in her king-size bed. She snatched a pinstripe suit and crisp blue button-down out of the closet but not before stubbing her toe against a suitcase. Two years in and Brandon still hadn't unpacked his last bag. For being so willing to love her, Brandon still had a few walls up, but Denyce was determined to break them all down. If she was anything, it was determined.

This was the longest either of them had ever been in a committed relationship and there were still a few bugs that needed ironing out. *That damn suitcase, for one*, Denyce thought as she quickly tied her hair back and headed downstairs. She wasn't free from scrutiny either, yet she'd be the last to admit she still had issues with their age differences. As much as she loved Brandon, she still wondered if he was the right one for her to settle down with.

"I know you've thought about it, girlfriend," Charlize teased during lunch later that day. Denyce texted Charlize, Natasha and, if she was in the city, Autumn, to meet her at a popular restaurant near her office. Natasha and Charlize arrived at the same time, joining Denyce at a table near the fireplace section of the restaurant. They ordered their food and a bottle of wine instead of hot apple cider or coffee.

"Thought about what?" Denyce said, playing dumb.

"Oh, come on!" Natasha blurted, "Do not play dumb with us, Denyce Mariah Wright. Have you guys even discussed the possibility of it? I mean, it's been *two years*, girl!"

Denyce rolled her eyes. "That is something I do not care to discuss at this point in time, thank you," she curtly replied while sitting back in her chair. She raised her wine glass and sipped while avoiding her friends' glares.

Charlize smirked and elbowed Natasha. "I'll bet Brandon's asked a dozen times and you just keep saying no! You're just the type of cold-hearted bitch to have a good man like that begging."

Denyce shot a look at Charlize that would have killed her in a heartbeat.

Natasha snapped her head at Charlize in shock and disappointment. "Oh my God, Charlize, she would never do something like that and you know it! I am positive that he's just holding out. And I think, that he thinks, that she thinks, she doesn't want him to."

"What are you ladies going on about?" Denyce, Charlize and Natasha looked up as Autumn strolled over to the last vacant chair at the table.

"It's about time you got your skinny ass over here," Charlize smirked. "We just about gave up on you. Figured you were somewhere in Paris by now."

"As a matter of fact, Charlize, I did a quick layover in Paris...FRANCE, not Texas, yesterday," Autumn said coolly. "Why are you acting like a jealous bitch all of a sudden?"

Charlize's eyebrows furrowed and her mouth opened to release ugliness in a way only she can, but Denyce threw her hands up in a 'stop' motion. "Ladies, please! Let's all play nice now."

Autumn leaned over and gave Charlize a hug and playfully pulled at one of her braids before turning and hugging Denyce as well. She sat down and waved at Natasha who winked in return.

"So," Autumn said "What were ya'll talking about before I so rudely interrupted?"

"We were wondering why Denyce hasn't locked down that gorgeous man of hers yet and Natasha here is fairly certain that, well, you go on an' tell her what you said, Nat," Charlize said.

"I said, I think, that Brandon thinks that Denyce thinks, that she does not want him to," Natasha said.

"To what? Autumn said.

"To possibly...possibly, pop the question," Denyce said. "Not that I don't want Brandon to. But he is aware that I am not the one holding back this time."

"Okay," Autumn said while nodding her head slowly. "Have you dropped subtle hints at him?"

Charlize rolled her eyes. "You know men don't understand subtleness! You got to hit them upside their heads fifteen times before they even start thinking that you might be trying to say something!"

The others looked at each other and mumbled in agreement to Charlize's theory.

"I'm just saying, Brandon is probably as blind to your subtle hints as a dog to a red ball in green grass," Charlize huffed, "you have to tell him speak what's on his mind! And tell him what's running in yours, shit!" Charlize grabbed her glass of wine and emptied it in one gulp and Denyce, Natasha and Autumn smirked before bursting into laughter.

Charlize looked at them while holding the empty glass. "What the fuck's wrong with you three?"

"Men are as blind as a dog looking for a red ball in the grass, Charlize." Denyce said while still laughing.

"Girl, what country shit is you on?" Charlize rolled her eyes and tipped her glass in their direction.

The table erupted in laughter, causing other lunch guests to glance their way for a second before resuming to their separate conversations.

"So," Autumn said after taking a breath, "Brandon hasn't asked you yet. Is this upsetting you?" Denyce paused before answering.

"No…but, I guess I never thought that I would want him to," Denyce said, "I mean I never thought I was looking to get married, let alone considering it as an option."

"But girl, it's always been an option," Natasha said.

Denyce laughed. "You know it wasn't for me."

"Well what the hell is wrong with that man, then?" Charlize added. "If I were him I would have bought you a ring the first time I fell into your satin sheets."

The women paused then laughed as Charlize rolled her eyes. "Brandon," Denyce started, then stopped. She wondered if she should be revealing how tender he really was.

"Brandon what?" Autumn asked.

Denyce paused. "He's just been holding back a lot, I know it. He acts like we're all in love, like we're going to last forever, but for all his sweet talking I know he's scared that I'm going leave him."

"Well, are you committed?" Charlize asked bluntly.

"Of course, I am," Denyce replied, "you know I am. You all know it."

"Yeah, but we also know you're scared," Natasha said. "He's a wonderful man, but he's also still a boy in a lot of ways, really."

A chorus of 'mmmmhmmms' left their lips.

"But here's the truth," Charlize stated, "He still would not be with your old ass after two years if he wasn't really committed to you. Whatever with all that bullshit fear and scaredy-cat shit." She paused and grasped Denyce's hand. "Denyce that man loves you; there's no reason for you to be afraid."

Weeks after their lunch date, Charlize's words continued to waver in Denyce's thoughts. Charlize may be outspoken and taken for a crass bitch at times, but Denyce knew Charlize was right. Men don't need subtlety, and Brandon sure as hell did love her. In her house Denyce sat at the dining room table sipping a Bloody Mary. She glanced every now and then towards the kitchen, particularly the kitchen table…where they made passionate love. Brandon opened her soul to love on every level: Philos, Eros, and Agape. He was not only her friend, he was her lover, and he seemed to love her unconditionally.

She glanced at her right hand and at the large diamond ring on her ring finger. This ring was a symbol of pride and independence. That she did not need a significant other to embellish her with diamonds, cars, and a home. She was able to do this by herself and on her own terms. Then she glances at her left hand and the bare, left fingers. In her mind Denyce watched the diamond ring on her right finger suddenly appear on her left ring finger, encrusted in a wedding band. She shook her head to clear the vision, but now sees that this 'independence' ring stood for what she no longer wants…loneliness. But even with Brandon's love, she was still alone. She took another sip of her Bloody Mary and scrunched her face. She no longer wanted it because of its bitterness. Or was she the one suddenly bitter? She rose from the dining room chair with the drink in her hand and walked into the kitchen. Dumping the drink in the sink Denyce glanced at the wall clock and realizes Brandon would be home soon. Brandon suddenly decided to start working on the weekends instead of spending them with her. Denyce was frustrated by the change since she cut back on weekend work and meetings for more quality time together.

"A man likes to put food on the table for his family, and you're my family, so you put two and two together," Brandon explained before heading out to a weekend job.

Denyce gave Brandon a quizzical expression. "What are you talking about? I don't need you to support me, and I've never asked you to. Besides, why can't you just be okay with the fact that I make more money?"

Brandon looked at her, completely flustered at what she just said. "Well, I'm not! Denyce, you couldn't possibly understand how emasculating it is for me – for any man – to have the woman they love earning not just a little more, but over three times as much as he does!"

Denyce held her tongue. She wondered how long Brandon felt this way about money.

Brandon continued, "But it's not just that. I like working, I like knowing I've done something with myself, that I've worked hard and I've got something to show for it." He paused, and took a deep breath. "You know this year's been hard on me. After the Sherls and Hughes job, there was nothing for me for a long time. I know you were okay with me leaning on you, and we made it through, even though I had to swallow my pride. But I got a chance now, Denyce, to make up for that time, to end the day with something more to show than empty pockets. I have to do this."

Denyce looked at Brandon as if it was her first time. It wasn't until after he had left for work that she sat down and thought it through. She'd never realized how desperate Brandon was to prove himself. More so, he needed to prove to her that his desire to work was not just about the money or being the man of the household. It was the same desire that she felt, the desire to be something in this world, to leave your mark and stop at nothing until you've achieved all that you possibly can. His drive was what every human essentially crave: accomplishment, no matter how insignificant.

But thinking about him on such a philosophical level made Denyce ponder her own motives. Perhaps what was driving Brandon to work was the same thing that was driving her desire for marriage now. Maybe marriage was just the next step or accomplishment on a long list of To-Dos for life. After marriage, then what? Would he want to start a family? Hell, could she even give him children; after all, she was 43 and regardless of the medical improvements of fertilization, adoption and surrogacy, would Brandon want to go through all of that? If they decide to have children, will her career end up in the back seat of their family car next to the children safety seat? Her life's goals would be defined by a different series of major events - first steps, first words, education, graduation, career, marriage, grand-children? Is that all there was to this life?

Denyce blinked her eyes realizing her mind wandered off too deep. She rinsed out the glass and reached for the pitcher for a refill, but changed her mind. She needed a clear head to reassess her reasons for wanting Brandon to propose marriage. At the same time, she needed to figure out why the thought of Brandon not proposing already, had made her insecure.

"Hey baby!" Denyce turned to the direction of Brandon's voice then his body as he shut the front door closed, cut through the living and dining rooms and entered the kitchen. Sweat from long hours on the job gleamed on his dirty and ruddy skin. She smiled as he approached her and kissed her cheek before entering the laundry room, his work belt dragging in his hands. While Brandon knew she never liked it when he got too close after a filthy day of work, Denyce did not flinch as he kissed her. Instead, she wondered how she would breach the subject of the next step with him.

She turned around and watched Brandon strip off his work clothes and fling them in the washer. He carefully measured a cup of detergent, dumped that in, shut the lid and hit the power button. Denyce scanned his body from head to toe, even though he was now in his boxers. Denyce felt a familiar twinge of lust take over her body as she appreciated the muscular physique on this 31-year-old young blood.

"How was work?" she asked.

Brandon let out a sigh and broke into a smile. "Same ol', same ol', Sugar. Hard day's work makes a man healthy, wealthy, and wise."

"I'm pretty sure that saying was in regards to bedtime and alarm clocks," Denyce added with a chuckle.

Brandon made his way to the fridge and pulled out a beer. "Yeah," he responded, "well, what else can get a man to bed early and up before the crack of dawn – besides sex?" He started towards her, a mischievous look in his eyes.

"Oh no you don't!" Denyce laughed as she scampered around the island, trying to get away from his sweat-drenched body.

"Don't what?" he teased.

"You know what!" Denyce shrieked as he lunged towards her, chasing her into the living room. "Brandon! No! Brandon, No!" She shrieked louder and laughed as they raced around the living room and up the stairs to the bedroom.

Denyce grabbed the same statue she had once nearly knocked him out with. "Don't you take one more step!" she threatened. "I got a weapon and I know how to use it!"

"Woman, your best weapon is not in your hands, and you know it," Brandon grinned with intent, "It's under those clothes!" He lunged towards Denyce again and managed to wrestle her to the bed, the statue landing softly beside them.

Brandon held her wrists above her head and let his lips brush softly over her neckline. "You are dirty!" Denyce protested and attempted to jerk her head away. "Oh, Brandon you're all sweaty! You need a shower first!"

When his tongue started tracing a line from her earlobe to her collarbone and eventually to her chest, Denyce sighed but begged one more time. "Brandon, please shower first! Baby, shower first, and I promise we'll begin where you left off."

Brandon stopped and raised his head to look at her. "Oh, no, Sugar. There's no stoppin' me now." Brandon suddenly picked her up carried her into the bathroom.

"Brandon!" She shrieked, "Brandon NO!"

Denyce's shrieks fell on deaf ears. He walked into the shower and turned the water on, then placed her at her feet, facing him. Water was running over both of them and Denyce still fully clothed while Brandon was in his boxers. Denyce screamed in protest and slammed her fists against Brandon's chest. He grabbed her wrists and laughed a low, guttural laugh. She stopped and rubbed her hands over her face and hair, staring at Brandon as water washed over her face. He wrapped his arms around her tiny, furious, frame and pulled her close.

Slowly a smile began to form at the corners of her mouth, but she pressed her lips together to hide it. His heart nearly pounding out of his chest, Brandon grabbed the bottom of Denyce's shirt and pulled it over her head. He leaned down and kissed her face and neck. Together they undressed and Denyce's anger and worries washed away. Brandon lifted Denyce and embraced her until they became one; moving together, making love as the steam from the shower clouded the glass walls and mirrors.

Brandon always had a way of clearing her mind. But no one ever told Denyce was how much more enjoyable sex became as she aged. Then again she'd never thought of having sex, let alone a relationship with a younger man. With Brandon's animalistic sex drive Denyce was worried at first about whether she could keep up with him. He made those worries disappear. The only problem was, the sex was so good she was easily distracted from important discussions they needed to conduct. Instead they always managed to tumble into her bed; the dining and/or kitchen table, the shower, discussing anything serious.

More time had passed and the issue of marriage was still pressing on Denyce's mind. If Brandon was thinking about discussing marriage, he did not show any signs. Denyce began to feel that maybe Brandon had no intentions of marrying her at all. She knew her thoughts were once again running amok. Maybe she was too old; maybe he was just waiting for another woman closer to his age to come along. Maybe he thought she was too old to settle down with and start a family. What if he never intended for them to last this long? She knew they needed to sit down and talk but fear kept Denyce from initiating the topic. What if her seemingly illogical thinking was what he was thinking in reality? She needed to get a grip. *Just talk to him, Denyce*, she thought. *It's Brandon for crying out loud.*

"Baby," Denyce said as they rinsed the dinner plates before placing them in the dishwasher.

"Yes?"

"We need to talk," she continued.

"About what?"

Denyce paused and took a deep breath. "Marriage."

Brandon set his plate down and lowered his gaze from Denyce. Then he ran one hand roughly over his face. Fear suddenly gripped her. *Oh no,* she thought, *he doesn't want to marry me. I've made an ass out of myself.*

"Okay," he said suddenly, still avoiding eye contact. "What is it about marriage that you want to talk about?"

Denyce fumbled for words. "Well," she said, "I guess I just want to know where you stand."

Brandon started loading up the dishwasher. "What do you mean?"

"I mean where do you stand when it comes to marriage?" she asked while wishing he would just look at her. "Do you want to get married?"

"Now?" he asked.

"No, not now, I mean – well, maybe. I don't know. I just want to know what you think about marriage in general, I guess. In regards to us, or not, what do you think about marriage period?" she paused. Brandon remained silent as his eyes focused on the dishes. Why was this so difficult? "Have you thought about it?"

Brandon slowly closed the dishwasher and straightened up. He crossed his arms over his chest and finally looked at Denyce, meeting her gaze with an intensity that nearly took her breath away.

"I have," he said.

"Well?" Denyce pressed.

"Well, what, Baby? I love you, you love me and we'll get married when the time is right. Right now things are good. Why are you rushing all this on me all of a sudden?"

"So you would want to marry me?"

"Is that what this is all about? You're insecure because you think I don't want to get married or marry you."

Denyce smiled sheepishly. "Yeah, I guess. I'm not getting any younger and you still have your whole life ahead of you."

"In other words, you thought I was holding back because you think you're too old to get married to someone as young as me."

"Basically," Denyce said, "only it sounds more stupid when you put it like that."

"Baby," Brandon sighed as he sauntered over to Denyce and rested his hands on her shoulders. "You have got to get over this age thing. If you don't, it will keep coming back to haunt us every step of the way and stir up problems where there are none. I love you, you know that. And yes, I want to marry you…when the time is right. Okay?"

Denyce relaxed as he pulled her into an embrace. Her ear rested against his steady heartbeat. She did love him, and she knew he loved her. Finally hearing from Brandon that he wanted to marry her -eventually - brought her a world of relief. But her clock seemed to be ticking louder than ever now. When would the time be right?

"Brandon," she said cautiously. "I know you love me, and…I hate to do this, but – "

"Then don't," he almost sighed in defeat.

"I have to," she said. "How long before the time is right, baby? I know you want me to get over the age thing, but I'm truly not getting any younger and we both know it."

Brandon groaned, released his hold and stepped back from Denyce. "Denyce, you know as well as I do that life doesn't revolve around your internal clock."

"That's not what I meant," Denyce shot back.

"Well, this is what I mean," Brandon said, "Marriage is a big step. And it's a step that we both have to be ready for."

Denyce turned away.

"I know you don't want to hear it. I don't want to say it. Maybe this is why it's never come up until now. But as much as hurts to finally say it out loud, I have to." He paused as she turned to face him. "I'm not ready for marriage right now, baby. I'm just not. You know we still have a few wrinkles to iron out, especially financially, and you have a job that you're not necessarily ready to downgrade…"

"Don't make this about me," Denyce shouted.

"I'm not, Denyce. And please don't make this into a fight…"

"So now I'm making this into a fight? Why you would think that? I was simply and calmly discussing your complete lack of commitment to me; nothing more, nothing less." As soon as the words were out of her mouth, Denyce regretted saying them. But her heart was too injured to pull back from a fight.

Brandon was surprisingly calm. Instead of flaring up, he reached out and gently pulled Denyce back into his arms.

"Baby," he said. "Look at me." He nudged her chin towards his face. "Look at me."

Denyce allowed him to turn her face towards his. The way she was behaving right now it felt as if Brandon was the oldest between them.

"You know I love you, Denyce."

She nodded.

"You know that I am 100% committed to this relationship."

She nodded again.

"You know that one day, when the time is right and when we're ready, we'll take that step – together."

She slightly nodded at his statement.

Brandon smiled and picked her up, holding her tight. "You can't be doing' this to me, woman. You can't be bringing up huge issues like this and lightin' a fire up under me for being honest with you." He set her down.

"I know," she answered weakly, embarrassed about her paranoia. "I just wanted to hear you say you wanted to be with me as much as I want to be with you."

"And I do. Don't ever think that I don't."

"Well, don't hold off too long, baby," she threatened lightly, "Or else I might get the wrong idea again."

"Don't you dare," he pulled her closer and let out a long sigh. "I love you, Denyce. Don't ever doubt it."

"I love you too, Brandon."

It took several more weeks before Denyce finally realized the thought of marriage hadn't crossed her mind. Still, she needed to feel that Brandon wasn't about to up and leave her for a younger, more attractive – more fertile – woman. She was facing insecurities she had never known before.

Her attitude at work changed as well. She was increasingly distracted and harsher on the younger women at the company. She had taken an especially cruel tone with Cheri although she barely realized it. Trevor also noticed a change in Denyce's behavior and finally coughed up the courage to intervene just as she was ranting at Cheri for a typo in a draft proposal.

"I expect more from you, Cheri. You've been working here how long? And I still have to correct your petty errors? Come on! Women your age don't get a position like this every day. Please don't make me question my judgment in keeping you on full-time!"

"Ms. Wright?" Trevor said, trying his best to stop Denyce before it got worse.

"Just a minute, Trevor," she demanded, "Cheri, I expect this to be completely re-written and left on my desk before you leave today."

"Yes, Ms. Wright," Cheri meekly replied while taking the letter from Denyce's unsteady hands.

"Denyce," Trevor said, this time a bit firmer, "Can I please have a moment with you in my office?"

Denyce turned to face Trevor and walked coolly towards his office.

Trevor caught up with Denyce and reached around to open the door for her. Still agitated, she jumped at Trevor's sudden gesture then walked inside his office. He followed her and shut the door. "Please have a seat," Trevor said as he pointed to one of two leather chairs facing his desk.

"I'm fine, thank you," Denyce said and stood behind the chairs instead.

"Denyce…I'm not begging."

Denyce stepped between the chairs and sat down in one.

"Denyce," Trevor started, "I've been meaning to talk to you and now seems like as good a time as ever."

Denyce shifted in her seat. "What's going on, Trevor?" she asked.

"I was going to ask you the same thing."

Denyce was taken aback. "What do you mean?"

Trevor moved the empty chair aside and sat at the edge of his desk facing Denyce. "What is going on with you? Is everything alright?"

"Yes, everything's fine."

"You're sure about that?"

"Yes, I'm positive. Why?"

Trevor smirked. "Honestly? Being around you lately has been a bit like being stuck in a house with a wild bear, and I'm pretty sure you're on the verge of losing the best assistant you've had in over ten years."

Denyce felt her breath catch in her throat. "I, I don't understand," she stammered.

"You've been on edge; icy is more like it, towards your assistant and any younger female working here," Trevor said. "You're especially hard on them, and without reason. Something is bothering you and you're letting it affect the way you work."

"Trevor, Cheri made an inexcusable mistake – "

"It was a clerical error, Denyce," Trevor interrupted. "It was a typo, and you threatened to fire her."

Denyce paused. Had she been unreasonably demanding lately? Perhaps she had. "I realize I might have been a bit hard on her for that, I'm sorry."

"Don't apologize to me; apologize to Cheri." Trevor got up and took the seat next to Denyce. "Now, what I'm concerned about are not Cheri's feelings; I'm concerned about you. What's going on?"

Denyce let out a deep breath. "I guess it's like you said, I've just been on edge lately."

"We've already established that. What I want to know is, why the edginess? What's going on with you?" "It's just personal stuff, Trevor. I'll get it under control."

Trevor scooted his chair closer to Denyce and leaned forward. "Don't do that, Denyce. Don't shut me out. You're not in this alone. We're practically partners, and we've been friends for years. Is everything all right at home? Brandon isn't mistreating you, is he? Because you know how I'd feel about that."

"No, no, it's nothing like that," Denyce replied. She took another deep breath and glanced sheepishly at Trevor. He was her friend, but she wasn't sure she wanted him to know about her insecurities. *Ah, to hell with it*, she thought. She let out a relenting sigh. "I just may be feeling a little *old*, lately, especially in regards to Brandon's age."

Trevor laughed.

"Don't laugh!" Denyce playfully hit him on the arm. "This is obviously serious. Lord, just look at how I've been treating Cheri!"

Trevor kept laughing. "Denyce, I thought you had some medical diagnosis or was on the verge of having a nervous breakdown!"

Denyce's mouth fell open. "No, no! I'm just being insecure."

Trevor patted her leg. "Darling, we're all getting more insecure with time. Trust me, you're not alone. But you have nothing, and I mean nothing to worry about, Denyce," Trevor assured her. "You are an amazing woman, truly exceptional, and if Brandon doesn't know that then he deserves to be with some young dumb heifer who thinks her body is the answer to everything."

Denyce threw her head back and screamed in laughter. "Ooh Trevor you need to stop! Then again," she said, "there are some seriously dumb heifers running around, huh?" She laughed again.

Trevor laughed and nodded. "Yes, yes there is and none of them will ever come close to your grace, class, and beauty, not in this lifetime. So you quit rolling heads around here. These poor creatures need a break. Show them the merciful goddess you have become, not the tyrannical one."

"Denyce the merciful," she chimed, "I like the sound of that."

Both stood up and Denyce headed for the door. She paused and turned around. "Thank you, Trevor. It means a lot that you can set me straight from time to time. It's nice to have a professional sounding board."

Trevor smiled. "No problem, Denyce. Anytime."

The Panthers Club

When Denyce got home later that evening, she found a note from Brandon on the counter.

Baby I am out with the boys.
Be home by midnight.
-B

Denyce didn't frown about Brandon not being home; some alone time will give her a chance to relax and think. How could she have let her insecurity run her emotions like that and not realize it? She decided to run a hot bath, complete with a few drops of bath oil As soothing jazz played in the background, she undressed and tied her hair up. She stepped inside her Victorian designed stand- alone tub and eased into the hot water and suds. Steam mingled with the scent from the oil and Denyce felt her rigid muscles relax as she got comfortable. She exhaled as she leaned back and rested her head on a bath pillow.

"Denyce? Dencyce baby wake up!"

Denyce shook her head without opening her eyes. She thought she heard someone say her name but she was alone. "Denyce," a deep male voice repeated, this time in a soft whisper in her ear. "Wake up, baby."

Denyce jerked awake as Brandon ran his hand in the now chilled bath water. "How long have been in the tub?"

"Huh?" Denyce blinked and then realized Brandon was kneeling by the tub with a concerned look on his face. She also realized the water was now freezing. "Damn it! Brandon what time is it?"

"It's about 11:30," Brandon said. He stood up, turned to a towel rack and grabbed a large Egyptian cotton towel. He opened the towel as Denyce stood up and wrapped it around her shivering body. She took his hand and stepped out of the tub. Brandon held her while rubbing his hands briskly up and down the sides of her body.

"I must have fallen asleep," she said.

"Evidently," Brandon said. "Baby you need a vacation."

"Bath time is the only time I have for a vacation," she said.

"Well then let's make time."

"What are you saying? You want to go halfway around the world to relax?"

Brandon smiled. "We don't have to go to the other side of the planet, but we need to go somewhere. Maybe someplace exotic, like the Bahamas. We can spend a week or two there," Brandon said, "You know you need and deserve it."

Denyce laughed. "I do need a vacation; but I never had the chance or the time to slip away. There was always some project in the way."

"You know what they say, no better time than the present," Brandon said.

223

"They also say, you can rest when you're dead," Denyce said.

"Don't say that! Baby, you've never taken time off? Not even a single day for yourself?"

Denyce shrugged her shoulders.

Brandon gave her a light squeeze. "Let's get away from all this, for a couple weeks, just you and me. What's stopping you?"

Denyce had always liked the idea of a vacation but time away from work was always crucial time lost. Could she really afford to take time off right now?

Brandon read her mind. "Now is the perfect time to get away. The expansion is finished and there's no new projects unfolding that need your attention. Baby what's holding us back?"

"Well, when you put it like that."

"Then let's go!" Brandon shouted while lifting Denyce into the air.

Denyce laughed along with his giddiness. *Yes*, she thought, *what better time than now*.

Chapter 4

Denyce gasped in amazement. *Waking up to a scene this beautiful should be a sin*, she thought. They arrived at the Caribbean islands the night before after catching the last flight of the evening. The water seemed as black and clear as the night's sky. Even as they rode in the limo from the tiny airport to their private getaway, the streets were dark with only the headlights highlighting a path before them.

The limousine approached a large and well-lit beachfront home ahead. This was their private holiday for 10 days, which was long enough for Denyce to spare. Despite the vacation, she insisted that she'd be virtually accessible to the company and demanded to keep her cell phone on and have Internet access. Brandon protested at first but relented when she put her foot down. This was her first time away from the office and she couldn't just go cold turkey.

When they entered the beach house, Brandon was awestruck at the decor. Denyce, however, frowned at the décor. She felt it looked too much like a tourist's dream with the bright walls and overly large floral prints. She would have preferred something a bit more modern, but this would have to do.

Brandon walked inside the master bedroom and took a running leap onto the king size, four post mahogany canopy bed. Denyce shook her head and laughed. "You're like a little child! At least take off your shoes."

Brandon made a face at her and kicked off his shoes. "Baby, you have got to relax," he said and took off his shirt. He flexed his chest muscles and smiled mischievously. "Now you have two choices; we can take a midnight swim or you climb into bed with me," Brandon said, "either choice, we are going to be naked!"

"Oh really?" Denyce said with a smirk. She slowly approached the bed while stepping out of her shoes. "Well I choose…" She reached behind her and tugged the zipper to her little black dress down. The dress dropped to the floor and she stepped over it. Brandon's eyes were intense with desire as Denyce stood in a black lace bra and thong set. She reached behind and unhooked the clasp. "I choose the option that involves…" the bra became airborne, landing on the arm of a nearby chair. "…my body feeling the magnitude…" Denyce slipped her fingers between her hips and the thin string section of the thong. She glided the thong off her round hips and until they hit the floor. She straightened her body and let Brandon indulge in the visual that was her sensual form. Brandon's erection from the crotch of his slacks strained and he swallowed loudly while staring. "…of the ocean waves hitting my body!" she shrieked as she ran out of the bedroom's French doors and down the patio steps to the beach.

"What the hell!" Brandon jumped off the bed and fought to take off his pants while hopping to the doors. He flung the doors open to the sounds of Denyce laughter as she rushed closer to the ocean.

Denyce screamed as she ran into the ocean's waves, the cold water hitting her body within seconds. She turned to head back to shore but Brandon scooped her in his arms and ran further into the sea. Denyce squealed in terror and delight as their bodies disappeared beneath the black water. She wrapped her arms around Brandon's neck and her legs locked around his waist. They allowed the ocean to carry them as they enjoyed the moment.

Denyce felt her heartbeat slow to a steady beat. She looked up at the moonless sky as the stars glowed brighter than any city skyline. "It's so *lovely*," she said while letting the beauty of the night envelop her.

Brandon's eyes were cast on the silhouette of Denyce's face in the water. "Yes," he whispered, "yes, it is."

They eventually headed back ashore and returned to the beach house. They took a shower, first washing away the salt and sand before they made love. They returned to the bedroom and climbed under the luxurious cotton sheets and fallen into a deep sleep.

The next morning Denyce awakened and eased out of bed. She grabbed her short, silk robe from the suitcase, put it on and walked over to the French doors. She pulled the doors open and was greeted with the magnificence of the sun. Her pupils adjusted and she saw the island at its most majestic beauty. She nearly dropped to her knees in awe.

"Brandon!" Denyce cried out. She jumped on the bed and started jostling him awake "Brandon, wake up!" Brandon sat up urgently and was prepared to fight. "What?! Who is it?!"

"Outside, Brandon," Denyce cried like a child, "Look outside! It's so beautiful I could just die!"

Brandon scrunched his face then shook his head in an attempt to clear it. "What?"

Denyce jumped off the bed and rushed out the doors and onto the patio deck. "Just come outside and look…look at this view!" Brandon threw the sheets from his body and stumbled out of the bed. Oblivious to being naked, he stepped out onto the patio and adjusted his eyes to the bright morning sun. His eyes widen at the scenery before them; like the pictures in the travel brochures and the commercials he's seen on TV, the sun displayed the Caribbean in all of its glory. The clear blue ocean flowed calmly against the endless white sand. The island was lined with the richness of plant life and palm trees. The sky was blue with starch white clouds serving as a backdrop for the suns endless rays of orange, yellow and gold.

"This is so much better than pictures in a magazine," Brandon whispered," "It's…"

"Surreal," Denyce said.

"Yeah," Brandon said. "I never knew such beauty existed."

"I think I finally understand why people love going on vacation now," Denyce admitted. "I never understood it until now. This literally makes you forget all of your troubles."

Brandon stood behind Denyce and wrapped his arms around her waist. She immediately relaxed in his embrace, resting her head against his chest.

"Well," Brandon said. "I'm up now so we may as well get some breakfast!"

After enjoying a breakfast of omelets and fresh, exotic fruit, they decided to begin their tour of the islands with the town market the first stop. They went to the back of the house where two 10-speed bicycles rested against the bike rack. "Let's go," Brandon said as they pushed off for a casual bike ride.

The sun and warm breeze was steady against their backs despite wearing t-shirts and shorts and Denyce's hair flowed in the wind. The scenery for most of the bike ride was trees lined along the road but the consistency did not bother her. It was much better than the traffic jams and clutter of buildings back in the U.S. When they reached the town market, they parked their bikes and began their journey, looking at cheap souvenirs and knock-off designer items.

"How about this one," Brandon said as he held up a hand-carved set of three monkeys. He made a face, covering his nose. "They forgot 'smell no evil,'" he laughed.

Denyce held up another hand-carved item: a mask with bulbous eyes and long, pointy teeth. "Or this might look good right beside your bedside, staring down at you at night while you sleep," she said in a ghoulish voice.

They both laughed and continued walking and enjoying each other's company. During their walk, Denyce found a well-made tie-dyed sundress that she bartered the seller down to $15 and Brandan purchased a hand woven sun hat with long, straw tassels. They also bought what looked like some of the juiciest mangos they've ever seen, but Denyce resisted the urge to sample one until they were properly cleaned.

Hours later they found a restaurant boasting to having the best fried fish on the island and lucked out on a table for two on the balcony. After ordering their meals, they held hands and looked out at the scenic beach view. When Denyce's order of red snapper came to the table, however, she almost shrieked. On her plate were not just pieces or filets of the red snapper, but the entire red snapper, including the head and eyes. After regaining her composure and laughing with Brandon, Denyce still would not touch her meal until Brandon cut the head off.

"I can't believe I actually ate that thing," she laughed later.

"I can't either," Brandon said, "Big ol' eyes looking up at you."

"It was good, though," she replied. "But I'll never order it again!"

They walked back to where their bikes were and began the ride back to the beach house. On the way, they noticed a vendor selling fresh coconut water from green coconuts. As they resumed riding, the afternoon heat bore on them, giving Denyce the urge to get back in the ocean as soon as they got to the house.

"Let's go snorkeling," she said as they leaned their bikes against the front porch.

"I was just thinking the same thing," Brandon said.

They threw on their swimwear and headed to the beach. Neither of them had ever worn flippers before and they struggled awkwardly to get into the water. Finally, after stumbling several times, Denyce managed to start floating on her back. She noticed Brandon was still having a hard time maneuvering the flippers and his body.

"Brandon, you have to do it like this!"

Brandon nodded and was soon on his back. They went backwards into the ocean and turned around once they were in a deep area. The further out they were, the calmer the ocean was. They dove under and looked at the underwater beauty while swimming.

From time to time, Brandon and Denyce would take out their mouthpieces to talk, but mostly they pointed at the different things and areas. Schools of fish darted maniacally below them, spooked by their unusual intruders. At one point Brandon saw a small lavender octopus, but it darted back into the coral too quick for Denyce to catch a glimpse.

When Denyce's legs began to tire, they made their way back to shore, realizing that the ocean had carried them nearly half a mile away from the beach.

"I had no idea we were moving without moving," Brandon said.

"Yeah," she said. "Makes you think how easy it would be to get swept out to sea and lost forever."

"That's kind of terrifying," Brandon said. "You be careful from now on. Don't go out there without me watching you. Last thing I want is to lose you on an amazing adventure like this. It would ruin me for life."

"You don't have to worry about me," Denyce assured him, "I will be very cautious. Scouts honor." She made an 'X' over her heart.

"That's my girl." Brandon hugged her close to him as they walked back to the house.

Once inside, they removed their swimwear and rinsed off in the shower before dressing for dinner. As Denyce finished her shower she called for Brandon to bring her a towel.

"Brandon I need a towel," she yelled. "Brandon!"

No answer.

"Where is that man?" she thought to herself while fumbling with her hands until she felt a shelf piled with towels. She suddenly heard Brandon's voice coming from the patio as he spoke quietly. She wrapped the towel around her head and walked out to the patio. "Brandon?" Denyce asked after noticing Brandon hanging up his cell phone. "What are you doing out here?"

Brandon turned and smiled at her. "Nothing baby. You almost ready?"

Denyce dropped her arms to her sides so Brandon could get a better look at the towels wrapped around her body and head. "Does it look like I'm ready?" she said.

"What did you need?"

"I needed a towel. Who were you talking to?"

"I was just answering some telemarketer. He wanted to know if I wanted to switch plans. It was nothing," Brandon said as he slid the cell into his pants pocket. "Sorry I wasn't there to help you baby."

Denyce looked at him then shook her head. "Well it looks like you're ready and I'm holding us up. I will be out in a bit."

"Okay, baby," Brandon leaned forward and kissed Denyce before she disappeared into the bedroom.

That was a tad strange, she thought. *Do telemarketers usually call cell phones?* She shook her head unconsciously and pushed the doubt from her mind. *Brandon wouldn't lie to me; I don't know what's gotten into me.*

They went to a more romantic restaurant and this time Denyce decided to forgo fish to avoid a repeat of lunch. They ordered Asopao, a soupy stew of chicken, rice, tomato, onions, bell peppers, ham, peas and capers. The main dish was paella and chutney and curry blended with allspice. After indulging in warm pineapple upside down cake, Denyce and Brandon talked and laughed while enjoying a bottle of Chardonnay. Denyce felt an exhilarating freedom she'd never known before. *She was now appreciative of the allure of a relaxing vacation.*

Denyce and Brandon took full advantage of their tropical escape. They snorkeled every other day, rode their bikes into town for any shopping or exploring, took a private tour of the island, and even tried boat fishing for a couple of hours one day. Denyce loved every moment of it, but mostly enjoyed lying around the beach, sunbathing, and simply relaxing. Not everything had to be so fast-paced, a race to see all the sights and sounds.

She wanted nothing more than to kick back and do nothing, say nothing, think nothing, for hours on end. It was a dream.

The day before they were scheduled to fly back to the U.S., Denyce wanted to spend the entire day at the house to savor their last moments there. She asked Brandon to walk the beach with her and comb for any conches they could find. She wanted them to enjoy the final hours of sand between their toes.

"I'm sorry, Baby," he said, "I just need to run into the market for a souvenir for my sister. I forgot, and I can't put it off."

Denyce tried to hide her disappointment.

"But you can come with me if you want," Brandon said, knowing her response would be no. "I'll only be an hour or so, promise."

"Brandon I didn't want to go into town today, and you knew that."

"I know, baby," he said, "And I'm so sorry. I'll be back quick." With that he grabbed his straw hat and kissed Denyce on the cheek before nearly running out the front door. "I'll be back soon," he called back.

"Mmm-hmm," was all Denyce said. She was angry Brandon chose to ruin their last moments here. *Everything has been so amazing until this point, and his forgetfulness has to go and wreck my mood,* she grumbled. She left the house and took a lonely stroll along shore of white sand and began beach combing.

By the time Brandon returned she'd finished combing the beach and was enjoying her last bath in the luxurious tub.

"I'm back, baby!" Brandon said as he walked in the front door. "You wouldn't believe the traffic downtown today; must have been some kind of event down at the fish fry. But I managed to find Sylvia some gorgeous shell jewelry. I know she'll love it." When Denyce did not respond, Brandon stopped talking and looked around. "Baby where are you?"

"I'm in here," Denyce called out. She was still angry over her unwanted alone time.

Brandon walked into the bedroom and set his bag down on the bed before heading into the bathroom. He held one hand behind his back and tipped towards the tub, trying to catch Denyce's eye but she wasn't looking.

"Baby," he cooed. "Baby, don't be mad." He knelt down beside the tub. "Don't be angry at me, please."

Denyce stared straight ahead. Brandon slowly brought a beautiful array of tropical flowers from behind his back.

Denyce looked at them and pushed them away. "You think you can buy my forgiveness with a little bit of sweetness?"

Brandon's shoulders fell then he glared at her. "Denyce are you seriously going to let my going to buy my sister a souvenir ruin this last day? I have that kind of effect on you that you can't let go."

Denyce finally looked at him and at first Brandon smiled. His smile vanished when he saw she was angrier than before.

Brandon jerked his head back and frowned. "Don't make me beg for forgiveness Denyce! I apologized before I left!"

Denyce didn't flinch.

"C'mon, Denyce, seriously?"

Denyce remained silent and stared at the bathroom wall.

"Alright, then," Brandon said, standing up. "I warned you." He suddenly stepped into the tub fully clothed, startling Denyce.

"Brandon! She shrieked, "What are you…"

"I warned you," he said and kneeled into the tub and pressed his body against hers, forcing her to lean back. The water overflows and soon the floor is drenched. "I warned you not to make me come in here and beg." His chest resting on her stomach, he looked up at her face. His big brown eyes pleaded her to look at him.

Denyce held on to her anger, deliberately looking through him.

"Don't do that, Denyce," he begged, "Come on, Baby. I'm sorry. I love you. Look at me, Baby."

Denyce met his gaze.

"I'm sorry, Baby. Please forgive me." He pulls himself up and gently kisses her cheek. "I'm sorry," he kissed her again. "I'm sorry." He begins kissing her full lips, over and over until Denyce is kissing him back.

She reached down and pulled his shirt up and over his head, letting his skin rest against hers. He lay down against her again and kisses then licks her ears. His tongue begins a trail to her neck, shoulder blades then her breasts. She gives into him, her body beginning to writhe beneath him. Brandon manages to take off his shorts and briefs and tosses them on the floor. He grabs the sides of the tub and rises up enough to get off his knees and for Denyce to bring her knees to her chin. He lowers his body in a sitting position and pulls her onto his lap. She straddles him and wraps her arms around his neck. Denyce lowers her head and kisses him deeply, moving her hands from Brandon's neck to cup his face. He grabs her hips and guides her into a rocking position then up and down. The increase friction results in synchronized moans as they increase the speed and pressure. Water splashes in rhythm with their love making as he massages one breast while massaging her ass as she rode him. Denyce's head falls back as she arches her body in ecstasy. She felt the surge of the orgasm climbing to its peak and moved faster and harder on top of Brandon. Brandon groaned and held her by her hips pushing her deeper as he thrust upward. Together they cried out, grunted and moaned as the waves of pleasure intense to an explosive climax. When it was over there was barely enough water in the tub and their bodies were instead drenched in sweat.

Brandon hugged Denyce and glanced over the tub. "I guess we're going to have to find a mop," he laughed.

The next day they packed their bags and checked if they had everything before loading up the limousine. The ride was quiet as they held hands on the way to the airport. Thirty minutes later the plane they were on, roared down the tarmac and took off. Denyce looked out the window and watched the islands evaporate as the plane reached its altitude. She was relieved their last day ended on a different type of explosive note that made her forget about how angry she was at Brandon. She reached across the seat and grabbed Brandon's hand. He looked at their hands and smiled at her before leaning against the airplane supplied pillow. Denyce leaned against her pillow and smiled. She was finally accepting the fact that this was not their last vacation. And that she was meant to be with Brandon.

Chapter 5

Days after returning, Denyce entered the corporate building knowing she was back to reality. Life continued to go on when she and Brandon escaped. Nothing's changed except for the extra tall pile of work on her desk as she swiped her office key card into the door slot.

"Cheri, have Pittmann call my office as soon as he gets in," Denyce said using the loudspeaker on her office phone. She settles into her chair, placing her purse and briefcase on the desk. "And make sure Trevor stops in to see me when he gets out of his meeting."

"Absolutely, Ms. Wright," Cheri's said. "It's good to have you back."

"Thank you, Cheri. Although I wish I could say it was good to be back, too." Denyce disconnects from the loudspeaker and reaches for the stack of files in her 'in' box. She uses one hand to turn on the desktop monitor dreading the trail of e-mails from her account. "Dang, this is going to take me a year to catch up to," she said.

"What's this I hear," Trevor said while walking into Denyce's office. Denyce looked up to see Trevor grinning from ear to ear. "The merciless goddess returns to her kingdom!"

Denyce stands up and walks around her desk and grabs his hand. "How are you Trevor?"

"A lot better now that you're back."

"Oh, I'm sure you managed fine without me," Denyce laughed. "But you could have at least done some work while I was gone. I didn't realize you were on vacation, too." Trevor looks over her shoulder at the stacks of paperwork on her desk.

"Well, I couldn't let you go thinking we didn't need you around here," Trevor said, "You might not have come back to us."

"You know that this company is my life, Trevor. How could I leave my pride and joy," she said with a smile.

"It's good to have you back, Denyce," Trevor said. "It's good to see your face. I didn't realize how much I missed it."

Denyce blushed. "Stop, Trevor."

He smiled and walked to the doorway. "We have a conference call at five tonight with McKinley. They're in LA and want to discuss a potential trip out there."

Denyce plopped into her chair and was going through the first stack of paperwork. "I'll be there," she said.

Denyce multitasks with the paperwork, checking her e-mails and talking phone calls. Leaving the office for ten days apparently set the world spinning off its axis. Cheri popped her head in at noon and announced she was off for lunch, asking if Denyce needed anything.

"Uh, no…Yes! Can you grab me a salad from P.F. Chang? You know what I like," Denyce said.

"Yes, Ms. Wright," Cheri said in a chipper tone.

The afternoon flew and Trevor poked his head in the office just as Denyce was setting the last file in its appropriate place.

"We're ready for you anytime, Denyce."

"What's that?" Denyce looked up, surprised.

"It's five o'clock. We have the conference call with McKinley?" He tapped his watch.

"Oh!" Denyce jumped up. "Be there in thirty seconds." She whipped around to a filing cabinet and pulled out her necessary documents and followed Trevor to the conference room.

The meeting was already underway as they slipped into the room. "We're looking to expand our offices into the Chicago area," a voice boomed from the phone's intercom. "We've already sent our scouts out to assess the market as well as the locale. We're pleased to say we're going ahead with our plans. We want to make sure you're on board for all our needs."

"Absolutely, Mr. McKinley," Denyce said in a smooth tone. "We are here for you, and we are ready with whatever direction and level you want to take this expansion to."

Trevor grinned at her from across the table. Just twenty-four hours ago she was lounging on a beach. Now she was back in the saddle as if the vacation was a dream.

Denyce got home late and wasted no time collapsing on the bed. She kicked off her pumps not caring where they land.

"Who's out there?" Denyce snapped her head at the sound of Brandon's voice. He was in the bathroom and the shower was running. "Who else would it be, baby?" Denyce said while entering the bathroom. "Were you expecting someone else at this time of night?"

"Actually, yes," Brandon joked, "You know my lady friends always come around this time of night."

"Uh-huh," she said.

Brandon stepped out of the shower and grabbed a towel. "You know how hard it is for me to keep the ladies off me. I mean, just look at this body." He held the towel off to the side and struck a pose.

"Get some clothes on before you hurt yourself," Denyce laughed, throwing a hand towel at him.

He caught the towel before it hit the ground and threw it in the sink. Brandon walked over and caught Denyce in an embrace and nuzzled her neck. "How was your first day back at work, baby?"

Denyce groaned and leaned into Brandon's body. "It was rough. You should have seen the pile of work waiting for me on my desk. I could hardly see over it. Then there were a billion e-mails to sort through; and the phone! Damn it, if I hear another phone ring tonight I swear I will hurt somebody."

Back in the bedroom, Denyce laid down again as Brandon tossed the towel from his waist and grabbed a pair of slacks. He could see from her expression and body language that she was extremely wound up.

Brandon reached down and gently pulls Denyce into an upright position. "I'm sure you handled everything with great ease. C'mon, let's get some food in your stomach."

Denyce groaned and wrestled from his grasp. "Just leave me here," she said, "let's order some Chinese."

"Chinese?" Brandon said, "Baby, you must truly be tired."

"And you know what the worst part is?" Denyce asked.

"What's that?"

"Nothing has changed. I mean nothing."

"So?" Brandon said.

"So I could have been taking vacations for years now! I can't believe I've been so stupid to think that the company would collapse without me. They did fine!"

Brandon laughed. "You know what they say, baby: hindsight is twenty-twenty."

Denyce groaned. She could still feel the pull of the ocean on her body.

"We can always go back anytime you desire," Brandon said, "No excuses!"

"Well it won't be for a while," Denyce said while browsing the take-out menu.

"Why's that?"

"I have a business trip to Los Angeles in two weeks. Hard to believe I am just returning from a trip, well, vacation. I'll be gone for five days," she said.

"You're going to L.A. for five days and the trip is in two weeks," Brandon said.

"I know," she said, "Baby, I'm sorry. After this I probably won't go anywhere for a while – even if it's a vacation."

"No, I understand, Brandon said. "Are you going alone?"

"No. Trevor's going also. Our newest client wants to meet both of us."

Brandon felt his neck muscles tense, but did not say anything as Denyce was on the phone with the Chinese restaurant. Thoughts filled his head about Denyce and Trevor being in L.A. for five days. Without him to keep Trevor's hands and everything else off her.

"Hold on," she said and looked at Brandon. "Baby what do you want from the menu?"

"Whatever you want baby, just make it a double order."

As Denyce resumed talking to the restaurant employee, Brandon's thoughts of Trevor sent his heart rate and blood pressure up.

"Twenty minutes will be fine. Same address as before, yes. Thank you!" Denyce set her cell down on the bedside table. "Did you hear that, Brandon? Dinner will be here in 20 minutes. Do you have cash on you?" Oblivious to Brandon's rising temper, Denyce started out the bedroom to go downstairs and wait on the delivery.

Since their last fight over Trevor, Brandon has put forth an effort to be civil with him. After all, Denyce was right. They've worked together for all these years without a single implication of an affair so what was he so jealous about? But Brandon did not let the fact that Denyce purposely failed to mention Trevor accompanying her on this business trip.

Brandon could not shake the images of them pulling all-nighters in the office while the entire building was empty sans security sleeping at the monitor desk. Trevor's hands lightly touching then caressing Denyce's shoulders as they constantly flirt and joke with each other. The veins in his neck throbbed and his jawbone nearly locked from his teeth clenching at every other scenario imaginable.

"Baby," Brandon said, "Do you really have to go to Los Angeles with Trevor and no one else?"

Denyce pauses in the doorway. "Brandon you know we work together and you know this is all about the business," she said.

"Are you going to be staying in the same hotel?" he asked.

"Are you seriously asking me that right now, Brandon? We just had the most amazing vacation in the Bahamas with a private beach. Our own little world…and you're asking why Trevor has to go on a business trip that affects our company," Denyce said.

Brandon sighed. Denyce continued. "You all riled up over a business matter involving a man I've never been with intimately nor am I interested in?" She steps closer to Brandon and rubs his arms. "Baby you have nothing to worry about so let it go, OK?"

Brandon wasn't about to let it go but relented for Denyce's sake and for the sake of the relationship. "Alright, Denyce," he said. "Okay. If you say it, I believe it."

"Thank you baby, you are such a good man." Denyce stood at the tip of her toes, kissed his cheek and rushed out as the doorbell went crazy.

"Mmm-hmm," he said. "Don't I know it."

The Panthers Club

The days leading to the business trip sped by as if to torment Brandon. It did not help that Denyce was spending more late hours at the office. He'd pretend to be sound asleep when Denyce finally showed up; he'd hear her tip up the stairs because her shoes were in her hand. It was to the point that Brandon knew the exchange over the cell phone; "Baby it's me. I'm sorry I have to be here a few more hours again. Don't wait up...I love you." Denyce wished Brandon would stop by the office unannounced so he can see for himself that Trevor's a professional and respecting man. One night Denyce did not walk inside the house until after 1 a.m. She takes off her shoes to ease upstairs when she notices a handwritten note on the side table.

> Sleeping over at Nick's.
> See you tomorrow night.
> –　B

It wasn't until Denyce read the note that she realizes she did not see Brandon's car parked in front of the house. She went to a window and peeped outside. Sure enough, his parking space was empty in front of her car. *Why in the hell was he sleeping at a friend's apartment?* She checked her messages to see if he had called to explain, but there were none. It was way too late to call him so she went to bed.

Denyce and Charlize sat inside a restaurant downtown for lunch. They were laughing and talking as the waiters and servers were in a blur with the other patrons. Denyce was famished. "What is taking the waiter so long with our food?" she asked Charlize.

"Girl, hang on, he's coming," her friend said without an edge in her voice.

Denyce looked at her, knowing any other time Charlize would be ready to cuss loudly for attention.

Charlize smiled at her while sipping a martini. "He's coming girl just you wait."

Seconds later the waiter brings their orders. When the waiter placed Denyce's plate in front of her, it was a cooked fish, with three heads. Denyce jerked her head back. "What the hell! Charlize! This fish has three damn heads!"

Charlize was already digging into her food. "You are tripping Denyce, ain't nothing wrong with your food!"

Denyce huffed and looked at the three head fish. "Don't worry," the fish heads said, "She can't climb trees like you can."

"What?" Denyce shrieked then looked up and saw Brandon at the other side of the restaurant. She tried calling him, but her voice wasn't loud enough for him to hear. She tried to get Charlize to motion for him to come

over, but Charlize was no longer sitting with her at the table. It was another woman, a total stranger, who was staring at Denyce angrily. Except for her expression, the woman was younger with exotic features and a beautiful figure. "Excuse you," Denyce said to the woman, "you are in my friend's seat!"

When the woman did not move or speak, Denyce attempted to get Brandon's attention again but he still did not notice her. "Look chick, I don't know who you are," Denyce said to the stranger, who was now gone. Denyce jumped from her chair and looked around until she was staring at the woman again. The stranger was now in Brandon's arms and they were kissing... She grew frantic, suddenly overwhelmed with the need to get his attention. Brandon and the stranger broke their kissing and looked at her clearly annoyed. Then they looked at each other, smiled and Brandon said, "I love you."

"What! Noooo! Brandon!" Denyce screamed. The louder her screams were, the happier and more intimate Brandon and the young, beautiful stranger became.

"BRANDON STOP!!" Denyce jolted from sleep soaking in her sweat. Her breathing was haggard and she could not stop shaking. She reached across the bed and turned on the lamp. Only then did she realize Brandon was not lying at her side and he was gone. "He's staying with a buddy," she whispered loud enough to hear it for herself.

Later that morning Denyce still could not shake off the dream or its message. The younger female seemed so clear and real, she even wondered if the image was of someone she knew or worked with. Brandon has yet to call and check to see if she was home or already at the office. By noon she was ready to call him but fought the urge to do it.

Denyce's cell rang just before 5 p.m. She hoped it was Brandon. "Hey baby," Brandon said, "how was work today?"

"Good," she said. "I missed you last night."

"Yeah, well...I'm going to be late coming home, but I'm not sleeping at Nick's again. That guy's place is a pig sty."

"Okay. So what time will you be in?"

"Well, if you're staying late at the office again, you won't even miss me."

Denyce felt her heart drop. "No, I'm not staying late tonight. I was actually hoping I'd see you."

Denyce was greeted with a pause then a rustling sound. "Brandon? What's...what's happened to the reception, I'm losing you!"

Suddenly muffled sounds filled Denyce's ear...along with a female voice. Denyce moved the cell from her ear and then brought it back. "Brandon! Who's there with you? I heard a woman's voice!"

"Denyce, I missed what you said. Are you there?"

"Yes, I'm here, Brandon. Who was that?"

Static appeared again. "Denyce," Brandon's voice broke through, "I have terrible service here. If you can still hear me, I'll see you later tonight."

Denyce stared at her phone in amazement. The call dropped. What had just happened? Did she really just hear a woman's voice with her man, or was she going crazy?

When Denyce got home later that night, she was still upset from the phone conversation and the female she knew she heard from Brandon's cell. Denyce also realized she was biting her nails. The last time she had nibbled on her nails was in sophomore year in high school. It was the night of Junior Prom, and Dwayne Scott, a linebacker on the football team was coming to pick her up. When he was a half hour late she started nibbling. By the time an hour passed she nearly chewed them down to the cuticles. After a few tears shed out of sheer humiliation and sitting on her parents' front porch in full prom array, she vowed to never let another guy hurt her again.

She threw her hands down in disgust and paced the den where the desktop computer was. She walked over and sat in front of the computer and pushed the power button. When the high-pitched jingle sound out, she pulled up Brandon's t-mail account and stared at the boxes demanding an e-mail address and password. Denyce stared at the screen contemplating hacking his account to read any suspicious incoming messages. They've been a couple for nearly two years and never has she felt the need to check his e-mails…until now. However, she could not bring herself to clicking the keyboard to open the account and eventually logged out.

She left the den and walked into the kitchen and pulled a bottle of red Pinot noir from the wine rack. While pouring a glass, Denyce stared at her cell phone and pushed it across the counter. After emptying the glass she looked at her cell again, picks it up and hits automatic dial. "Charlize? Uh-huh, yeah, put some clothes on, I'm picking you up," she said.

"Uhm, bitch it's late," Charlize mumbled from the other line.

"Are you OK?" "I'm just peachy," Denyce said. "Now put on some clothes! I will be there in 15!"

Fifteen minutes later Denyce was leaning on the car horn. Twenty minutes later she and Charlize were entering a crowded nightclub on Michigan Avenue. She was dragging Charlize by the arm to the bar and before Charlize could adjust her outfit, a round of shots was lined up just for them.

"What is going on with you, Woman?" Charlize shouted over the music.

"What?" Denyce shouted back, "I can't hear you! Music's too loud!" She tossed back both shots and demanded another round.

Charlize's eyes grew wide. "Next round, I'll share – promise!"

Denyce stood in one spot but her shoulders and hips were moving seductively to the beat. She did not bother to adjust the one shoulder blouse she was wearing and her black jeans looked painted on. "Are you wearing a bra?" Charlize shouted. Denyce heard what her friend said but only smiled as she knocked out another shot.

When they finished the next round, Denyce charged towards the dance floor. "Come on!" she screamed. "Let's dance!"

Charlize's eyes were still wide in amazement. She hadn't seen Denyce like this in years, but she didn't mind. She followed close behind and they pushed their way through the crowd until they found the center of the dance floor and let the music take over. Denyce closed her eyes and let the rhythm wash over her, the bass echoing in her soul.

By the time midnight rolled around, she could feel the coolness of sweat down her back and under her breasts. She finally motioned to Charlize that she was ready to go. She walked outside and let the cool air overwhelm her body. Her eardrums throbbed and the start of what will be one hell of a hangover was creeping on her, but Denyce did not care. Her worries about Brandon had disappeared.

"What the hell was that all about?" Charlize's voice broke through her revelry.

Denyce let out a deep breath. "I just needed to get out of my head for a while," she said while digging for her car keys.

"Oh no you don't," Charlize said and grabbed the keys from Denyce. "The car is parked in a safe spot and neither of us is fit to drive." Denyce shrugged and stepped closer to the curb, trying to hail a cab.

Charlize shook her head. "Woman, I have not seen you like that since that asshole Donovan tried to smother your ass into submission," Charlize said. "I know you. This was about a man, and there's only one in your life at the moment, so I'm assuming Brandon's caused you some heartache."

The reminder instantly irritated Denyce. "Charlize," she warned, "now would be a good time to shut the hell up."

Charlize took her cue and opened the cab door to let Denyce in. Denyce nearly fell into the back seat. "Scoot over," Charlize said. The cab dropped Charlize off first. "All right chick," she continued, "Call me tomorrow. You sleep tight, and don't let that man ruin you. You are stronger than that."

Denyce waved her off and Charlize slammed the cab door shut and gave the driver the house address. The cab pulled up in front of her house and Denyce opened her purse to pay the driver. "The ride's free, honey," the driver said, "as long as you are not behind the wheel."

Denyce smiled, opened the door and slid out of the cab. She closed the door and walked backwards from the curb waving at the driver.

Denyce staggered to the front door, took the key out of her purse and fumbled trying to put the key into the slot. The door suddenly flew open and Brandon was standing there, looking at her. Denyce straightened up and looked at Brandon before she smiled. "Thank you baby," she slurred as he stepped aside to let her in. "Where have you been, baby," she slurred again and then stumbled forward.

Brandon grabbed her and helped her inside. "I should be asking you the same question," he said. Denyce attempted another step while trying to take off her shoes. Before she toppled over again, Brandon picked her up and carried her upstairs.

"My hero," Denyce said and rests her head on his shoulder. "Why did you take off and hurt me like that? You should be sweet all the time."

Brandon entered the bedroom and gently placed her on the bed and removed her clothing. "I'll get you a bucket," he said and went to the bathroom.

Denyce suddenly sat up. "Who was that woman, Brandon? I heard a woman's voice!"

"There's no one here except you and me, Denyce," Brandon said as he placed the bucket near the bed. He eased her back into a laying position. "You need to sleep this off."

"I am telling you, I heard her," Denyce mumbled incoherently until her eyes rolled back. She'd passed out hopefully for the night. Brandon walked around the bed and sat on the other side. Denyce began to snore and Brandon put a light blanket on her. He'd have to wait until tomorrow to have a talk with her.

The next morning Denyce's head was still spinning from the night before. Thankfully she hadn't needed the bucket that Brandon left beside the bed, but what she did need was a bottle of Gatorade and a couple of vitamins. She crawled out of bed in only her bikini panties and found her way downstairs where Brandon was eating breakfast.

"Good morning, sleepy head," Brandon said in a way too cheery tone. She frowned. "Why is everything so bright down here?" she asked and reached for the light switch. She realized the switch was in the 'off' position. Brandon pointed at the windows. "It's called sunshine and there's no switch for it," he said with a chuckle.

Denyce groaned again and opened the fridge. There was only a bottle of orange juice on the shelf so she took it out, opened the lid and poured a glass. She opened her other hand filled with the vitamins and cupped it to her mouth.

"So," he said.

"So?"

"How was your night out?"

Denyce tried to remember the night before but it was all a blur. "I think I had a good time," she said, "but I can only remember bits and pieces. Charlize paid for my cab ride home."

"Oh Charlize tagged along," Brandon said. "That's good, you were not alone."

Denyce took a gulp of orange juice and glanced at Brandon. The tone in his voice when he emphasized her not being alone struck a nerve. "I really don't want to talk about this right now," Denyce said while rubbing her head. She slid off the stool and walked out the kitchen.

"Denyce where's the car?" he yelled as she headed to the staircase.

"Huh?" she said.

"Your car," he repeated, "where did you leave the car? Did Charlize drive it to her house after taking the keys?"

Denyce paused at the bottom step. "Shit!" she mumbled then attempted to run upstairs. "I need to take a shower!"

Brandon ran out of the kitchen and followed Denyce upstairs. "Do I need to call Charlize? DENYCE! Where the hell is your car?!

"It's parked in front of the nightclub we went to," Denyce shrieked, "I'm going to go get it!" She bolted into the bedroom, slammed the door and locked it before he could grab the knob.

Brandon banged on the door. "Denyce open the door!"

The sound of the shower coming on angered Brandon until the doorbell chimed. He rushed downstairs and unlocked the door. Charlize stood on the porch staring wide-eyed at him and holding Denyce's car keys. "I...I brought Denyce's car back from downtown," she said while handing the keys to Brandon. "She did not get ticketed and a friend followed me so I don't need a ride back home."

Brandon stared at Charlize then looked at the keys. "Thanks for bringing the car back, and for keeping her from driving home," he said and closed the door.

Brandon placed the keys on the nearby table and walked upstairs to the bedroom door. He went to knock but noticed it was slightly open. "Denyce," he said while walking in. Denyce stepped out of the bathroom in a robe with a towel in her hand. "Denyce, you may not want to talk about this right now, but we need to."

Denyce walked past Brandon and sat on the foot of the bed. "Why would you go out last night when you knew I wasn't spending the night at Nick's again," he asked.

"Brandon not now," Denyce said.

"Yes, now, Denyce!" he yelled. "You're working late hours and suddenly you and Charlize decide to hang at the club, get drunk as hell. You could hardly walk let alone take off your clothes! Since when do you go to the club?"

Denyce took off her robe and picked up the towel to dry off and block Brandon's voice from her head.

"I don't understand you, woman. Ever since we got back from the islands you can't make time for me. What the hell's going on?"

Denyce stopped drying off and stormed to the dresser, yanked a drawer open and snatched out a bra and panty set. "You want to fight Brandon? Fine, let's do this! I work late because that is what my job entails me to do sometimes. You've been with me for what, two years and you're bitching about me going out and getting drunk?   And...and, you bitch about me working late hours? It's my job that paid for that ten-day vacation, sweetheart. You suggested we go away, but it was my freaking credit card that made your suggestion happen!" Denyce stepped into her panties and fought to put on her bra. "Who are you to question my late nights at the office; I have to work to pay that credit card bill! I have to work because it's what I've been doing long before you even learned to go to the bathroom all by yourself!"

Brandon opened his mouth to say something when Denyce pointed her finger in his face. "But wait a minute...I came home one night earlier than usual and I get a note saying you're doing a sleepover at your boy's house," Denyce shrieked, "What the hell's that about, Brandon? Then you call me later and I can barely hear you for the bad connection on your cell...

Brandon threw his hands up. "Now, I can explain –"

"And in the background," Denyce yelled over him, "I hear another woman's voice. But do you think I get an explanation or an 'I love you, Baby' or even a call back when you get service again? You just hung up on me and that was that. So why the hell do you think I felt the need to go out and have a few drinks with my best friend last night?"

She turned away from Brandon and stormed into her walk-in closet, snatching a pair of jeans and a shirt from the hangers. Her head felt 10 times worse than the hangover but she did not care. All she wanted to do was get out of his sight. Then it dawned on her.

"Get your ass out of my house," Denyce said while tossing her clothes on her bed.

Brandon looked at her. "Baby..."

"Noooo, nooo, no," Denyce said and pointed to the bedroom door. "This is my house, been mine for 20 damn years...I worked to buy and pay for it. Get your sorry ass out!"

Brandon blinked then grabbed the overnight bag and some clothes. He threw the strap on his shoulder and quietly left the bedroom, went downstairs and left.

Moments after hearing his car leave, Denyce sat on the foot of the bed and covered her face. When she blurted out about hearing a woman's voice on his cell, it was no mistake that Brandon did not say a word afterwards. It was all too clear that her world was falling apart.

The next few days before the business trip were a confusing blur. Her workload hadn't let up; it did not matter how late she worked because Brandon stayed away from the house, just like she demanded. Some days seemed worse than others, but all of them were heavy with waiting. She did her best to avoid thinking about Brandon and where he was…or who he was with. The tables have turned and Denyce wore the green eyes of jealousy.

Her flight to Los Angeles in 48 hours and Denyce feared Brandon won't ever call. She's only had one lengthy conversation and that was with Autumn, who hooked her up with discount roundtrip airfare. "My pleasure, honey," Autumn said.

"After all, what good is it being a flight attendant if I can't treat my girls to great deals?" Denyce smiled, but solemnly returned the conversation back to Brandon. She filled Autumn in on the drama and was seeking her honest opinion. "So do you think I should call him?" Denyce asked.

"I don't know what to tell you, honey," Autumn said, "I feel that with the way things went down, it's his responsibility to call you and explain everything."

"And that's exactly why I haven't called Brandon. I feel as if he betrayed me, not the other way around!"

"Well, I'm sure he feels like he isn't the only one in the wrong," Autumn said. "It's just complicated. You were busy, maybe he started to feel neglected…"

"Are you saying I made him cheat?" Denyce yelled.

"No, that's not what I'm saying! I'm saying maybe you two just drifted apart. It's not like your relationship was easy. It took work. And if you let a couple of things slide, before you know it, you're grasping at air trying to keep it together," Autumn said.

Denyce knew she was right. Had she forced Brandon into the arms of another woman? She would kill herself it she had. "I just never realized we were on such shaky ground," Denyce said. "Everything was perfect until our trip." She suddenly remembered something. "Oh my God," Denyce shrieked.

"What?" Autumn asked.

"The phone call."

"What?" Autumn asked. "What phone call?"

"When we were in the Bahamas, he got a call from someone. He said it was a telemarketer…"

"Since when do telemarketers call cell phones?" Autumn interrupted.

"Exactly! I thought the same thing but we were having such a great time I just let it go."

"You don't think?" Autumn asked.

"Brandon was cheating on me the whole time," she cried. "That bastard!"

"No," Autumn said, "I don't believe it."

"There's only one way to find out," Denyce said. She walked in the den, sat in front of the desk and turned on the computer.

"Denyce what are you doing?" Autumn asked. "I heard your computer come on…you are not hacking into his account!"

Denyce ignored Autumn and began typing Brandon's e-mail address and password. "I deserve to know if he is cheating on me," Denyce said while she waited for his page to pop up. "If he doesn't have the nerve to call and tell me the truth, then I will search for the truth…or rather, lies," she said. "And I don't have to hack; I already know the password."

"Denyce I really don't think this is a good idea," Autumn said.

"I really need you to be a supportive friend right now, Autumn…." Denyce paused then pounded the desk with her fist. "Son of a bitch changed his password!" Denyce ran her fingers in her hair trying to think of any clues. She and Autumn tried everything; names, food, runner/jogger. Each attempt led to an 'error' statement.

"Denyce just leave it alone and wait until Brandon calls you," Autumn pleaded.

Denyce looked around the office for another hint. She noticed a corkboard on the upper right side of the wall and a map of all the running trails highlighted. Denyce snapped her fingers and typed lakefront trail. The page immediately opened. "Yes, I'm in!" Denyce yelled in Autumn's ear.

"No way!" Autumn shouted, "Oh, my God, my heart is racing! I feel like we're doing something illegal."

Denyce clicked on the inbox and scrolled the current message topics. "Nothing here but junk and coupons for penis enlargement drugs," she laughed.

"Try the sent box. A lot of people never clean that out and it saves everything you send," Autumn said.

Denyce clicked the link and tons of messages from the past year appeared. She did not recognize any of the subject matter on most of them. "There is at least 20 e-mails to a Jen Hampton," Denyce said, "I don't know a Jen Hampton, Autumn." Denyce's hand that held the mouse trembled. "Do you think this is the other woman?"

"I don't know," Autumn said. "Are you sure you want to open them?"

Denyce noticed an e-mail dated two days ago. She held the cursor at the link but was hesitant to click the mouse. "I don't know Autumn." All the answers to Denyce's suspicions could be in this e-mail and yet panic rushed her senses.

"Did you open it?" Autumn asked, "Denyce? What does it say?"

Denyce looked at the link. She moved the cursor to the upper right corner of the screen. Autumn's voice rose to break the silence. "What did it say?"

"I can't tell you," Denyce said, "I logged out." She then turned off the computer and sat back in the chair. Tears rolled down her cheeks and she sniffed.

"Oh Denyce," Autumn said. "What are you going to do now?"

"I don't know," Denyce sighed. "I know you don't want to, but you're going to have to talk to Brandon about this. You two can't keep running circles around each other forever. This has to get resolved."

"Yeah I know," Denyce said. She thanked her friend again for the tickets and promised to call her when she returned from Los Angeles.

Pushing her body out of the chair, Denyce went to her bedroom and started packing. Talking to Brandon will have to wait until she got back.

Chapter 6

Because of Autumn Denyce and Trevor were flying first class to Los Angeles with no layovers. When a flight attendant arrives with champagne, Denyce immediately grabbed a flute, emptied it in one gulp and signaled for a refill. "Whoa there," Trevor said, "What's the hurry?"

She smiled at the attendant who topped the flute. Denyce then tilted her seat back and rested her head. "I plan on having some peace on this flight. She tilted the flute in his direction. "And this is going to give it to me a hell of a lot faster."

"You know our first meeting with Darrell is this evening," Trevor said while adjusting his seat.

Denyce glanced at her watch. "That gives me just over seven hours of rest and relaxation and almost half of that will be spent on this aircraft, so I'm good."

"All right then," Trevor said and reached over with his flute for a refill. He sat back noticing Denyce closed her eyes. "I take it things are still tense at home."

Denyce kept her eyes closed. "I don't want to talk about it right now, Trevor," she said. "Let's just get this week over, and this deal settled with McKinley. I'll manage my own affairs."

Trevor gulped his champagne and rested the flute on the tray. "No problem, boss lady."

The first three days of meetings and arrangements went smoothly. Being in a new city and facing the challenges organizing the McKinley deal exhilarated Denyce and took her mind off things back in Chicago. The trip hit a snag when on the fourth day Darrell McKinley announced that he needed to rescheduled the meetings.

"I truly apologize for the delay. We'll have to finish everything at tomorrow morning's meeting," Darrell said. "Again, my apologies, but family matters are never predictable."

"Don't worry about it, Darrell," Trevor said. "We'll be able to settle everything tomorrow, no problem."

"Yes," Denyce added, "Trevor and I will work on finalizing everything tonight and we can neatly tie up this deal tomorrow." They shook hands and promised to meet at 8 a.m.

Denyce and Trevor exhaled as soon as they were out of Darrell's sight. "So what's the plan boss lady?" Trevor joked as they walked the foyer to the building's exit. Denyce glances at her watch. "Well, it's after 10 a.m. and we've had breakfast. I guess we can do whatever we want."

"Sounds good," Trevor said as he holds the door open for her to walk out. "Anything in particular you want to see?"

"I guess I could look over the details later today, say for dinner." Trevor caught her arm. "No, I meant did you want to see anything in the city; go sight-seeing?"

Denyce thought about it. "I wouldn't mind taking a dip in the pool. Not quite this warm in Chicago yet. Maybe I can work on my tan." She held her arm out and examined her dark skin. "Maybe not," she smiled.

Trevor grinned back. "All right, I'll meet you at the poolside bar in half an hour. Sound good?"

"Sure," she said, "I'll even buy you one of those fruity girlie drinks with the umbrella." Trevor flinched at the offer. "Yeah, not going to happen but I will meet you poolside anyway!"

Back in her suite Denyce admired the reflection in the stand alone mirror. She brought along a black two-piece swimsuit instead of a one piece. Her curves filled the bikini nicely; in fact better at 43 than in her 30s. Having not dealt with the physical aftermath of childbirth as some women do, her body is still one to reckon with. She turned around so to look over her shoulder at her backside and smiled. "Wait until Brandon…" Denyce froze then walked away from the mirror. She could not believe she brought up Brandon knowing damn well he was somewhere else and likely with someone else. A sudden panic rushed through her body as she thought about walking along the poolside for Trevor. She looked at her body thinking she should have brought the one-piece. What will Trevor say when he sees me in this bikini? What will he think? Denyce walked up to the mirror again. "Screw it," she said and tied on the red and black sarong. She stepped into a pair of red flip flops, grabbed her key card and left the suite.

Trevor was sitting at the poolside bar wearing a pair of board shorts and sunglasses. He saw Denyce immediately and waved her over.

Denyce smiled and sashayed over to the bar, pretending to be oblivious to the male onlookers following her every sway. She dug in her bag for a pair of sunglasses to block the searing sun. She took the stool beside Trevor and nodded at the bartender.

"I beat you to it," Trevor said, as he handed her a strawberry daiquiri decorated by a florescent green paper umbrella. "Just what I needed," Denyce laughs and takes a sip. "Where's yours?"

Trevor raised a glass of rum and Coke.

Denyce took another sip from her drink and tries to avoid scanning Trevor's body up and down. For a man in his late 40s Trevor had a damn near perfect physique. He's been hiding all of that under those suits?

"Denyce!"

Denyce snapped out of her daze. "Huh? Oh, what were you saying?"

"I said you look great in your swimsuit ensemble," Trevor repeated with a wave of his hand.

"Thank you," she said praying her face isn't flushed with embarrassment.

"I'm almost afraid to ask if you wanted to go for that swim!" he went on to say.

"What! Let's go," Denyce said and hopped off the stool. Trevor pointed out the lounge chairs he reserved and with dramatic flourish, Denyce took off the sarong and stepped out of her flip flops. She placed everything in one of the chairs and rushed to the pool.

SPLASH!

Denyce looked ahead and noticed that Trevor ran past her and jumped in the deep end of the pool. "You got me wet," Denyce said then wished she could take the words back.

"Oh, come on!" Trevor yelled, "Just jump in here! I thought you were Miss all that!"

Denyce raised an eyebrow and picked up her pace to the edge. Instead of jumping in, she turned and walked to the ladder of the diving board. Trevor did a backstroke while watching Denyce walk to the edge of the board. After two bounces, she did a perfect dive into the pool.

As Denyce come up from underwater Trevor applauded. "I am Miss All That," she said with pride.

"Bravo! And I will never doubt your title again," Trevor said as he swam towards her. An odd silence came between them as Trevor watched Denyce run her hands over her hair which was in a tight ponytail. His eyes panned her body from head to toe as the water rippled against her body.

"Okay, Trevor," Denyce said, "You can stop staring now."

"My apologies, but it's hard not to look."

"Mmm-hmm," Denyce pursed her lips together. "You're not so bad yourself," she said as she swam towards the other side of the pool, leaving him in the center.

"Wait," Trevor said, "did you just give me a compliment?"

Denyce laughed as Trevor mimicked unbelievable shock. She sat on an underwater bench in the corner and shook her head. "Did I? I better take it back then!"

"Typical woman," Trevor laughed. He swam to the bench and sat next to her. Denyce mocked being insulted and splashed water at him. "I resent that!"

"Sure you do. You know how you women are; will change her mind at a finger snap," Trevor teased. "However, you, Miss Wright, are a woman of mystery."

Denyce looked at Trevor with surprise. "I guess that's a compliment," she said. Trevor continued to look at her and soon Denyce felt hot despite the water's coolness. "It is a compliment…and you're welcome."

As Trevor continued to look at her like a man looks at his girlfriend…or wife, Brandon invaded Denyce's thoughts. "Hey," Trevor said, "Where'd your mind go this time?"

"You don't want to know," she said. "How do know that?"

"Brandon walked out on me," Denyce sighed, "Correction, I kicked his ass out of my house. I did it because I think he's been cheating on me."

Trevor's head drew back. "This has to be a joke…"

"No, it's true. I kicked him out and he did not fight it," she continued. "He grabbed that damn bag, put some clothes in it and walked out. I've not heard from him since." Trevor stared at Denyce who looked ahead of her as if watching the rest of the hotel guests enjoy a day at the pool. "Remember how I was such a bitch to the women at the office, especially to Cheri? Yeah well what I suspected turns out to be true."

Trevor wrapped his arm around her and pulled her close for a hug. Denyce did not stop his embrace; instead she relished it. "Denyce I am so sorry. I should have questioned your mood earlier," Trevor said.

Denyce sighed in Trevor's embrace. "You did not know what was going on." "I knew enough that you did not deserve this," Trevor said, "and he did not deserve you. Not then and not now."

Denyce blinked at Trevor's words and soon felt uncomfortable. She moves his arm from her shoulder and stands up from the bench. "I think I'll go back to my suite and maybe take a nap," she said and reaches for the side grip.

"Denyce do become a hermit in that suite," Trevor said while swimming to the edge. "What purpose will it serve to punish you for something that jerk did?"

"A big bed, a couple of free movies, room service and the deluxe mini bar is not punishment," Denyce chuckled while grabbing the complimentary towel from the chair.

Trevor lightly grabbed Denyce's arm. "You are not going to spend the rest of the day crying over some asshole who didn't know what he had right in front of him."

Denyce gently pulled away from Trevor's hold, puts down the towel and brings the sarong around her waist. "I'm a grown woman Trevor and can do whatever I want on this sudden free time." She picked up her bag, pulls out the key card and brushes past him. Trevor grabs his towel and follows Denyce inside the hotel. "Where are you going?" she said.

"I'm walking you to your suite," he said and ignores any objection she throws at him. When they get to her suite door Denyce swipes the card and waits for the green light to appear on the door. Nothing.

"Ok," she mumbles and swipes the card again. The light on the door remains red.

"Let me try," Trevor said and he takes the key card and swipes it. "This is your key card…"

"Yes Trevor it's my key card," Denyce snaps and snatches the card from his hand. Trevor takes her hand and pulls her away from the door. "Let's go to the front desk and have them look at the card."

They head to the desk and give the young woman the card. She attempts to swipe it from a machine. "I'm sorry, ma'am but it looks like a chip glitch."

Denyce nods. "OK, so can I have a replacement?"

The woman blushes. "I'm not authorized to give you a replacement and my supervisor is on his lunch break. I'm sorry."

Denyce's mouth drops open and she spins away from the desk throwing her arms in the air. "Unbelievable!"

Trevor leans over the desk counter and tells the woman to call his room when the supervisor returns. He then places his hands on Denyce's shoulders and pushes her forward. "We can go to my suite and you can dry off and relax. I'll order us some room service and you can watch all of the sappy chick flicks you desire."

They got off the elevator and went to Trevor's suite. He swiped his key card and pushed the door open. Denyce walked in and headed straight for the mini bar. She grabbed two bottles of vodka and a bag of peanuts. "Make yourself at home," Trevor said as Denyce plopped down on the sofa.

"I'll pay you back for these." "Don't worry about it," Trevor said and picks up the phone to order some food. "Is there anything in particular you want?"

Denyce smiles. "A big piece of chocolate cake with vanilla ice cream…and a slice of cheesecake!"

"A three course meal," Trevor jokes. He gave the order and added a couple of turkey club sandwiches and pop. "Our order will be here in 20," he said. Trevor sat down besides Denyce who then swings her feet onto his lap.

"So…what are you going to do about Brandon? Does this mean it's over between you two?"

Denyce emptied one mini bottle of vodka and placed it on the side table. "I don't know. You'd think I've made up my mind but love is not all black and white; it has turned into a funky shade of gray," she said.

"I can't argue with that. But sometimes you got to put reason ahead of love. It's not the way they sing about it in love songs and if you don't put reason first then you're playing dumb," Trevor said. "You have to protect yourself sometimes."

"Is that why you're still single?" Denyce asked.

Trevor laughed. "I thought we were talking about you?"

"Well, I don't see you taking any risks in love, and I've known you for a long time, Trevor. What's your story on hearts of the matter?"

Trevor looked away. "We don't need to go there right now. I want to make sure you're okay."

Denyce sat up. "Oh no you don't; spill it! There is someone in that heart of yours."

Trevor nervously glanced at her. "You want to know who the love of my life is, Denyce?"

Denyce smiled in anticipation.

"You," Trevor said and looks at her. "It's you, Denyce and it has been since the moment you walked into the office."

Denyce's eyes widen and when she tried to speak, the words were nonexistent.

"When I said Brandon didn't deserve you, I meant it," he went on. "You are more woman than any man on this earth deserves to have. You are smart, funny, gorgeous and sexy. You are a strong and independent woman."

Denyce felt the blood rush her face and her heart pounded so hard it felt as if it was fighting to break free from her body.

"These past few months have been excruciating for me; hell, the past two years have been heartbreaking, watching you fall in love with another man. And despite you being with Brandon we were growing closer, and I hoped…" his voice trails off. "I just hoped."

"Trevor…I..." Denyce said.

"I know," Trevor said. "It's impossible, right? Working so closely at Sherls & Hughes, it would be impossible for anything to happen." He looked away. "It doesn't help that you still love him. The moment I saw your eyes light up talking about him, I knew I'd never stand a chance."

Denyce sat there, speechless. She did love Brandon, but he ruined it. Denyce looked at Trevor and dropped her feet from his lap. She scooted closer to him and gently placed her hand on his thigh. Trevor eyes dropped to her hand and he slowly looked at her. He turned to Denyce, grabbed her hand and with a quick yank, pulled her forward. His mouth crushed against hers as he cupped her face. She felt his tongue push inside her mouth and she returned the force of their tongues tangling. She leaned until she was on her back and Trevor climbed on top of her. Their bodies rubbed against each other with Trevor's hips grinding against her. The hardness in his swim shorts sent waves of heat through her.

Suddenly there was an abrupt knock on the door. "Room service!" a man's voice rang out.

Trevor and Denyce stopped, searching each other's eyes for the next action to take. He sighed in frustration and stood up. "Just a minute," he called out.

Denyce bit her lip and sat up. "It's okay," she whispered then sat up and smoothed her hair.

Trevor opened the door, tipped the bellhop and pulled the cart inside. He kicked the door close and rolled the cart to the couch. "Your…dessert, madam," Trevor joked while lifting the lid. Denyce laughed as he walked around the cart and sat next to her.

"Yeah," Denyce said while pushing the cart away. "I was already having dessert." She leaned forward and kisses Trevor while pulling him back on top.

Trevor's hands caressed her body; his left hand finds the knot of the sarong and tugs at it. Denyce raised her hips to make it easier for him to remove it and push her bikini bottom past her hips. She fumbled with the drawstrings of his shorts, finally pushing them past his ass. Their bodies wiggled on the limited space the couch provided…

"Riiiiiiiing!" Both freeze as the phone repeats its untimely interruption. Trevor rested his head on Denyce's shoulder. "Seriously?" he mumbled while climbing off of her and grabbing the receiver.

"Yes hello? Oh, good. Thank you." Trevor looked at Denyce. "The supervisor is back from lunch and has your replacement key card."

She gave him a slight smile and sat up. "Trevor…I think we should hold off on doing this." Trevor sighed and sits back on the couch. "It must be a sign; an omen, something," he laughed.

Denyce leaned over, picked up the sarong and standed up to wrap it around her waist. "Consider it bad timing. Besides, I am too unstable right now and what's going on between me and Brandon needs closure."

Trevor rubbed his face and smiled. "If something were to happen between us," Denyce stroked his face, "I would want you to have all of me – mind, body and soul – because you deserve that."

She headed for the door, turning before leaving. "I'm sorry," she whispered.

"Don't be," Trevor said, still sitting on the sofa. "This won't change anything. I still love you and the world will never be the wiser."

Denyce took the elevator to the lobby and retrieved the new key card. She walked back to the elevator to return to her suite, her mind on what took place and how far it almost went. It was a moment of weakness that happened because of unfinished anger and bitterness towards Brandon.

A feeling of guilt seared her heart as she realized that she almost took advantage of Trevor's true feelings for her selfish act of revenge. The elevator doors opened at the floor they were staying on and Denyce rushed past Trevor's door to get to hers three doors down. She let herself inside and snatched off the sarong, the bikini and headed for the shower. She rinsed away any evidence of touching and even grabbed the complimentary bottles of shampoo and conditioner to wash her hair. Stepping out of the shower 20 minutes later, she dried off and put on the provided bathrobe. She marched over to the mini bar and took another bottle of vodka out and some snacks, cursing herself for not taking her orders of cake, ice cream and cheesecake with her when she left Trevor's suite.

Denyce jumped in the bed, grabbed the TV remote from the nightstand and pushed the Power button. Alcohol, cookies, peanuts and a movie is all she can take the rest of the day.

Denyce breezed into the conference room the next morning as if she did not indulge in alcohol and for a brief moment, Trevor. "Good morning, everyone," she said to the assistant and a server setting up the continental breakfast table. She walked past Trevor with a slight nod. Trevor watched her as she found a seat two chairs away from him. She felt his eyes and looked at him with a smile.

"Is everything alright Trevor?"

Trevor blinked and then a solemn expression covered his face. "Everything is great," he said with a forced smile that made Denyce uncomfortable. She opened her mouth to say something when McKinley walked in and immediately regained a professional composure.

The meeting ended 90 minutes later and Denyce rushed back to her suite. She called for a bellhop from her cell phone while looking to see if she was missing anything. Instead of waiting for the late afternoon flight with Trevor to Chicago, she went online last night and was able to bump to an earlier flight within the next hour.

She left the hotel without bumping into Trevor and rushed the airport. After dealing with TSAs and baggage check, Denyce sat in first class relieved that she could relax. She politely declined the complimentary champagne, remembering her 2 a.m. wakeup call from the vodka and junk food. She reclines her seat and closes her eyes as the plane picked up speed on the runway. She wonders what she will face when she returns home and walks in her door. She checked her cell for messages or texts from Brandon and got nothing. As she dozed off she hoped to have one last chance to see and speak to Brandon. She hoped for one last chance to mend what was chipping away.

Hours later Denyce made it home and unlocked the door. She dragged the wheeled carry-on into the living room and glanced to her right. Brandon was sitting at the kitchen table reading the newspaper and eating a BLT. "Hello," she said while standing in the doorway.

He jerked his head away from the paper and jumped up. Denyce stood with her arms folded as he wiped bread crumbs off his face then clothing. He chewed and swallowed a portion of the sandwich and dropped the paper on the table. "I thought you would not be home until this evening," he said.

"I took an early flight," she said.

"Oh," he returned.

Denyce turned away, removed her coat and walked to the living room closet. She placed her purse on the side table.

Gordon entered the living room. "I know this is…complicated."

"You think?" Denyce replied.

"I meant to call…"

"Do you even still live here?" Denyce interrupted.

Brandon paused. "I'm not sure what to say to that."

Denyce grabbed her suitcase and started upstairs.

"We need to talk, Denyce," Brandon called after her, his hand resting on the banister.

"It would've been nice to hear you say this weeks ago!"

"I know," Brandon said, "I deserve that…"

"Whatever," Denyce said and walks inside the master bedroom then returns to the top of the staircase. "I'm sure you and Miss Hampton have blissfully counted every day of peace you've had."

"Who?" Brandon asked.

"I did not stutter Brandon! Nearly a month goes by without a single phone call, text or e-mail after I find out you're messing with another woman and now you're playing dumb?"

Brandon runs up the stairs, "Another woman? Denyce, hold on…"

"It doesn't matter anymore," Denyce continues, "I've moved on." She hurled her bag on the bed and unzips it.

Brandon stops in the bedroom doorway confused. "Moved on? What are you talking about?"

"Don't change the subject. This isn't about me. This is about you. If you're not already here to get your things or to give me a proper explanation, you can pack the rest of your things and leave!"

"You're trying to throw me out?"

"It's not like you live here anymore and, by the way, this is my house," she said. Brandon entered the room and tries to grab Denyce by the arm. "Can you please sit down so we can talk about this…about us?"

"Don't you touch me!" Denyce shouted.

"I'm sorry I didn't call, Denyce. I know what it looks like but you have got to trust me."

"Trust you?"

"Yes," he pleaded. "Please, just trust me. I would never cheat on you. I never did and I never will. I love you, Denyce. It's just complicated. I promise, I'll explain everything in time."

Denyce just stared at Brandon not knowing what to believe. She did not expect him to be in the house, let alone listening to him spill all sorts of excuses at her. She felt like throwing up.

"Will you please say something?" Brandon asked.

"Who is Jen Hampton?"

Brandon looked at Denyce. "All I can tell you…Jen is a friend who is helping me with some personal issues."

Denyce blinked at Brandon, shook her head and blinked again. "I don't hear from my man; a man who said he loves me, is living with me…and you're saying this Jen is a friend helping you with some personal issues?"

"I know it sounds crazy," Brandon continued, "But that's why I put off calling or seeing you for so long. I think…"

"I kissed Trevor," Denyce blurted out.

Brandon froze. He stared wide-eyed at Denyce hoping he did not hear what she said. "We had some free time between meetings and, we went for a swim and went back to his suite because my key card would not work," Denyce rambled, "and we almost…"

"Don't," he interjected.

"But nothing happened."

"I can't hear this," Brandon said and starts to walk out of the bedroom.

"Brandon!"

He spun around and charge towards Denyce. "You're accusing *me* of cheating, when *you're* the one off running around, while I'm *completely* faithful?!" He turned again to leave. "Hold up! How did you know her name is Jen Hampton?"

"I…I opened your account…" Brandon threw his hands up and on top of his head.

"You went into my e-mail account Denyce?! Seriously, you spied on me?"

Denyce took two steps back. "No, I mean yes, but I did not read the emails, Brandon! I just noticed who they were from! But Brandon, nothing happened with Trevor and we did not sleep together! I was emotional and stressed from not hearing from or seeing you. I could not go through with it because I love you!"

"I can't be here right now," Brandon spat out," I gotta get out of here!" He ran down stairs, grabbed his coat, flew the door open and slammed it shut behind him.

Denyce stood at the top of the stairs listening to the wheels of his car screech on the pavement. She returned to her bedroom as tears wet her face. Denyce was more confused than ever. She felt if she admitted what almost but didn't happen with Trevor that Brandon would decide to open up and reveal the personal issues he decided to handle with another woman. Instead, Brandon left in a rage that made her have second thoughts. He truly looked heartbroken, she thought. "Shit, I don't know what's going on with me!" She dropped down on the bed and released her emotions in endless sobs; she truly does love Brandon and blamed herself for not being more understanding.

Chapter 7

It was an hour before Denyce finally pulled herself off the bed. Her eyes were puffy and red and she felt a headache coming on. Brandon had not returned and she feared that he wouldn't. It would not surprise her if he'd eventually show up with a moving truck to get his things. More than ever she wanted to cocoon herself from the outside world and escape from this madness call love. She's lost Brandon and she had to return to work and face another man she ran away from. Kissing Trevor was a mistake along with bumping and grinding with him on that damn couch. I should have waited in the lobby for the supervisor to return, she thought. It was too little, too late. She messed around with someone's feelings because she assumed the man in her life – the man who loved her and she loved in return – was with another woman. She was jealous of this Jen Hampton and did not have a fucking clue about her connection with Brandon.

And Trevor, who confessed his love for her. Things at the office will never be the same after Los Angeles. There was no way in hell Trevor will act like that moment of passion did not happen. He is smart enough to know by now that she was using him for her selfish needs. Denyce planned to return to work the next day but after all of this she was going to call Cheri and tell her she was taking another week off. Hell she may just turn in a letter of resignation, sell the house and move to another state. Again with the running! Sherls & Hughes was her corporation for twelve years and she'll be damned if she was going to run from the company.

Her call phone rang, jarring her from her thoughts. Trevor Langfield appeared on the caller ID. Denyce groaned and pressed the silent button. She was about to empty what had to be a dozen messages from him since she left L.A. but felt the need to hear the message he left moments later. "Denyce it's Trevor again. I know you are probably just getting in a settling down but….we should talk. Call me." Denyce cleared the message and continued to clean out the voicemail box. She tossed her phone on the bed and went downstairs to get something to eat.

While fixing a small salad, Denyce picked up the receiver from the landline and dialed Cheri's office number. "Sherls & Hughes, this is Cheri speaking; how may I help you?"

"Hey Cheri, it's Denyce."

"Oh, hi Miss Wright! I was not expecting a call from you today. Is there something wrong?"

Yeah, everything. "No, I am just checking in. Uhm, is it real busy over there?"

"No ma'am, everything is running smoothly," Cheri said. "Although Mr. Washington is here and he's acting kind of bizarre…"

"I'm sure he's fine," Denyce chimed in, "if he came in straight from the airport, he's probably just tired."

"Yes you are probably right," Cheri said.

Denyce paused for a moment. "Uhm, Cheri I also called because I won't likely return to the office for another week."

"Oh, I see," Cheri said. "I'm pretty tired myself from the trip and I may be coming down with something," Denyce said while rolling her eyes. "I will check in from time to time."

"Ok Miss Wright. You take care of yourself." Denyce hung up and stared at the salad before putting it back in the refrigerator, her appetite gone for the night.

The following week came and went without a word from Brandon. Denyce kept herself busy with housework, grocery shopping(although she bought half the amount of food), reading and sleeping. She barely kept telephone conversations with Charlize, Natasha or Autumn past 10 minutes and turned down lunch and dinner dates. The Saturday before she forced herself back to work was spent in the bed eating, sleeping and watching shows she recorded on the DVR. She was back in a deep slumber when the phone on the nightstand practically screamed. She put the pillow over her head and prayed for the voicemail to click on. Instead a male voice came from the intercom. "Denyce it's Trevor. The company ball is tonight and you and Brandon are scheduled to be there. Uhm, if you've forgotten, Greg Powell and Darrell McKinley will also be there and you two are sitting at their table." Denyce sat up and tossed the pillow to the side. "If Brandon can't make it I can meet you at the door and be your escort for the evening. So, call me."

Denyce looked at the time. She had approximately two hours to get ready for the event and Brandon was still not talking to her. She fought the urge to crawl back under her blanket cave and dragged into the bathroom. "GAAAAAAAAAAAAH!" Denyce caught a glimpse of herself in the mirror; her weave was nappy, she had raccoon rings under her eyes and her nose looked like a clown's rubber nose. She stripped off her pajamas and jumped in the shower with a wash cloth, soap and a comb to detangle her weave. Thirty minutes later she was lathering her body with lotions and her eyes with cream. She blow dried her hair and grabbed the styling gel to transform her locks into a sleek ponytail.

Running to the closet with nothing on but a thong, Denyce pulled out a Marc Jacobs fuchsia satin gown with a plunging front and back. She accessorized with a Mauri Pioppo gold and amethyst ring, and authentic Indian gold and diamond bangles. She stepped into a simple pair of Chie

Mihara flat-soled sandals. A quick makeup job and she looked nothing like the self-pitying crybaby she's been all week. She grabbed her clutch and headed out the door alone.

Denyce walked into the lobby of the ballroom where the event was held and took a breath. She'd checked her fur at the door and got smiles and compliments on her dress. She wished Brandon was standing at her side, holding her hand and sneaking a fight with the tuxedo she would have insisted he wear. Instead, Denyce walked into the ballroom and found the table where Trevor, Powell and McKinley were seated. "Good evening gentlemen," she smiled as the men stood up. "Miss Wright, it's an honor to see you again," Darrell said while shaking her hand. She shook Powell's hand and nodded at Trevor who pulled out a chair for her to sit.

"Thank you Trevor," she said while looking at him. Trevor pushed the chair up and turned to greet guests at a nearby table.

"Psst, Trevor," Denyce whispered while grabbing his hand.

"What's wrong," he asked.

"I know I am supposed to deliver a thank you speech, but I did not prepare one," Denyce said.

"Don't worry about it," he said then walked off. The entire evening went fast even when Denyce would catch Trevor glancing at her. She talked to Powell and McKinley then went to every table for a quick chat with the guests. With three hours in Denyce felt it was OK to leave for the night. She could only pretend to be Miss Marketing Professional for so long. She said her good-byes and went to the coat check to retrieve her fur. She was almost out the door when a hand grasped her shoulder.

She turned to see Trevor standing behind her. "What are you doing?" Denyce asked as Trevor gently guided her outside.

He did not bother to get his coat and walked her to the side of the centre. "I should be asking you the same thing," Trevor said while watching the doors. "You owe me a few minutes of your time; after all I did the courtesy of delivering the thank you speech at the podium.

Denyce tightened her coat and nodded. "Fair enough. What do you want?"

Trevor leaned closer to Denyce who smelled alcohol on his breath. "Why are you leaving so early? You don't return my calls, you take a week off after a business trip and by the way I did figure out that you took another flight. And now you're taking off on what is the company's biggest event...and still ignore me?"

Denyce stared at him but felt her blood pressure rise.

"I thought we had something, Denyce," he continued. "At least, I thought we were friends."

Denyce moved her head back from the alcohol induced scent Trevor was giving off. "Well you thought wrong!"

"I thought wrong?" It was obvious now that Trevor had been drinking heavily. "Oh come on, Denyce! I know you liked it! You felt the same way I've been feeling for years! Tell me that I'm lying!

"Excuse me?" Denyce said.

Trevor moved close enough against Denyce to crush her with his body. "Come on baby just give me a chance. I can give you so much more than Brandon can imagine; he's just a freaking kid! He doesn't know how to satisfy a woman like I do." Trevor was slurring his words and he attempted to put his hands on Denyce's waist.

She slapped his hands away. "Trevor, you've gone too far and you need to back off…NOW!"

Trevor attempted to wrap his arms around her again.

"Stop it!" Denyce cried, trying to shove him away. She grabbed him by the shoulders and swiftly brought her knee to his groin, sending him reeling in pain.

"You Bitch!" he shouted.

Suddenly Denyce heard the whooshing sound of the double doors open. Two buff security guards charged outside and grabbed Trevor. "Are you okay, Ms. Wright?" one of the security guards asked.

"Yes, yes I am fine," Denyce said and stepped aside. "Mr. Langfield attacked me."

The other guard nodded. "The security camera caught all of it. We'll take it from here." The guards went to both sides of Trevor and walked off with him.

"Mr. Langfield!" Denyce yelled out. Trevor and the guards turned around. "Boxes containing your things will be at the front desk in the lobby Monday morning."

"Screw you, you deceitful whore!" he called back angrily.

Denyce picked up her clutch, adjusted her coat and walked to her car. Her hand shook as she attempted to unlock the car. She gave up and pushed the keypad that automatically popped the lock and climbed inside. Denyce started the car but waited five minutes before putting the car in gear and pulling off. More than anything she wished Brandon was here for her right now even if she'd have to post bail for him after what Trevor did.

By the time Denyce got home her shaking had nearly subsided. She walked tiredly into the house, still wishing Brandon was there to calm her. She took a few more steps and noticed Brandon sitting at the bottom step of the stairway. A set of bags were propped against the railing.

"Brandon," Denyce whispered.

"Denyce," Brandon said, "Just let me talk." Denyce nodded and removed her coat.

"I love you Denyce, I truly do. But you have made it hard on me sometimes."

"I …"

"Just let me say my peace, Denyce," he said firmly.

"I understand why you kissed Trevor. I let you down and I drove you to him."

Denyce took a step back. She couldn't believe what she was hearing. Brandon was blaming himself for what happened with Trevor. "No Brandon, I need to tell you…"

"Woman! Brandon snapped, "You need to let me finish!"

She closed her mouth again and held her breath.

"I want you to know that if you feel you need my forgiveness, you have it. But I take full responsibility for not letting you know what was going on sooner. I neglected you, I let you think we were over and for that I am truly sorry."

Denyce's eyes filled with tears. Everything was her fault and he was taking the blame.

Brandon looked at his bags. "We really did not get the chance to talk about everything, but you seem to have made up your mind." Brandon stood up. "If you want to move on then I can't do anything about it but leave. You just say the word."

Denyce felt her legs go numb. She never wanted Brandon to leave. That's what caused all the trouble in the first place. She wanted him to stay, to love her and be with her always. She was blinded with jealousy without know the whole story. But she never wanted to lose him.

"All I want to know Brandon is…who is Jen Hampton?" Denyce asked. "Please tell me!"

Brandon reached into his coat pocket and pulled out a form. He unfolded the document and held it out to Denyce. "The answer's right there," he said.

Denyce took the document and began reading. It was a certified document announcing Brandon's completion of a project management class.

"I don't understand," Denyce said.

"I've been going to school in Bloomington," Brandon said. "Miss Hampton is my course instructor and my advisor. She's been guiding me along and figuring out the best course of action to become a real estate developer."

"I still don't understand. Bloomington is two hours away," Denyce said. "You've been commuting all this time to take a class in Bloomington?"

"Yes, but only because that school had the program available at the time," Brandon said. "The colleges and universities in Illinois were not teaching the program for another year." Brandon stepped closer to Denyce. "That's why I've been out late at night; the reception during that commute is horrible! And I wanted to surprise you after I passed the program."

Denyce felt relieved and embarrassed. She's accused Brandon of so much wrong doing and he was doing right all this time! "Brandon you could have told me! Why would you keep this from me?"

Brandon reached into his other coat pocket and pulled out a small black, velvet case. He looked down at it and caressed the tiny box in his hands. "It was for this," he said quietly. "Because I needed to prove to you – and to me – that I could be worthy of your love."

Denyce's eyes widened at the sight of the box. Tears and mascara streamed down her cheeks. Brandon took a deep breath. "Denyce if you want me to stay, I will stay with you forever. You have made me a better man and I want to achieve things I never thought would be possible. You inspire me with your determination and dedication to your company and your life. I am so proud to be in your life and I want you to know that I can be the same as you." The tears increased and all Denyce could do was watch Brandon kneel down on one knee and open the little black box. A beautiful Tiffany platinum and diamond engagement ring sparkled.

"Denyce, if you let me, I will love you beyond forever. All you have to say is 'yes.'

Without hesitation, Denyce fell to her knees and threw her arms around Brandon's neck, ignoring the ring. "Oh Brandon Yes," she sobbed, "Yes, yes, and yes!"

Welcoming the embrace he missed for so long, Brandon held Denyce tight while kissing away her tears.

"I love you, Denyce," he whispered before locking his lips with hers.

"I love you too, Brandon," she whispered back.

Chapter 8

Denyce rolled over in bed, her hand hitting an empty pillow beside her. She opened her eyes in a moment of fear. Then she remembered; they were staying in separate suites at the Elysian, and today was the day.

Charlize and Natasha were set to arrive around 9 a.m. which gave them five hours to get everything ready. Autumn, however, was in Hawaii, and wouldn't arrive until after their luncheon and would only have time to throw on her dress and fix her hair. Denyce relished having a little time to herself before the madness began. She climbed out of bed and walked to the large Jacuzzi tub that was in the suite's master bathroom.

She pinned up her hair as the Jacuzzi filled with bubbles. She looked in the mirror and was relieved to not see one blemish on her face that would ruin her wedding day. "I'm getting married," she said aloud. She removed her night gown and stepped gingerly into the Jacuzzi, easing in a sitting position while getting adjusted to the heat. After adjusting the jets to a relaxing speed Denyce finally sat back and relaxed. She realized this day almost did not exist. She reflected on the past two years she and Brandon shared and damn if they weren't bumps, bruises and challenges. Denyce grabbed a loofah and gently massaged her body, smiling about the first time Brandon explored every inch of her. The rollercoaster ride that was their relationship seemed to derail at every little thing! She was beyond insecure about being in an uncommon relationship that society still frowns on, yet men old as Father Time could damn near date an infant without judgment. Through it all Brandon stayed around – even when he wasn't physically present, he was still in love with her. Brandon's love was the reason why today is happening and not her insecure, paranoid actions. God's truly blessed me with an amazing man, Denyce thought.

She let her hands fall to her lower abdomen. She imagined having Brandon's child. Given that she was now 45 years old, it was a medical risk, but she has yet to experience signs of menopause. If I want to be a mother we better start after the preacher pronounces us man and wife! She was so proud of Brandon in the last months before today. He was taking the steps needed to be a real estate developer and has matured beyond his now 33 years. They've talked about her leaving Sherls and Hughes and she's mentioned wanting to be his business partner. With her experience in overseeing and putting award winning projects together and his drive they would be a kickass team! It's only a thought because for now she wanted to be the supportive and loving wife Brandon deserves. And she knew he will be the perfect husband.

The Panthers Club

Denyce stepped out of the tub and wrapped herself in a luxurious bathrobe. She let the tub drain and left the bathroom. Denyce entered the main area of the suite and sat at the vanity table near the bed. She delicately unpinned her hair and combed it out, smoothing the frays and kinks of last night's peaceful slumber. She picked up the clips that would soon be attached with tiny orange and yellow roses. She held one up to her head, imagining how her hair would be styled: should she wear it up, back, or down? Shouldn't she have already made this decision?

She glanced at the clock on the wall. Any minute now Charlize and Natasha will rush inside the suite gushing with giddiness and excitement. They will surround her with love and friendship, mixed with nervousness as if it were they too, was getting married. "I owe it all to you for encouraging me to call Brandon back and say yes to a date," Denyce said to Charlize and Natasha as they helped her get ready.

"Damn skippy you owe it to us," Charlize said without hesitation. Natasha pinched Charlize's arm. "Ow! Girl I bruise easily," Charlize shrieked as Denyce laughed. "Ok ladies! While I know as the bride I need to look better than you all, but I can't have you looking like Ike beat your asses," she laughed.

They all laughed until they heard a knock on the door. "Just a second!" Charlize yelled as Natasha blocked Denyce.

"That better not be Brandon! It's bad luck to see the bride before the wedding!" Natasha said.

Charlize slowly opened the door and young man stood behind cart covered with silver trays. "Room service for the bride to be," he said and wheeled the cart inside. The man left and Denyce got up and lifted the lids. Platters of various treats were beautifully displayed; chocolate covered strawberries, waffles with fruit and whip cream, Danish pastries, fresh coffee, a pitcher of mimosa and a beautiful bouquet of pink roses and yellow lilies.

"*My goodness who is responsible for all of this?*" Denyce wondered as Charlize grabbed a strawberry. Natasha shook her head at Charlize and picked up an envelope.

"Maybe this will tell you," she said, handing it to Denyce.

She opened the envelope and pulled the card out. She recognized Brandon's handwriting immediately.

To my beautiful bride with whom

I am able to give many breakfasts in bed.

To the great future that lies ahead of us.

Much love,

- B

She placed the card on the cart and picked up a chocolate covered strawberry. Denyce bit into the fruit and relished its sweetness. Damn the diet she went on to make sure she'd fit the dress; this was a preview of mornings to come. She devoured two more until Natasha slapped her hand away and yanked the cart from Denyce's reach. "That's enough! You can have plenty of that and more after the wedding," she said. "But this will be wasted," Denyce pouted.

"No it won't," Charlize said and stabbed a fork into a slice of waffle covered in whipped cream. "I'm wearing an adjustable girdle under my bridesmaid dress. I have nothing to worry about!" The friends resumed getting ready for a Girls Day and headed to a limousine that whisked them to a spa. Denyce was scheduled for a massage and for all three, manicures and pedicures.

Denyce lulled into a deep sleep during her massage. She dreamed she and Brandon were walking a path together in a lush green forest, with two small girls running ahead of them. She longed for the girls to turn around so that she could see their faces, but they were always out of reach. When she began to feel disheartened Brandon's hand miraculously found hers, and she smiled at him. She couldn't see his face clearly but she knew it was Brandon and together they walked the beautiful path of the forest.

Denyce awaken from the dream just as the masseuse was massaging her scalp. She smiled at the thought of the dream. When the massage was over, she joined Charlize and Natasha in raised chairs for their pedicures. "So," Natasha began, "Do you have cold feet yet?"

"Nope," Denyce said.

"You aren't afraid at all?" Charlize asked.

"I am eagerly anticipating being Brandon's wife."

"Even after all those years alone?" Natasha pushed.

Denyce leaned her head back against the seat. "I guess I'm just ready now. I spent all that time afraid; now I no longer have to be. Brandon makes me fearless."

"Well that settles it for me," Charlize said, "If you're happy and content with this decision then we are happy for you and Brandon." Charlize reached over and squeezed Denyce's hand.

Denyce smiled. "I love you girls."

"We love you too," they said.

After a light lunch at Balsan's they returned to Denyce's suite. The stylist and assistants were already there waiting for their return. There was a little more than two hours to finish the hair and makeup.

Denyce sat at the vanity and the stylist created a plaited bun with clips garnished in rose petals and the tips covered with tiny flowers and an embellishment of long white feathers. Denyce then chose to apply her own makeup, allowing the stylist and assistants to work their magic on her friends.

Natasha began to blink as the stylist grabbed a tissue to blot away tears. "Natasha I know you are not crying!" Charlize said, "You are going to get Denyce started and ruin her makeup!" "I'm sorry," Natasha said while blotting her eyes. "I am just so happy for Denyce!"

Denyce smiled and blew a kiss to her friend. "Are you going to be OK?" Natasha smiled and straightened up for the stylist to continue. After their hair and makeup was done, Natasha went to the hanger and grabbed the wedding dress. It was a perfect choice; Greek style halter top with a flowing white chiffon skirt and a wide, diamond encrusted silver waist by Romona Kaveza. It costs a fortune but Denyce did not care and it was memorable.

The dress fitted her body without a hint of the breakfast she indulged showing. Natasha handed Denyce her bouquet, a floral bulb of orange, yellows and pastel green that matched the decorum in her hair. "How do I look?" she asked her friends. "Oh Denyce," they all chimed, "go to the mirror." Denyce slowly walked to the full length mirror and caught her breath. For the first time, her nerves began to rattle a bit. It suddenly felt real…she was getting married today.

Charlize and Natasha stood beside her in their orange and salmon bridesmaid dresses. Charlize touched Denyce's shoulders. "Are you ready for this?" Charlize asked.

Denyce grinned and nodded yes. "I'm getting married," she said, enjoying the sentence leaving her lips. "I'm getting married."

"Yes, you are, honey," Autumn shrieked while walking in the door with only minutes to spare. She was already dressed in a matching orange dress, similar in color but not in style to Charlize's.

Denyce whipped around. "Girl you finally made it! We were wondering if you'd be running down the aisle behind me!" The two women carefully hugged without crushing their dresses or ruining their makeup.

"It was so hard to leave Hawaii, but I knew I had a higher calling' to attend to!" Autumn joked.

The ladies fussed over each other as time moved quickly. Denyce's hired wedding coordinator, Andrew, had arranged everything in the ballroom for the ceremony. Just as the girls were straightening out the final touches, he popped his head in the room.

"Any moment now, ladies!" he bellowed in a high pitch voice. "Denyce, we are going to take you down last. Girlfriends you can head to the ballroom now, but please wait for me by the entrance!" The three giggled as Andrew shooed them out of the suite. He closed the door and faced Denyce. "Honey you are a dream!"

Denyce blushed. "I feel like a dream!" She could not wait to see Brandon standing at the altar. She was nervous now but that will change once she sees him while walking down the aisle. Andrew delicately checked for any mishaps or possible wardrobe malfunctions and began going through the itinerary one more time. I just want to be sure that everything is fabulous and you and Mr. Gordon have a stress-free day," Andrew said with a smile.

Denyce nodded. "And we've kept Mr. Gordon at bay; not just for the obvious bad luck thingy, but no pre-wedding hook-ups," Andrew said with mock seriousness. Denyce nodded and held her breath to keep from bursting into laughter. Suddenly a chime went off in Andrew's hand and he rushed out of the suite, making Denyce nervous.

Seconds later Andrew reappeared and spoke into the tiny radio. "We're on our way." Andrew motioned for Denyce to leave the suite. She stood up and held the dress and carefully passed Andrew who held the door open. They walked into the elevator under the admiration of other hotel guests not invited to the wedding.

On the ride down Andrew was chatting away with the last minute details but Denyce heard nothing. Her mind focused on what was about to take place. When the doors opened, Andrew was yakking about Brandon almost getting lost on the way to the hotel. She smiled and continued to follow Andrew.

Finally they were standing outside the ballroom. Denyce felt her hands begin to grow sweaty and she resisted the urge to wipe them on her wedding dress. Charlize, Natasha and Autumn stood in their designated spots in front of her. They looked over their shoulders and winked at her. Denyce just focused on taking deep breaths and holding her posture perfectly. When the music started, Andrew ushered each girl forward through the doors. He stood to the side of the door watching without distracting from the processional before him. The men were already standing at the altar with the preacher, watching the bridesmaids approach them.

Suddenly the familiar music of "The Wedding March" flowed through the speakers and the audience stood from their seats and turned to the doors. "It's your moment to shine, sweetie," Andrew said as he stepped further away. Denyce smiled and steadied herself. Taking a deep breath she walked to the doorway and glanced at the crowd. Her eyes settled on the handsome young man wearing a white tuxedo. He smiled at her. Denyce let out another breath and her nerves melted.

She was getting married today.

Autumn

Chapter 1

It was the last day of October and the sounds of children squealing in joy and terror filled the night's chilled air. Chicago's streets and neighborhoods were like those across the U.S. who celebrated this festive and frightening holiday; filled with parades of children in costumes, teens in their everyday wardrobes and parents bundled up to go through the mundane ritual of being the distant escorts. The sky wore an endless sheet of black with a scattering of stars and a moon that seem larger and more ominous than the average night. Candle lit Jack-o-lanterns and decorative paper bags assembled along sidewalks and porches as a guide to houses offering sweet treats. "Trick or Treat!" echoed throughout the neighborhoods as parents or bored teenagers gave out candy to smiles hidden by scary and amusing masks.

"So now you want to be a plastic surgeon?" Autumn was having her weekly telephone conversation with her daughter Danyelle while finishing preparing a pot of beef stew. "Why are you suddenly so fascinated in plastic surgery? And why do people even bother to do all of that crap?"

"I just find it interesting about plastikos or plastos," Danyelle said with a touch of irritation.

"Wait, plasti-what? Do you mean plastic? Cause if that is what you mean then say plastic!"

"Mom, plastikos or plastos are the Greek terminology for plastic! Either way it means molding or shaping."

"Well, it's all Greek to me how people want to waste money re-shaping and molding their faces, bodies, titties…"

"MOM!" Danyelle's shriek of embarrassment pierced Autumn's left eardrum and it was all she could do not to shriek in laughter at her sensitive baby girl.

"You've always been the brains of the family," Autumn managed to say without snickering at her earlier, 'appalling' remark. She heard her daughter release a slow sigh then a giggle. Danyelle shared her stubborn attitude to letting things go but was quicker to move on. And just that fast Danyelle continued talking about the history of plastic surgery including how the procedure helped in the treatment of World War II soldiers. Another 15 minutes went by and Autumn's stew was coming to a boil. "OK baby I need to let you go so I can finish dinner. Give Eric my love and I will talk to you later." "OK Mom. I love you!"

"I love you too, Baby girl."

Danyelle was almost 21 years old and in her third year of pre-med; but she will always be Autumn's baby. It's unbelievable that Danyelle was in the throes of deciding whether to become a plastic surgeon. Autumn supported any decision her daughter made and with the continuing trend of women…and men seeking anything to stop Father Time's aging process she will never be out of a job. But she had plenty of time to solidify her decisions between her internship and residency. What mattered to Autumn was Danyelle's education and happiness. Danyelle never had to worry about finances or having to ride out a semester because of a lack of money because Autumn stayed on top of writing the checks and sending them to the necessary offices. And she prayed before, during and after each bill was paid that Danyelle stayed diligent in her studies and continue to not be distracted. So far Danyelle's kept her proud and worry-free.

SLAM!

The sound of the back door startled Autumn and she turned from the stove to see her 17 year-old son join her in the kitchen. Terrence stopped long enough to give her a familiar look. "When's dinner going to be ready?" "Well, Denver will be home soon so let's say 30 minutes." Autumn then scanned her son from the top of his matted hair and dirty face to the numerous sweat stains located on various parts of his funky clothes. "Terrence before you do anything else I want you to get cleaned up! You stink," Autumn looked at his barely recognizable gym shoes. "What have I told you about walking through my house in those gym shoes?"

Terrence stepped out of the shoes and bent over to pick them up. "Sorry mama; I figured since I am already funky I would not offend you more by having you smell my feet!"

Autumn opened her mouth to say something when Terrence rushed to her and kissed her cheek. The dampness from his brow connected with the side of her face causing her to jump back. "Ugh! Boy, get away from me!"

He laughed and ran out of the kitchen. She watched Terrence's long, slender frame take the stairs two at a time and shook her head. Autumn felt that every time she blinked Terrence sprouts another two inches and his appetite was legendary which is why she used the largest pot she purchased to make one of his favorites, beef stew or chicken and dumplings.

She did not complain about cooking large meals for her son or being a homebody sometimes. Being a flight attendant for a major airline for nearly 20 years only allowed her to spend time at home in sporadic times. The best times was when she was able to return home at night after a day of work, but that shuffled with schedules when she was gone for three days at a time. Being on international routes meant at least working 12 to 15 days a month, but even then those days can increase at whim. Over the years she decided against leasing an apartment in another part of the U.S., especially when Danyelle and Terrence got older and finances were steep with school tuitions, dances and such. She would either stay at a hotel or room with another attendant who was single or had family nearby. Autumn was gaining seniority and could choose to cut back on her schedule, but with the unknowingly changes due to the recession and wondering if the airline suddenly clips its wings in employees and budgets she tries to maintain a full work schedule. She was riddled with guilt when Danyelle and Terrence were smaller, missing important moments like plays and games and it was worse when she'd worked holidays. But it was all for them. They see her a little more now and she laughed at the fact that she is with them during

Halloween weekend compared to missing their costume debuts years ago. The children never seemed to complain and immediately forgive her when she came home with gifts and souvenirs from the numerous cities and countries she had layovers. Whether it was routes within the U.S. or later when she began working the international routes, she enjoyed her traveling perks and seeing her children's faces light up when given bags filled with souvenirs. Her then husband Phillip however, always reminded her that she was not being the mother and wife she signed up to be. Even though they married young – and had Danyelle immediately-they were happy until Phillip was becoming more demanding of her duties as a wife and mother.

He knew when she took the job at 22 years old that both would have to work to keep a roof over their heads, food on the table and clothes on their backs. As far as he was concerned he 'suffered' through the majority of the marriage and the last straw was when he left her for a younger, more physically fit woman. No, scratch that. He left her for a little girl because the chick was a year older than Danyelle and as far as Autumn was concerned, Danyelle was still growing. Phillip may as well been dating one of Danyelle's classmates.

Autumn never blamed the job as to why he left them instead she blamed it on her post-pregnancy, shape-shifting body. She dropped the extra pounds like a brick after having Danyelle; exercising and going on liquid diets, but gained it back and then some after Terrence. She never told anyone except her girlfriend, Denyce, that she had some liposuction done on her stomach and hips one year after Terrence was born. And when he was 5 she had her breasts lifted and re-shaped, lips injected with collagen, botox in the frown lines, and another liposuction procedure on her arms. Thanks to good genes the scars were not hideously visible. The only ones privy to that secret was the insurance company, the hospital and the doctor who performed the procedure. Add physical and mental stress and there you have it. Over time she got over her ex-husband's decision but the mental scars still throb on occasion. The irony that Danyelle is considering a career as a plastic surgeon still would not convince Autumn to go under the knife again to make someone else happy.

"Baby, I'm home!"

"I'm in the kitchen!" Autumn said. Denver's walk picked up and she smiled when he kissed her cheek.

"You will not believe the nightclub I toured downtown today! It's off the chain like Leo promised! Autumn remained silent as Denver continued to boast about a building that was the home to what she already knew will be the latest 'hot spot' in Chicago owned by her man. It was in his voice that he loved the place already. She quit stirring the stew and let it thicken while washing the flour off her hands. "I thought you were still working with Jet on that other spot, Falago, Fango, Flame-O..."

"Fuego," he corrected. "It means fire in Spanish and yes, I'm still working with Jed on his club, absolutely. But I got to get more clubs under my belt – and bigger and better ones at that. I got to make a name for myself, you know that." He wrapped his arms around Autumn and nuzzled her neck.

"I know, Denver. I just don't want you to have too much on your plate. You remember how things ended up last year when you managed over five clubs at once?"

"Honey those clubs were nothing drastic. I'm doing this so you can finally leave your job," he said and kissed her again. "I miss you."

"All right, guys," Terrence suddenly interrupted, "Break it up."

Denver releases Autumn and greets Terrence with a fist bump and hug. "My man! How was basketball practice? You are scoring nothing but 3-pointers, right?"

"You know it!" Terrence then mimics faking a free throw and his arms nearly knocked a couple of pots off Autumn's hanging pot rack.

"Hey!" she shouted. "Not in the house, T! You are not a little boy anymore."

Terrence carefully re-adjusts the pots. "Sorry about that, mama."

"I told you before you are too damn tall to play in the kitchen or the house! If you use the brain God gave you, you would not have to apologize so much!"

"Whoa, baby, take it easy on him," Denver said then slapped Terrence's arm. "The pots aren't destroyed and it was my fault; I provoked him."

"Sometimes, you two are nothing but trouble. Sometimes I feel like I'm still a single mother with three – not two – children to raise!"

Terrence laughed but Denver paused at Autumn's last remark. He was 27 years old, making him 6 years older than Danyelle and 10 years older than Terrence. And Denver is 14 years younger than Autumn who just celebrated her 41st birthday.

Denver was more like an older brother or cousin than a father to Terrence and Danyelle. He never wanted them to think of him as Dad or even a father figure. As long as they liked him and knew he loved and respected their mother, nothing else needed to be discussed.

"Baby when are you going to start getting ready?"

Autumn turned and gave Denver a puzzling look. "Get ready for…"

"Tonight's Halloween party at the club? I have Maroon 5 playing for Jet. I get all of the covers plus 8.5 percent of the liquor sales! My boy Graham hooked me up baby and we have to be there for face time!"

Terrence's eyes bulged at the mention of the hot pop band. "Maroon 5? Mama, can I come with you guys?"

"Absolutely not," Autumn said without hesitation. "You are four years away from legal club-hopping! Dinner is ready so please set the table."

"Dang mama," Terrence groaned, "It's not like I'm going to try and buy liquor…"

"Uhm, little boy! First, don't groan at me and second, you don't have any business even saying liquor! Now do as I say!" Autumn put on a pair of oven mitts and grabbed the pot's handles to place the pot on the table. "Besides I probably won't be going myself."

Denver followed her to the table. "And why is that, honey?"

"I have a 5 a.m. flight to Moscow and I'll be back in four days."

"We've planned for months for this party, Autumn!"

She cringed as Denver's voice escalated while Terrence slowed his pace setting the table. The last thing she wanted was a loud argument. "I know that, baby, but I got the call before you got here and a couple of attendants are off and they are short. I am filling in for someone. I'm sorry sweetie but it's my job and you know it's unpredictable."

"Wow," Denver said walking away in a huff. "I know now more than ever that I need to hurry up and make enough money so you can tell the airlines you are permanently grounded!"

Autumn rolled her eyes at the trite metaphor he used, but hated to see him upset. "Baby, are you joining us for dinner?"

"Nope," Denver yelled as he went upstairs. "I will get something at the party. I need to get ready, so you and Terrence go ahead and eat. I will talk to you on my way out."

Autumn inhaled and shook her head.

"Mama?"

Autumn turned to look at Terrence as he pulled out a chair with one hand while holding a plate of cornbread muffins in the other. She smiled at him while taking her seat. Terrence rushed to the chair next to her, placed the muffins on the table and grabbed the ladle for a massive scoop of stew for his bowl. "I know this stew is off the chain! Let's eat."

Forty minutes later, Terrence was cleaning the kitchen. Autumn went upstairs to the master bedroom. Denver was in front of the stand alone mirror double-checking the long-sleeve, muscle hugging t-shirt, dark jeans and short black boots. His almond skin tone was a perfect complement to his strong jaw line, full lips and piercing dark eyes. He preferred the bald look, and so did Autumn. Denver glanced at her through the mirror's reflection.

"Autumn, I am sorry about my attitude earlier…"

"No, you don't need to apologize, baby. This is my fault."

"No, it is the airlines' fault," Denver said while turning to face her. "But I know you have to work, so I will be fine."

Autumn stepped forward and stretched her arms around his neck. Denver followed by wrapping his arms around her waist, his hands gently resting on her butt. "I am so sorry that I am going to miss tonight," Autumn said, "but I appreciate your understanding and I know you will make sure everything is alright with Terrence while I'm out of town."

"Of course I am going to look after him as I always do! And as far as tonight, he has my cell number for emergencies and will not bother you if you lay down early. Plus I will only be out a few hours. I will be snuggled up next to you when that stupid alarm goes off!"

Autumn laughed and lightly kissed his lips. Denver lowered his head and kissed her gently, then with a little more pressure. Autumn melted into his kiss as their tongues found each other. He held her tighter and she felt him rising against the inseam of his jeans. "Mmmmm, we better quit," Autum said while pulling away. "I need to finish packing and you need to get to Maroon 5."

After watching Denver drive off, Autumn walked into the TV room where Terrence was watching a horror movie on the 45-inch flat screen while eating a bowl of popcorn. He had permission to spend the night at a friend's house but changed his mind. "Where in the world does all of that food travel?"

"It spreads out," Terrence said without looking at her.

Autumn plopped down on the couch next to her son and grabbed a handful of popcorn before he could move the bowl away. "Honey, I want to apologize to you for seeing me and Denver fight. And I am sorry for the attitude I gave you earlier for playing in the kitchen."

"Don't worry about it, Mama. Couples fight all the time, right? And I knew better than to be clowning in the kitchen."

Autumn grabbed the remote and lowered the volume. "Yes couples do fight but we just don't want to upset you."

"Mama, it's all in the past," Terrence said while reaching for the remote. "Besides Denver texted an apology from upstairs."

The Panthers Club

Autumn laughed at the thought of texting to avoid facing the person. "OK then. Well I am going to finish packing and then go to bed." She leaned over and kissed her son's cheek. "Don't stay up too late and turn off all the lights except the hallway and the porch…"

"Shhhh, ma, I'm missing the best part," Terrence said while waving her off.

"I will call you from the airport, smartie!"

An hour after doing last minute checks on everything and calling Danyelle again to check on Terrence occasionally, Autumn drew a hot bubble bath to relax. Resting her head against the neck pillow, her body gave in to the steaming heat and scent of jasmine from the tubful of bubbles. Autumn reflected on the events earlier that evening and still felt bad for talking to her soon to be 18 year old son as if he were 10. Terrence was taking mandatory exams that would hopefully lead to graduation next June. He had sent transcripts to at least 20 colleges and universities. He hinted at staying close to home and attending the University of Illinois or DePaul but was also considering going out of state. Autumn planned to go with him on some of the college tours during Christmas break or spring break. She was not going to be on a damn flight somewhere and miss out like she did with Danyelle who went to the college tours with her dad or an older female relative as chaperone.

Autumn was determined to look into her December schedule right away to make vacation time for the holidays at home with Terrence and Denver. Maybe they could pick up Danyelle and road trip it back home if the weather wasn't too bad. Traveling around the world was the main reason she became a flight attendant. And while every layover promised something exciting, Autumn now felt it would only be more exciting with Terrence and Denver joining her.

Not that she's never invited Denver to fly in and meet her at the layover destinations. It's not like he couldn't work it around his job. She was friends with a guy who would take a flight on Friday afternoons anywhere and return in time to get ready for work. He would literally get off the plane early Monday morning and be at his job at 9 a.m. "Where do you go?" Autumn inquired on day.

"Anywhere," he would say to her. "I just decide I need to take a trip and check the fares online, get a roundtrip ticket and go!"

Denver, however, scoffed at the suggestion, saying a weekend was not enough time to spend in another city, let alone another country. "And the cost of the ticket would kill me, Autumn!" Denver would say, ignoring the fact that she could get him a discount or better yet fly free through her employee perks. He always gave an excuse not to join her. When they were younger, Danyelle and Terrence would meet her at one of the U.S. layovers and Terrence even met her in Paris, France after a chaperoned flight when he was 14. But he was too busy with school, games, friends and girlfriends now. And she gave up asking Denver to meet her.

Autumn stepped out of the tub and let the water out. She sat at the vanity table then grabbed a jar of moisturizing body crème she purchased while on a layover in Sweden. The crème claimed to smooth out any visible signs of cellulite especially on the thighs and buttocks. Sitting naked on the vanity stool, Autumn opened the jar and scooped a generous amount with three fingers then set the jar on the table. She began rubbing and massaging her upper right thigh vigorously as the instructions on the jar read. After moisturizing her face and body, she slipped into a long, oversized t-shirt and walked out of the bathroom into the hallway. She leaned over the banister and saw that Terrence really did listen. All the lights except the downstairs hallway and porch were off. He had the volume down in the TV room and was likely dozing off on the oversize plush couch. Autumn walked into the bedroom, pulled back the covers and bed sheet and climbed in. She did not even bother to turn on the lamp on the nightstand to read a little, instead falling into a deep slumber.

Just as soon as she closed her eyes Autumn was stirred awake. "Terrence what's wrong? It's not even 5 a.m."

Suddenly she felt extra body weight on top of her and her t-shirt rise above her hips. "Denver? No, No, baby I need more sleep and I'm not quite right!"

Denver had gotten home around 1 a.m., slipped in the bed and fell asleep but woke up at 4:30 to give Autumn a nice sendoff.

Denver reached over to the lamp and turned it on. "Sexy, you are just right with me," he said as he tried to kiss her.

"My breath stinks!" Autumn said and pushed Denver's head away. She wiggled from his grasp and bumped him off of her while eyeing the clock. "Shit, I may as well wake up!"

Denver moved further to his side of the bed and propped up on his elbows. "I'm sorry," he said as Autumn got up to go to the bathroom.

When he heard the shower Denver tipped to the door and eased it open.

"DENVER!!" Autumn shrieked when he yanked the shower curtain back and stepped in also naked in all his muscular glory. "Shush girl, you'll wake Terrence up!"

Autumn laughed. "That boy can sleep through two tornadoes and an earthquake!"

"Oh well, we don't have a problem, then," Denver said pulling her into his embrace. "Denver…I have. To. Get. Ready," Autumn gasped as he backed her against the shower stall and lifted her up. Her legs automatically wrapped around his waist, her ankles locked together. The water from the showerhead pelted off his back leaving sprays of water to hit her face and most of her body. Denver entered her body with one swift move, pressing her more against the wall while thrusting upward. "You won't be late," he grunted, "I promise."

Autumn gasped and moaned while holding on to him to keep from falling in the tub. She knew he'd never let her fall and get injured, but the thrill of holding on to his muscular back as he loved her drove her crazy with desire.

Ten minutes later they were soaping each other's bodies as the warm water washed over them. "Ok, I need to finish getting ready," Autumn said as she grabbed a towel and wrapped it around her body while stepping out of the tub.

Denver stepped out also and grinned while wrapping a towel around his waist. "I told you I would not make you late!"

Autumn rolled her eyes at Denver and laughed as he opened the walk-in closet doors. "Whoa!" Denver eyes nearly jumped out of their sockets. He noticed a female costume hanging from the built in rack. It was a white button-up one piece with pink pinstripes and a matching miniskirt. A pair of white thigh high stockings and a pair of 5-inch white stilettos were perched on a nearby shelf. "Is this yours?"

Autumn glanced in his direction while starting to get dressed in her flight attendant uniform. "Oh yeah, that was my Halloween costume I was going to wear for you when we returned from last night's party," she said while adjusting her pants. "But when everything changed I just put it back in the closet."

Denver's eyes glazed over at the thought of what could have happened the night before. "Promise me you will wear this Tuesday night!"

Autumn walked over and kissed long enough for him to miss her, but short enough to tease him. She was glad to be sexually compatible with Denver; in the beginning their sex life was, lopsided. While his youth was one of the pluses between them, Denver was limited when it came to experimentation in the bedroom. She figured it was because the women before her were only use to missionary and a few minutes of doggy style, thinking they had him on lock and poor thing did not realize his full potential.

Autumn relished on her wardrobe of sexy costumes like the French maid, naughty nurse or the lustful librarian and sex toys. She kept her 'black bag' overflowing with all types of equipment, creams, body oils and edible you name it. In their early months of dating, she thought she'd scared Denver off with her daring outfits and toys. He showed some discomfort at first and then realized she was trying to school him in the art of pleasure. As time went by he asked her to put some space between the toys and costumes. "I sometimes feel as if I am, you know, cheating on you with another woman," Denver said one time before sex while she stood wearing a very grown version of a girl's school uniform.

"But it's me baby," Autumn said while leaning forward to show off her pushed to the max breasts spilling from the white tie-on shirt.

"I know it's you, somewhere in there. You don't have to do this constantly to turn me on. I'm turned on when you walk in the house hair messed up and your work uniform disheveled. Dress-up is fine…sometimes. But I want you."

So the costumes night slowed for a bit, but was slowly starting to increase again. Maybe, because the costumes built up Autumn's confidence in some strange way, making her feel more secure about herself. No matter how hot their love making sessions were, Autumn still felt the need to give him more.

He watched Autumn grab her purse then he grabbed the handle to the carry on suitcase. They quietly left the house and went to Denver's car. He pressed the key pad to unlock the trunk, put Autumn's luggage inside and closed the trunk. Denver rushed to the passenger's side to open the door for her. Climbing into the driver's side, he started the car and pulled out of the driveway. As they headed to O'Hare Autumn heard the chime for her text messages. "Tell those pilots to bring you back safe and unharmed! Love, T." Autumn laughed and replied with <3!

"Terrence's goodbye text I presume," Denver said while keeping an eye on the road.

"Yes indeed. Giving the usual orders I have to pass to the pilots."

The drive to the airport was 40 minutes long but felt longer as neither started a conversation.

Denver finally broke the silence. "Autumn? Is everything cool?"

"Huh? What are you talking about?"

"Waking you up this morning before the alarm. Making love in the shower."

Autumn glanced at him but re-focused on her cell phone checking messages and texting Danyelle. "Autumn, are you angry about what happened in the shower? I just wanted to send you off in a good mood."

"Denver," she sighed, "Everything is fine and this morning was great…"

"But…"

"But I like to be ready and prepared for our sessions."

"Our 'sessions?' Since when is our sex life a series of sessions?" Autumn shifted her body in the passenger seat to face Denver. "Session was the wrong word. I just don't feel right in the morning when you decide to ambush me and I need to freshen up and look nice."

Denver gripped the steering wheel tighter. "Here we go…"

Autumn jerked her head back at Denver's response. "Excuse you?"

"Autumn, for someone who is spontaneous with costumes and sex toys, what is wrong with being spontaneous without those things? If I am in the mood of pleasing my woman she can be wearing mismatched bra and panties for all I care! It's not like I am analyzing your outfit like those judges in one of those fashion makeover reality shows!"

Autumn fumed at Denver's words. "I just feel ugly sometimes and want to look my best for you!"

Denver blew out a breath. "Baby you are not ugly. You are the most beautiful, intelligent and sexy woman I've ever been with! All I want to do when I look at you is be all over that curvy body."

"I've gained five pounds," Autumn said while slapping her stomach.

"AUTUMN, I don't care if you gain 50 pounds! Stop beating yourself up. Next thing you'll be talking about plastic surgery."

Autumn darted her eyes away from him and straightened up in the seat. "You're right baby. I'm sorry."

Denver reached across and grabbed her hand. "We're cool, sexy. I love you."

The drive home had Denver going through what went down while dropping Autumn off at O'Hare. He was not trying to send her off with a fight but he was getting tired of the self criticism she gave her body. He looked past her physical flaws but she was always ready to point them out and make him say something negative. Denver knew better than to trip up like that. Had he agreed with her on one flaw all hell would have broke loose. Why could she not accept the fact that he truly loved her? If all he cared about was her looks he'd left her for the sheer fact that she was masking her face to look like someone else. Women his age and younger were all about showing off their looks and bodies to get noticed. Autumn should be comfortable and secure about her body and looks. Hell, isn't that how a 40-something woman suppose to act? Confident, secure and sexy? He's crossed paths with some unattractive women who carry themselves like they were Vanessa Williams, Halle Berry and Jada Pinkett-Smith rolled up into one! Maybe I should tell her to consider cosmetic surgery, Denver thought as he pulled into the driveway. Yeah and maybe I don't want to see 30!

Denver unlocked the front door and closed it behind him after entering. "Terrence, you awake?" He walked down the hallway and made a right turn to a shorter hallway that led to T's bedroom. He could hear Terrence snoring through the closed door so he turned around and headed to the kitchen. He washed his hands, opened the refrigerator door and took out a package of bacon, carton of eggs, a small block of jalapeno pepper jack cheese and a small bag of white potatoes. Opening the bag of potatoes Denver peeled six medium size potatoes, then sliced and diced them in the food processor. Grabbing the skillets and placing them on the stove, he seasoned the potatoes with salt and pepper then diced some red peppers and tossed all into an oiled skillet to make hash browns. He then cracked some eggs, seasoned and lightly whisked them then poured into another oiled skillet and topped the eggs with sliced cheese. The bacon was cooking in the microwave.

"Dang it smells good in here," Terrence said as he entered the kitchen.

"I knew something would wake you up. Get the plates man and… good morning," Denver said.

****

Autumn checked in and entered the employees' cafeteria to grab a cup of coffee and see what was available to eat. She decided on a sausage, cheese and egg burrito and a blueberry muffin. She sat down at one of the tables, unwrapped the large burrito and stared at it. "I should have eaten at home," she thought, "but I didn't because Denver wanted to break me off before I got to work." She reluctantly took a bite into the burrito and forgets that it is swimming in calories. "I'll make up for it by going to the hotel gym when we arrive in Moscow," she thought.

After finishing her breakfast and talking to a couple of attendants for another flight Autumn headed to the plane to meet with another attendant and the captain. The captain briefed Autumn and her colleague on emergency evacuation procedures, coordination of the crew, the length of the flight, weather conditions and special issues involving passengers. After the briefing, they made sure the first-aid kits and emergency equipment was working, check on food, beverages and blankets.

Autumn paused in the back near the attendants' quarters and re-adjusted her uniform in anticipation of going to the entrance to greet passengers as they come aboard. After the passengers are seated and demonstrations on seatbelts, emergency equipment usage and escape routes were shown, Autumn and her co-worker – who was younger and fluent in Russian - wished all a safe flight. It was going to be a little over a 12 hour flight so Autumn and her partner sat in the back of the plane, buckled their seatbelts and prepared for takeoff.

When the plane landed in Moscow 12 hours later, Autumn was thankful that she checked the weather conditions before going to bed. She was also thankful for Terrence reminding her in a text before he turned in that it was practically winter in Moscow. After the passengers exited the plane she and the other attendant did a thorough check of the aisles, seats and overhead bins for anything left behind, safe or suspicious. She then put on her triple down coat and a huge hat with lining and a pair of warm gloves. She and the crew rushed down the stairs and across the tarmac to enter the airport and grab their luggage. From there she took a cab to the hotel where she reserved a suite online.

It was 7 a.m. in Moscow and 7 p.m. in Chicago. Arriving at the hotel she headed to the front desk where the concierge handed her a key card right away. "spa-see-ba," she said, thanking the concierge. She took the elevator to her suite and inserted the key card. Walking in she was happy to see the king size bed, a welcome basket filled with bottled water, souvenir bottles of lotion, snacks and flowers on the nearby table. She placed her carry-on against the wall near the bed, removed her hat, coat and gloves and tossed them in the chair.

Autumn sat down on the plush bed and took a deep breath. She could hear footsteps pass her door, knowing other guests were on their way to breakfast or site-seeing on an early Sunday morning. She was about to take a long nap, but not before checking in on the home front. She grabbed her cell phone to dial and realized the battery was dead. "Shit," Autumn mumbled while digging in her purse for the charger and came up empty.

She unzipped the carry-on and checked the side pouches. "Damn it, now I have to use their phone to make a phone call!" She picked up the room phone and dialed for the operator. "Uhm, Vy gavareeteh pa anglisky?"

"Yes, ma'am, I do speak English," the operator replied. "Oh thank you Lord!" Autumn said before asking the operator to make a call to Chicago. The operator took the number and name and within seconds the line was ringing.

"Hello," a deep male voice flowed into Autumn's ear making her smile.

"Hello sweetheart! I am in Moscow safe and sound!"

"Hey baby so glad to hear your voice!" Denver said then added, "Terrence! Your mom's safe in Moscow!"

Denver stared at his cell phone screen for a second. "How come you did not use your cell?"

Autumn smiled at the concerned attitude coming from Denver. "My battery died and I forgot my charger."

Denver sat down on the couch. "So what time is it in Russia?"

"It's after 7 a.m. on a freezing Sunday morning! But I am good. What are you two up to on a Saturday night?"

"Well I am going to relax a bit before I check out the capacity of a couple of the clubs. I want to make sure everything is alright. T is doing OK despite a minor issue earlier this afternoon."

Autumn sat up at the mention of 'issue' which meant T was in trouble. "What happened, Denver?"

"It's nothing for you to worry about Autumn, there was a scuffle with some friends of his that he hung out with and the police…"

Autumn jumped to her feet and walked down the foyer before realizing she was not at home, let alone the U.S. "POLICE?"

"Calm down baby, the police contacted me and I picked him up at the park. He was the one breaking up the scuffle."

"OK," Autumn sighed and sat back down on the bed. "Let him know I will be talking to him when I get back Tuesday!"

"He knows honey. So, anyway I am going to check on my venues since people were buzzing positive stuff about the Halloween concert featuring Maroon 5."

Autumn slapped her hand upside her head; she'd forgotten to ask him about the concert while getting ready to fly here. Well the sex made her forget about asking the concert's outcome. But she was also irritated about that morning. "Denver? I am so sorry I did not ask about the Halloween concert. And I want to apologize for the argument on the drive to the airport."

"No problem, baby. I know you have a lot on your mind with the work schedule and everything."

"Alright, well I will let you go," Autumn said, "you and Terrence be good!"

"Well Terrence is no problem...and I have no choice but to be good since you are not here," Denver said.

Autumn hung up and breathed a sigh of relief regarding Terrence and the minor issue. The last thing she needed was Terrence to be in trouble and risk all he's worked for with his studies and acceptance letters from colleges.

Autumn was also thankful for Denver being there to watch things and handle situations. The police probably thought Denver was Terrence's older brother and turned him over to his guardianship. The minor issue could have been a lot worse without Denver being there; Terrence could have ended up in juvenile, especially if he decided to argue with the officer. But even his father, Phillip, told him as a child to never, ever raise his voice at a police officer and to always be respectful when answering questions. And look the officer in the eye when speaking. She gave Phillip credit when it came to instructing their children on self-respect and respect for others. They were a great team...when he wasn't barking about her being gone most of the time and how his parents had to play babysitters because he had a job too. Her former in-laws knew things were getting uglier and uglier between them but stayed out of it, thankfully, without pointing fingers of blame at her. They were disappointed when their son walked away with another woman but it was out of their hands.

Autumn was also stressed with her job. After 9/11, terror alerts, and the security changes, flight attendants almost had to train like military soldiers or special agents to prepare for whatever or whoever decided to go crazy or act too suspicious. Pre-9/11 the most she, fellow attendants and the crews had to worry about was a baby crying or a passenger having too much to drink.

Autumn was not ready to retire and there wasn't a mandatory retirement age for a flight attendant. She read and heard of stories about flight attendants retiring after more than 50 years on the job. Hell there was one story years ago about an 89-year-old flight attendant! Autumn figured she could do another 20 years on the job unless Denver makes it big as a club owner and promoter. He would be 47 then and probably looking for a 20-something for arm candy purposes. *Will Denver still be in my life 20 years from now?* Why am I even thinking about this right now, Autumn thought while removing her clothes to get some sleep. Paranoia will do nothing but make my ass older and crazier than I already am.

Chapter 2

Autumn returned from Moscow Tuesday afternoon and took a cab home since Denver was out taking care of business at the Loft, a nightclub where he had a standing contract. She was tired and eager to take a bath and get some sleep. After her bath Autumn walked in the bedroom and past the standing mirror; she took a few steps back and dropped the towel. Standing naked and soaking wet she began twisting and turning her body to check her reflection and her flesh. Her breasts were fuller from weight gain but still sat decently upright since her surgery 10 years ago. Her stomach was a little thicker but still flat thanks to on and off exercise.

She hesitated before turning slowly to look over her shoulder and glimpse at her butt. It was still curvy but some reshaping might be in order. A co-worker tried to talk her into getting an ass lift but she thought that was way too dramatic and crazy. She checked out the back of her legs and her thighs for any lumpy cheesy formations, praying that Swedish cellulite cream was working.

After a thorough inspection Autumn picked up her towel, went to the dresser and grabbed a bottle of cocoa butter lotion. She wanted to get as much sleep as possible. She had another international flight in 48 hours because she is filling for another attendant. Autumn made sure that for that fill-in she'd get 4 days off. She wanted to be able to relax and have a little fun with her man. Denver had been waiting for her to be off to enjoy a night at The Loft and she confirmed that after this sudden trip she would indeed enjoy a night out with him.

****

A few days later when Autumn returned from her trip, she took along nap then started getting ready for a good time with her man. She showered, styled her hair and put on a little black dress that hugged the right curves and concealed the wrong ones. She stepped into a pair of black Louboutins Denver bought her some time ago, checked her reflection once more and walked out of the bedroom.

"What are you doing?" Denver called from the bottom of the stairs. "We're all waiting on you, Autumn!"

"Yeah, hurry up and bring your slow ass downstairs," a female voice shouted. Autumn walked downstairs and at the last step flipped Charlize off.

"Yeah I love you too, bitch," Charlize said while finishing off her shot of vodka.

"I know good and hell well you are not drinking all of my liquor!"

"Well you need to dress faster!"

Just as Autumn was about to unleash another smartass remark, Natasha stepped in between the two while Denver laughed with amusement. "I am so glad you two just love each other to death," Natasha said as Charlize draped one arm around Natasha's shoulders and her other hand grabbed Autumn's hand and yanked her off the step.

"I am so glad we are taking a limo to the club," Denver chuckled.

"We are glad too," Charlize said as she smoothed back her long micro-mini braids from her face which was already flushed from the liquor.

"Let's go," Natasha said while shaking her head.

****

They could hear the music blaring as the limo stopped in front of the club. Denver and the driver helped the ladies out then they headed past the velvet rope and the long line as the limo pulled off. "Hey Denver what's happening," said the bouncer as he made a path for them to enter.

"It's all good, Keith, thanks a lot."

Once inside, Charlize and Natasha headed straight for the bar, while Denver escorted Autumn to a V.I.P. booth on the right side of the dance floor. A man who looked mixed with Italian and African-American features sat alone at the booth. He was concentrating on whatever was on his laptop.

"Leo, my man!" Denver yelled over the noisy crowd and loud music.

Leo waved them over and another tall and bulky guy in a suit moved another velvet rope barrier back, smiling as he gestured for Denver and Autumn to step inside. Leo scooted out of the booth and stood up to greet them. He was barely 5'7 in height and his caramel complexion glowed from the strobe lights hanging overhead. "Denver! It is so good seeing you tonight," Leo said while turning his attention to Autumn. "And who is this exquisite beauty standing beside you?"

"This is my girlfriend Autumn. Autumn this is Leo Gillian."

Autumn smiled as the owner took her right hand to his lips, lightly kissing it.

"It is indeed a pleasure to meet you, Autumn."

Leo then stepped aside, waving around the V.I.P. section. "Make yourselves at home! You are my guests tonight."

Just then Natasha and Charlize appeared after searching for Denver and Autumn for the last 10 minutes. "Here they are in the V.I.P. section," Charlize said imitating a snobbish attitude. They took another step when the suited bouncer blocked them.

"Excuse you," Charlize snapped.

"It's OK buddy, they are with us," Denver said and the bouncer stepped aside.

"Hmph, you better act like you know," Charlize said then took a sip out of her galss and winked at the bouncer as he watched her with intensity.

Charlize pranced into the V.I.P section with Natasha smiling until she saw Autumn glaring at her. "I'm sorry!" Charlize mouthed, no words coming out.

"Natasha, Charlize. This is Leo, owner of The Loft," Denver said. They nodded and shook hands before joining all of them in the booth.

"Welcome and the drinks are on me tonight," Leo said while raising a glass.

"I'll drink to that," Charlize said and all clicked their glasses.

Autumn took in The Loft's atmosphere from the booth, taking in everything Denver described to her weeks ago. The interior had the look of a large studio apartment in one of those old warehouse structures. There was plenty of dance space and the surrounding wall to wall seating areas gave the crowd a perfect view on the two floor levels. The bar was accessible from either direction and the DJ had his own section. A kitchen was in the back so if you wanted to eat something to line your stomachs before drinking you could order wings, mini-burgers and other appetizers from the menu. And the waiting staff was professional and the strict dress code kept trouble at bay. And Leo wasn't such a bad guy. "Baby, I think this is my favorite of the clubs you are working with," Autumn said to Denver.

"You really like it, huh?"

"Yes I do," Autumn said.

The DJ was playing old school R&B mixes and the crowd was dancing nonstop. Denver stood up and grabbed Autumn's hand. "C'mon let's dance!"

Autumn nodded and left her purse with Charlize and Natasha who were placing food orders to a cute male waiter.

Denver led Autumn to the main level and moved their way onto the dance floor. The music was vibrating the floor and they blended with the crowd making their own moves. Autumn absorbed the music and the all around vibe felt from the crowd. She danced in those Louboutins as if they were ballerina flats, moving her body and swaying her hips to the rhythm. She felt the eyes of men and women on her; some were closer to Denver's age and she could tell they were wondering what she was doing with him. Autumn closed her eyes and continued to move. She felt a pair of male hands embrace her waist and slide to her hips. She knew it was Denver who had moved closer and danced against her body matching her moves. Soon he was grinding against her, she smiled, and opened her eyes. They began their own rendition of dirty dancing to everything from Rick James to George Clinton to Vanity 6.

By the time Denver and Autumn made it back to the booth, they were glistening with sweat. Charlize and Natasha looked up from their plates as Denver patted his face with a cloth napkin. "Well damn, did you two have sex on the floor?" Charlize asked as Natasha laughed.

"Not quite," Autumn said and laughed back. She grabbed her purse and got the bouncer's attention. "Where's the ladies' room?"

The bouncer pointed to the far end of the V.I.P. section to a Mahoghany wood door with a gold door handle and "Ladies" etched in cursive. "Thanks. Charlize, Natasha, I'm heading to the ladies room to freshen up."

Charlize jumped up and picked up her handbag. I'm going with you!"

Autumn walked ahead of Charlize and past the bouncer, but Charlize purposely brushed her body, which was poured into a red dress with a plunging neckline, against the bouncer.

"Girl, leave that man alone," Natasha yelled from her seat. Autumn did not even bother to look back to see what her friend was doing.

Autumn and Charlize entered the ladies room and a bright light greeted them. The sitting area looked like a separate lounge with plush brown chairs and a loveseat. A wall that was a complete vanity area with basins was decorated with marble countertops and gold faucets. Around the corner were six roomy stalls and standing mirrors. Shelves throughout the facility were filled with potpourri and fresh flowers. A bowl containing travel size bottles of lotions and hand sanitizers was on the counter and in the sitting area were mini-packs of breath mint strips and peppermint candy. "Now this is a ladies room," Charlize said as she walked inside a stall.

Autumn grabbed one of a stack of complimentary hand towels from the corner counter and patted the sweat off her chest. She patted her face and then touched up her makeup.

Charlize returned to the sitting area and washed her hands. "Girl this place is off the chain! Denver's done well with this contract," she said.

Autumn nodded in agreement. "I really like this place."

They headed out and back to the section until Charlize noticed Natasha on the dance floor with two tall, chocolate and muscular men. "Oh that heifer is sharing," Charlize said while heading to the dance floor.

Autumn laughed and joined Denver and Leo back at the booth. Seeing Denver was talking business with Leo, Autumn waved the waiter over and ordered two rounds of Jäger Bombs for the table. She loved the mix of licorice and fizzy sour of the two when combined – plus the Red Bull left her with a nice burst of energy that kept her body moving. She toasted the men before throwing back both shots. She then saw Natasha signal for her from the dance floor, so Autumn left the booth and worked her way through the crowd and to Natasha and Charlize. All three friends danced with each other and people in the crowd. The buzz from the shots hit Autumn and she danced harder with a mixture of wildness and seduction.

Charlize and Natasha kept up and were soon getting cutting side-eye glances from the twenty-something females and lustful stares from the latter's dates, husbands or boyfriends. They danced and accepted drinks from men and a couple of women and turned down notes with cell numbers and special requests. Autumn, Charlize and Natasha grew tired of dancing and led each other by the hand back to the V.I.P. section when Autumn suddenly stopped at the second step.

A gorgeous Latina female who looked to be around 25, was making her way to the booth where Denver and Leo sat. The woman had to be 5'4 in stocking feet but the stilettos she wore tonight made her four inches taller and accentuated her big shapely legs. She wore a curve-hugging short dress in teal blue and her long black hair rested softly on her shoulders. Autumn watched as she stood by the booth's table talking and grinning at Denver. "Excuse you," Autumn said while nearly shoving the woman out of the way. Autumn leaned into Denver to the point that he had to lean back. "What is she doing here?"

"Hola gentlemen," the woman said after regaining her standing. "Mind if I join you?"

"Yes," Autumn snapped while glaring at her, "Yes we do!"

Denver stepped aside and moved Autumn at the same time. "We don't mind at all. We will make room."

Autumn glared at him and suddenly stepped in front of the woman and blocking any chance of her sitting in the booth. Charlize and Natasha watched everything unfold from the steps before the section. Autumn stepped closer to the woman who was now glaring at her. "What a surprise seeing you here, Candi."

"I was invited," she said with a slow smile.

"Actually I called her," Leo said. "I could not discuss the contract without Denver's partner."

Leo's words punched Autumn's eardrums like a jackhammer on a stubborn piece of concrete.

"PARTNER?! Autumn turned to Denver, her face flushed with a mixture of anger, shock and too many shots. Leo looked uncomfortable as Autumn was getting louder.

"Candice- uh Candi – Maria Riverez has been working with me for 7 years and she is very good at what she does," Denver said to Autumn's disbelief.

Candi smiled at Denver, her glossy lips revealing a row of perfect white teeth. She turned to Leo and placed her hand on his shoulder. "This is going to be a fantastic partnership," she said as Leo took her hand from his shoulder and kissed her palm.

Autumn peered at Candi, jealously, imagining herself choke slamming her. The teal halter dress Candi wore left little to the imagination from the halter top to the short hem. Autumn rolled her eyes in disgust but at the same time hating her little black dress.

"Let's move to another booth to prevent cramping," Leo said and gestured for Candi and Denver to sit in the booth behind the one Denver, Autumn, Natasha and Charlize were seated. Autumn watched as Candi placed herself between Denver and Leo, laughing and taking turns touching their hands.

"Uhm, Autumn," Charlize whispered while nudging Natasha closer to the booth. "Let's sit down."

Natasha and Charlize sat down across from Autumn who sat with her back to Denver, Candi and Leo. Autumn did not touch another drink or nibbled on an appetizer. Instead she sat still and eavesdropped on the conversation. "I thought his partnership was over with that Latina bitch three years ago," Natasha whispered.

"Well apparently it's not," Charlize said. "Autumn, don't let that heifer get to you!"

Autumn looked at her friends and leaned forward. "Denver did not tell me that he was still professionally working with her again! He kept that part of his contracting with clubs secret!"

Natasha and Charlize leaned back against the booth seat, gasping in unison. "Shit girl he is wrong for that," Natasha said, "but still you have nothing to worry about! Denver is madly in love with you! He does not want her; you are 100 times better than she is!" Autumn wished she could believe Natasha's words of confidence, but she could not help but feel jealous and deceived. What was really going on?

As hard as she tried to listen, Autumn barely made out what the three was discussing but heard Candi's annoying fake ass laugh clear as a bell. Autumn felt her blood pressure rising as her neck tightened and her muscles tensed. "Autumn you are going to have a fucking stroke if you don't take a breath!" Charlize said while reaching across the table to grab her hand. "Let's get some fresh air, hell, call the limo driver and we can go to my apartment…"

"No." Autumn shouted above the noise. "I am not leaving Denver with that bitch!"

Natasha scooted to Autumn's side and hugged her. "Denver is not like Phillip." Autumn jerked her head angrily towards Natasha. "You don't know that!"

"OK let's go," Charlize said. "I'm texting for a cab to pick us up. We've had free drinks, food and danced our asses off. You are coming with us back to my townhouse and we are going to chill!" Autumn stared at Charlize and did not move. Charlize stood up and walked to Autumn's side. "You are not going to give that bitch the satisfaction of you being insecure and weak. Get your ass up from this booth, say goodnight to them and tell Denver I will bring you home in the morning!"

Autumn got up and did what she was told, even wearing a smile and being pleasant to Candi. Candi did not know how to take it but managed to smile back. Autumn kissed Denver on the lips, said goodnight to Leo and followed Natasha and Charlize out of the V.I.P. section and out the club.

****

Thirty minutes later they were getting out of the cab and waiting for Charlize to unlock her front door. Once inside, Natasha ran past Charlize and Autumn, kicking off her shoes while heading to the bathroom. "You better not throw up on my floor!" Charlize screamed.

"I don't have to throw up, I have to pee!" Natasha shouted and slammed the door.

Charlize laughed while dropping her purse on the coffee table and stepped out of her shoes. Autumn plopped in the recliner and wrestled her feet out of the Louboutins. "I don't think I will be able to wear these shoes for another month!" She said while rubbing her feet.

"Well you can loan them to me," Charlize then disappeared into her bedroom and returned minutes later wearing a pair of pajama bottoms and a t-shirt. She threw one set on the sofa and handed another set to Autumn who was stepping out of her dress and the spandex that held her curves together.

Natasha opened the bathroom door and stepped into the living room half naked, grabbing the last pajama set from the couch. Autumn and Charlize stared at Natasha before bursting into laughter.

"What? Shit I was hot!" Natasha said, joining the laughter. Once the laughter died down and all three friends were comfortable and free of dresses, spandex, heels, jewelry and makeup, they sat on the L-shape couch sipping coffee and listening to the sounds of Miles and Coltrane. "Bitches Brew" flowed from Charlize's surround sound speakers and Autumn smirked.

"What's that smirk about?" Natasha asked.

"This is Candi's theme song," Autumn said while sipping her coffee. Another burst of shrieking laughter overwhelmed the music as they raised their mugs in unison. "Girl you are on it! But why are you acting all jealous and scared that Denver will leave for her? Charlize asked.

"I don't know. I guess I was pretty stunned seeing her show up at the club. I thought she left Chicago after Denver ended their personal relationship. Maybe he feels indebted to her for helping him get national contracts. I don't know..I don't know…"

Denver and Candi were the IT couple in high school during his senior year and into college. He was a DJ in high school since he was a sophomore at Roosevelt High School playing at sock hops and school dances. Candi was in middle school when she first laid eyes on him at a dance where he spun records and developed a serious crush. Being he was from Gary and she lived in East Chicago she was limited to running into him if only to say hi. When she finished middle school Candi was determined to get closer to Denver so she had an aunt living in Gary request a special transfer to Roosevelt and moved in with her. He was a junior when she arrived as a freshman but Candi looked older thanks to puberty hitting the right places and she wore makeup and made sure he noticed her. They were dating on the low before she was a sophomore. She even followed him to college after graduating from high school and would cause major scenes at the frat and sorority parties when Denver was dee-jaying. By then he called his mobile DJ service Nyght Life Entertainment and had a team of DJs and assistants – all men because Candi was not trying to have any competition.

Time went on and business grew leaps and bounds. Candi would brag on how she was the inspiration behind Denver going from a mobile DJ playing for school dances and boring wedding receptions, birthday and retirement parties to the up and coming club promoter in the hottest spots in the Chicago area. And she even got him a couple of opportunities in New York.

While he was appreciative of all she'd done for him, Denver said Candi started pushing him about taking their relationship to the next level with marriage. Denver told her he was not ready and was not sure he wanted her as Mrs. Harris. She insisted at how they can become a mega-entertainment empire with her networks and his business savvy.

"Well apparently – and no offense to you or Denver – his ass is still working with night clubs in Chicago," Natasha said. "And while he's done some stuff in New York, Denver's not even touched the surfaces of New York or Los Angeles."

Autumn adjusted her legs to sit Indian style at the corner of the sofa.
"No offense taken. Do you know when Candi found out he was dating someone else and an older woman at that, she laughed at him and said it was 'just a thing' and he'd be back."

"That was three years ago and he is still with you, old lady," Charlize chuckled.

"Yeah but she's back in his world," Autumn said quietly. "Or maybe she never left."

Natasha jumped up and stomped into the kitchen. Seconds later she appeared with a platter adorned with thick slices of 7-UP pound cake with cream cheese frosting. "We are changing this mood," Natasha said.

"Uhm who told you to go in my kitchen and steal my cake?" Charlize asked.

"I did not steal your damn cake. If I was stealing it my ass would be in a getaway car…or cab."

Natasha placed a slice on a paper towel and handed it to Autumn who frowned and shook her head. "I'm big enough as is."

Charlize sat her coffee mug hard on the coffee table and pointed at Autumn. "That's what this is about! You are worried about getting big and older and losing Denver to a younger woman!"

"Girl you better eat this slice of cake," Natasha said, placing the paper towel on Autumn's lap. "Men like thickness, don't let them damn magazines and the media tell you different!"

"Did you see how he was looking at Candi? It was as if he was having a flashback," Autumn said.

"Candi is no skinny bitch, Autumn! She has curves too and big legs…" Autumn glared at Natasha who shoved a piece of cake in her mouth and looked away.

Charlize rolled her eyes. "Autumn, Natashaa is just saying you are built too! And you worked that dress and them expensive ass shoes, which by the way Denver bought them for you! I scanned Candi's outfit; the dress is from that department store carrying celebrity cheap knock-offs and the shoes are Louboutin rip-offs!"

Natasha nodded in agreement. "Plus you are a mature, intelligent, professional and beautiful woman. Don't stoop to that little girl's level," Natasha added.

Autumn broke a piece from her slice of cake and popped it in her mouth. The cream cheese frosting melted along with the lightness of the cake as she chewed. She felt guilt-free about the cake, but guilty about not telling her girls about the cosmetic surgery and liposuction she had after the children. If they knew about that Charlize would kick her ass into a new shape and Natasha would just look at her with disappointment on not being told. "Charlize, you know you can bake the hell out of a cake!" Autumn said while breaking another piece.

"You are right guys. I don't need to feel inferior or insecure about Candi's so called return, but I do plan on asking Denver about the secrecy."

"And if he does not explain," Charlize said while grabbing the mugs and headed to the kitchen for coffee refills, "then you can leave him the fuck alone and do better."

"HOLD ON!" Autumn shouted while unfolding her legs from the sofa. She walked in the kitchen and blocked Charlize from grabbing the coffee pot. "I thought you said no childish games! Now you want me to give him an ultimatum?"

Charlize placed the mugs on the counter. "Look I had flashbacks too when Candi walked up to us tonight. I remember how uncomfortable Denver was when he introduced you to his friends early in the relationship and how Candi crashed the party and talked about you to their friends until he put her out. I remember you had me come with a date for support and I ended up being blocked from snatching that little heifer off the floor!"

Autumn smiled at the memory of that party three years ago. Candi was still reeling in disbelief about being dumped for Autumn. Denver had the party because some old friends were in town and felt it was the right time to introduce people to his new girlfriend after four months of dating. The introductions went smoothly to Autumn's surprise – a lot of the guys thought it was damn hot for Denver to be with an older woman and the women gave her the 'you go girl' approval. While in the middle of the party and Autumn was talking to some of Denver's friends, everything stopped when Candi's loud mouth shrieked in the apartment. "How dare you leave me for that old ass puta!" Most of the crowd gasped and 'oohed' at what Candi screamed but Charlize had snatched off her earrings and put all of her rings on one hand and was about to pounce the girl. Charlize's date caught her mid-leap while Autumn prepared to defend herself if Candi came at her. Denver, however, grabbed Candi and dragged her out of his apartment as she cursed in her native tongue.

"Charlize, Denver will be truthful to me! He gets along great with Terrence and Danyelle and I love him," Autumn said.

Charlize threw her hands up in defense. "Hey I'm saying if he is back sniffing around her and not keeping it business like, it's been a fun three years! You have to be happy sweetheart."

Charlize pulled Autumn into a hug. "But you can't be happy unless you love yourself first."

"And Denver's not a bad guy!" Natasha yelled from the living room. "And can I have my coffee back please? I want to wash down this cake!"

Charlize dropped her arms, refilled the mugs, gave Autumn hers and grabbed the other two. "I'd spike her mug if I remembered which one she's drinking from," Charlize mumbled as they left the kitchen.

"I heard that," Natasha said and grabbed the green mug. "Anyway, yes I would ask him about the secrecy but don't rant like some maniac. That'll either scare Denver or piss him off. Besides, he was not paying attention to her…not like you think."

Charlize and Autumn sat back on the couch and looked at Natasha. "So he was not eyeing her handkerchief dress?" Charlize asked.

"Of course he noticed the dress, duh, all men are going to look at a skimpy dress unless some 300 pound chick stretched it on!"

They all laughed.

"The thing is, once you look at the dress, the average guy is going to want more than the goodies. Your back was to Denver, Candi and Leo, but while you were all hot and huffy, Denver was hot and bothered…about you!"

Autumn stopped mid-sip. "What do you mean?"

"Girl, you've been with that boy, I mean, young man for three years and you can't feel when the guy is watching you?"

When you cme back from the bathroom, did you not see him lick his lips?"

Autumn paused to think.

"Apparently not! And when you kissed him and turned to walk away, his eyes were in slits of lust. He was not giving that chic any vibe!"

Charlize gave Natasha a fist bump. "Tell it Natasha! Girl, you are on that spying shit! Go get you another slice of cake!"

Autumn burst into laughter as Natasha jumped off the sofa and headed for the kitchen. They laughed and talked until they heard the buzzer. "Who the hell is hitting that buzzer at…3 a.m.!" Charlize said then stood up. She walked to the closet and grabbed a shoe box off the shelf.

"Aw hell," Natasha said while pulling a box cutter from her purse.

Autumn looked at them in amazement. "Why not ask who it is?"

Charlize pulled her 9 mm from the box, cocked it, and eased up to the door. "Look Autumn, it's 3 o'clock in the damn morning, so either you hit 911 on speed dial or grab something to beat the hell out of the mother…"

"AUTUMN! Are you in there? It's Denver!"

Autumn jumped to her feet while Natasha quickly put the box cutter back in her purse. Charlize, however, hesitantly put the safety back on the gun.

"Move Charlize, it's Denver!

Charlize stepped aside and returned her gun to the box and the closet shelf.

Autumn unlocked the door. Denver walked in and looked around. "Y'all having a slumber party? How come I was not invited?"

Charlize was closing her closet when she turned and spoke to Denver. "You know you should of called or texted before coming over, young blood."

Denver ignored her, wrapped his arms around Autumn and kissed her longingly. A minute later he pulled back from Autumn who looked at him with glazed eyes. "I miss you," he said while stroking her butt.

"Hey you two need to get a room and my rooms are closed!" Charlize yelled from the sofa.

Natasha grinned while finishing off her second slice of cake.

"Can we go home?" Denver asked.

"I need to change back into my dress…"

"Girl no you don't!" Natasha yelled. "Who is going to pay attention to you in pajamas in the middle of the night?"

"Right," Charlize added. "Everybody wearing PJ's as clothes now anyway. Well, not me, but take your ass home! You can take your dress and come back later for your those shoes."

Autumn and Denver left the townhouse and got in the limo. "So, how did your meeting with Leo…and Candi go?" Autumn asked while snuggling close to Denver.

He draped his arm around her. "It went well. Candi hated to see you leave…"

"No she didn't," Autumn said.

"OK, OK. But I wished you hadn't left."

Autumn relaxed her head on his shoulder and stroked across his shirt. That kiss at Charlize's made her hot and despite two mugs of coffee she was still buzzed from all the shots she, Natasha and Charlize tossed back at the club. Autumn began kissing Denver's neck while unbuttoning his shirt. "Baby, what are you doing?" Denver asked. He tried to stop Autumn from unbuttoning his shirt and really tried to stop after she began fumbling with his belt buckle. "Autumn, the chauffeur will see us!"

Autumn broke away and scooted to the privacy window. She looked around until she noticed a button and pressed on it. The tinted window and soundproof barrier rolled up. "Now," she said while moving towards him. "See no evil, hear no evil."

Denver chuckled nervously as Autumn got on her knees and unzipped his pants. "Wait, baby, I don't think…"

"Shhhhh," Autumn whispered as she gently took his erection out of his briefs. She began licking and then bathing it with her tongue, sending Denver into a dizzying moment.

"Damn," he moaned. His breath was caught in his throat watching Autumn engulf his erection into her mouth. Denver bit his bottom lip as her head bobbed up and down while she made slurping sounds. "Autumn…Autumn," he sighed as she sped up her pace then slowed down. She continued this through the ride home and when she heard the limo slow down she released him with a 'popping' sound and placed him back in his briefs. Denver fumbled with his zipper and belt while Autumn opened a complimentary bottle of ginger ale and drank it all. "That was amazing," he managed to say. "Oh I am not done with you yet," Autumn said and winked.

The limo pulled up in front of the house. The driver got out and opened the door for them. Autumn stepped out and thanked the driver then Denver cautiously stepped out and handed the driver a $200 tip. "Thanks a lot my man," Denver slapped the driver on the shoulder and followed Autumn to the front door.

Autumn unlocked the door and walked in while Denver followed. He turned to close the door when he felt himself hit the door hard. "The hell…" he managed to say before Autumn snatched him around and pressed her body against his. She kissed Denver long and deep while grinding against him. Within seconds she'd yanked off the t-shirt and pajama bottoms and continued grinding against his clothes.

"Shit Autumn," he managed to gasp. Before he could take control, Autumn yanked his pants and briefs down and pressed against him again, grinding against his erection.

"You like that, baby?" She moaned while nibbling his neck.

Denver's head hit against the door as he responded with a groan.

"Yeah…you like that."

Autumn climbed his body, wrapped her arms around his neck and continued to slide and grind against him until she had him breathing heavier. Denver grabbed her waist, step away from the door and spun around until her back was against the door. He stepped out of his pants and briefs and thrust up and inside her. Autumn locked her ankles above his hips and braced her back against the door as Denver thrust then pounded into her, making her scream with desire. "Oh baby, yes, yes!" She raked her nails on his back as he nibbled her neck. He ran his teeth gently up and down her neck and earlobe. "Do you want me to stop?" he growled in her ear.

Autumn shook her head too hot to answer him.

"I said," he flicked the tip of his tongue against her earlobe while pumping inside her. "Do you want me to stop?"

"No, no, please don't!" Autumn panted.

Denver obliged and continued pumping, stopping to grind against her then pumping again. Autumn was delirious with desire as their bodies slipped against each other from the sweat. An orgasm surged through her body as she screamed and held Denver tighter before becoming weak. He felt her sliding down the door and he followed suit ending with him lying on top of her. He took off his shirt and began kissing her neck, collarbone then between her breasts. Autumn soon caught her breath, relaxing and stroking his arms as he licked and kissed her breasts and large brown nipples. His mouth continued to make its way to her navel and then pushing her legs further apart, he began devouring her sweetness. "OH!" Autumn shouted while trying to sit up, but her body betrayed her, forcing her to lie back on the hardwood floor. Besides moaning and screaming all Autumn could do was look up towards the ceiling and be thankful Terrence was spending the night at a friend's house.

Denver sent Autumn through another wave of orgasmic bliss before helping her to her feet. They headed to the guest bedroom across from Terrence's room. "Wait," Autumn said as he laid her on the bed. "Let me get the black bag..."

"Autumn," Denver said while crawling over her. "I'm your black bag tonight."

Autumn woke up around noon refreshed and well rested. She stretched and smiled after noticing the bed spread and sheet were on the floor. She looked down at her naked body and saw her skin was still flushed after the early morning sex romp. Reaching behind her to grab the pillows she noticed marks on the wall where the headboard scraped and banged against it. She eased off the bed and upon standing had to take careful steps. "Damn he did a number on me," she thought. She heard a soft tap on the door and it opened slowly. Denver walked in wearing black pajama bottoms and carrying a tray loaded with a breakfast for a queen.

"Morning sexy," he said while motioning her to get back in bed. Autumn scooted back and propped the pillows behind her. Denver came to the left side of the bed and placed the tray across her lap. He made ham and cheese omelets, bacon, hash browns and biscuits with apple jam. A bowl of fruit and a tall glass of orange juice were also on the tray. "Oh I definitely need to replenish my energy," Autumn said. "You get my vitamins too?"

Denver nodded and put the bottles of iron, vitamin B and a multivitamin on the tray. He leaned forward and kissed her. "Mmmm, thank you Denver." He smiled and left the room.

The last 24 hours had been amazing...with the exception of running into Candi. But all thoughts of Candi left with a quickness when Denver showed up at Charlize's place. When he walked up to her and passionately kissed her, she felt as if she were in another world. She smiled at the thought of being in a daze when he broke from the kiss. In her mind she flashed back to the first time she met Denver.

Autumn was doing another attendant a big favor when she filled in for her. It was a commercial flight from New York to Chicago and she was already in New York after working an international flight. Autumn was taking care of the passengers in first class and was beginning to serve complimentary champagne after the plane reached altitude. She arrived at one seat and noticed a young man in deep thought. "Sir, would you like some champagne?"

The man looked up at her and a huge grin spread across his face. "Yes, I would," he said.

Autumn poured the champagne into a plastic flute as steady as she could because he was watching her. "Here you go," she said and handed him the flute. He took it but was so busy staring at her that he nearly spilled it. "Careful!" she laughed.

"Thank you…beautiful."

Autumn smiled and went to the next passenger all the while noticing that the young, handsome man was still watching her. After serving all of the passengers she turned to dispose of the bottle and her eyes locked with his. When they landed in Chicago Autumn was getting her luggage and about to run inside the employees' lounge when she noticed the flirtatious young man waiting nearby with his luggage. "My name is Denver Harris," he said stretching his hand out.

"Mr. Harris…"

"Please call me Denver." Autumn shook his hand.

"Denver is an odd name for a man."

"Well, Autumn is kind of odd, but beautiful…like you," he said. "Uhm, I was wondering if you'd like to join me for a drink or dinner sometime."

Autumn looked at him thinking he could be her son. Hell he can't be but a year older than my daughter. "I'm sorry, Denver but I will have to say…"

"Please don't say no," he begged. "I can tell we had a connection. We kept looking at each other."

She caved in and they went out for coffee and ended up talking for 6 hours. She checked on her children and they were fine. After exchanging phone numbers Autumn thought that would be the last time she'd hear from or see Denver. Luckily she thought wrong. Their first official date ended in bed and she knew that would be the end of it. Again he proved her wrong.

As they continued seeing each other Autumn had to decide when it would be a good time to introduce Denver to Danyelle and Terrence. Danyelle was 18 and preparing to be a college freshman and Terrence was 14. They knew she was dating off and on and seemed happy for her after interrogating past dates. But this was different because she was only seeing Denver now and there was the age thing. "I want to introduce you to my son and daughter," she said during a night at his place. "I think it's time I let them in on my secret."

"OK. You want me to stop by tomorrow? It's the weekend so maybe I can show up early before they take off with activities," he said.

"Stop by around noon after they've finished their chores," Autumn said. "Maybe we can all have lunch afterwards."

When Denver arrived at the house Danyelle thought it was someone called to do the lawn or repair something. "Mama, there's some repair guy here!"

Autumn approached the front door, laughed and told Denver to come inside. They walked into the TV room where Danyelle was sitting next to Terrence who was concentrating on a video game. "Terrence. Terrence!" Autumn shouted then reached around him and turned off the game.

"Hey!" he said while watching his mom and Denver walk in front of the TV.

"Terrence...Danyelle...this is Denver Harris," she paused. "The man I've been seeing for two months."

Terrence's mouth dropped open. "Alright, Mama!" he said then jumped up and shook Denver's hand.

Danyelle stared at Denver so hard he had to look away. "How old are you?" she asked.

"Twenty-four," Denver said nervously.

Autumn stepped towards Danyelle. "Sweetie..."

"TWENTY-FOUR? You're six years older than I am!" Danyelle yelled and stood up.

"Baby calm down; that is not how you talk to an..."

"Oh mama please don't say adult! He is a baby! He could be my big brother! Are you kidding me?" Danyelle asked.

"Danni why are you tripping?" Terrence asked. "Dad took off with a chick at least five years younger than Denver – by the way, that's a cool first name..."

"Thanks," Denver said awkwardly.

"So why can't mama do the same thing?"

Danyelle glared at her brother, mother and Denver. "You're joining dad in robbing the cradle?" Danyelle offered. "Why don't you both just go to a pre-registration day for high school students!"

"DANYELLE!" Autumn yelled as Danyelle stormed to her room.

That was definitely a day I won't forget, Autumn thought while finishing her special breakfast. She was glad to finally get Danyelle's 'approval' after seeing Denver was not going anywhere and Terrence liked him from the start. Autumn finished her breakfast when she heard the landline ring in the living room. "Don't move baby I got it!" Denver yelled.

Autumn reached for her orange juice, taking a sip.

"Autumn!" Denver yelled as he rushed into the bedroom and headed to the closet where he snatched a pair of jeans from the hanger and began putting them on. "Baby we have to go to the hospital!"

Autumn dropped the glass, the orange juice spilled across the bed. She moved the tray to the other side of the bed as Denver tossed her a pair of jeans, a shirt and her shoes.

"Denver what's wrong?"

"Terrence's been in an accident!"

****

Denver and Autumn burst through the E.R. doors at Chicago Trauma Center, ran down the hallway and stopped at the registration desk. A nurse calmly looked at them while going through medical charts. "May I help you?"

"Yes my son was in an accident..."

"What's his name?"

"Terrence Daniels. He's 17 and we got a call from his friend's father..."

The nurse gestured for Autumn to follow her to triage. "OK, come with me." She paused for a moment then turned toward Terrence, "Excuse me," the nurse said while looking at Denver. "Is this your son as well?"

"Lady, this is my wife," Denver blurted.

The nurse nodded and led them inside triage. Denver held Autumn's right hand as they rushed behind the nurse. After passing the nurses center and closed curtains with other patients, the nurse finally slowed down and stopped in front of #5. "Hold on," the nurse said, pulling the curtain back enough so she could step in.

Autumn heard beeping sounds and voices besides the nurse and squeezed Denver's hand tighter. "T is going to be fine baby," Denver said.

"He's fine I know it." Autumn nodded while blinking back tears.

The curtain was pulled back some more and a male doctor emerged. "Are you his parents?"

Autumn and Denver nodded.

"I am Dr. Artison and I am the emergency room and trauma director. Terrence has been in and out of consciousness so we are going through a series of tests including a CT scan and X-rays for broken bones. Right now he does not seem to have internal bleeding but we have to keep a watch on that as things change."

Autumn felt lightheaded and grabbed her stomach. "Baby what's wrong?" Denver asked and tightened his grip on her.

"I'm not feeling so good..."

Autumn broke away from Denver and ran to the nearest garbage can by the nurses' station. Denver and the doctor caught up with her and steadied her as she vomited. "Get her some water and a cold compress!" the doctor ordered. As Autumn straightened up, another nurse showed up with the items.

"Thank you," she mumbled as the nurse and Denver walked her to a chair. The nurse handed her a towel to wipe her mouth and the cup of water. Autumn slowly sipped the water as Denver rested the cold compress on the back of her neck. "Are you better, sweetie?" he asked.

Autumn nodded. "Please continue doctor."

"Terrence is roughed up a bit; a lot of bruises and abrasions and swelling. Right now we are monitoring him to check that there isn't trauma or pressure on the brain."

"A friend's father called us and said there was an accident," Denver said. "What exactly happened?"

"Yes there was a bad two-vehicle accident. The medics and a traffic police officer said the car your son and his friend were riding in was struck by a semi-trailer who ran a red light in the downtown area and side swiped the car. The impact from the semitrailer knocked the car on the West end of the street and it hit the curb and crashed into a bus stop."

Denver's eyes widened as he held on to Autumn who slumped forward in the chair. "Autumn!" he yelled, dropping to his knees.

"I'm OK," Autumn said while taking a breath. She straightened up and looked at the doctor. "Can we see him?"

The doctor nodded and Autumn got up with Denver's support and followed the doctor to the curtain.

Chapter 3

Autumn gasped as she entered the triage room and looked at her son. Terrence was lying on the stretcher wearing a temporary neck brace and his head wrapped in gauze. His face was swollen like a balloon and black and blue bruises were visible near his eyes. His mouth was also swollen. They had planks along his body to keep him from making sudden moves and IVs were in both arms. His sweat pants were now useless as they were cut off him by the medics. Dried blood was on his body and monitors were recording his blood pressure, pulse and heartbeat. Autumn released Denver's hold and carefully walked to the stretcher and leaned over the safety rail. "Terrence, baby? Mama's here," she said while lightly stroking his arm.

"mmMama."

Autumn leaned in closer. "I'm right here sweetheart."

Terrence slightly opened his eyes and tried to move his head. "No baby, stay still," Autumn said while looking into his eyes. "You are going to have to be still for me OK?"

Terrence closed his eyes. Denver stood beside Autumn and rubbed Terrence's hand. "Hey my man, everything is going to be alright. We're not going anywhere."

Suddenly, the monitors started beeping louder than before and the graphs for Terrence's heart rate became haggard. "Oh my goodness!" Autumn yelled as Dr. Artison and nurses rushed in. Terrence began seizing and Autumn screamed.

"Get them out of here right now!" The doctor yelled as a nurse moved Autumn and Denver out of the room.

Autumn and Denver sat in the triage's waiting room, hugging each other for support. "Terrence is going to be fine. The doctor and nurses are taking care of him," Denver soothingly told her.

"I just want to hold my baby," Autumn cried.

Seconds later they heard footsteps rushing to the waiting room. "Girl, we got a text from Danyelle about Terrence!" Charlize said as she scooped Autumn from the chair and into her arms.

Autumn burst into tears holding on to her friend. Natasha joined them, rubbing both their backs. "He went into a seizure moments ago! I am so scared!" Autumn cried.

Natasha walked over to Denver and hugged him. "Has the doctor come out with an update since the seizure?" she asked.

"No, not yet," Denver said. Autumn and Charlize sat down still holding each other.

"Well that means they are still working on him. We have to pray and pray hard," Charlize said.

Denver filled them in on the details of the accident. "We don't know what happened to his friend. But I do know, they brought him here too," Denver said.

Fifteen minutes later, Dr. Artison walked in the waiting room. "We've stabilized Terrence and we are going to move him to ICU. There is some swelling in the brain but we are going to keep an eye on that for now. The seizure was a minor one despite what you saw," the doctor said. "He may need surgery depending on the results from the tests but right now he is breathing steadily."

Autumn sighed in Charlize's arms. "Thank you, doctor."

"You're welcome. When we are ready to move him the nurse will alert you and you and your husband can come and see him for a little bit. We don't want him overly excited." All four nodded as the doctor walked out.

"Hey doctor," Denver called out. "What happened to Terrence's friend?"

The doctor shook his head. "I had to tell his parents that he did not make it. Neither did the driver of the semitrailer."

Autumn hugged and cried in Charlize's arms again as Denver plopped in a chair and covered his face. Natasha sat next to him and rubbed his back. "I will text Danyelle on Terrence's update. She said she is catching a flight after class," Natasha said while taking out her cell phone.

"Thanks Natasha," Autumn replied then Autumn moved out of Charlize's embrace and walked over to Denver.

Denver stood up and hugged her. "I think I would have gone crazy if that nurse kept me from coming back here with you," he whispered in her ear.

Autumn hugged him tighter. "I am so glad you are with me," she said. "We should look for the other boy's parents and give our condolences." Denver agreed and told Charlize and Natasha to text them when they start moving Terrence out of triage.

Denver and Autumn found the other boy's parents inside a comfort room where they were joined by other relatives. "Excuse me, Mr. Edmonds?" Denver asked a man holding who appeared to be his wife.

"Yes?"

"I'm Denver Harris and this is Autumn Daniels, Terrence's mother."

Autumn stepped forward to the couple. "I am so sorry about your son Mr. and Mrs. Edmonds," she said. The woman walked up to Autumn and stretched out her arms. Autumn embraced her as they cried.

"Terrence and Trent always hung out together. How is Terrence?" asked Mrs. Edmonds.

"They are taking him to ICU," Autumn said. "He had a seizure but they stabilized him. I'm guessing they were on their way to our house."

The woman nodded. "Yes Trent was taking your son home. He's such a good driver, but that semi…"

Mr. Edmonds placed his hands on her shoulders and she stepped back into his arms. Just then Denver heard his cell beep. They're ready to move Terrence. "Baby I got a text from Charlize; we have to go," Denver said.

They hugged the Edmonds again and headed back to the triage area. Denver and Autumn returned in time to see a male nurse pushing Terrence's mobile bed out of the room. Two female nurses were at both sides of the bed making sure Terrence was comfortable and to hold the IV bags during the transition. Dr. Artison handed Autumn a handful of papers and forms, plus Terrence's overnight bag the traffic cop brought to the hospital. "He dropped it off at the nurses' station," the doctor said.

"Thank you," Denver said while taking the bag from Autumn. They followed the nurses and Terrence to the other side of the center to ICU.

After Terrence was situated in one of the rooms, Autumn sat at a table near his bed and answered the nurse's questions about him. Denver stood behind Autumn, watching the other nurses reconnect Terrence's IVs and monitors. They adjusted his bed and placed a circulatory device on his feet to keep his blood and circulation going and prevent clotting.

Denver lowered his gaze to the bag collecting Terrence's urine as a catheter was inserted earlier. All of this scared the hell out of Denver as he was not use to seeing Terrence in this state. He's not Terrence's biological father but in the three years he's been dating Autumn he's grown accustomed to being a father figure to her son. If someone told him years ago that he would be in a relationship that included a teenage boy and a girl in college when he'd not paid off his college tuition, he'd called that person crazy.

Now as he watched the nurses do their jobs with a keen eye, Denver had no regrets getting involved with an older, divorced mother of two. "Ok Mrs. Daniels all the forms are filled and signed and Terrence is resting comfortably," one of the nurses said, oblivious to the fact that Denver and Autumn were not married. "We have everything monitored from the nurses' station right outside and your son will be checked constantly while in ICU. If you and your husband need anything, push this button or come to the desk."

Autumn nodded while writing Danyelle's and Phillip's names on a list of people permitted to visit Terrence during ICU hours.

Autumn felt her cell phone vibrate and checked the text. It was from Natasha. 'Dad's on his way to ICU. He should be there any minute.'

Autumn texted OK and shoved the phone in her jacket pocket. She glanced up just in time to see Phillip rushing in the door. "Phillip's here," she informed.

Denver nodded and turned around in time to see Phillip hurrying toward them. "How is he…" Phillip stopped a few steps from the bed looking at Terrence breathing steadily with help from a breathing tube.

His shoulders slumped like a boulder was hoisted onto his body. Autumn got up and walked over to Phillip, embracing him. They slowly walked to Terrence's bedside. "Hey, buddy," Phillip said to his son while lightly touching the top of his head.

"The doctor put him in a drug induced coma in hopes that the swelling in his brain goes down," Autumn said. "I tried calling you on the way here."

"You and Danyelle must have been calling at the same time; she was the first voice I heard when I listened to them." Autumn nodded and squeezed Phillip's arm. She filled him in on everything as Denver sat at the table looking on.

Phillip met Denver not long after Danyelle acted like an overpaid drama actress leaving back to back messages and texts on his cell, home and office phones within 15-minutes of storming out of the house and sitting in her car. Autumn invited him to stop by in between his errands including taking Monique, the younger woman he left Autumn for and eventually married. That wedding day was memorable as Danyelle put on a show before the ceremony refusing to wear the bridesmaid dress Monique had designed then starting a food fight with Terrence at the reception. It took a lot of apologies and an extended week in Hawaii to calm Monique down.

Autumn did not know Phillip was on her property until she heard Danyelle sputtering "Daddy!" in high pitch levels while she and Denver sat in the living room. The next sound they heard was Phillip opening the front door with Danyelle at his heels.

Danyelle walked around to the front of her father. "I'm sorry for being childish when I am old enough to vote and drive a car. Mom I am sorry for being rude and disrespectful under your roof. I will not disrespect you or your house because I know my ass will end up on the street without the car you paid for and I will likely have to find a way to go to college and make ends meet." Denver's eyes widen after listening to this apology that was more like a speech.

"Uh, apology accepted, but try not using the word ass" he said. Denver looked at Autumn who was wearing a blank expression to keep from laughing. Phillip then introduced himself to Denver and hung out for a couple hours talking getting to know each other.

Phillip made his way to where Denver was sitting. "Thanks for being here, man" he said to Denver as they shook hands.

"It's not a problem Phil, that's my buddy there."

"Yeah he's a great kid." Phillip looked back at his son and Autumn. "How is she holding up?"

Denver stood and motioned Phillip to the corner of the room. "She was in hysterics of course. When we saw him in triage she was so upset she threw up."

Phillip shoved his hands in his pants pockets. "I'm just glad you two were home when you got the call."

"Actually, we were at The Loft last night," Denver said. "It was Autumn's first time there and really her first time having a few days off in a while."

"Those international routes are a bitch," Phillip said.

After a few seconds of uncomfortable silence, they turned their attention to Autumn who was holding a conversation with Terrence. She'd pulled up a chair as close as possible to the bed and locked her fingers with Terrence's right hand.

"Excuse me."

All three turned to the door where a nurse and nurse's aide walked in. "We have to change his dressing and do vitals. Can you please step outside?"

Autumn panicked at the thought of leaving her son for even a second. "Please can I stay? I'll sit at the table on in the corner near the window."

The nurse looked at her and nodded. Autumn released Terrence's hand and went to the corner on the opposite side of the room.

Phillip and Denver stood for a few minutes then decided to go have a seat in ICU's waiting room.

"Denver if you and Autumn need anything don't hesitate to let me know. I'll be here for awhile. I called my office already and informed them I will be off on family emergency until further notice," Phillip said.

"Thanks Phillip, but we will be fine. Let's focus on Terrence and Danyelle."

They sat in silence until both heard their cell phones beep. It was Danyelle sending messages to both men that she should be in Chicago later that evening. Both men text OK then chuckled when they said in unison it was Danyelle. "I guess it's a good thing both of us answered it huh?" Phillip said. And they laughed.

Autumn stayed at Terrence's bed side the entire day, leaving only to use the bathroom. When Denver and Phillip walked in with lunch from the cafeteria she'd eat in the chair while they sat at the table. Phillip brought his laptop and earphones to send messages to his woman, Monique and his relatives. He also relayed updates to his supervisor who hired Terrence as an intern the last couple summers. Later that day just before dinner, Phillip got a text from Danyelle that she was at O'Hare. "Hey Denver I'm going to pick Danyelle up from O'Hare."

"Do you want me to go instead?" Denver asked.

"No I'll go ahead." Denver nodded knowing it's best that Phillip go. Danyelle wanted her daddy and he understood that. "I'll call you if there are changes while you're gone," Denver said.

Phillip got up and walked to the bed. He rubbed Autumn's shoulder. "I'm going to get Danyelle from the airport. You need anything?" Autumn shook her head no and Phillip left the room.

Charlize and Natasha walked the hall that led to ICU. They were about to go into the waiting room when Denver stepped out and caught up with them. "Hey! Sorry we left you guys in the E.R.," Denver said.

"Don't worry about it," Charlize said. "We left anyway to give you all some privacy. We got something to eat and Natasha had to run some errands."

"Yeah we figured we should come back and at least sit in the area," Natasha said.

"Thank you," Denver said.

"Oh, we called Denyce who is away on a business trip but she said call or text her with updates no matter the hour and she will talk to Autumn later," Charlize said.

"Yeah well I'm sure she understands that Autumn is in that room for the long haul," Denver said looking behind him. "She is not moving and she shoved her cell phone in my hand."

Charlize and Natasha walked over to the ICU window and looked at Terrence then Autumn. Tears ran down their faces and they hugged each other. "We are praying for all of you and the families of the deceased boy and the driver," Natasha sniffled.

"Did you ever find out what the deal was with the truck driver?" Charlize asked.

"I called the traffic officer who left his card with the E.R. and trauma director. The officer said it was a combination of a lack of sleep and talking on the cell phone," Denver said.

"Damn! That falling asleep at the wheel is some dangerous shit, especially when driving a semitrailer," Charlize said.

****

Chapter 4

"Daddy!" Danyelle ran into her father's arms as soon as she spotted him near luggage claim.

"Hey angel, how are you?" he said, hugging her tight and kissing her forehead.

"I'm OK…could be better."

"Yeah I know me too." Phillip took his daughter's suitcase and they headed to the parking lot.

"I was hoping to not come home until Thanksgiving weekend, but, we can't control all things," Danyelle said.

Phillip opened the trunk and put her suitcase inside. "Nope, no we can't sweetheart."

They got in the car and Phillip pulled off. "How long are you here?"

"At least a week, but the professors said if I need to stay longer I can send my papers and do my tests online," Danyelle said. "I may consider that option because Thanksgiving is not far and it would not make sense to fly back to Atlanta then turn around for the holidays."

"Don't you have a job?" Phillip asked.

"No I took a break this semester because of the heavy load I have. Mama felt it was best so I would not go crazy and then pass the craziness down to her," Danyelle said.

Phillip laughed. "Well that was very noble of you!"

"Daddy is Terrence going to be OK?" she asked.

"He's pretty bad sweetie but he could have been worse," he said. "His friend died from his injuries as did the semitrailer driver. But we are all going to be there for Terrence and your mom."

Danyelle did not respond, instead she focused on the scenery. They were away from O'Hare and coming in the city. She looked at the Thanksgiving and Christmas decorations along the houses and business districts.

"Is Denver still at the hospital?" she asked, breaking the silence.

"Yes he is. He is by your mom's side," he said then glanced over at Danyelle. "Charlize and Natasha are there too. They're hoping to see you."

"I can't wait to see tee-tee Charlize and Natasha," Danyelle said.

"And you will speak to Denver, right?"

"Of course I'll speak to him…wait," Danyelle said. "How is he in ICU with mom? They're not married!"

"Your mother probably told the nurse in E.R. that Denver was her husband."

Danyelle's mouth dropped open. "OK I know they've been together for three years and he likes us but…"

"Danyelle we are not having this discussion! Denver has been a part of your mother's life for awhile and he is apparently in for the long haul. You will not enter that hospital disrespecting him and upsetting your mother!" Phillip said. "You are 21 years old and you need to accept once and for all that your mother is a grown ass woman who can see who she wants and that is that!"

Danyelle recoiled in the passenger seat as they got closer to Chicago Trauma Center. "I'm sorry Daddy," Danyelle said as Phillip parked in the center's public lot. "I just wish sometimes you and mama made the marriage work."

Phillip turned off the ignition and grabbed Danyelle's hand. "I know you do Danyelle. We're sorry it didn't but that does not mean we love you and Terrence less. Things happen and we have to move on. There's respect between the four of us and while it was not easy at first it is working out in the end," he said.

"I love you Daddy," Danyelle said and lean forward to hug him.

"Ditto angel, ditto."

Danyelle was the spitting image of Phillip with a cocoa complexion, hazel eyes and square jaw line framed with a medium length bob of dark brown mixed with highlights. Terrence was a darker version of Autumn with a serious expression on his face that vanished when he smiles. His tall, lean height came from either side of the family while Danyelle stopped at 5'7.

Phillip and Danyelle entered ICU and walked inside Terrence's room. "Mama," Danyelle's voice shook as she looked at her little brother attached to tubes and IVs. Autumn jumped up and pulled Danyelle into her arms.

"Hey baby girl. How was your flight?" Danyelle did not respond; she looked over her mother's shoulder at Terrence.

"Mama T looks awful!" Danyelle cried out and stepped away from her mother's embrace.

Phillip turned his daughter around and held her. "It's OK sweetie. C'mon, let's go to the other side and you can talk to him," Phillip said.

As he guided her around the bed Danyelle looked at Denver who stood by the table watching. Danyelle moved from her father and approached Denver with a hug. "Hey girl," Denver said hugging her tight.

"Hey. Thank you for being here to help," Danyelle said, pulling back to wipe the tears off her face.

She joined her father at the left side of Terrence's bed leaned down to his face. She kissed his cheek twice. "T I'm going to need you to get better

OK? You have to get better so you can visit me on campus, eat up all the cafeteria food, flirt with my friends and tell guys my secrets," Danyelle said.

Everyone laughed.

"Good evening everyone. Visiting hours in ICU are now over," a voice on the intercom announced interrupting their moment. "You can return tomorrow as the schedule here is 45 minutes per hour beginning at noon and ending at 6 p.m. Goodnight and thank you."

Autumn looked at everyone. "I'm staying the night. The nurse gave me permission to stay over. An aide is bringing in a folding bed."

"Mama I will go home and get some things and bring them to the station for you," Danyelle said while putting on her coat.

Phillip grabbed his car keys and walked over to Autumn. He kissed the top of her head. "I'll be back tomorrow. Call me on changes or if you need something."

Autumn nodded and squeezed Phillip's hand. Danyelle bent over and hugged her mother. "I'll be back shortly. They walked out the room. Denver walked over to the bed and Autumn stood up and went in his arms. "I'll be OK honey," she said and kissed him. "I know you will. I'll check on you later. Call me for whatever. I'll be home," Denver continued.

Denver then rubbed Terrence's hand. "See you tomorrow, T."

"Looks like Charlize and Natasha left before we got here," Phillip said to Danyelle as they entered the parking lot.

"I'll text them to let them know we'll be at the house in ten minutes," Danyelle as she turned on her phone.

When they arrived at the house Charlize's car was parked on the street. Danyelle and Phillip walked to the front door and she unlocked it. As they entered Danyelle stopped to hang up her coat while Phillip headed toward the bathroom.

The doorbell rang.

Looking through the peephole, she saw two of her mother's bestfriends. Danyelle had barely opened the door when Charlize rushed in with arms stretched out for a hug. Danyelle and Charlize hugged until Natasha made her way across the threshold.

"Stop hogging the love!" Danyelle moved from Charlize and ran into Natasha's arms. "Girl you look good!" Natasha said as she kissed Danyelle's face. "How's my future cosmetic surgeon coming along with her studies? I may have to come to your practice one day."

Classes are hell but I can handle it! Why are you talking about plastic surgery now? You don't need it!" she said.

"Girl I'm reserving my spot to be under your knife in 10 years!" Natasha laughed.

"Well mama's staying overnight at the center so I need to throw some things in an overnight bag."

"Uuuh, I hate to interrupt this reunion but didn't I see Phillip's car in the driveway," Charlize asked.

"Yes, Daddy's here. I think he's in the bathroom."

"Well, back to the subject of your mother's bag. We stopped at the store on the way here and put a bag together for her. We bought her pajamas, robe, underwear, a pair of jeans, blouse and gym shoes. And in the side compartment of the bag we added some toiletries. We knew she was not going to come home and who would expect her to? Anyway, it's all in the car. We'll give it to you before we leave," Charlize informed.

"You two are the best," Danyelle said as she sat on the living room couch.

"Oh, one more thing." Charlize held out an envelope. Here's a card for my sister-friend."

"I'm sure she will appreciate it," Natasha said while placing it on the arm of the sofa.

Phillip came from around the corner looking at his cell phone. "Hello, ladies. Sorry but, I have to leave you right now. Mrs. Monique Daniels is calling me 911." He went to the couch, bent over and kissed his daughter on the cheek. "Did your mom say where her car keys are?"

"I know where she usually keeps them. I'll talk to you later Daddy." Phillip waved at Charlize and Natasha and left.

"Alright, now that dad's gone," Charlize said as she plopped on the couch next to Danyelle. "What's going on with you and Eric?"

Danyelle laughed as Natasha sat in the recliner. "Yeah he's not taking you away from your books, is he?"

"No tee-tee Natasha and Charlize! Eric and I are doing fine. He wanted to come with me but I told him to stay. I have to tell mama Eric asked about her," Danyelle said.

Charlize pat Danyelle's thigh. "Are you OK staying here with Denver? Because if you're not you can stay with me or Natasha," Charlize said.

"Thanks but I will be OK. I think Denver will likely be at the center a lot so it's not like I am going be around him alot," Danyelle said.

Charlize and Natasha got quiet.

"What?" Danyelle asked.

"Denver may stay out of the way with your Dad around…out of respect," Natasha said.

"And we know you are still kind of iffy about Denver and your mama," Charlize added.

Danyelle looked down. "Just seeing us together like it was when Terrence and I were younger…we're a family you know? I like Denver a lot but it's just hard."

"Denver is well aware that you've never fully accepted him and a lot of it is because you feel your mama should not be with another man," Charlize said. "But weren't you the same way about your dad when he was seeing Monique?"

"Yeah remember what you did at the wedding and the reception?" Natasha said.

Danyelle smirked at the memory. "I guess if I pull that stunt on mama when she and Denver get married, I will end up going to witness protection!" They laughed until they heard the front door open.

Denver's voice surprised them all. "Are you ladies decent in here?" he asked.

"We're in the living room!" Natasha yelled.

Denver entered the living room and sat down in the other recliner. "I got Autumn to eat dinner. I brought her some steak tacos," Denver said. "It's a wonder Terrence's eyes did not pop open at the smell of those tacos," Charlize laughed. "Oh, a specialist came by and he said Terrence is doing well under the induced coma and they will run some tests early in the morning," continued.

"They do tests on Sunday?" Danyelle asked.

"When it comes to situations like Terrence the specialist said they are around the clock. But that's any situation because it's a trauma center," Natasha said.

Danyelle hopped up. "I need to take the bag to mama." She went to her mama's room and grabbed the car keys. She ran downstairs and to the door where Charlize and Natasha were standing.

"I'll bring the things for your Mom to the car," Natasha said. "Denver we'll be seeing you, she added reaching for the knob.

"Later, Denver," Danyelle added indifferently as she headed out the door. "I will be back in a little bit."

"Yeah Denver, we'll holler at you later. I know it's a lot going on but don't forget to call Autumn's job to let them know what's going on, Charlize informed.

Denver walked over and embraced both, Charlize and Natasha before they exited the house. "I'll take care of it. Thank you ladies for everything. Drive safely."

"Denver get some rest if you can," Natasha threw over her shoulder as they made their way down the side walk leading to the car.

"First, I have to eat. I'm starving."

Thirty minutes later, Danyelle let herself in the house and an aroma hit her hard. "Ooh that hamburger smells good!" she said walking in the kitchen.

"There are two in the skillet. Do you want one?" Denver asked.

"Thank you!" she said while pulling off her coat and hanging it in the hall closet.

She made her way to the kitchen where she pressed on the bottle of hand sanitizer on the counter then grabbed a paper towel. Denver placed two plates on the table, a hamburger and buns on each one. A bowl of fries was on the table, along with all the condiments and pre-wrapped slices of pepper jack cheese. They sat down, blessed the food and began making their own version of a cheeseburger. Denver jumped up and opened the refrigerator to retrieve cans of grape pop.

"Thanks," Danyelle said.

They bit into their piled high burgers and savored the juiciness of the thick patties with the just the right flavor of seasoning. "This burger is so delicious Denver," Danyelle said as she grabbed a handful of crispy fries.

"Glad you like it. I did not feel like having tacos. I just wanted your mom to eat something," he said.

"Well I am glad you are here for her," she said.

"Yeah well I will probably take a step back now that your dad will be around to help out," Denver said as he took another bite.

"Denver mama needs you by her side too. Daddy is only going to be there every now and then because he does have a wife and a little stepson."

"I keep forgetting about that little boy," Denver said. "Well he's taken off a lot of time to be near Autumn and Terrence so that's why I figured…"

"As much as I like Monique, she is not going to have daddy spent all of his vacation time in the trauma center with mama," Danyelle said. "She is still insecure because of his relationship with mama. She loved it when mama was witching all over the place after daddy left but when mama started getting over it and they were back on speaking terms for our sake, Monique's been faking the understanding," Danyelle said.

Denver looked at Danyelle and quietly thought about how Autumn didn't play when it came down to her man and another woman. She was livid when Candi showed up at The Loft the other night, which was why he had the limo driver take him to Charlize's townhouse. He wanted to dismiss any perception that he would go home with Candi. Candi was his past and he wanted Autumn to know that. Autumn never even mentioned anything about Candi being at the club or why he was still communicating with her. Denver guessed Autumn worked out all of her concerns and insecurities when they made love afterwards.

The sound of Danyelle smacking on her burger took him away from his thoughts. "Danyelle…I love your mother and everything about her, including those little insecurities, he said feeling the need to confess that.

Danyelle paused before finishing off her cheeseburger. "Mama's always had some insecurities, especially about her body. She was that way before she met you. It was one of the reasons daddy left her…" Danyelle froze and glanced at Denver.

"Really?" Denver said.

"I said one of the reasons," Danyelle continued. "But he did not like her being away from us constantly. He's kind of old school. He is almost 50."

Denver laughed. "What does his age have to do with anything?"

"Daddy won't admit it but he has that 'women need to be at home raising the kids' personality," she said.

They finished dinner and cleaned the kitchen. Danyelle took her suitcase in her old bedroom upstairs.

Denver walked around the house and finished tiding up. He spotted the envelope on the arm of the sofa addressed to him and Autumn. He opened it and read the hand-written saluation first. It read "To the only two people I know who put the F-R in the word "Freaks". After reading the sentiments, Denver saw it was signed by Charlize. He couldn't help but laugh, thinking that even in a time like this, you can always count on Charlize to put a smile on your face.

Chapter 5

Days went by with Terrence's progress improving more and more. Denver occasionally took Autumn home or out for a bite to eat while Phillip, Danyelle, Charlize and Natasha alternated staying with Terrence. Danyelle even had a couple of friends stop by and they'd play cards at the table, promising Autumn they would not scream or slam on the table.

After being at the hospital on the regular, Autumn came home one day, too exhausted to make it to her room. She fell asleep on the couch. Denver came in the livingroom and decided to carry her to the bedroom. He walked in and laid her on the bed, knelt down and took off her shoes. She squirmed a bit then was still again. He did not want to chance waking her so he put a comforter on her and turned off the light.

The next morning Autumn's cell phone ringed loud and clear. She sat up and looked around the room slowly realizing she was at home. "Hello." She said then paused a few second. "OK, thank you", she continued. Autumn pushed the comforter off and swung her legs to the side.

Denver walked in the room. "Morning baby. Was that the center?" he asked.

"Yeah the doctor said they are going to slowly take him out of the induced coma today," she said, stretching.

"That's great! What time do we need to get ready?" Denver asked.

"They're doing it at 10 a.m. and it's only 8 a.m. so we have time to eat breakfast." Autumn looked down noticing she was in yesterday's outfit. "Guess I slept like a rock huh?"

Denver came to the bed, sat down and smiled. "You were knocked out on the couch. I had to carry you in here."

"I hope I didn't injure you," she joked.

He kissed her. 'You were light as a…"

"Don't even finish that lame ass line," she said.

He laughed. "You go ahead and shower while I fix breakfast."

Autumn smiled and stood up to go through the closet. It was a few minutes picking out her outfit then on to her bath. Thirty minutes later she followed the scent of turkey sausages and maple syrup.

"Pancakes? What are trying to do, put me back to sleep?" Autumn said. She sat down and Denver place three hot fluffy pancakes on her plate with two sausage patties. He already put pats of butter between each pancake and the maple syrup was heated.

"Enjoy baby," he said.

Autumn cut into the stack after pouring the syrup and put a forkful in her mouth. "Oh my goodness, this is sooo good!" she said.

Danyelle walked in the kitchen and sat at the table. Denver plopped three pancakes on another plate, added two sausage patties and placed them in front of Danyelle with a glass of cold milk.

"Baby the center called and said they are going to slowly wake Terrence," Autumn said before stuffing another forkful. "

That's great!" Danyelle said as she poured hot maple syrup on her pancakes.

Denver was about to fix him a plate when the doorbell rang. He placed his plate and silverware on the counter then went to answer the door.

"Hey Phillip," Denver said and stepped aside.

"Hey Denver how's it going?" he said.

"Everything's cool. They're in the kitchen eating breakfast. Come on and join us."

Phillip stopped in the kitchen doorway. "I should have called first. Sorry about that."

Denver nudged him in the kitchen. "Have a seat, I'll make you a stack of pancakes."

"No, I've eaten already but thanks. I guess I am a little excited because the center called me about Terrence," Phillip said.

He sat next to Danyelle who waved 'hello' with her fork.

He laughed and winked at Autumn. "Hey Phil," she mumbled with her mouth full.

"Wow your pancakes must be off the hook Denver," Phillip said.

"Oh Dad stop trying to be hip!" Danyelle groaned.

Denver and Phillip laughed at her.

"Yeah we got the call too," Autumn said while wiping her mouth. "I figure we'll go there shortly."

Denver fixed his plate and sat down by the small island near the table.

"Denver, please take my seat," Phillip said, pushing his chair back.

"Sit down. Don't worry about me," Denver said and bit off a sausage patty. Denver ate and watched as Danyelle had her parents' full attention talking about classes and her boyfriend Eric. He was giving Danyelle space and respect by not intervening on her time with them. This was a crucial time for them with Terrence and he did not want to push himself in their circle.

After the ladies finished breakfast. Danyelle offered to wash the plates. "No I will put them in the dishwasher," Denver said and took her plate from her hands. "It's after 9 so you all better go."

Autumn and Danyelle went to the bathroom and returned grabbing their coats. "Denver, aren't you coming?" Autumn asked.

"I'm coming right behind you. You all go ahead," he said.

"Are you sure?"

"Yes, I have a few things to do. It won't take long, go ahead."

"OK baby," Autumn said and kissed Denver lovingly. She moved back and stroked his face making him smile. "I love you."

"I love you too."

Phillip interjected, "it makes no sense for every one to drive so you all can ride with me."

Denver watched the car back out of the driveway and head down the street. He finished loading the dishwasher, turned it on then walked in the living room. The sound of his cellphone singing arrested his attention. Digging in his pocket he pulled out his cell phone, read the text and pushed speed dial. "What? … I will be there in 15 minutes," Denver said and ended the call.

****

Denver walked inside a local coffee shop called Joe's Cup and scanned the crowd. The place was the size of an average café but had the atmosphere of a friendly diner. Moms who dropped off their children at daycare or elementary school blended with those looking for jobs and some taking advantage of the free Wi-fi. All together they were enjoying cups and mugs of coffee or hot chocolate with a pastry or a small sandwich.

None paid attention to Denver, except for Candi, who stood out in a red wool trench coat, black leggings and undoubtedly a sweater with a plunging neckline underneath. She waved Denver over to a corner table a little distant from the other patrons. "Denver, hey," she said and reached out to hug him.

"Why did you text me Candi?" he asked and sat down with his back to the crowd.

Candi sat down and wrapped her hands around her mug of hot chocolate. "I saw on the news about the horrible accident involving Autumn's son, his friend and that truck driver. How is Terrence?"

"Terrence is doing fine; in fact the doctor is going to slowly take him out of the drug induced coma," Denver said.

"Oh that is wonderful! When are they doing it?" Denver glanced at the clock on the wall. "They should be prepping Terrence right now."

"Wait…they're working on him right this minute and you are not with Autumn?"

Denver looked at her. "I'm heading there after I find out what you have to say that is so urgent."

Candi looked at him then raised the hot chocolate to her lips and sipped. "I don't understand why you are not there right now…"

"Autumn and Danyelle rode with Phillip to the trauma center," Denver said.

"Who's Phillip?"

"Autumn's ex-husband and Terrence and Danyelle's dad."

"Oh," Candi said. "Feeling like the odd man out?"

"I am giving them the respect and privacy that a family needs at this time!" Denver said. He looked around and noticed he was a bit loud.

"Everything OK, sir?" a waiter behind the counter asked.

"Yes, everything's fine. I'm sorry for the loudness," Denver said.

Candi touched Denver's hand. "I did not mean to upset you like that. I just figured Autumn would want you with her at this moment."

Denver pushed his chair back and stood up. "You are 100 percent right Candi. Whatever you need to tell me can wait."

"You're right. We can talk about the clubs another time."

Denver looked at her. "This is about a club? I'll text you later about that," he said and walked away.

****

Autumn, Danyelle and Phillip sat in the lounge not far from the operating rooms on the second floor. It had been 20 minutes since Terrence was taken in to begin the procedure. The doctor informed them that the procedure was complicated and could not be done all at once or there would be complications. "We will continue to monitor Terrence and draw blood to determine the amount of medication needed," he had told them.

"Anybody want coffee?" Danyelle asked while grabbing her purse.

"Yeah I could use a large cup," Phillip said. "Autumn, do you want coffee?"

She shook her head no.

"I'll be back," Danyelle said and left the lounge.

Phillip scooted next to Autumn and draped his arm across the back of the chair. "He is going to be fine. I have complete and utter faith," Phillip said.

"I know. I am just thinking about what Terrence's been through these last few days," Autumn said. "He will pull out of this but he will have a long recovery. He will likely have to repeat senior year and all of that preparation is gone…"

"Honey we have to pray on this," Phillip said. "We don't know what God has in store for Terrence. He could wake up and turn around so quickly! He's already a miracle in that he survived the accident. Let's just take his recovery one day at a time."

Autumn nodded.

"Hey look who I found," Danyelle walked in with hot coffee cups in a cardboard cup holder. Denver was on her heels. He walked over to Autumn and she stood up and kissed him.

"Sorry I'm late. Are they still working on Terrence?"

"Yeah but they should be out soon," Autumn said. "This is only the first in a series of weaning him out of the coma."

Denver took off his coat and sat next to Autumn. Danyelle handed her parents their coffee. "Denver did you want me to get you a cup?" Danyelle asked.

"No I'm good."

They all sat in silence for ten minutes then the neurologist walked in. "Mr. and Ms. Daniels, your son is being taken back to ICU. It's so far, so good with this initiation to wean him off the barbiturates and he is stable."

"Thank you very much," Autumn said as Phillip shook the neurologist's hand.

"As I've said before this is a complicated process and if there's a setback we may have to induce him again. Right now he is doing OK," the doctor said before leaving.

"Thank goodness the first step is complete," Autumn said as Phillip hugged her. She hugged Danyelle then Denver.

"I guess we can head back to ICU and visit for a while," Phillip said.

They all stopped in and watched Terrence sleep. "Hey son, you're doing great," Phillip said and placed his hand on his son's chest.

Terrence blinked twice then stopped.

"Did you see that, Autumn?" Phillip said, grinning from ear to ear. "He heard me!" Autumn squeezed Phillip's arm and hugged Danyelle close to her side.

Denver smiled. "That's right Terrence, let us know you are coming back strong!" he said.

After being advised to let Terrence rest, they left the hospital. All were smiling about Terrence's updates and his reaction to Phillip touching him. Danyelle sent a text to Charlize, Natasha and Denyce, who texted back with smiley faces and words of praise. Autumn and Danyelle rode home with Denver while Phillip went to meet with Monique. As Denver pulled up the driveway his phone went off but he missed the call. No sooner than they made it to the front door, Denver's cell went off again. "Sounds like someone's hunting you down," Autumn said.

Denver checked the phone. "It's not the hospital so it goes to voicemail," he said. They walked in the house and Denver disabled the alarm system. After Autumn and Danyelle hung their coats and headed to separate bathrooms, Denver's cell beeped alerting him about a text message. "Just checking to see if all is OK with Terrence."

Denver typed furiously. "Everything is cool. STOP CALLING ME!"

****

Autumn and Danyelle went back to the center that evening and walked in to see Phillip and Monique in the room. "Autumn, Danyelle," Monique said as she approached them. She hugged and kissed Autumn first then Danyelle who gave her a slight squeeze. "And you must be Denver," Monique continued and stretched out her hand.

Denver shook her hand and smiled. "Yes I am. It's nice to meet you."

"I wish it was under better circumstances," Monique said as she turned and looked at Terrence.

"Yes well I am sure Phillip told you about the beginning of weaning Terrence out of the induced coma this morning," Autumn said.

"Yes and that is wonderful news! Terrence is in my prayers for a perfect recovery."

Autumn smiled and walked to the bed. "Mama's back sweetie," she said, bending down to kiss his forehead.

Terrence blinked twice in response causing Autumn to gasp. "He's been blinking quite a bit from what the doctors and the nurses told me," Phillip said. "They may do the second step tomorrow or early Friday."

Autumn gently brushed her lips on her son's forehead. "Keep fighting baby I know you can do it."

Danyelle stood next to her mom, stroking her brother's hand. "Hey little brother it's Danni," she said. "You have to come back so I can watch you devour Thanksgiving dinner!"

"Geez, I have not even thought about getting a turkey or any damn thing," Autumn said. "Thanksgiving is in another week!"

Monique walked over to Autumn. "If you like you all can come to our house for Thanksgiving. That is if you want to," Monique said.

Danyelle cut a side glance at her mom who turned and faced Monique. "We appreciate the offer Monique. Who knows, we might just take you up on that invite," Autumn said.

Monique turned to face Denver. "You're welcome to come along too of course. I am sure Phillip doesn't mind, right?"

Denver raised an eyebrow then slowly smiled. "Of course, thank you."

All of them stood in awkward silence with the machines beeping providing the only noise in the room. "OK then, Monique and I have been here for a while, so we are going to let you have some time with Terrence until the intercom announces for everyone on this floor to leave," Phillip said.

He held Monique's coat up as she slipped in it. "It was nice seeing you Autumn…Danyelle. And nice meeting you Denver," she said and strolled out.

Phillip walked over and said his goodbyes to Autumn, Danyelle and Terrence. He turned to Denver, shook his hand and left.

"Wow," Denver said after Phillip and Monique were out of earshot.

"Yep," Danyelle and Autumn said in unison.

****

That night when Danyelle turned in, Denver walked in the bedroom and watched Autumn put on a night shirt. His eyes wandered as she raised her arms to put the shirt over her head. Her breasts were full and upright; her nipples were inviting. He scanned her curves from her belly to her hips. Denver wished her bikini panties were not there but he could change all of that. Autumn struggled with the head opening of the shirt and could not see Denver sneaking up on her until she felt his hands cup her breasts. "What the…Denver, no," she whispered while trying to move away without tripping.

Denver laughed and snatched the shirt off her head, pulled her in his arms and kissed her. Autumn pressed her hands on his shoulders and tried to push him away. He held her tighter and pushed his tongue in her mouth.

"Denver stop!" Autumn said breaking free from the kiss.

"What's wrong?" he asked while stroking her sides.

"I'm not in the mood and Danyelle is here!"

Denver stepped back and looked at the ceiling. "This door is closed, Danyelle's upstairs and probably has her iPod plugged in her ears to block any 'disgusting' noises we are likely to make," Denver said with a laugh. He stepped closer to kiss Autumn again and she backed away and grabbed her night shirt. "I said no and I meant it!" she snapped.

Denver quietly watched Autumn put the night shirt on and turned to the door. "I just don't feel like having sex tonight," she said to his back. "I'm tired and these days have been long…"

"I understand and I'm sorry," Denver said as he opened the door and walked out.

Autumn turned off the light and went to bed. Denver closed the door and stood in the hallway. She did not even ask if I was coming to bed, he thought.

Denver walked into the TV room, turned the TV on and lowered the volume. He was half watching a night time talk show when his cell beeped. "I thought you were going to call me tonight so we can talk about the club?" Denver hit speed dial. "Are you at home? Good, I'll be there in 30."

****

Candi opened her front door still wearing her black leggings and a black, low cut sweater. Her hair was flowing perfectly and her makeup, especially her cherry glossed lips was refreshed at 10:30 p.m. "Hey Denver, come on in," she said, stepping aside. He walked inside her home and noticed the fireplace was lit and warming the living room. Candi took his coat and hung it on the coat rack. She walked ahead of Denver and gestured at the sofa facing the fireplace. He walked over and sat down. The coffee table in front of him had a portfolio lying on top along with an open laptop. "Can I get you something to drink? Coffee or a shot of whatever?" she asked.

"No I want you to sit down and tell me what you have to say about a club," Denver barked. "Which club and why?"

"OK you need to chill," Candi said as she sat down next to him. "What's wrong babe? Autumn's son hasn't gotten worse has he?"

"No he is doing fine. They started weaning him out of the coma this morning and he has been responding to touch and voices by blinking," Denver said.

"Oh Denver that is amazing news!" Candi reached over and hugged him.

Denver then noticed that Candi was braless underneath her sweater. He shrugged away from her and scooted away as well.

"I'm sorry; I am just happy to hear about her son," she said, looking at him. "I read in the paper the boy who died, his funeral is Friday," she said. "That is so sad for that family not to have a beautiful Thanksgiving."

Denver took a deep breath and looked at Candi. "What club are you talking about?"

Candi grabbed the portfolio and hit a button on the laptop's keyboard. "The Loft and Fuego actually. I talked with Leo some more about doing a big collaboration with that guy Jet who owns Fuego? If these guys partnered, it would bring bigger crowds, more income and their reputations would overwhelm all the other nightclubs in Chicago," Candi said, smiling.

"Wait, you talked some more with Leo? And you met up with Jet without my knowledge or input?" Denver yelled. He was so furious with Candi at that moment he could have choked the shit out of her. He glared at her and snatched the portfolio out of her hand. Skimming the pages and pausing to read some of the documentation Denver could not believe his eyes. "Wow you have a freaking blueprint with graphics and a budget tablet and everything!" He tossed the portfolio on the coffee table.

"Denver, listen with everything going on with your woman I did not want to disturb you. And I know she doesn't like…"Candi stuttered.

"But you suddenly decide to hit me up AFTER the fact. You've done secret meetings and put together shit that was probably done months ago before I showed up with Autumn at The Loft last weekend!" Denver yelled. He stood up and pushed the coffee table aside with his right leg. "That's why you brought your ass to the club! You knew what was already going down when you walked in there flaunting your body and laughing with me and Leo. When Leo told Autumn he invited you, I should have known!"

Candi stood and faced Denver. "I am only looking out for us and our business! It is not my fault that you did not tell Autumn that you reconnected with me a year ago because you did not want to lose profits on some of the contracts I drew for you!" Candi yelled back. "You have some business sense, Denver, but it was not enough! I may have followed you all over the place when I was younger but I damn sure know how to make deals now. You forget my Mom owned three restaurants in East Chicago and Poppy was a self made businessman!"

Denver looked at Candi and dropped back on the couch. Candi eased on the couch next to him. "You asked me to come back and help you out on the low and that is what I am doing," she said. "We've been doing fine. But you should have told Autumn back then that we were still business partners."

Denver looked at Candi and laughed. "Autumn can't stand your ass, remember? If I told her that we were still working together she'd knocked my head off," Denver said.

"She would have cussed you out, but maybe she'd got over it," Candi said.

Denver rubbed his face and heard the logs crackling. He got up, grabbed a poker iron, removed the safety gate and moved the logs around.

"Denver you are so angry tonight. I've never seen you act this way." "Well Candi you do this bull…"

"Oh no, you were pissed before I told you about this," Candi said and walked over to him. "I could see it on your face when you came inside."

Denver sighed. "It's just been so frustrating these last days with Terrence and Autumn. Danyelle is kind of tolerating me for Autumn's sake but I know she still does not like me. And since Phillip…Autumn's ex-husband and the kids' dad, has been with them, I feel left out. Hell even Phillip's second wife took pity on me to invite over for Thanksgiving next week," he said.

"I am so sorry Denver," Candi said. She stroked his arm and smiled at him. Denver looked down at Candi as her hand rested on his left arm. The crackling of the firewood grew louder and it was getting warmer. He stared at Candi who feigned a concerned expression…and pull her into his arms. Denver's mouth covered her full cherry glossed lips as he roughly kissed her. His tongue found hers and their passion increased with every lick. They lowered their bodies on the floor inches from the fireplace; Denver sat down and pulled Candi on his lap. She was facing him and had her legs on both sides of his body. Denver grabbed the bottom of her sweater and pulled it over her head, her breasts waiting for his lips and tongue. He buried his face in her chest, licking, sucking and caressing her with his tongue. "Denver," Candi gasped, cradling the back of his head. He raised her up by her hips and began peeling her leggings down. She stood up and removed them.

Just as Candi was about to sit back on his lap, Denver tightened his grip to keep her standing and dove into her pleasure spot. "Shit!" she screamed when she felt his tongue. Candi trembled as his head moved sideways and up and down. Denver then steadied Candi so she wouldn't fall and kept at it until she cried for joy. He managed to get out of his jeans and briefs while on the floor and eased Candi onto his lap until she cried out again. Denver then laid on his back, watching Candi ride him with abandon. He watched the shadows from the fireplace dance all over her body as his hands caressed, pinched and slapped. Candi was lost in the passion as their bodies glistened with sweat. She collapsed on top of him, trying to control her breathing. But Denver rolled over, placing Candi on her back. Feeling him spread her legs further apart let Candi know Denver was not ready to end the moment.

****

The next morning Autumn walked in the kitchen to get a cup of coffee when she realized the coffeemaker was still clean. Denver occasionally made a fresh pot while she slept, timing it just right for her to pour a large cup. "I guess he's still irked at not getting any last night," she thought to herself while removing a can of coffee beans from the top cabinet. She did not feel bad about turning him down; in fact she was surprised he came on to her so strongly.

Since Terrence's accident Autumn understandably has not been in any type of mood for sex and Denver has been supportive and respectful. However she noticed he's been distant at times, especially whenever Phillip was around. She did not think Denver was insecure or jealous of the closeness between her and Phillip. When she and Phillip went through the initial phases of ugly arguments and the divorce both calmed down enough to see their children were affected by the nastiness. Terrence's grades were dropping and Danyelle was losing weight and her hair was thinning from all of the stress and emotional pain she bottled in. They knew then a truce had to happen. No matter what, they agreed that if something happened to the children all ugliness and pettiness went to hell. Terrence's critically slow recovery was their biggest challenge yet. Autumn turned the coffee maker on and went upstairs to see if Denver was in their bedroom. She walked the hallway and paused to peek in Danyelle's room. Just as Denver said last night, she was still asleep wearing earplugs with the iPod resting on the pillow next to her. Autumn carefully pulled the door up and continued to the master bedroom. She turned the doorknob and pushed the door open. Denver was sprawled in the center of the bed snoring away. She closed the door and went back downstairs to fix some breakfast.

"Morning," Danyelle said two hours later as she passed the living room to go in the kitchen. Autumn was sitting in the middle of the couch with her laptop checking messages. Her cell phone was on the charger placed on the coffee table.

"Morning baby girl," she called out.

"Man I slept like someone hit me with a brick! Danyelle said, opening the refrigerator and grabbing the carton of eggs, a loaf of wheat bread and a package of bacon. "I did not hear anything except when the alarm code beeped that it was armed."

Autumn leaned her head back. "The alarm was set?"

"Yeah, like after midnight," Danyelle said while oiling a skillet. "I did not think to set it before going to bed because you were still up. Didn't you set it?"

Autumn paused to think. "No I did not set it either because I was just as tired. Denver must have set it."

"Oh yeah that makes sense," Danyelle said. "He probably stayed up and before going to bed noticed it was disabled. It's just funny how no matter how hard I sleep I can always hear that alarm code."

****

Denver laid on the bed staring at the ceiling and listening to Autumn and Danyelle talk. He could not make out all of the conversation but clearly heard Danyelle mention the house alarm. He panicked for a moment because he made every effort to ease in the house after leaving Candi. "You don't have to leave," Candi said, watching Denver zip his jeans and grab his shirt. She sat on the floor still naked and glowing on her own since the fireplace was no longer lit.

Denver didn't say a word as he buttoned his shirt and grabbed his shoes. He plopped on the couch to put them on, never looking at her. "Whew, I need to drink a gallon of orange juice or an energy drink! You took all of my energy away," she said, smiling.

Denver stood up and grabbed his coat.

Candi stood up and hugged her body. "I don't regret what happened and I know you don't either," she softly spoke. "You're tense about what's going on with Aut..."

"Don't say her name!" Denver snapped and buttoned his coat.

325

"Oh now her name is sacred," Candi said, dripping with sarcasm.

Denver went to the door, yanked it open and stepped out. He stopped and looked over his shoulder. "We will continue the matter about that collaboration."

Candi did not move as he slammed the door behind him.

It had been after 1 a.m. when he punched the alarm's security code and tipped upstairs to the master bedroom, figuring if he tried to slip in bed with Autumn she'd wake up and snap at him again. He jumped in the shower and put on a pair of navy drawstring pajamas before climbing in the bed. If any time he should have been more understanding was last night; the stress of everything going on finally taken toll on Autumn's body and she needed to rest. But no, he let his horniness get to him and figured he could take Autumn's mind off of things for at least an hour.

"Denver, are you up yet?" Autumn said from the other side of the door.

Denver sat up and swung his legs to the side of the bed. "Yeah baby, come in."

Autumn walked in with a cup of coffee." "You were really tired," she said, handing him the cup. "I peeked in a couple hours ago and you were sprawled on the bed like a child."

He rubbed his head and neck, smiled at her. "Yeah I guess we all needed a good night's sleep," he said.

Autumn sat next to him. "I want to apologize for giving you an attitude last night. I was just so tired and my body caved after running on fumes these last few days," she said.

Denver placed the cup on the nightstand and pulled her in his arms. "You deserve the apology for me being an ass," he said, stroking her hair. "I was being selfish and should have never tried to force sex on you." He pulled back and looked at her. "Please accept my apology."

Autumn leaned in and kissed him. "I accept."

Chapter 6

Danyelle dropped Autumn off at the trauma center at 1 p.m. so she could run some errands and have a video conference with her professors. She decided to ask the professors to e-mail any mid-term tests she needed to take and she'll complete and send them back Thanksgiving eve. It was hard to believe Thanksgiving was a week away and Autumn had yet to buy a turkey and groceries to make a holiday meal. She did not even want to think about Thanksgiving without Terrence at the table trying to take both turkey legs and half a bowl of dressing, candied yams, fresh string beans, turnip and mustard greens, homemade rolls and a whole sweet potato pie. The last two Thanksgivings, Denver sat and watched in amazement at how much Terrence put away. He also witnessed and laughed hard about it, how Danyelle would hurry and fix her plate immediately after saying 'Amen' because she knew it would be a lost cause if she moved too slowly.

Autumn smiled at the ICU nurses while heading to Terrence's room. She walked in and noticed cut out decorations of a turkey, pilgrims, corn and other symbols of fall and Thanksgiving taped on the walls. They blended with the get well cards, posters and notes from his classmates. A huge bouquet from the airlines sat at the center of the table with a sealed envelope sticking out. Autumn placed her coat and purse in a chair and eased the envelope out of the bouquet. Taking the card out and opening it, Autumn gasped as signatures from some of the flight crews she's worked with covered the entire card. A smaller envelope contained five gift cards – two from a major credit card service, three from major retail and department stores. A gift certificate to a weekend spa with no expiration date had Autumn's name printed on it. Autumn was speechless and touched by the gestures from her co-workers. She shoved everything back in the big envelope and put it in her purse.

Autumn walked to the bed, leaned over and kissed her son lightly on the lips. "Hey sweetie I hope you are doing better," she said, stroking the top of his head. There was less gauze wrapping on his face and from what she could see the black and blue marks from the bruises were fading and the swelling was going down. "You have a lot of love in this room. The wall in front of you is covered with cards from friends and someone's decorated with Thanksgiving stuff. I would love to have you home in time for Thanksgiving, just so you can be with family." Autumn watched her son's face for a reaction and soon he began blinking. "I see you baby, she said.

The nurse's aide walked in to check his vitals. "Hello Ms. Daniels," the young friendly aide said while walking to the left side of Terrence's bed.

"Hi sweetheart," Autumn said, sitting in the chair at the right.

"I hope you don't mind but me and another aide decorated the wall and we taped all of the cards and stuff."

"Oh no I don't mind, thank you so much," Autumn said. "It's very lovely."

The aide smiled while taking Terrence's blood pressure. "The doctor was here early this morning with the nurse. I will tell her you are here and she can give you details on the visit."

"Thank you," Autumn said as the aide wrote everything down.

"Terrence is doing pretty well; his blood pressure is decent and his heart rate is steady," the aide continued. She wrapped everything up and rolled the portable blood pressure machine out of the room.

Autumn pulled out her cell phone and checked messages.

"Ms. Daniels?"

Autumn looked up to see the dayshift nurse enter. "I'm Rose and I was here with Dr. Artison at 7 a.m."

"Oh, yes, the aide said she'd look for you."

"Yes ma'am. Well Dr. Artison said Terrence is progressing well and so far no withdrawal symptoms are visible from the first weaning of barbiturates. He wants to do part two tomorrow morning at the same time as before, 10 a.m.," the nurse said.

"OK sounds good. Thank you for informing me," Autumn said as the nurse left the room. Autumn sat back in the chair and grabbed the remote. She turned to a sports channel, inching the volume to a level where she and Terrence could hear the sports analysts talk. She then called Phillip to give him an update and texted the others with the same message. Putting the phone in her pocket, she looked at her son. "You're getting stronger each day baby," Autumn said, rubbing his arm. "I am so proud of you."

****

"Jet, answer the damn phone!" Denver punched redial on his cell phone a dozen times and left messages that ranged from subdued to raging lunacy. He could not believe that Jet would agree to collaborate with Leo and The Loft without consulting him. He knew a lot of it had to do with Candi seducing them into the agreement. She had Leo on lock that night flirting with him, sometimes in Spanish – even though Leo is part Italian-American, he spoke Spanish and Italian fluently – and kept pressing her body against him. She probably slept with Jet or threatened to have his liquor license revoked if he did not show a slight interest. Jet promised him Fuego was going to stand on its own with the elaborate design, including the club's name lighting up with digitally enhanced 'flames' flickering under the letters just above the entrance. The interior was shades of reds yellows and orange with state of the art sound system and a venue fit for entertainers to

328

do impromptu concerts. Denver signed a contract with Jet but Candi's documents showed a different contract with blank spaces meant for his signature joining signatures from Candi, Jet and Leo set in permanent ink. He also needed to talk to Candi again. And just talk; what happened last night was something to take the edge off his needs. It meant absolutely nothing to him. "She messes me over so why not return the favor," he thought.

Denver gave up trying to reach Jet for now and decided to pay Leo a visit at his office above the club. Leo owned the entire building which included two additional floors that he turned into office space. The floor above the club was filled with small office spaces, two bathrooms and a small kitchen.

The top floor was renovated exclusively for Leo with art pieces and furnishings that inspired his diverse ethnicity. Leo's father was a second generation Italian born in New York City who owned a couple markets that specialized in Italian breads, spices, sauces and more. His mother was an African-American woman who was a secretary in Harlem by day and a seamstress for various people of high society three nights a week. They met when one of his mother's customers insisted that she go to the market to pick up ingredients to make a buffet inspired by Italy. Growing up Leo never worried about what people said or their stares because he had to focus on studying and working hard. Neither of his parents gave a damn about race and color, the only color that mattered was the one that could provide them a decent living.

Denver parked in the back of the building and walked to the door, pressing the doorbell. The door flung open and a tall, burly white guy wearing all black stared Denver down. "Is Leo here?" Denver asked without smiling.

"Do you have an appointment?" the guy said.

"You must be new around here," Denver said. "Tell Leo Denver needs to speak with him."

The guy smirked and pressed a button on his cell phone. "Mr. Gillian, there's a Mr. Colorado to see you."

"Who?" a voice boomed from the loudspeaker.

"Leo it's me, Denver!" he shouted, becoming irritated with the smart ass joke for security.

"Let him up and no need to pat him down. He's a friend of mine," Leo said, hanging up. The guy stepped aside and Denver measured him up while walking in. Denver rode the elevator to the top floor, stepped out and into what is the main seating area. Black leather couches and chairs were meticulously placed around a long glass coffee table with black trim. A built-in bar covered a portion of the left wall in the waiting area with every spirit you can imagine. Bookshelves filled with first editions and beyond lined the other walls. Denver walked through the waiting area to a section that was Leo's office. More bookshelves, an entertainment center and a huge desk set topped with a desktop and laptop computers, framed photos of family spread out. Behind him was an exquisite painting done by a famous African American artist. The surrounding walls were covered with pictures of Leo posing with celebrities from his childhood to the hottest stars today.

"Denver, how are you my friend?" Leo said as he walked around the desk and offered his hand. Denver shook his hand, smiling. "I'm not doing too good Leo. I feel insulted."

Leo gestured at Denver to take a seat in one of two chairs facing the desk. "What's wrong? Is it Autumn's son?"

"No Leo it's about you, Candi, Jet and this new partnership," Denver said, looking up at Leo.

Leo rubbed his chin and shook his head. "Denver you are still part of The Loft and Fuego. We just decided to team up and strengthen the industry market," he said.

"How is it that you three go behind my back," Denver argued.

"We did not go behind your back, son. You are a hired contractor not an owner. The new contracts just acquire your signature so it is solid and you are not left out of your duties. Your pay as a contractor increases so you come out a winner!"

Denver leaned forward. "I was supposed to be part owner of Fuego! You should have contacted me!"

"No, Jet should have contacted you," Leo said, pointing his finger for emphasis. "Jet was running low on finances and his credit is kind of shaky. When I heard about this I contacted Jet. He suggested we contact Candi because of her background in finances. We did nothing behind your back," Leo said.

Denver knew nothing about Jet's money problems because Jet never mentioned it. "OK so maybe Jet was afraid to say anything me. Maybe he thought I would end our pending partnership. It's still unfair that I have to find out after the fact," Denver said.

"Well you need to get a hold of Jet or Candi. The way she was talking that night I thought you knew," Leo said, getting up from the chair.

Denver stood up and shook Leo's hand. "Thanks anyway, man. I'll catch up with them hopefully soon," Denver said and walked out of the office to the elevator.

Denver was getting in his car when his cell phone beeped. He looked at the screen, frowning at Jet's name. "Sorry I missed your calls. I'm home."

Denver started his car, hit reverse and screeched out of the parking space. He arrived at Harrison Townhouses within 15 minutes, pulling up at the gate. After a security guard buzzed him in, Denver drove through the community of townhomes until he found Jet's place.

Jet inherited the townhome via his parents' will five years ago. He once held loud parties until the association threatened to have him evicted. Now the only noise heard is an occasional argument from one of his lady friends. Denver told him that unless he was serious about a woman to never let them know where he lived or he will never get rid of them. Denver jogged to the door and pressed the buzzard. He could hear footsteps approach the door, then the deadbolt come undone. "Denver man I am sorry…"

Jet did not see Denver's right fist coming. He looked up from the floor holding his jaw. "Man, what the fu..,"

Denver grabbed Jet by his sweatshirt collar, pulled him to his feet and punched him again. This time Jet's left eye closed shut and he screamed. "Denver what the hell is your problem?"

"Why didn't you tell me about this collaboration with Candi and Leo?" Denver asked, releasing his grip on Jet and making his way to the living room.

Jet staggered around. "Man I can't see!"

Denver stomped into the kitchen opened the freezer door and grabbed a frozen bag of peas. He walked over to Jet and shoved the pack in his hand. "Press it on your eye," Denver mumbled, shoving Jet to the living room and on the couch. "Why didn't you tell me you were having money problems regarding Fuego? I thought we were partners," Denver said.

Jet sat back in the couch. "Man I had to do something right away because the bank was threatening to take the club! The first person I thought to call was Candi because she has that experience handling money problems."

"Did you get a loan from Candi?" Denver asked.

"Man…" Jet hesitated.

Denver leaned into him. "You need to say something or that right eye is swelling."

Jet threw his hands up. "We went to the bank and she talked to the guy and handed him a check." It wasn't her money it was Leo's.

Denver's mouth dropped open. "Sounds like she sweet talked Leo into saving your ass, created a new contract where she would get a percentage for saving your ass!"

Jet nodded his answer. Denver got up and headed to the door. "You may want to stay home for a few days; let those injuries heal," he said and left.

Phillip and Monique tipped inside Terrence's room. Autumn dosed off in the chair holding Terrence's hand.

"Autumn…Autumn," Phillip whispered while gently shaking her shoulder.

"Huh?" she jumped and blinked her eyes. "Oh hey Phil, Monique."

"Hi Autumn," Monique said, sitting down at the table.

"How long have you been asleep?" Phillip asked.

"I don't know, maybe an hour," Autumn looked at the clock on the wall. "Yeah about an hour or so." She stood and stretched, moving aside for Phillip to get closer to the bed.

"Hey champ, its dad," Phillip said, kissing Terrence's forehead.

Terrence blinked and took a deep breath.

"He is responding a little better huh?" Phillip said with a smile.

Autumn nodded and turned to Monique. "How are you doing today, Monique?"

"Oh I am fine, thanks. Are you doing alright?"

"I'm better rested compared to the last few days. The doctor said they will resume weaning Terrence from the barbiturates tomorrow morning, same time as yesterday."

Phillip looked up. "That young man, Langston Edmonds' funeral is tomorrow at 1 p.m. Maybe we should stop by the funeral home tonight and pay our respects," he said.

"I agree. We can leave here early enough to freshen up and head over there," Autumn said.

"Where's Denver?" Monique asked. "Has he been here today?"

"No. Danyelle dropped me off to run errands," Autumn said and pulled out her cell phone. She dialed Denver's cell number and waited for him to answer. It went to voicemail. She sent a text. When he did not answer immediately Autumn frowned. "He is not answering anything. Maybe he's at one of the clubs," she sighed. "I'll text Danyelle and see if she is on her way back."

****

Denver read the text and listened to the voicemail message from Autumn then turned the phone off. He was sitting at Candi's dining room table with his back to the living room and the fireplace. When she let him inside he could barely look at her and think about last night. She was wearing a charcoal gray body-hugging sweater dress with a wide belt cinching her waist and a pair of black leather boots. Her dark hair was pinned up with loose strands falling along her face. "I see you've been quite the businesswoman today," he said as she handed him a drink.

"Jet sent me a picture of what you did to his face Denver. That was not cool," she said, taking a seat across from him.

332

"His ass will be fine and he had it coming for not being honest with me," Denver said, taking a huge gulp of his drink.

"I was going to tell you all about the changes but you were busy with…Autumn and her family," Candi said.

"I am being a supportive friend, Candi."

"If that's the case why are you running around beating up people, having talks with others and most of all, why are you in my house?"

Denver looked at her. "I saw you checking your phone then you turned it off. Did you tell Autumn about last night?"

"NO!" Denver shouted and pushed his chair back.

"Look you may have punched Jet around but you sure in the hell not jumping me! I'll call the police and Autumn. She will be devastated," Candi said calmly.

Denver looked at her then scoot his chair to the table. "I came here to deal with you about the behind my back bullshit," he mumbled.

"And now you have my answer," Candi said, rising from her chair. She walked around the table and stood over him. "Now that you know everything you can go home…if you want."

Denver looked at Candi, then at his drink. Candi walked away from him and continued to the staircase. He sat for a few seconds, got up with drink in hand, and followed Candi.

Danyelle joined Autumn, Phillip and Monique in Terrence's room holding a bouquet of roses and a gift bag. "I stopped by the house and a delivery man was knocking on the door with this," Danyelle said.

She handed them to Autumn who placed the vase on the nightstand and reached in the gift bag. "Aw it's a teddy bear with Terrence's name stitched on a basketball jersey," she said. Autumn pulled out a card that revealed it was from a couple of female classmates.

"And you said he was too shy," Danyelle said, laughing. "Terrence got game he just didn't want to tell his mama!"

Autumn rolled her eyes and placed the stuffed toy next to the bouquet. She put the card beside them. "I thought Denver was here since he wasn't at the house?" Danyelle asked.

"Nope he has not been here this afternoon and he is not answering my calls or texts," Autumn said.

"Wow. Maybe he just wanted to give us some space," Danyelle said.

"Yeah…maybe," Autumn said to herself.

Later that evening Autumn, Danyelle, Phillip and Monique stopped at the funeral home where Terrence's friend Langston Edmonds laid for viewing. They arrived in time for family hour and embraced the grieving family.

"Thank you for coming," Mrs. Edmonds said, tears running down her cheeks. Autumn hugged her again and rubbed her back.

"Again we are so sorry for your loss and if you need anything, do not hesitate to call me," Autumn said.

"I've been praying for Terrence. Raymond and I only met Terrence a couple of times but he is a nice young man and he and Langston played ball a lot and had a couple of classes together," Mrs. Edmonds said.

Autumn squeezed her hands. Phillip and Monique talked to Mr. Edmonds and Danyelle talked to some of the relatives. They stayed through the family hour and gave the Edmonds sympathy cards. Thirty minutes later they returned to their separate homes. Danyelle pulled up the driveway as Autumn glanced around from the passenger seat. "Did you try to reach Denver again, mama?" Danyelle asked while getting out of the car.

"Yes I did," Autumn said, clearly irritated. They walked in the house, hung their coats in the closet and walked in the TV room, seeing it was pitch black.

"Looks like he left this morning and hasn't been back," Danyelle mumbled while flipping on the light switch and grabbing the remote. She turned to a movie playing on one of the digital channels and walked in the kitchen. "I'm getting a bowl of cookies and crème do you want a bowl?" Danyelle called out.

"No baby I think I am going to browse my laptop," Autumn said while speed dialing Denver's number for the third time. "Denver where are you?" Autumn said while leaving a message on voicemail. "Terrence is going through another weaning in the morning. Call me back to let me know if you are on your way home."

****

The doorbell rang an hour later; Autumn opened the door when she noticed Charlize's car parked on the street. "Hey you two, come in," she said. They hugged and Autumn took their coats.

Charlize and Natasha followed Autumn in the TV room. "Hey Danni!" Charlize and Natasha said in unison before sitting down on both sides and kissing her cheeks.

"Hey tee-tees!" she said, smiling.

"You're not going back to Atlanta Monday?" Natasha asked.

"No, going to take my exams online…speaking of which, I need to go upstairs and study some more before the professors start sending those attachments," Danyelle said, grabbing her empty bowl and standing.

"I will give you three some privacy and catch you tomorrow." Danyelle kissed all three and left.

Autumn filled them in on tomorrow's events with Terrence. "OK we will come by sometime during the procedure," Natasha said while Charlize propped herself against two throw pillows.

"So…what's this about Denver being absent and unresponsive to calls and texts," Charlize said, surprising Autumn.

"Danyelle text us while you all were leaving the center," Natasha added. "You know she can walk and text at the same time like all of the young people."

Autumn sighed and stood up. "Does anyone want martinis?" she asked, walking to the kitchen.

"Are you making and serving them because I'm too comfortable to get up," Charlize said.

Autumn got the ingredients and the glasses. Natasha walked in and pulled out a pitcher from the cabinet. They returned to the TV room 10 minutes later, Charlize bringing the martini glasses and Natasha the pitcher. They filled their glasses and downed the first ones right away. "OK, Autumn said while pouring another glass, "Denver did not stop by the trauma center today, period and he's yet to return my messages. He hasn't even been here since this morning."

"Did you two have a fight?" Natasha asked.

"Well, kind of," Autumn said, taking a sip. "The other night I was so tired from the full day with Terrence and you know the weaning…all of the days' stress caught up with me and my body was crashing. I was trying to put on a damn night shirt and Denver sneaked up on me and began fondling me and I was not trying to have that."

"OK, so you told him to quit," Charlize said, pouring her second martini. "Yes I did and he kept messing with me and I snapped at him. He backed off, apologized and left out of the room."

"He probably feels bad," Natasha said.

"Well I thought everything was cool because I talked to him early this morning before heading to see Terrence. I guess I was wrong," Autumn sighed.

"He is probably hanging out with some of his buddies and now doing a check on those clubs he's contracted with," Natasha said. "Maybe he just needed some space. He'll call you or show up in here later tonight."

"Yeah while we're asleep because I doubt if either of will be fit to drive," Charlize said, laughing. Autumn laughed hard. "Well you two know where the guest bedroom is. I'll go to my own bed tonight, maybe he will climb in."

"Shit he better go in your room because we're beating the hell out of him if he tries to climb on top of us!" Natasha said and laughed.

Autumn took the half full pitcher in the refrigerator, wished her friends a good night and went upstairs.

The next morning Autumn woke up and turned to the left side of the bed. It was empty, not even a dent in the mattress or pillow, but she already knew that. She had her phone on the charger with the volume up for text alerts or calls but none came.

Glancing at the alarm clock it read 8:30 a.m. "Mama, are you up?" Danyelle said while knocking on the door.

"Yeah baby I'm awake. I'm heading to the bathroom right now," Autumn said, pushing the covers back. She got up and walked to the dresser, opening her underwear drawer. She grabbed a pair of panties and a bra, closed the drawer hard and stomped into her master bathroom. "This was getting ridiculous," Autumn thought to herself while turning on the shower. She put on her shower cap, yanked back the curtain and stepped under the warm water. *Where in the hell was Denver and why hasn't called back? If he got drunk and is sleeping it off at a buddy's house he could at least send a note.* Autumn let all kinds of thoughts run through her mind about Denver and she was starting to get a headache. "No I am not about to run my pressure up about Denver. I have to be calm for my baby," she thought again while rinsing off.

Twenty minutes later she jogged downstairs fully dressed in comfortable clothes and shoes. She was about to call out for Danyelle when she remembered Charlize and Natasha were in the guest bedroom. She walked down the hall and tapped on the door. "Natasha's in the shower," Charlize said while opening the door. She was combing her hair and wearing a different blouse from last night.

"Where'd you find…good morning…where'd you get that blouse?" Autumn asked from the doorway.

"It was folded in my big-ass purse, along with a fresh pair of panties," Charlize said nonchalantly.

"You know I'm always prepared for anything! I even have my own travel size soap, lotion, deodorant and a mini-toothpaste set. Don't act like you don't know us!" Autumn fell out laughing.

Natasha came out of the bathroom in her underwear heading straight to her purse, pulling out a small kit with her items and a lavender pullover sweater. "Did that man-child call or text you yet?" Natasha said while moisturizing her legs.

"No and right now I don't care. I sent a message last night about Terrence today and I'm leaving it at that," Autumn said.

"Oh girls," Danyelle called out. "Breakfast and coffee is on the table, nice and hot!"

Everyone except Denver was at the trauma center inside Terrence's room. Autumn, Phillip and Danyelle kissed Terrence's forehead before the nurses wheeled him to the unit for his second weaning. They all joined

Charlize and Natasha in the waiting area. Monique stayed home with her son who was fighting a cold.

Phillip leaned into Danyelle's ear. "Has Denver popped up yet?"

Danyelle looked at her dad and shook her head. "Mama's not happy either," she whispered, her eyes focused on Autumn sitting in the corner between Charlize and Natasha. She did not even have her cell phone out, just the pager from the nurse to let them know Terrence's procedure was done and he was heading back to ICU.

****

Denver sat up on the bathroom floor wishing his head would stop pounding. He overdid it with the drinking and just completed praying to the porcelain god. He was in his navy blue briefs and nothing else. He barely remembered where he was until an hour ago before he ran in the bathroom. His cell phone was in his coat pocket, turned off but he knew Autumn's left a ton of voicemail messages and texts. Positive he'd completely emptied his stomach Denver grabbed the side of the bathtub and slowly pushed his body to a standing position.

"Are you alright in there?" Candi yelled from the other side of the door.

"Yes…shit," Denver mumbled while holding his head. He turned on the shower and stepped out of his briefs. He let the cold water hit him first, gritting his teeth as the spray felt like sharp needles stabbing him. Two minutes later he turned the hot water on and grabbed a bar of soap. When he left the bathroom he was in his jeans and shirt. He put on his shoes and came downstairs.

Candi walked over, handing him a glass of water and two ibuprofen tablets. "You need to eat something," she said, standing in a short black robe with her hair down.

Denver grabbed his coat, took his cell phone out of the pocket and turned it on. Sure enough his voicemail was full and he's received 25 text messages between Autumn and Danyelle. "I'll grab something to eat on the way…SHIT!"

Candi walked over and tried to look at his cell screen. "What's wrong?" she asked.

Denver pushed her out of the way, grabbed his car keys and yelled for her to unlock the door. Candi grabbed her keys, undid the locks and jumped when Denver yanked the door open. "I have to get to the trauma center!" Denver yelled while running to his car.

Denver's car screeched into the center's parking lot, pulling into the nearest space. He jumped out of the car and ran inside the center and all the way to the unit where Autumn and the others were in the waiting room. Autumn looked up when she heard footsteps stop in the entrance. Everyone else looked at her then in the direction of her vision. Denver quietly walked in, hands shoved in his coat pockets. He felt all of their eyes on him and the guilt beat him down. He turned toward the corner of the room where Autumn, Charlize and Natasha sat against each other.

"Autumn…" Charlize raised her right hand in the air, cutting off his speech. Natasha glared at him as Autumn looked away.

Denver turned around, nearly colliding into Phillip who stared him down. "I don't know where the hell you've been for nearly 24 hours, but you can either sit down, shut the hell up…or you can leave," Phillip said without flinching.

Denver looked at Phillip, his blood boiling but he knew better than to react. He drew a breath and walked to the other side of the waiting area and sat down. Phillip returned to his seat next to Danyelle who grabbed his hand.

****

"CODE BLUE! CODE BLUE!"

Autumn jumped up after hearing the alert, dropping the pager. Phillip and the others stood up and gathered in the doorway as nurses and doctors rushed past the waiting area, heading around the corner.

"Oh my goodness, who are they rushing too?" Natasha said, her voice trembling.

Charlize squeezed her shoulders and grabbed Autumn's arm. "Come on and sit back down. We'll have to pray for that person."

Autumn turned to sit back on the couch when the pager lit up and buzzed on the floor. She kneeled down and picked it up. "Terrence's procedure is done," she said smiling. "The doctor should be here any minute."

They all sat down and waited.

Five minutes later the nurse who gave Autumn the pager walked in. "Ms. Daniels…can you and Mr. Daniels follow me please."

Both stood up and Autumn handed the nurse the pager giving her a smile. The nurse returned a slight smile and led them to another room. Danyelle jumped up looking terrified and ran out of the waiting area. "Danyelle, wait, they'll be back…" Charlize yelled. They suddenly heard a sound that stopped Charlize in her tracks; Natasha began to cry and Denver frozen wide-eyed in the chair.

"NOOOOOOOOOOOOOOOOOOOOO!" Charlize managed to run in the direction of the screams and slowed her pace when she saw Autumn slumped in Phillip's arms and Danyelle jumping up and down in hysterics.

Two nurses grabbed Danyelle and placed her in a chair trying to get her to take deep breaths between her sobs. A male nurse helped Phillip put

338

Autumn on a stretcher and worked on waking her up and Phillip dropped into a chair, burying his face in his hands. Natasha joined Charlize, standing by her side with her arm around her waist. They sobbed as the medical staff and pastoral representative worked to calm and comfort the family. Denver remained in the waiting room unable to will his body to stand up.

****

Two hours passed since Terrence was pronounced dead by the doctors. During the procedure he suffered an aneurysm and went into a grand mal seizure. Doctors were unable to save him. Autumn and Phillip silently signed papers for death certificate, hospital and funeral documentations. Charlize and Natasha surrounded Danyelle who was rocking in a chair, tears still streaming down her cheeks.

Denver managed to leave the waiting room 15 minutes after the rest followed Autumn and Phillip and heard the news. He knew when the nurse walked in the waiting room Terrence was gone. He felt it in his heart and when his pulse rate quickened. His blood pressure also peaked and the dull pain from his hangover tripled to the point that he thought he'd gone into shock or had a stroke. As if anybody noticed or cared. Strangers sitting in the waiting area while their loved ones were undergoing a procedure of some sort shared looks of sadness and pity as they watched Danyelle run out of the room. They knew the message as well and were probably relieved it wasn't for them to receive it yet.

Denver followed Autumn, Phillip, Danyelle and the others to the offices, but at a distance. When Autumn looked at him as he approached her, it was a look of disdain. He stepped away before Phillip could approach him. Now Denver was so distant from their walking paces others would think he wasn't with them. And as far as they were concern right now, they were right.

After gathering Terrence's belongings, cards and flowers they left the center. Natasha drove Danyelle's car, Danyelle rode with her parents and Charlize followed them. Denver got in his car and put the key in the ignition…and broke down in tears pressing his head against the steering wheel. When Phillip, Natasha and Charlize pulled up in front of the house they noticed another car pulling up behind them. Autumn stepped out of Phillip's car and ran towards the fourth vehicle.

"Denyce!" Autumn cried, running into her arms.

"Oh Autumn, sweetie," Denyce said as she held her friend tight.

They embraced each other as Danyelle made her way to them. Autumn stepped back and Denyce grabbed Danyelle, cradling her head against her chest. They walked up the sidewalk to the front door, Phillip unlocking and pushing the door open. They gathered in the living room where Denyce hugged and kissed Phillip, Charlize and Natasha.

Phillip took Denyce's car keys to get her luggage from the trunk as she'd made up her mind after receiving Natasha's text that she was staying with Autumn and Danyelle. "Autumn whatever you, Danyelle and Phil need us to do, we're doing it," Denyce said as Charlize and Natasha nod in agreement.

"Thank you, thank you all," Autumn said. "I just want to lie down for a while. I can't believe my baby boy is gone!"

Phillip walked Autumn upstairs and got her settled in bed. He returned downstairs and to the TV room. "I have to go home and check on Monique and Marc," he said. He went to the couch and kissed Danyelle who was curled up looking blankly at the TV. "I'll be back sweetie," Phillip said.

Charlize hugged him and walked him to the door. "We'll take care of them," she said as he headed to his car. "Unbelieveable how T leaves us the same day as that other boy's funeral," Charlize said to Denyce as they walked in the kitchen.

"Oh my goodness yes it is! But what else is unbelievable is how Denver suddenly disappeared on Autumn!" Denyce said while making a grocery list.

"Natasha sent me texts and Autumn did too a couple of times, but I'd figured he was back by then. He actually did not show up until 30 minutes into the procedure and moments before Terrence coded?"

"Yep," Charlize said. And he better not show his ass over here tonight. Wherever Denver was all this time, he better buy some new clothes and draws and keep his ass there!"

****

Denver drove to Harrison Townhouses and asked the guard in the security booth to buzz him. After getting the go ahead, he drove to the back of the property. When he got out of the car Jet already unlocked the door so it was ajar. Denver walked in as Jet sat down with an icepack on his eye. "I have not done anything else to get a beat down…"

"Terrence is dead," Denver mumbled.

Jet lowered the icepack. "Wait, your girlfriend's son? What happened…I thought they were taking him out of the medicated coma," Jet said.

"He had an aneurysm and a big seizure. They could not bring him back," Denver said sitting in a recliner.

"Aw man, I'm sorry! Give Autumn my condolences…wait, how come you're not with her?"

"Because I screwed up," Denver said. "I had not been back at the house since dealing with you yesterday. I did not check my messages and I was late heading to the trauma center during the procedure. Terrence died 15 minutes after I got there."

Jet leaned forward, placing his arms across his lap. "Where were you all this time, Denver?"

"You'd been at Leo's and came here beating my ass, so where'd you go....aw hell!"

Denver lowered his head.

Jet sat up. "Dude, tell me you were not with Candi all this damn time!"

Denver remained quiet.

"Man what if she stops by the house? You know it's going to be on the news tomorrow or Sunday because of the accident!" Jet continued.

"I'm going to send her a text," Denver said, sitting back in the recliner. "I was running out of her house after I finally turned my phone back on to check messages."

Jet shook his head. "I'm guessing you need some place to stay for a while huh?" Denver nodded.

Chapter 7

Autumn came downstairs in pajamas and slippers. From the house being a little brighter inside she figured it had to be late into the night. Then she smelled food from the kitchen and heard sounds coming from the TV room. Natasha emerged from the kitchen after hearing the floor creak. "Hey sweetie," she said to Autumn who looked around and then at Natasha as if confused.

"What time is it?" Autumn asked.

"Its 5:30 p.m. You've been sleep for a good while," Natasha said.

She took Autumn by the hand to guide her to the kitchen. "Are you hungry? Let me fix you a small plate."

Autumn slowly followed Natasha into the kitchen, waiting as she pulled back a chair. Autumn sat down and Natasha walked to the stove. She grabbed a plate off the counter and took lids off the pots. "Denyce went to the store and got a few things, so we have baked chicken, rice and green beans..."

"Do you have any soup?" Autumn asked softly.

"Soup? No baby we don't have any soup. Damn I should have figured you'd want something light," Natasha said, frowning at her lack of thought.

Autumn pushed the chair back and stood up. "There are a couple cans of chicken noodle in the pantry over there," she said, walking to the pantry. Charlize walked in from the TV room.

"Hey I thought I heard your voice. Why are you getting canned soup from the pantry when we have..." "I WANT SOUP!" Autumn screamed then froze with the cans in her hand. Autumn lowered her head and begins to sob uncontrollably.

Charlize rushed over to Autumn and wrapped her arms around her. "I'm sorry baby, I am so, so, sorry," Charlize stroked her back and walked her to the kitchen chair. She took the cans out of Autumn's grip and walked to the stove, placed the cans on the counter and grabbed a pot from the overhead rack. "I'll fix you a nice bowl, OK? And if you want, we have some cornbread muffins warmed up in the oven," Charlize continued.

Natasha sat next to Autumn hugging her and cleaning her face. "Is it still Friday?" Autumn sniffed.

"Yes baby," Natasha whispered, stroking her hair.

Autumn sighed, her shoulders dropping. She blew her nose and straightened up, smiling at Natasha. "Right now Terrence would see this food and damn near eat out of the skillets if I let him get away with it," Autumn chuckled. "Oh I miss him."

"I know baby, I know," Natasha said, squeezing her shoulder.

Charlize place a big bowl of soup, then a cornbread muffin and a spoon on the table in front of Autumn. "Here you are, sweetie," she said.

"Charlize I am sorry I snapped at you," Autumn said, tears welling up in her eyes.

"It's OK Autumn, no need to apologize," she said. She leaned over and kissed Autumn's cheek and wiped away a tear.

Autumn ate as much soup as possible until she felt full. "Thank you, I feel better now," she said, pushing her chair back and standing. "I don't know what I would do without you all." She walked out of the kitchen and into the TV room.

Denyce was reading from her e-book tablet and wearing headphones. Danyelle was no longer asleep on the couch. Autumn came around the couch and lightly nudged her friend. "Huh…hey Autumn," Denyce said, taking off the headphones and putting her table on the coffee table. She stood up and hugged Autumn for a long time. "Sit down," she said, making room for Autumn.

Autumn sat down, squeezing Denyce's hand.

"How are you feeling? Did you get something to eat?"

"I've been up for nearly an hour and Charlize fixed me a bowl of soup. I know there's a full meal on the stove but I just felt like something light for now."

Denyce nodded and pointed at the iPod and tablet "Well now you know what I was doing that I did not hear or realize you were up and around!"

Autumn laughed. "Where's Danyelle? She was stretched out on the other end of this couch when Phillip took me upstairs earlier."

"She's upstairs in her room. She woke up about an hour after you went, made some phone calls, helped cook dinner. She said she was going to send e-mails to her professors and tell them about Terrence," Denyce said, pausing at the reality of her last words.

"I want his funeral to be a week from tomorrow," Autumn said suddenly.

"Oh, OK," Denyce said, grabbing her tablet and deleting the book she was reading. She pulled up a calendar on the screen and circled the date. "I'll contact the funeral home in the morning to get the arrangements together," Denyce said. She pulled Autumn against her side. "We'll take care of you Autumn."

****

The rest of the weekend was busy with activity preparing for Terrence's home going. Members of the media called the house and Natasha made herself the spokesperson for the family. Friends and some of Autumn's colleagues called or e-mailed messages saying to keep them update on the services. The principal from Terrence's high school stopped by Saturday afternoon with flowers, adding that she will arrange for counselors to meet with and talk to students who were classmates or knew Terrence personally. Autumn pulled herself together and received well wishes face to face and took phone calls, but would cry herself to sleep. Phillip and Monique came with Marc who was still fighting a cold but they brought his medicine. Danyelle offered to look after him, taking him in her room letting him watch cartoons on her laptop.

Monique sat chatting with Natasha, Charlize and Denyce in the TV room and Phillip with Autumn in the living. "How are you holding up?" he asked.

"I'm doing just that…holding," she said, smiling at him.

"We are all going to make it through this. I know it's hard because Thanksgiving is coming up."

"Yeah but we kind of had Thanksgiving if you think about it." Phillip looked at her.

"How so?"

"We got a chance to be with our son every day since the accident and he communicated with all of us through blinking his eyes. Plus his room was decorated for the holiday. We have to be thankful for that," Autumn said, tears rolling on her cheeks. Phillip hugged Autumn and they continued holding each other for hours.

****

"We have a sad update to a story we last reported last weekend. Terrence Daniels, the third person involved in a two-vehicle crash that included a semi-trailer…died yesterday morning during a procedure to wean him out of a drug-induced coma. The 17-year-old Norton High School senior suffered critical injuries when the semi-trailer, driven by Matthew Anderson, went through a traffic signal and crashed into the car containing Daniels and 17-year-old Langston Edmonds, who, ironically was laid to rest yesterday. Anderson was laid to rest last Wednesday. Friends and family members…,"

Denver hit the mute button on the TV remote and continued watching news footage of Natasha speaking on behalf of the family. He sat in Jet's living room wearing sweats Jet purchased at an area retail store, too numb to leave the townhouse. He stopped counting how many times he'd picked up his cell phone to call Autumn or text a message and dared not show up on her doorstep.

He had keys to the house but it was her name on the mortgage papers after the divorce proceedings with Phillip. He no longer felt the need to fight Phillip after he scolded him like a misbehaved child; Denver knew he deserved it, now more than ever. How in the hell did he allow himself to

344

spiral to this level? Phillip never mistreated or disrespected him or his relationship with Autumn. The man is comfortable in his own skin and moved on to have a working relationship with her. From meeting Monique Denver could sense a little attitude but it was neutralized to a point where it was almost nonexistent and she was at least 34 years old.

"Hey man you want to go out for dinner and a couple of beers?" Jet asked while walking in the living room.

"Naw, you go ahead, I'm not hungry," Denver mumbled. Jet walked to the couch and looked at the TV. He noticed the crawler mentioning Terrence's death and figured the story ran moments ago. He grabbed the remote and hit 'Off.' "I know it's only been a day but you've got to eat something Denver," Jet said.

"I'll make a sandwich," Denver grumbled.

"Did you try calling…"

"JET, leave me alone, OK?"

Denver slouched further into the couch staring into space. Jet picked up his keys, grabbed his coat from the chair and left. Denver remained on the couch for another half hour until he got up to go to the bathroom. He came out a couple minutes later and heard a hip-hop song flowing from his cell. He went to the couch and picked up the phone. "Candi, I don't feel like talking," he said, moving his thumb to disconnect the call.

"Denver, please don't hang up! I saw the story on the news," Candi said, sniffing.

"I'd be at home comforting Autumn with her family and friends right now if not for you!" Denver yelled.

"Hold on…hold on Denver what are you talking about? You're not at the house?"

"No I'm at Jet's. By the time I got to the trauma center the doctors were already doing the procedure and it's wasn't even 15 minutes when a code blue alert was announced," Denver continued.

"Everyone thought it was somebody else but I had a feeling it was Terrence…unfortunately, I was right. Autumn's friends would not let me talk to her when I got there and her ex-husband snapped at me. When everything went downhill I was invisible to them."

"Denver I am sorry Autumn lost her son, I really am, but you can't blame me for you not being there!" Candi said.

"What the fuck you mean you're not the blame," Denver yelled.

"No one told you to come to my house again," Candi yelled back. "No one told you to come over, get drunk and sleep with me!"

"You could have put me out!"

"I told you to leave but you started drinking and I did not want you to drive!"

Denver got quiet and just held his cell phone. "You went all ape shit over a simple change in partnership that did not affect you and this is how it ends up," Candi said.

"You are not the blame for Terrence's death, Denver! You were not that truck driver or you'd be dead too. You were not there for your girlfriend because…you did not want to be."

"You are a damn liar!" Denver screamed into his phone.

"Oh, really? Like I said…you came over that first time apparently frustrated, horny and Autumn could not provide you with what you wanted. You got the edge off, but the second time you're at my house, drinking my liquor? That was all you, papi. I just took care of you like old times," she said and hung up.

Chapter 8

The rest of the weekend flew by and Monday morning Denyce joined Phillip and Autumn at Madison Funeral Home to make the arrangements. They sat in the director's office, Autumn holding a manila envelope with a photo of Terrence smiling. It was one of her favorite pictures of him. Phillip carefully placed a navy three-piece suit, a medium blue shirt and print tie splashed with various colors that complemented the suit and shirt in a compartment bag on the chair besides him. A small shopping bag contained tokens Autumn wanted placed in the casket with Terrence; the small teddy bear from his classmates, some handwritten poems from friends, a jersey bearing the number of a basketball player from his favorite team and a note from Danyelle.

Danyelle could not bear to come to the funeral home, preferring to wait until the visitation to take everything in. The director talked to them and went through the process smoothly. They ordered programs and floral arrangements on behalf of the family. Autumn reminded the director to have a small, heart-shaped arrangement with 'Love you T, Danyelle' stitched in the pillow centerpiece. An hour later they walked out of the funeral with a confirmation to view the body Wednesday morning to make sure everything was properly done. They stopped at a restaurant for a light lunch before returning to the house. Autumn sighed in the booth as Denyce and Phillip drank their glasses of pop.

"What's wrong Autumn?" Phillip asked.

"I guess we won't have Thanksgiving dinner."

"We can if you want too," Denyce said.

"It doesn't matter, right now it's just another day," Autumn said, pushing the remaining portion of a chef's salad around with her fork.

"Well I am sure we won't have to with the food coming in from friends and members of the church. If there's any non-perishable food left over we should take it to that community shelter near the house."

Denyce and Phillip nodded in agreement.

They finished their lunches and left. As they pulled into the driveway Autumn noticed a figure standing on the front porch. Phillip put the car in park and turned off the ignition. "Who is that?" he asked Autumn and Denyce while opening the car door.

Autumn stared hard then gasped. "It's Denver," she said, hurrying to open the passenger door and get out before it registered to Phillip. By the time she got out of the car it was too late; Denver turned around and Phillip charged at him.

"Phillip, No!" Autumn yelled as Denyce climbed out the back seat, running behind her. Denver threw up his hands, bracing for the impact as Phillip leap towards him. Both men hit the front door hard with Denver taking the brunt of the pain. Phillip stood up, pulling Denver to his feet and was about to punch him when he felt his right arm being held back. "Stop, Phillip, STOP!" Autumn screamed and held his arm back with all her strength. Denyce wedged her body between Denver and Phillip, trying to loosen Phillip's left hand off Denver's coat and shirt.

The door flew open and Charlize was holding a butcher's knife in her hand ready to cut who ever banged on the door. "What the hell?" Charlize screamed, dropping the knife on the floor and struggling to see who Phillip was trying to hit.

Danyelle ran to the door, her mouth opened in shock. "Daddy let go of Denver," she yelled. "Daddy, please!"

Everybody stopped moving; Denyce finally loosened Phillip's grip, causing Denver to fall in the doorway and to the floor. Denyce stumbled back until Phillip caught her arm and pulled her forward. Autumn released Phillip's right arm and stood still catching her breath.

When Charlize looked down and saw Denver trying to get up, she turned around, eyeing the butcher's knife on the floor and looked at him. "Uh-uh," Danyelle said as she zipped past, kneeled and grab the knife handle, walking to the kitchen.

"Get out of Autumn's house!" Phillip yelled as Denver jumped to his feet.

"I...I live here too, Phillip," Denver stuttered while fixing his coat. "Phillip, let's go in the kitchen," Denyce said, gently guiding him past Denver. Autumn stepped inside, looking at Denver. "Let's go in the living room," she said, walking in front of him.

Autumn took off her coat and hand it over to Charlize who was determined to sit in on the conversation. "Where's Natasha?" Autumn asked.

"She had to make a run," Charlize said, watching Denver sit on the couch.

"Where the hell have you been, Denver?"

"Charlize,.."

"No, Autumn I want him to answer the question! I can speak on your behalf!"

Autumn touched Charlize's shoulders and squeezed. "Charlize, he is my boyfriend; I'll talk to him."

Charlize stared at Denver who did not look away. "I'll be in the kitchen," Charlize said and walked off.

Autumn sat next to Denver and turned to face him. Denver looked at her shamefully. "I'm sorry about Terrence. And I'm sorry I wasn't here for you," he said.

"What happened to you, Denver? Where were you all of this time?" Autumn asked.

Denver took a breath and rubbed his hands over his face. "I've been at Jet's place," he said, withholding the rest of the story. "I was just out and needed to think. Plus you all were with Terrence, as you should've been and I felt like I was in the way."

Autumn looked at Denver and shook her head. She was still upset with him and could not understand why he would feel out of place. "I called you, text you…so you could see him before the procedure," Autumn said. "None of us ever put you out of ICU Denver. You've been there all this time and suddenly decided to vanish?"

"I know and it was wrong for me to do that," Denver said. "I deserve your anger. But if you let me, I will support you from here on out."

Autumn looked at him then nodded. "You are going to have to apologize to them, too," she said, moving her head in the direction of the kitchen. Phillip, Denyce and Danyelle were sitting at the table watching them. Charlize stood by the counter where Danyelle took the cutlery set away and placed it on the table near her.

"You're right," Denver said, standing up. Autumn joined him and they walked towards the kitchen.

"Hey everyone, I'm back," Natasha said while stepping in the house. She stopped when she saw Denver walking alongside Autumn.

Danyelle appeared in the kitchen doorway holding on to the cutlery block. "Hey Natasha," she said while eyeing her mother and Denver in the kitchen. "Danyelle…"

Danyelle waved her hand. "You missed it…leave it at that."

****

The days leading to the visitation were as relaxed as they could be; the front door was constantly opened and families and friends were in and out. Danyelle's boyfriend Eric arrived Tuesday night and some of Autumn's colleagues flew in using an extended holiday to arrive early. Thanksgiving Day almost felt like the usual holiday gathering; Phillip, Monique and Marc came over and the house was filled with sounds of conversations and football bowls coming from the TVs. Denver participated in small talk with a few of Autumn's other friends and some relatives from out of town, but mainly watched the games.

Autumn was surrounded by people all day making her laugh, at times louder than she normally sound. He watched her from time to time, happy to see her talking and smiling. As the evening set, some of the twenty-something relatives and friends of Danyelle and Terrence carried paper plates filled with desserts or another helping of dinner, beer and pop to the basement where card tables were set up. Denver slowly walked the stairway to the basement, looking at them picking their partners, sitting at the tables and opening fresh boxes of cards. Someone turned a laptop placed on the corner bar into a stereo with a mix of old school and new school R&B and hip-hop blaring. Denver walked to a nearby couch. "Hey Denver, I need one more player!" Danyelle yelled from a table off the right side of the room.

Denver walked over and pulled back a chair. "We're playing spades," Danyelle said while cutting cards. "Terrence was my partner whenever I was home on break or he'd visit the campus for the weekend."

Denver smiled and waited for her to deal.

It was close to midnight when Danyelle, Denver and the others returned to the main level of the house after cleaning up. Seeing that Autumn was nodding off on the couch, the guests whispered their goodbyes and slipped out of the house. Denver grabbed his coat. "Where are you going?"

He turned and Autumn was stretching her arms above her head. "Well I was going back to Jet's," Denver said.

"No, go upstairs," Autumn said, walking around the couch. "I'll be up in a minute."

Denver paused and looked around. Phillip, his wife and stepson were already gone, Natasha and Charlize were in the guest bedroom and Denyce was chatting with Danyelle who was about to take three full garbage bags outside. "I'll take those out, Danyelle," Denver said, walking in the kitchen.

"Thanks," Danyelle said. He picked up two of the bags and left out the kitchen's side door and walked to the garage.

Autumn threw a jacket on and followed him. "Denver I mean it, you are welcomed back here," she said.

"Then I will sleep in Terrence's bed…"

"Denyce is sleeping in there."

They stood quietly by the garbage cans. "OK. I will stay…and sleep on the couch," Denver said.

Autumn walked up, cupped his face in her hands and kissed him. Denver returned the kiss, savoring Autumn's mouth and wet tongue. He pulled her closer, stroking her hair and running his hands down her back. She broke from the kiss. "Come to our bed," Autumn said, grabbing his hand and leading him inside the house.

****

Friday's visitation and Saturday's funeral overflowed with people coming to pay their last respects. Friday night Autumn and Phillip were touched after finding out Norton High School's basketball team had a moment of silence for Terrence, Langston and the truck driver prior to the night's game which they won. The next day it seemed as if the entire school showed up with other mourners including some of Danyelle's college classmates and two professors. All of her professors waived her mid-terms against her wishes.

The service was beautiful and humorous at times thanks to stories shared by Danyelle, Phillip, Autumn and some of Terrence's classmates. The caravan was long as they headed to Chicago Cemetery for the burial ceremony. Denver stood Danyelle's right side as she and Phillip held Autumn who broke down at the end of the prayer then asked people to leave as the cemetery workers lowered the casket.

As everyone parted to their cars to go to the repast Denver looked to his left and saw Candi standing a few feet away from the crowd, dressed in a long black wool coat, pumps with her hair pulled back in a bun. "What are you doing here?" he whispered when he got close enough.

"I am here paying my respects," Candi said. "I was at the funeral too. It was so crowded that I end up sitting in the balcony."

"Well you should not be here!" Denver said, his voice pitching a bit.

"I have nothing to hide Denver. Besides I talked to Autumn on the phone a few days ago. She thanked me for the bouquet and card I had delivered to the house."

"I did not see them," Denver said.

"They weren't for you…wait… you're back in the house?" Candi asked with surprise. "You must not have said anything about us."

"No I'm not and neither will you!"

"No problem but if you are in need of conversation…" Candi said, taking out her car keys. "You know where I live."

****

Autumn was glad the weekend was done and over with. Out of town relatives left, Danyelle was packing to head back to Atlanta with Eric and Phillip, Monique and Marc went back home. She informed the airline she will return to work after the first of the year. Natasha and Charlize went back to their separate homes minutes away but still insisted staying with her. "Are you sure you are happy having that little boy back?" Charlize said while grabbing her suitcase, "Because I can put him out."

"I don't have enough money to bail your ass out Charlize," Natasha said as she came down the hall.

Autumn laughed, walking both friends to the door. "I'm fine Charlize. I'll talk to you two sometime this week," she said, waving as they jumped in the car.

Denyce walked in the kitchen. "Well I see Denver took the leftovers and went to the community shelter."

"Yes he left before Charlize could grab his neck and threaten him," Autumn said, laughing.

Denyce slice a piece of pecan pie and placed it on a paper plate. She sat at the table and stabbed her fork into it. "This is so good! Your auntie put her feet in this!" Denyce said.

Autumn sat at the table with a slice and a scoop of vanilla ice cream on top. "I'm going to be rolling all over the house if I keep eating like this," Autumn said but did not stop putting a spoonful of pecan pie ala mode in her mouth.

"Autumn…is everything back on good standing with Denver?" Denyce asked.

"We're taking it day by day. We really haven't seriously talked with the house being full of people, but I am glad he's back home. I miss him," Autumn said.

Denver reached over and squeezed her hand. "As long as you are happy, I'm cool."

Denyce left Tuesday morning, returning to Gary and her workaholic personality. While she could have easily commuted to Autumn's this was the closest thing to a getaway regardless of the circumstances. Autumn enjoyed the company of her friends and family but she loved having the house back with just her and Denver.

****

Denver and Leo met for lunch at The Loft later in the week to go over the contracts Candi showed him. He took Leo's pen and signed on the dotted lines. "I am glad we are now on good terms Denver," Leo said while sipping cognac.

Denver nodded. "Yeah I guess I let my temper get the best of me. Again my sincerest apologies."

"Well at least I did not get socked in the jaw and a swollen left eye," Leo said, laughing. "Are you and Jet cool again?"

"Yeah we are. I crashed at Jet's a couple of days after Terrence's death, you know. Due to the fallout and me being a jerk."

Leo took another sip and signaled the waiter to bring a dessert menu. "Yeah you were a jerk to leave because she wouldn't…satisfy you. But you're a bigger jerk for sleeping with Candi."

Denver froze and stared at Leo. "I don't know what you're talk…"

"Denver, Candi told me while we were discussing business over the phone a few days ago," Leo said calmly.

Denver suddenly felt sick to his stomach. The cognac he was drinking now had a bitter aftertaste and the filet mignon, baked potato and creamed spinach began to swim inside him. *Why in the hell would Candi tell Leo about them having sex?*

The Panthers Club

"I'm not planning on holding it over your head," Leo said. "But you need to be careful and pay a little more respect to your lady....Autumn I mean."

****

The holidays were in full swing as December rolled in and shoppers packed the Magnificent Mile along downtown Chicago for days leading to Christmas. Denver was surprised how festive Autumn was seeing she lost her youngest child, but she dragged out boxes of outdoor decorations to put up. Denver was on a ladder during a nice sunny but cold day, stringing lights along the roof while Autumn set up yard decorations of Frosty the Snowman, Santa and his reindeer and tall plastic candy canes lined up and down the sidewalk and driveway. When they finished, they tested the lights making sure they all worked. They went inside, rested and warmed up for an hour and then assembled the to the ceiling green Christmas tree. It wasn't until sunset that they finished decorating, eating cookies and drinking hot apple cider. Autumn ran outside with a digital camera to take a photo of the tree in the living room picture window and the outdoor decorations. "This is a perfect picture," she said, showing Denver after coming inside.

"Wow it did come out nice! Now that it's dark outside the decorations can join the rest of the block and show out," he laughed.

They sat together on the couch, snuggling and watching the lights dance on the tree. The ornaments were a combination of those purchased at department stores, a collection of souvenirs from Autumn's flights and handmade ones by Danyelle and Terrence. A black angel carved in wood with silver wings made of twine and wire sat on top of the tree. "Terrence made that angel in craftsman class, or as I told him, 'in old school in was workshop.' He was so proud of that angel and I thought I lost it. I was digging through the boxes and there it was," Autumn said looking up.

Denver looked at the tree then at Autumn. "I am glad to see that beautiful smile again," he said and lightly kissing her on the lips. He applied more pressure in his kiss and she welcomed it.

Autumn shifted her weight so to be closer to Denver, wrapping her arms around his neck. He held her tighter and caressed her lower back. He moved his mouth to her neck and began to lightly nibble on it. His hands slipped under her shirt, caressing her breasts. Autumn sighed and moved so he can get better access to her breasts. She felt his hands slide to her stomach and then leave from under her shirt and stood up. Denver pulled Autumn to her feet, held her hand and led her out of the living room to go upstairs.

Once in their master bedroom they tore at each other's clothing, alternating between kissing and groping. Autumn walked backwards to the bed, allowing herself to fall. Denver leaned forward, climbing on the bed and laying above her body. He kissed her slow and deep, lowering his body

353

on top of hers. He used his mouth to explore every inch of her, causing her to squirm with desire. The further Denver's mouth went, the louder Autumn's moans and sighs were. When she was more than ready for him, Denver reached in the nightstand drawer, pulled out a condom and put it on. "I love you Autumn," he said, entering her.

"I love you too, Denver," she moaned, holding on to him as he thrust inside her. Autumn opened her legs wider so Denver could go deeper.

"Oh Autumn you feel so good," he said, picking up the pace. He grabbed her wrists and brought her arms above her head, put more weight on her and moved harder and faster. Autumn screamed and gasped, driving him to grind against her.

"Oh Denver, don't stop!" she moaned, raising and circling her hips. Denver pressed on top of her, kissing her neck and nibbling her ear, never breaking his stride. Both reach orgasm together, trembling, trying to catch their breath.

"You're beautiful," Denver said while kissing Autumn's face. She hugged and kissed him back.

****

Denver was enjoying the days and nights with Autumn. Because she took the entire month of December off, Autumn was able to spend more time with him and attend a couple of The Loft's holiday themed events like "Mistletoe Mondays" and "Sexy Santa Saturday." One event Denver was looking forward to taking Autumn to is the 'grand-opening' celebration of The Loft/Fuego partnership Saturday before Christmas. It was going to be a huge event and Denver, Jet, Leo and Candi held numerous meetings and teleconferences preparing for it.

Whenever they met at the club or in Leo's office the greetings between Denver and Candi were cordial and business only. Candi only called if Leo was on the other line for an event update and she stopped texting Denver. Autumn went shopping with Charlize and Natasha one day, taking advantage of slashed prices on clothes, shoes, accessories. Autumn always saved extra money for her December shopping sprees but spending time with her buddies was an extra treat. They took a lunch break at a café in the middle of Michigan Avenue, dragging the bags they've yet to stuff in the car. "Girl we need a moving van for all of this stuff," Natasha said, laughing.

Charlize and Autumn also laughed, trying to push their bags underneath the table and still have leg room. "It's going to be a good Christmas, Autumn said as the waiter approached them.

"Good afternoon ladies are you ready to order?"

"Yes I will have the double cheeseburger, ring fries and a strawberry shake," Autumn said.

"Oh that sounds good, I'll have the same," Natasha said.

"Bring me a bacon burger with everything, onion rings and a chocolate shake," Charlize added.

"Thank you for your choices, your order will arrive in 20 minutes," the waiter said, taking the menus and walking off.

"I know Natasha and I are not worried about the pounds, but you ordering a double cheeseburger, fries and a shake," Charlize said.

"Are you hiding something?" Autumn's eyes widened. "Fool I am not pregnant! After…Terrence I put an end to that."

Natasha reached over and pinched Charlize. "OW! I'm sorry Autumn. Natasha that shit hurt!" she said, rubbing her arm.

Autumn laughed as the waiter brought their shakes. "Hmmm this is heaven," Autumn sighed, taking another sip.

"Is Denver still behaving?" Charlize asked while eating the cherry that come with the shake.

"Yes sweetie! We have not been this close in a while. Then again I'm usually 30,000…40,000 feet in the air," Autumn said.

"Well I'm glad it's working out for you," Charlize said.

"Despite what we've gone through it has brought us closer and he is more attentive than ever," Autumn said.

"I am so happy for you; right Charlize?" Natasha said eyeing her friend. "I said I'm glad!"

"OK ladies let's keep this positive. Besides," Autumn saw the waiter coming with a big tray. "We need to focus on our other addiction…food!"

Chapter 9

The Loft/Fuego event was hours away, Denver and Autumn spent hours getting ready. Autumn spent the morning at a salon getting her hair styled, a manicure and a pedicure. Miraculously enough there's only been a couple of light snow showers in the last week and the weatherman said Saturday before Christmas was going to be perfect without the worries of slipping and sliding everything during a night on the town. Autumn took over the master bathroom getting ready so Denver had to use the bathroom down the hall.

During that last shopping spree with the girls, Autumn spotted a gorgeous emerald green off the shoulder dress that stretched and hugged her curves right down to the slit at the left leg. She found a pair of 4-inch, open-toed silver shoes and a matching handbag. She wore her hair down in a medium length layered bob, subtle makeup and diamond crusted tear drop earrings with a matching choker. Denver wore an all black ensemble topped with a black tie with emerald green designs and black shoes. He went to the barber early that day to get his head shaved and buffed and trim the goatee he decided to grow much to Autumn's delight. "Hey baby, are you ready?" Denver yelled in front of the closed door.

"I'm coming; go downstairs!" Autumn yelled back.

Denver chuckled and jogged the steps to the main level.

Denver stood in front of the mirror in the hallway for one last look then turned around when he heard footsteps. He froze as Autumn came downstairs in her ensemble. "Damn," he muttered under his breath.

Autumn smiled as she was pleased with Denver's reaction. "Thank you sexy," she said, reaching for his hand.

He pulled her close then raised her hand to his lips. "I'm having the honor of doing this before Leo sees you," he said, laughing.

Autumn slowly ran a finger down his firm jaw line bringing a smile to his face. "Be careful hotness, we may just stay home," he said.

"Oh no, get our coats and the car keys," Autumn said, giggling and walking from him. "I'm flaunting all of this tonight!"

They arrived at The Loft's new valet section where men and women rushed to open car doors and carefully park their cars in a secure and well-lit spot. Denver handed the valet his keys and beat the other valet in opening the passenger door to help Autumn out. They entered through the V.I.P. doors and went straight to the second floor. "This was a smart move for Leo to change the entrances," Autumn said over the music.

"I couldn't agree more," Denver said, guiding her to a table that already had a bucket of champagne and glass flutes. Twenty V.I.P. tables and booths were filling up fast. A short line was at the buffet table as people loaded their plates with hot wings, shrimp, mini-quiche, quesadillas, veggie trays and more. Another table had pans of lasagna, baked fish, spaghetti and Italian bread. The lower level also had buffet tables lined up with the choices from the first order.

Autumn noticed Charlize and Natasha coming their way. "There's Autumn," Natasha yelled and pointed. "Girl you are looking hot! Why did you choose emerald green?"

"I figured a lot of women were going for red because of Fuego, so I wanted to be different," Autumn said.

Natasha wore a black jumpsuit with a wide silver belt and 4-inch boots. Charlize wore a rich brown texture wrap dress with gold accessories and brown stilettos.

"Hey emerald princess," Charlize teased. Autumn laughed, stepping closer to hug them. Charlize and Natasha hugged Denver and joined them at the table.

"Where's Leo?" Autumn asked.

"He's here," Denver said. "I texted him and he said he'd be down from the office shortly."

The music flowed and the crowd was a sea of Christmas colors on outfits that ranged from shy to extreme. The dance floor was packed and the deejays kept the music flowing. "Is Candi here, too?" Autumn asked.

"She's supposed to be here. She'll probably make a grand entrance," Denver said while taking the champagne bottle out of the ice bucket.

He popped the cork causing Autumn, Charlize and Natasha to squeal in delight, then filled the flutes. "To a beautiful night surrounded by three beautiful women," Denver said, raising his glass to them.

"Damn straight!" Charlize said and clicked her glass against Denver's.

Autumn, Charlize and Natasha got up and went to the buffet tables to fill their plates while Denver text Leo. "Hey man, are you about to make your appearance soon? Autumn, Charlize and Natasha are asking for you!"

Denver took a sip of champagne when his cell beeped. "You know P-dud, Poofy or whatever he calls himself now has nothing on me ;-) Will be out shortly."

Denver put the phone back on the table. Autumn returned placing a plate in front of him before sitting down with hers. "Thank you sweetie," he said.

Natasha and Charlize were close behind, placing their food on the table and taking their seats. "Denver this is going to be better than it already is," Natasha said, digging her fork into a slice of lasagna.

"Thanks. I hope we get this crowded from now on," he said.

Suddenly the deejay started playing the "Wobble" song and folks on the dance floor went crazy assembling lines for the dance. "Oh can we squeeze in there," Charlize said.

Autumn looked down, shaking her head. "Nope, we better wobble here," she said, noticing a short line already happening near their table. "Come on!" she yelled, pulling Denver up with Charlize and Natasha jumping out of their seats.

They joined the short line in the V.I.P. section bouncing, leaning back, dipping low, backing up and turning around to repeat. The club filled with chants of "Yeah, Yeah!" and "Get in there!" from both floors as the patrons dance up a sweat. After the long version ended people in the V.I.P. section laughed, delivered fist bumps and hi-fives while fanning and returning to their tables and booths.

"Whew I love that song!" Charlize said, plopping in her chair. She grabbed a napkin and patted the sweat off her bosom. Natasha, Autumn and Denver found their way back to the table and grabbed their glasses of champagne.

Suddenly the lights over the main floor and stage between the deejay booths dimmed and one large spotlight came on. Dramatic music flowed through the speakers and Leo stepped out from behind the thin curtains to a round of applause. He wore a fitted black turtleneck and black slacks. The light gave extra shine to his salt and pepper hair that was cut short to keep the natural finger curls tamed. "Girl that Leo is a fine piece of Black Italian!"

Natasha said, making Autumn, Charlize and Denver laugh. Leo raised his hands to quiet the crowd and they fell into silence. "Thank you all for coming here tonight! I am honored to be the owner of The Loft…but even more honored to join forces with Jet or if you grew up with him, Jeremy Ellis Turner," he said as the crowd burst into laughter.

"Damn Leo just put Jet on blast with his government name!" Denver laughed. "Come on out Jet if you are not blending with the crowd!"

Jet emerged from backstage smiling and shaking his head at Leo. They did a short hug and Jet stepped aside. "I know my V.I.P. section is pretty packed, but surely one of the biggest and best contractors in the Chicago area is up there front and center…Denver Harris where are you?"

The spotlight moved to the second level and Denver stood up, waving and acknowledging everyone. "Thanks for being here, Denver and hello to your gorgeous girlfriend Autumn," Leo said. Denver took Autumn by the hand as she stood and nodded.

Leo stepped to the left of the stage. "Now we have one more mastermind behind this collaboration. She is beautiful but also has brains! Candi Riverez!"

Candi entered the stage from the back; the spotlight shining on her. The applause was deafening and everyone was on their feet but Denver, who dropped into his seat. Autumn bent over caressing his face. "Denver, what's wrong?" she asked as Denver's face ashen.

Natasha gave Autumn a glass of water to give to Denver who did not reach for it. He stared at the wall monitor that had a shot of the stage. "Now ladies and gentlemen," Leo said and reached for a glass. "I want you to raise your glasses for a champagne toast! Well all except Candi....she is expecting a little piece of candy!"

Everyone laughed and raised their glasses as Candi turned sideways in her flaming red orange halter swing dress, her baby bump clearly showing. "Oh she pulled a Beyonce'!"

One patron screamed from the dance floor as laughter erupted, oblivious to the scenario unfolding. Autumn dropped the glass of water and looked down at Denver who was sweating profusely. Natasha and Charlize also stared at Denver in total shock and disbelief. Denver continued to stare at the monitor as Candi smiled, waved and blew kisses at the crowd. She caught the camera aimed at her that was connected to the monitor facing the V.I.P. section and blew another kiss. "Hey Big Daddy" was the words she mouthed out directly into the camera.

"WATCH OUT!" someone screamed as Charlize managed to grab the champagne bottle and swing at Denver. Another male patron was able to dive and knock Denver on the floor before contact and Autumn and Natasha jumped back.

"You dirty lying punk bitch!" Charlize screamed as she attempted to move the table and jump on Denver. "How do you do this to my friend?"

Natasha grabbed Autumn who was still in shock. "Come on baby, we have to go now!" Natasha screamed, pulling Autumn to the stairway.

Leo and Jet rushed to the elevator that goes to V.I.P. while Candi remained onstage watching the fiasco. The bouncer Charlize flirted with a while back snatched her away from Denver who was now balled up against a booth defending his body from Charlize's kicks, punches and scratches.

Charlize reached behind her and poked the bouncer's left eye, causing him to release her and scream in agony. Charlize shoved her way downstairs to the exit without her coat.

"Charlize, over here," Natasha yelled. "I got us a cab, come on!"

She ran to the cab and climbed in the back, falling across Natasha and Autumn's lap. The cab pulled off and Charlize managed to sit up and move to where she was between Natasha and Autumn. Autumn stared straight ahead not saying a word. No one opened their mouths the entire ride to Autumn's house.

The bouncer managed to pull Denver out of the crowd, many who grabbed their coats and left before something uglier went down. The bouncer got to the elevator with Denver in tow and they went to the top floor. When the doors opened Denver broke free and ran into the office where Leo and Jet stood waiting. Denver drew his fist back to hit either one of them but another bouncer caught his left jaw, sending Denver to the floor. "How long did you know," Denver yelling and holding his face.

"Denver I swear I did not figure it out until today," Jet said trying to understand it all.

"LIAR!" Denver got to his feet but the bouncer shoved him in a chair.

"Man I'm telling the truth! I've not seen Candi in the last week; she would update me on tonight through texts! Leo's the only one who has seen her face to face."

Leo looked at Jet then Denver. "She found out late last week and it did not start showing until now," Leo said. "And she was getting irritable whenever she came by for meetings."

Leo walked over to the chair where Denver sat, deflated. "You my friend should have worn protection. I understand about get all hot and out of control…in the moment. But you should have thought with this," Leo poked the top of Denver's head, "instead of that."

Denver got up, slowly walked to the elevator. He stepped inside and waited for it to take him to the V.I.P. level. Stepping off, he was blinded by a dark material. Denver snatched at it and it was his coat shoved in his face by the bouncer. Denver put it on and stepped outside. The place was still crowded because the deejays calmed everyone down and announced free champagne on Leo – who approved the announcement while waiting for Denver.

Denver retrieved his car from valet, tipped the guy and climbed in. He pulled off and drives three blocks away and pulls over. He did not see Candi anymore after the bouncer shoved him in the elevator nor as he left the club. He could not blame her or say she tricked him into getting pregnant; like Leo said, his penis got the best of him. But in the end he lost the one person he wanted to work out. Denver drove to a hotel and paid for a room with his credit card, knowing better than to show up at Autumn's house.

Autumn, Natasha and Charlize walked in the house, slamming the door behind them. Autumn walked in the living room and stared at the Christmas tree blink in tune with the music on the stereo. All the lights were connected from the tree to the house and the yard decorations.

Charlize marched upstairs, shoes in her hand and Natasha quietly joined Autumn at her side. "The condoms," Autumn muttered.

Natasha looked at her. "What sweetie?"

Autumn sat on the couch. "We've been making love since we decorated the house and this tree. He started wearing condoms again that night."

Natasha slowly sat beside her.

"We had sex after our first date three years ago and I had him wearing condoms for at least a year because I did not know how long we would last. He kept condoms around but we never used them again. This explains why he is using them again. He was sleeping with her."

Natasha wrapped her arm around Autumn. "You deserve much better Autumn. He humiliated you and even though a lot of people in that club had no idea what was going on or who you were, Candi and those bastards knew what they were doing!"

Autumn suddenly looked towards the stairway. "What is Charlize doing upstairs?"

Both of them got up and headed to the stairway when Charlize met them halfway coming down. "I was looking for stuff that belonged to that bastard so I can burn them." Natasha and Autumn looked at each other and chuckled.

Charlize walked past them. "I don't see what the hell's so funny."

Autumn turned and pulled her friend into a hug. "Charlize I am going to be fine…I've figured it out."

Charlize looked at both of them confused.

Natasha explained to her about Autumn's conversation which only made Charlize angrier. "I need to find him and take him out…."

"Charlize!" Natasha shouted.

Autumn laughed then grabbed her car keys. "What are you doing?" Natasha asked as Autumn re-buttoned her coat.

"I'm dropping you two off. I will be fine by myself," Autumn said.

"Are you sure?" Charlie asked. "Because we can stay over in case Denver tries to come by."

"Denver's not coming through; he knows it's over," Autumn said.

"But he will need to come and move his things out of here," Natasha said,

"Are you going to let him in?" Autumn looked at them. "Do you actually think he will physically show up with a moving truck? I'm willing to bet money that he will not show his face again because, one, he's ashamed; two he's scared to death of you," Autumn said, pointing at Charlize. "Three, when Phillip finds out about this through you or Danyelle, Denver knows he will turn up missing. Don't worry about me."

Natasha and Charlize put on their coats, grabbed their purses and followed Autumn out of the house.

Forty-eight hours later a professional moving van arrived at Autumn's house and alerted Autumn of their arrival. She let the four men in with the last one handing her a set of house keys. "Mr. Harris asked that I pass these to you ma'am," the guy said.

"Thank you," Autumn said, following them inside. She directed the movers to the properties belonging to Denver and sat in the TV room.

"Ma'am?" another mover called out. "All of these oversize black plastic bags contain Mr. Harris' belongings?"

"Yep," Autumn said without leaving the couch. "His clothes, shoes and coats are stuffed in the first two bags…that he purchased with his own money. The other bag contains some electronics he also purchased and that's it."

One of the movers walked around the couch with a clipboard in his hand. "Ms. Daniels, this list I have reads a stereo, a flat screen TV, clothes, exercise equipment, shoes, boots, leather coats and more."

Autumn looked up, smiling at the mover. "Yes those were his things…because I bought all of that in three years. And I have the receipts for most of it. But since I did not need most of it, let Mr. Harris know the three men shelters, an after-school program and a small library are enjoying early Christmas presents courtesy of him. Oh and tell him congratulations on the baby…Candi finally got what she wanted."

Epilogue

Chanale sat back and watched the three strangers divulged into their stories of lovers younger than all of them and chuckled. It was funny how she came to Visonz during a second run around with Duke only to be stood up again. Maybe, she thought, maybe she just needed to take a break from men period. After listening to the oldest of the group Camille talk about her hot life with this local and young top chef maybe she should reconsider dating more younger men. Hell Camille almost reminded her of herself.

Chanale finished off another martini and waved her hand at the waitress.

"Baby girl don't you think you've had enough," asked Camille while Autumn and Denyce watched from across the table.

"I'm not ordering another drink; I'm paying my bill," Chanale said.

The crowd was thinning out at the art gallery/nightclub and the event was a success. "Ok well do you need a ride, Chanale? I am about ready to leave," Camille said while pulling out a receipt for the art piece she purchased for Roman. She was going to walk to the gallery side where Dayon was still there and pick up her package to put in the car.

"No I will get a taxi," Chanale said while absentmindedly playing with her hair.

Denyce and Autumn looked at each other. "Whew, if you strike a match in front of her she's likely to explode," Denyce said making Autumn drop her head in laughter.

"I will be fine...I think," Chanale said as she grabbed her purse. She reached in and pulled out her cell phone to call a cab company.

"Honey? Honey! The cab service is already outside waiting to take no need to be driving folks like you home," Autumn said with a smirk.

Chanale blinked a couple of times at both of them and started laughing.

"Hey Chanale." The male voice behind Chanale made her, Denyce and Autumn turn in his direction.

"Desmond? Is that you," Chanale leaned forward and squinted in the dim lights.

"Yes it's me," he said while watching her.

"Are you OK? Do you need a ride home?"

"Nope, I'm leaving the car here and going to hail..."

"One of us will be taking her home," Camille intervened while resting the wrapped piece of artwork against their table.

Desmond looked at Camille who gave him a stare that could cut the thickest piece of glass while Denyce and Autumn stood up and slipped on their coats. "OK," Desmond said, looking at Chanale, "It was good seeing you."

Desmond walked off but not without looking back at Chanale a couple of times. She watched him return to a group that included a couple of women and men. None of the women favored Adrianna from what she could tell. She turned back to the group of strangers who were now likely to become her friends and smiled.

"All right," Chanale said while snatching her coat from the chair. "Which one of you old bitches is giving me a ride home!"

Author's Bio

Lisa D. DeNeal is a freelance writer who currently works for the Post-Tribune as a correspondent and weekly columnist. She's also written articles for the Kiwanis and Port of Harlem magazines and the Gary Crusader weekly newspaper. She is co-author of the 2008 memoir, "Unflappable," a coming of age story on Carolyn E. Mosby, daughter of the late Indiana State Senator Carolyn Brown Mosby.

Miss DeNeal is the youngest of four children to Robert DeNeal, Jr. and the late Ada DeNeal , an alumna of Roosevelt High School and Calumet College of St. Joseph. She currently resides in her hometown of Gary, IN.

Author's Bio

A self-proclaimed master of relaxation, Alethea finds her best times to write are early in the morning after prayer and meditation or late at night when everyone is asleep. The sight and sounds of rain and thunderstorms also enrich the creative process for her. Alethea finds that this process calms her enough to create a heartbeat for each character.

What causes this author's heart beat to accelerate in real life? God, her man, and two daughters.

When not writing, Alethea loves to indulge her passion for traveling, attending church, giving forgiveness workshops, watching movies, reading fiction and non-fiction, chatting with friends, shooting pool, watching NFL and NBA games, and shopping.

Alethea is the author of four books, Bag Lady, Womb Child, Help Wanted, and Forgiveness for the Man's Soul.